Deutsche Luftwaffe

Uniforms and Equipment of the German Air Force (1935-1945)

Gustavo Cano
Santiago Guillén

ANDREA PRESS

Authors: GUSTAVO CANO MUÑOZ and SANTIAGO GUILLÉN GONZÁLEZ

Archive photographs: SANTIAGO GUILLÉN GONZÁLEZ collection, unless otherwise noted.

Weapons: FUNDACIÓN DON RODRIGO

Editor-in-chief: JOSÉ MARÍA LÓPEZ

Coordination: RICARDO RECIO CARDONA

Text edition: KEVIN MORAN (English) and DANIELA TUTAS (German).

Design and Layout: ANDREA PRESS - DISEÑO ENTRE2 in partnership with VANDALIA SERVICIOS EDITORIALES

Photography and image processing: JOSÉ IGNACIO PÉREZ LOZANO

Cover main photo: A grouping of *Luftwaffe* flight equipment and uniforms. Top left: An Me 109 pilot wearing the LKp N 101 net flight helmet and hinged rigid-framed *Splitterschutzbrille* goggles. Botton left: *Oberstleutnant* Erich Leie, a famous German fighter ace.

Inside front and back covers: Luftwaffe aircraft taken from the 1943 Official Pocket year book of the National Socialist Flyers Corps as seen in pages 102, 103, 104 and 105.

All the specimens that appear on this book belong to the collection of SANTIAGO GUILLÉN GONZÁLEZ, except for the mask shown in pages 192 and 193, which belong to the collection of MANUEL ÁLVARO REQUENA, whom the authors wish to thank for his assistance and cooperation. We would also like to express our profound gratitude to the board of directors of the FUNDACIÓN DON RODRIGO for the constant assistance and generosity shown during the preparation of this book, for giving us access to their weapons collection and for allowing us to photograph some of them for the book, shown in pages 324 to 345.

Printed in: GRAFILUR, ARTE GRÁFICO (Spain)

Published by ANDREA PRESS
C/ Talleres, 21 - Pol. Ind. de Alpedrete - 28430 Alpedrete (Madrid)
Tel.: +34 91 857 00 08 - Fax: +34 91 857 00 48
www.andreapresspublishing.com
sales@andreapresspublishing

Distributed in the UE by:

ANDREA EUROPE, S.L.
C/ Talleres, 21 - Pol. Ind. de Alpedrete
28430 Alpedrete (Madrid) Spain
Tel.: (34) 91 857 00 08
Fax: (34) 91 857 00 48
orders@andreaeurope.com
www.andreaeurope.com

Distributed in USA and Canada by:

ANDREA DEPOT USA, INC.
1822 HOLLY RD., SUITE 110
CORPUS CHRISTI TX 78417
TEXAS - USA
Phone: 361-334-1625
Fax: 361-334-2955
orders@andreadepotusa.com
www.andreadepotusa.com

ISBN: 978-84-96658-39-4
DL: M-9828-2013

TABLE OF CONTENTS

Hans-Joachim Marseille, ace of aces. Recipient of the Knight's Cross, Oak Leaves, Swords and Diamonds. He scored 158 kills in 382 missions. He died in a plane crash on September 30, 1942.

This Gefreiter *poses for the camera before the war, wearing a* Sommermütze *peaked cap.*
The eagle national emblem belong to the first pattern, with a drop tail, while the piping cord with the Waffenfarbe color is still present in the collar of his Tuchrock *tunic.*

Preface

The 8th of May, 1945 was not only the day that marked the end of the war in Europe, but also the final point of one of the most unique and fascinating eras in the history of military aviation. This book is intended to give anyone with an interest in the history of the *Luftwaffe* a clear visual idea of the men who fought in the German Air Force through one of the most captivating aspects of their wartime experience: their uniforms, flight gear and equipment. It comprises a detailed compilation of some of their *"tools of the trade"*, with a special emphasis on the visual aspect of the objects described; showing highly detailed photographs of some of the most prominent pieces of uniforms and equipment used by the men who flew in the German air force during the Second World War. The use of color throughout the book gives the reader the opportunity to appreciate the different varieties of materials and fabrics produced during the war, in the hope that it provides useful information to a wide range of readers including militaria collectors, modellers, illustrators and studio wardrobe departments. The readers will notice the relatively large number of period photographs depicting Spanish pilots who served in the *Luftwaffe* as part of the volunteer *15. Spanische Staffel* fighting on the Eastern Front. The documentary wealth of such photos in the author's archive, coupled with their quality showing flight uniforms and equipment and the fact that most have never been published before have been the main reasons to be selected to appear in the book.

The book is intended to give a brief overview of the most identifiable elements, and by no means a profound study or systematic display of each and every piece of equipment and uniform, a venture that would require several books to accomplish and is well beyond the scope of this book. The authors have limited the identification data and the captions to the basic information in order to include as many photographs as possible. The difference between this book and others that have been published before lies in the fact that the emphasis has shifted from quantity to quality. Out of the vast collection of artifacts at our disposal, the task of choosing which items would appear in the book and which would be discarded was not an easy one to make. It was finally decided to showcase those pieces that were most commonly used by the average German pilot and crewman, and in some cases a rare or unusual artefact of clothing or equipment which the authors believed would be appealing to more advanced connoisseurs and enthusiasts of *Luftwaffe* militaria.

All of the specimens shown in the book are, to the best of our knowledge, of original wartime manufacture. They belong to the collection of one of the authors or have been graciously lent by other advanced collectors. At the same time, every effort has been made to verify the information contained within these pages, including the study of a vast amount of available bibliographic resources, frequent consulting with experts in the field, as well as careful examination of all the specimens photographed. The authors expect a certain amount of conjecture and acknowledge there might be different opinions regarding some of the facts reflected in this book, as with all things historical. However, any mistake or omission found in these pages can only be blamed on the authors, and by no means to any other person or institution that helped in the preparation of this book.

We have really enjoyed producing this book and sincerely hope the result will give the same pleasure to our readers.

Gustavo Cano Muñoz
Santiago Guillén González

A Luftwaffe *anti-aircraft flak unit moves to the front. The officer guiding the convoy is wearing a* Fliegerbluse *and an officer belt.*

I. INTRODUCTION:
HISTORY OF THE LUFTWAFFE

When the *Luftwaffe* was officially disbanded by the allies in 1946 following the defeat of the Third Reich, one of the most fascinating and controversial chapters in the annals of aviation history had been written. The eleven years of existence of this feared fighting force, whose fame was shaped by the groundbreaking machines and the high-spirited men who flew them, forged a record that will always be remembered. The following pages contain a brief history of the *Luftwaffe*, which will help to set the context for the uniforms and equipment of the men that this book intends to portray.

The defeat in the First World War in 1918 and the subsequent conditions of the VersaillesTreaty signed by Germany with the victors after the armistice eliminated the aircraft as a weapon from the German arsenal. Germany was denied access not only to new armaments such as the submarine, the airplane and the tank, but the conditions of the armistice also severely limited the size and capability of the German armed forces. Despite the limitations, the Germans began deep studies and reflections about the role of some of the new weapons used in the war that had just ended. The Weimar Republic, the new state that was born at the end of the war, was allowed to have only a small defensive military force, the *Reichswehr*. Its size and composition were controlled by the Allies to prevent future German military aggression against its neighbors. The *Reichswehr* consisted of a limited-sized army, the *Reichsheer*, and a small defensive navy, the *Reichsmarine*. However, there was no provision for an air force. Hans von Seeckt, a Prussian aristocrat from a family with a long military tradition who reached the rank of *Generalmajor* during the First World War, was designated to organize the new German army. Foreseeing the potential of a strong air force in future conflicts, he made sure that its advocates possessed some voice within the new army. Thus, he made provisions for the new army to include a small cadre of veteran officers with ample experience in the conduct of the air battles of the First World War.

Limitations imposed by the allied nations forced German aviation to work with severe restrictions. The only way to circumvent the limitations of Versailles was to develop an ambitious program destined to the development of military aircraft and training of men that would become the basis of the future German air force. One of the first measures was to guarantee the survival of the German aviation industry. Thus, the government applied a policy of handing extensive subsidies to civil aviation. The bid paid off, and Germany's advance in civil aviation was impressive. By 1927, the German *Lufthansa* airline was much stronger than all of her European competitors together. This experience in long-distance flying, navigation, and instrument flying obviously had a positive impact on the future development of the *Luftwaffe*.

The Flieger *of the photo is wearing an overseas cap. On his lower left breast he is bearing the Civil Gliding proficiency cloth badge. The three gulls indicate a "C" certificate, awarded to those students that have flown a glider for five minutes without losing height and have passed an oral exam. The badge qualified the recipient for the official soaring license.*

Military aviation factories were constructed and disguised as civil factories, airdromes were built and aircraft which later could be used as military prototypes were developed. This cover-up of the real intentions of the German authorities continued in the form of so called "recreational" flying schools and in secretly subsidized sports flying clubs for flight training. In 1932, the major German club had some 60,000 members. A paramilitary air force, the *Deutscher Luftsportverband* (DLV or German Air Union), was formed with Ernst Udet, a famed German fighter ace who achieved 62 victories during World War One, as its head. The uniforms designed for use by the DLV personnel and many of the insignia would later be adopted with minor modifications by the new *Luftwaffe*, although during the DLV period the ranks were given designations that made them sound more civilian than military. At the same

The pilot badge was instituted by Reichsmarschall *Hermann Göring on August 12, 1935.*

time, German scientists began extensive technical research and experiments with the aim of developing superior flight clothing and equipment and better flight instruments for aircraft navigation. Germans flew and worked for civilian air lines in foreign countries, especially South America; these airlines later provided a good number of air and ground personnel to the German Air Force. But the most important advance during the twenties and beginning of the thirties came with the collaboration with the USSR.

Cooperation with the USSR

The situation of the Soviet Union after the war was precarious. The civil war was still raging and the country was internationally isolated. In this context, both nations started negotiations to create a framework of cooperation. After a series of negotiations, Germany and the USSR signed the Rapallo Treaty in April, 1922. One of the most important agreements of the treaty was to begin an effective German-Soviet military cooperation. On August of 1922, the German *Reichswehr* and the RKKA (Workers' and Peasants' Red Army) reached an agreement which allowed the Germans to establish military bases on Soviet soil. These bases were to be primarily used for research and development and for personnel training, specifically in those disciplines which were expressly forbidden for Germany by the Versailles treaty. In return, Germany would allow the *Reichswehr* to perform military exercises alongside the Red Army and it would also agree to share industrial and military technological advances made by German scientists. As part of the deal, a number of Soviet military officers secretly trained in Germany in a variety of disciplines. However, the Germans managed to get more from the USSR than what they gave to their counterparts. The cooperation was fruitful in terms of technical innovations in military aviation, but also in tactics and strategies. During the summer of 1931, German and Soviet forces conducted a series of joint air maneuvers designed to devise the most effective attack and defense techniques. At this point, over 1,200 *Luftwaffe* pilots had been trained at Lipetsk, one of the largest bases in Soviet territory.

In 1932 Adolf Hitler decided there was no need to continue cooperating with their ideological enemies and began to cut ties with the Soviets. Finally it was the USSR who officially asked the *Reichswehr* to shut down the Soviet facilities and depart. The Germans finally left in September of 1933. However, diplomatic contacts would not be completely severed, continuing steadily throughout the following years and culminating with the Molotov-Ribbentrop Pact of 1939, a ten-year nonaggression pact in which each signatory promised not to attack the other, and included an economic agreement to exchange German manufactured goods for Soviet raw materials. The pact also contained a secret clause that provided for the partition of Poland and the rest of Eastern Europe into Soviet and German spheres of interest. Still, the problems facing the Germans in the road to creating an air force that could serve as an effective tool of diplomatic and military policy were enormous. In May of 1933, the German Air Ministry was created and Hermann Göring named Air Minister. He immediately combined all private flying clubs and expanded all aviation schools. Students and officers were put into uniform. Old airfields were made larger and new ones built.

Finally, on February 26, 1935, Hitler ordered Göring to form the *Luftwaffe*, breaking the Treaty of Versailles. Neither Britain and France nor the League of Nations did anything to oppose the unilateral action taken by Germany, even after admitting the existence of some 1,000 military aircraft and 20,000 trained officers and men. Under the direction of Göring, the newly formed air forces began to accumulate a growing strength, and often received preference in the allocation of funding and resources. As an example, it is worth mentioning that the total of the antiaircraft artillery and the necessary signal organizations were stripped from the *Heer* (the land component of the armed forces) and transferred to the *Luftwaffe*.

The Condor Legion Experience

In July 1936, while the Germans were in the process of completing the first stages of rearmament, a civil war broke out in Spain after a conservative-backed military coup to depose the legitimate republican government failed to gain control over the whole country. Hitler decided to provide aid to the rebels, who had similar ideological principles, especially in the air. The man appointed to lead the expeditionary force was Wolfram von Richthofen, one of the chief technical assistants of the German air force and cousin of the famous *"Red Baron"* Manfred von Richthofen, Germany's leading flying ace of the First World War. Richthofen arrived in Spain as Chief of Staff of the Condor Legion (name given to the volunteer expeditionary force), and soon realized that the traditional tactics or air powers were not compatible with the reality he found on the ground. The lack of important strategic targets and an unsuitable artillery led Richthofen to use his air power as a weapon to support the land offensive of the troops led by the leader of the rebel forces, General Francisco Franco, who was at that moment in the process of taking control of the Basque region of Spain.

Richthofen led the development of new techniques and tactics of close air support for ground forces in offensive operations. Overcoming great difficulties, he developed a

A crew poses in front of a Junkers Ju 86 bomber wearing the service uniform. (Militaria Arganzuela)

system based in the close cooperation and improved planning between ground and air units, establishing close communication links and recognition devices, and saw the need to have *Luftwaffe* liaison officers to serve directly with front-line units. Meanwhile, the lessons of strategic bombing were uneven. Even though it was recognized that the bombing of cities, especially those with insufficient anti-aircraft defenses, was indeed an effective instrument to disrupt morale within the population, others believed that this experiment in psychological warfare served only to make the populace more defiant. Even though the Nationalists were able to destroy large "rebel" cities such as Madrid, Barcelona or Valencia with incendiaries, they had refrained because of the delicate political problems involved in a civil war. Both winners and losers would have to live in the same country after the war was over and having large cities turned into a pile of rubble was not deemed to be a wise political decision for the rebels. Whatever the attitudes towards the effects of bombing, the Spanish Civil War confirmed in some Germans' minds the belief that fighter aircraft and civil defense measures would have a great importance in the coming war, as they would appreciably reduce casualties in an air attack.

For the *Luftwaffe*, Spain was a helpful testing ground for its aircraft and tactics. The Germans learned priceless combat lessons in Spain which they quickly incorporated into their doctrine. Apart from the lessons learned regarding close air support and the cooperation with the army, another important lesson learned from the war in Spain was the difficulty of hitting targets both day and night. The experience obtained from night attacks proved generally beneficial, while the problem of hitting targets accurately in daylight missions helped push towards a conception that every bomber

This Messerschmitt Bf 109G-2 of the 9. /JG54 "Grünherz" *is parked beneath a camouflage net. The photo was probably taken in Oldenburg in 1943, during the Defense of the Reich.*

should have a dive-bombing capability. At night, the Germans discovered the difficulties not only in finding targets but also hitting them. This led to the belief that the use of navigational aids was critical under bad weather conditions and night operations. Soon, scientists began to experiment with radio direction systems as an aid to navigation and as a technological answer to the problem of bombing targets in conditions of limited visibility. The result was the *Knickebein* system, used for the first time in the Battle of Britain.

The attack on Poland

In September 1938, Neville Chamberlain, the British Prime Minister, met with a defiant Hitler in Berchtesgaden, a mountain retreat in the Alps, to try to appease Hitler, who had threatened to invade Czechoslovakia if Britain opposed his plans to take over the Sudetenland, a Czech region inhabited mostly by ethnic Germans. After discussing the issue with Edouard Daladier, the French Prime Minister, Chamberlain opted for an appeasement policy and informed Hitler that his proposals were accepted. But the German dictator perceived that both Britain and France were unwilling to go to war, and was ready to use that weakness for his own benefit. A few days later, he demanded not only the annexation, but the total occupation of that region by his army. After Britain and France rejected these new demands, the Italian dictator Benito Mussolini suggested Hitler to hold a conference of Germany, Britain, France and Italy as a way of solving this issue. The meeting took place in Munich on September 29, 1938. Desperate to avoid war, Chamberlain and Daladier agreed that Germany could have the *Sudetenland*. In return, Hitler promised not to make any further territorial demands in Europe.

This easy and misleading triumph over Czechoslovakia enabled not only Hitler, but also his military subordinates to make the decision to attack Poland the following year. In March 1939, with the excuse of Czech political troubles, Hitler threatened the new Czech leader, Dr. Emil Hacha, declaring that if Czechoslovakia refused to accede to German demands and sign the surrender of the country, the city of Prague would soon be in ruins from bombing, and that this would be only the beginning. This political move using the *Luftwaffe* as a powerful instrument of terror was to be one of the last of Hitler's peaceful conquests. The seizure of Prague finally forced the British government to react and send a warning to Hitler. Yet, the new British position was due more to internal political pressure than to a fundamental change in the government's attitude.

On July 3, Hitler and Göring paid a visit to the *Rechlin-Lärz Luftwaffe* test station, the main testing ground for new aircraft designs, to inspect the latest in research and development. The technical experts did a thorough job to assure that aircraft and equipment in the design and test stages were close to production. The demonstration provided one more confirmation to the *Führer* that the *Luftwaffe* not only possessed current superiority over its opponents, but that it would be capable to maintain such superiority for the foreseeable future. It was an impression that was far from real. This was the last confirmation Hitler needed to decide the offensive against Poland.

In the early morning of September 1, 1939, German bombers and fighters launched a series of heavy attacks on targets inside Polish territory. The German attack caught the Poles in the process of mobilizing. The first clash between *Luftwaffe* and Polish fighter aircraft took place over the airfield of Balice, near Cracow At the same time, another fight was about to take place over the outskirts of Warsaw. The *Polish Pursuit Brigade* intercepted a large formation of He 111 bombers escorted by Bf 110s. In the ensuing fight, six He 111s were shot down. Heavy fighting over Warsaw resumed later in the day, when a second German bomber raid, escorted by both Bf 110 and Bf 109 fighters, was again intercepted by Polish fighters, which could not replicate the success of the morning engagement, as the German fighters attacked them before they could reach their objectives. Soon first German bombs fell on Warsaw. In the following days, the attacks continued. Taking advantage of the superior features of its aircraft, the *Luftwaffe* used small groups of bombers approaching the target from several directions at different altitudes, while Bf 109s and Bf 110s flew sweeps in the target area. The Polish Air force was forced to retreat and by September 10 all but one Polish fighter wing were moved east of the Vistula, where they could do very little against the far superior force they were facing. Except for occasional skirmishes, there was little the Polish armed forces could do to resist the attack of the Germans. Warsaw surrendered on September 27 and by October 6, the campaign was over.

The Germans used about 2,000 aircraft in the attack against Poland, losing a total of 258 to all causes. About 400 pilots and crewmen were killed or missing and an additional 120 wounded. The Polish air force *(Lotnictwo Wojskowe)* had lost around 330 aircraft, 260 as the result of enemy action. 61 airmen were killed, 110 were missing and 63 were wounded.

War in the west

There was little France and Britain could do to interrupt the German conquest of Poland except to declare war

This soldier on guard duty is protecting his head from the extreme cold with a Luftwaffe *pattern Pelzmütze fur covered cap.*

A Focke-Wulf Fw 187 Falke *(Falcon). The aircraft was produced in the summer of 1939 and intended to compete against the Messerschmitt Bf 110 as a fighter.*

A group of Ju 52 transport aircraft arrive to an Afrikakorps *airbase in the desert with supplies. Several Bf 110s are also visible in the photo. (Signal)*

German ground crew at work loading ammunition on a Messerschmitt Bf 109.

A row of combat-ready Messerschmitt Bf 109B fighter aircraft stand in line waiting for the pilots.

on Germany and proclaim the general mobilization of its armies. The following period of six months of inactivity in land operations led the press to speak of the *"phony war"*. But it was the calm before the storm. Hitler's military plans had always been directed at conquering the eastern European territories, especially the Soviet Union. But in the face of Britain and France's unwillingness to sign a peace treaty with Germany, he decided that the necessary preliminary step before attacking the Soviet Union was to defeat his western European enemies and thus avoid a war on two fronts. On May 10, 1940, Germany surprised the allies by launching an offensive against Holland and northern Belgium. German armored vehicles stormed through the Ardennes area. The *Luftwaffe* had the initial mission to destroy the opposing allied air forces and their ground bases. The equipment available to the Dutch and the Belgians was mostly obsolete and their armies were incapable of mounting any serious opposition. The British had stationed a strong force of bombers and fighters in France to support the British Expeditionary Force. Before the attack, The French air force was mostly obsolete, as it was still in the process of manufacturing and equipping squadrons with new aircraft. The first *Luftwaffe* air strikes accomplished the mission and effectively eliminated the Belgian and Dutch air forces. The British and French also suffered heavy aircraft losses on the ground and in the air. But the victory did not come easily. On the first day of the offensive, the Germans lost 83 aircraft, including 47 bombers and 25 fighters and on the following day, the losses grew a further 42 aircraft, including 22 bombers, 8 dive bombers, and 10 fighters. To secure the advance, *Luftwaffe* airborne forces seized strategic bridges throughout Belgium and Holland, while German glider forces captured the Belgian fortress of *Eben Emael,* a supposedly impregnable stronghold. The success of the operation created a stunning impact on the allied command, leading to the false impression that the German paratroopers were a much stronger force than it was in reality.

In the north, Dutch resistance finally collapsed on the third day of attack, after the German 9th Panzer Division reached the outskirts of Rotterdam. On May 14, a bombing raid destroyed the center of the city and killed over 800 civilians, even though negotiations to surrender the city were still taking place. Some argue the bombing took place by mistake due to difficulties in communications, while others indicate that this tactic followed a familiar pattern of the *Wehrmacht*, designed to reach their objectives through terror directed at otherwise non-military targets. Mistake or not, the fact is that the Dutch Commander in Chief signed the capitulation document of all his forces in Holland on the next day, fearing that the *Luftwaffe* would destroy another city.

On May 13 the forces of Field Marshall Ewald von Kleist crossed the Meuse river in three different sectors. Kleist's performance in the Polish campaign at the command of a Panzer Corps had been so valued that he was now at the command of a *Panzergruppe*, an armored unit formed by several Panzer Corps. At Sedan, in French territory, waves of German dive bombers pounded the French defenders of the south bank of the river in what turned out to be heaviest air bombardment made by the German Air force in the war. German troops started to cross the river in rubber boats and on rafts and the course of the following days the tanks swept across the bridges. General Heinz Guderian, an old school military man who had fought in the First World war and is generally considered as one of the advocates of the *"Blitzkrieg"*, a military doctrine involving quick, deep strikes into enemy territory, spearheaded by armor with close air support, widened the Sedan bridgehead

Musicians of a Luftwaffe *band in the foreground performing during a parade. The man at the front is holding the regimental Schnellenbaum: a traditional artifact present in all German military bands. (Militaria Arganzuela)*

advancing to the west in open country in the direction of the English Channel. Soon the advancing German forces established an operational base close to a small town west of the Meuse River called Charleville, where a fleet of Ju-52 aircraft transported much needed fuel, aircraft spare parts, ammunition and ground crews to support the land forces.

The final phase of the operation became one of the most controversial episodes of the campaign: the escape of most of the British Expeditionary Force and large numbers of French soldiers through the beaches and harbor of the coastal French town of Dunkirk. It was the first serious blunder of the *Luftwaffe* in the war. The operation to evacuate the British Expeditionary Force from France, codenamed Operation *Dynamo*, began on May 26. Unlike what had happened during the previous phases of the campaign, in this occasion Germans fighters and bombers fought with disadvantage against British aircraft. Although they had managed to capture several enemy airfields, some of their planes were on the limit of their range, having much less effective time over the target than the British Hurricane and Spitfire fighters which came to defend the evacuation from southern England. This meant that the full power of the

A Junkers Ju 88A-4 in flight. This multi-role aircraft served in all the fronts of the Second World War. (Militaria Arganzuela)

Ready for a high-altitude mission , this pilot is equipped with winter flight gear. He is wearing a HM5/15 series oxygen mask.

Luftwaffe could not be used due to the lack of air superiority in the area. Whenever the German bombers attacked the harbor facilities or the beaches, the RAF (Royal Air Force) fighters were there to disrupt the bombings, causing significant losses on German aircraft. However, on May 27 the *Luftwaffe* managed to bomb the harbor and disable most of its facilities. Despite the pressure, many thousands of men on the beaches were ferried out by a myriad of small craft pressed into service by the Royal Navy and some of them manned by amateur seamen. After nine days of evacuation, the operation came to an end in June 4. The RAF had lost 177 aircraft and the Germans 240. Some 198,000 British and 140,000 French and Belgian troops had been saved, but virtually all of their heavy equipment had to be abandoned.

The Battle of Britain

After the fall of France, the British government was certain that Germany's next target would be the islands. Even though Hitler did not have a definitive plan for an invasion, he ordered the outline of an operation called *Seelöwe* (Sealion). Hitler knew that there was no way he could invade Britain on the ground without first gaining air superiority, and the British military leadership also knew that stopping the *Luftwaffe* would be the key to their survival. Once sure air superiority could be gained, he hoped to break Britain's will and defuse his only enemy in the west before concentrating on the attack on the Soviet Union. At the beginning of the battle, the British possessed some 600 frontline fighters to defend themselves, while the Germans had about 1,300 bombers and dive bombers at their disposal and about 1,200 fighters, stationed in bases from Norway to the coast of France.

These pre-production Focke Wulf Fw 190A-0 fighters await the test pilots in a German air base. (Militaria Arganzuela)

View of a Heinkel He 111 in flight. This medium bomber was designed at the beginning of the thirties and masqueraded as a transport aircraft to circumvent the restrictions of the Treaty of Versailles. (Militaria Arganzuela)

It is generally accepted that the battle started about the 10th of July and ended on the 31st October of 1940, but others believe that the point which marked the end was actually the moment when the *Luftwaffe* withdrew their bomber units from the battlefield in preparation for the attack on the Soviet Union. The *Luftwaffe* had no systematic or consistent plan of action. However, the campaign can be roughly divided in four phases: The first comprised air battles in the English Channel and the attack of British vessels, ending on the 11th of August. The second phase started with the attack on coastal airfields and the disruption of the radar stations, lasting until the 24th of August. The next phase was directed at the airfields and Fighter Command and ended on the 7th of September, when the *Luftwaffe* decided to shift their targets to the city of London.

Operations began in early July 1940, with a series of bomber attacks against British vessels along the English Channel and also targeting several ports located in southern England. In early August, the number of aircraft engaged in the battle was still relatively small. The radar early warning gave the Fighter Command a clear view of the direction of enemy groups approaching British soil and allowed them to direct their fighter forces at them to prevent them from bombing. When the Germans realized that the radar provided some early warning against German raids, the first attempts at blinding them took place. Several stations were damaged, but were repaired and worked again in less than seven hours. The *Luftwaffe* failed to mount repeated attacks in order to knock them down definitively. Neither Göring nor his subordinates realized how vital the radar stations were to the defense of the Island, and soon ordered to stop the attacks on the radar chain.

Two ground crew workers cheerfully load belts of 20 mm ammunition for the MG 151 guns of a Messerschmitt Bf 109 fighter aircraft.

A row of Dornier Do 217 "flying pencil" *light bombers lined in an airfield. (Militaria Arganzuela)*

The attention was then turned to the destruction of Britain's Fighter Command and airfields. The RAF had the advantage of flying in their home soil. Pilots who were forced to bail out of their aircraft were usually back at their airfields within hours to continue fighting. Meanwhile, any *Luftwaffe* pilot or aircrew forced to bail out on British territory became immediately a prisoner of war, or had the risk of death by drowning or exposure if the aircraft was shot down over the English Channel. Pilots and crew members began to suffer a form of combat fatigue known as the *Kanalkrankheit* or *"Channel Sickness"*.

The *Luftwaffe* was losing planes and pilots at an alarming rate, and even though they never lost the superiority of men and machines, the strategy of attacking airfields put increasing strain on the resources of the remaining forces. Thus, on the 7th of September, the first raid was launched again the docks in the East End of London. The attacks continued with massive raids pounding the docks and also the city itself. The change of target, though painful for the population of London, was the turning point of the battle, as it gave the RAF a critical rest to reorganize at a moment when its forces were on the limit. The German fighter escorts had a limited fuel capacity and they could stay with the bombers only ten minutes of flying time before having to return to their bases. This left many of the bombers completely undefended, with the result of a great number of casualties inflicted upon the enemy by the RAF.

Finally, on 19 September, Operation *Seelöwe* was postponed indefinitely by Hitler. It had been the first time in history when air power alone had decided the outcome of a major battle. The German air attacks against Britain were massive, but their initial intensity could not be maintained by the Germans, considering the high losses they were sustaining, as twice as many aircraft as the British. Indeed, by the battle's end, the *Luftwaffe* had lost 1,700 planes to 900 British planes.

War against the Soviet Union

"Barbarossa" was the code name for the German operation to invade the Soviet Union. The plan was announced by Hitler to German officials in the summer of 1940, and was to be carried out in the spring of 1941. It comprised the largest force ever assembled for a single operation in the annals of military history, meant to fight in a front of over two thousand miles. Three Army Groups had been tasked to deliver the attack on Soviet territory. Leningrad and the Baltic region would be secured by Army Group North, while the conquest of Moscow would be the duty of Army Group Center. *Generalfeldmarschall* Rundstedt, commander of Army Group South, would be in charge of the southern thrust, aimed at occupying the Ukraine region.

The attack started on the morning of June 22, 1941. In total, the Germans used three million soldiers, more than 3,500 tanks, 7,200 artillery guns, 1,800 aircraft and 750,000 horses. The *Luftwaffe* managed to wipe out the Red Air Force from the skies during the first days of the operation, a demonstration of its technical competence and one of the most important tactical victories of the beginning of the campaign. Much of the Soviet aircraft were destroyed on the ground. The Germans used the element of surprise to their full advantage and the superiority of the German aircraft became evident from the initial skirmishes. But the success can also be attributed the fact that Stalin refused to believe the intelligence reports indicating an attack from

A Luftwaffe *static anti-aircraft flak unit in action. Over the course of the war, the continuous attacks by first RAF, then USAAF bombers on German cities led to increase the number of flak units deployed.*

The impressive Me 323 Gigant *cargo airplane unloads a VW type 82* Kübelwagen.

their former allies was imminent. The *Voenno-Vozdushniye Sily* (VVS or Soviet Air Force) was one of the largest and most powerful air forces in the world. Stalin foresaw the importance of a strong air force and used immense resources to develop a modern and powerful fighting force. Scientists and engineers designed new planes, incorporating several groundbreaking technical features. The Polikarpov I-16 fighter was the world's first monoplane fighter with a retractable undercarriage. The Tupolev TB-3 bomber was the world's first long-range monoplane heavy bomber. However, the VVS suffered from a series of weaknesses. One of them was that the rate of production of modern planes was not going as fast as planned, so when the war started the Soviet air force still possessed a high amount of obsolete aircraft in their arsenal. The new MiG-3s and LaGG-3s composed only a small percentage of the fleet of the VVS. The second weakness was the lack of a modern operational doctrine and the third was an incompetent leadership. The purges that Stalin had made during the thirties affected the combat readiness of the service. The weakness of the Red Air Force was exposed during the Winter War against Finland, but no effort was made to correct the problem, because of the fear of voicing an independent opinion, a very dangerous thing to do during the Stalinist era.

The result of the *Luftwaffe* victory was the complete air superiority over the battlefield, enabling even the most obsolete airplanes in the German forces, such as the *Stuka* dive bombers, to be deployed in support of ground operations without fear of being attacked. Air superiority and close battlefield support were key components of the attack. Without the practically complete air superiority achieved in the first days of the campaign, the spectacular advances achieved by the tanks would not have been so broad. The attack also concentrated on major Soviet cities, which were mercilessly pounded by the *Luftwaffe*. Unfortunately for the planners of *"Barbarossa"*, the range of German bombers was shorter than many Soviet war industries, which were rapidly moved beyond the Urals. Even though the bomber fleet was perfectly fit for the relatively limited campaigns in the battlefields of Western Europe, the USSR presented new challenges. Being a tactical force, designed to support the ground force advances, the *Luftwaffe* made no provision for a strong strategic bombing force. Major bombing operations were mounted only when the soviets kept their ground and successfully resisted the German advances. The Soviet resistance was stronger than expected and the campaign dragged on into the winter, for which the German troops were unprepared. A Soviet counteroffensive launched in December 1941 brought the German advance to a halt. The failure to defeat the Soviet Union meant that the war in the East would continue into a second year and further deplete Germany's military resources.

As the Russian winter relented in the spring of 1942, the German High Command planned a fresh offensive for the summer with the code name Operation *"Blue"*. This offensive was less pretentious and smaller in scope, focusing mainly on the south. The aim was to cut both the oil and the lend-lease shipments that were coming through the

Production line in the Messerschmitt factory in Augsburg. The workers are mounting the instrument panels on the cockpits of the Bf 109E fuselages.

Volga River. The thrust would also sweep and seize the oil fields in the Caucasus, setting the stage for a future advance into the Middle East. On the 28th of June, 1942 Army Group South started the advance toward Voronezh. After encountering a heavy resistance, the troops were ordered to by-pass the city and push eastward to Stalingrad. The *Luftwaffe* began to bomb the city furiously as the 6th Army moved toward it and provided the aircraft with forward bases. This time, however, the Volga made it impossible to encircle the city. The rubble and destroyed buildings created by the air raids created barricades and areas where small units could take cover and set up strong points. Soviet soldiers could move from one building to another through holes made in walls, and through the sewer system, presenting a new challenge for the attacking troops. Once the 6th Army entered the city the fight was usually conducted at such close quarters that bombing was very limited in order to avoid casualties by friendly fire. The battle, which lasted six months, produced more than a million and a half casualties and meant the destruction of an entire Germany army and half of another. Stalingrad was a significant battle that marked the turning point in the war on the Eastern Front. While the ultimate outcome of Germany's war effort in the East probably was determined by its failure to defeat the U.S.S.R. in its 1941 campaign, Stalingrad was the high water mark of Germany's eastward advance. After its defeat at the city named after the Soviet dictator, the Reich never occupied as much Soviet territory for the rest of the war, and with some exceptions, would be in continuous retreat until their defeat. The campaign also had serious consequences for Germany in terms of manpower, material and morale. The *Luftwaffe* was already overstretched, having not only to support German armies in the east and also fight against Allied armies on the ground of north Africa and Italy, but also had to face the growing Allied strategic bombing campaign over the skies of the Reich. In the west, the British were beginning to acquire the capability needed to attack German cities by night, while the first units of the U.S. Army Air Force would soon appear over the daytime skies of Western Europe. In the Mediterranean, the Germans had virtually lost control of the skies. Germany was faced to fight in multiple fronts against increasing enemy strength using forces that barely reached pre-war levels.

The *Luftwaffe* suffered from the lack of an efficient management. Many factors converged to weaken the German air force, starting with the failure to draw objective conclusions from the attrition rates of 1940, an arrogant attitude after the early victories and especially the refusal to recognize the fact that modern war was a struggle of industrial production as well as a conflict on the battlefield. Germany was facing a strong coalition of nations with an air force that was already in serious trouble. The fact that it managed to recover from this situation and managed to hold on for the next years is a remarkable achievement on the power of the German people and their military institutions.

The defense of the Reich

While military events and production decisions taken during 1940 and 1941 had sealed the Third Reich's fate, strategic decisions taken in 1943 determined how events would unfold. The western air war had remained mainly a peripheral theatre, and only focused the interest of Hitler and the *Luftwaffe* staff after several British successes such as the May 1942 Cologne raid. However, the threat in the west remained no more than that for the remainder of 1942. However, in the summer of 1943, and for the first time since 1940, aircraft losses in the west reached a sizeable proportion of total losses. Deprived of precious fuel, its units ravaged by the summer attrition, the *Luftwaffe* was a force that no longer exercised any influence on the conduct of either air or ground operations. The price that American bombers paid to keep the *Luftwaffe* down was at times high. The attacks on the synthetic fuel factories of early September cost the Americans no less than 91 bombers, but the destruction of fuel capacity and aircraft kept the Germans from any substantial recovery. On November 2, 1944, Eighth and Fifteenth Air Forces launched a massive attack on the German fuel industry. Of the 490 fighters that took off to meet the invading formations, the *Luftwaffe* lost no less than 120 aircraft with 70 pilots killed and wounded. Approximately 40 American bombers fell.

The end

In 1944 the *Luftwaffe* was no longer a force that could affect the course of the war. By April, the task facing the *Luftwaffe* had become palpably beyond its capabilities. The Allied air strategy against Germany's transportation and oil production infrastructures placed Anglo-American air efforts within the framework of overall Allied strategy. The pressure of Allied air and ground forces, landed and supported by their navies, caused the *Wehrmacht's* entire defensive structure in France to collapse. That collapse threatened to become complete at the beginning of September, but the Allies missed their chance to finish it. Germany's enemies now based their aircraft in France and Belgium, and even Spitfires were in range far to the east of the Rhine. For the Allied air forces, the problem was how to turn their air superiority into final victory. At the end of September, control of Allied strategic air forces returned to the air commanders. Like the ground commanders, Air Chief Marshal Sir Arthur Harris and General Carl Spaatz searched for their answer to the question of final victory. They thought that defeat would be achieved by bombing what little remained of Germany's cities. But the final collapse would only arrive when the foot soldier moved through the broken wreckage of what had been the Third Reich.

Continued, tenacious German resistance only insured that the Reich would suffer even worse physical destruction and mounting casualties. It is not easy to understand how the German pilots were able to fly against such overwhelming odds. The most obvious reason seems to have been the fact that from the summer of 1943, German fighter pilots were desperately struggling to save their homeland from Allied bombing. In such circumstances and considering the loyalty, teamwork and brotherhood that existed between *Luftwaffe* personnel, it is not surprising that German pilots continued to fly in the face of terrible odds. The outstanding quality of middle-level leadership also explains it. Squadron and flight commanders kept their organizations together based in an inflexible refusal to lower the standards in the officer's corps. There was one additional element in the Germans' ability to continue the flight. When units had

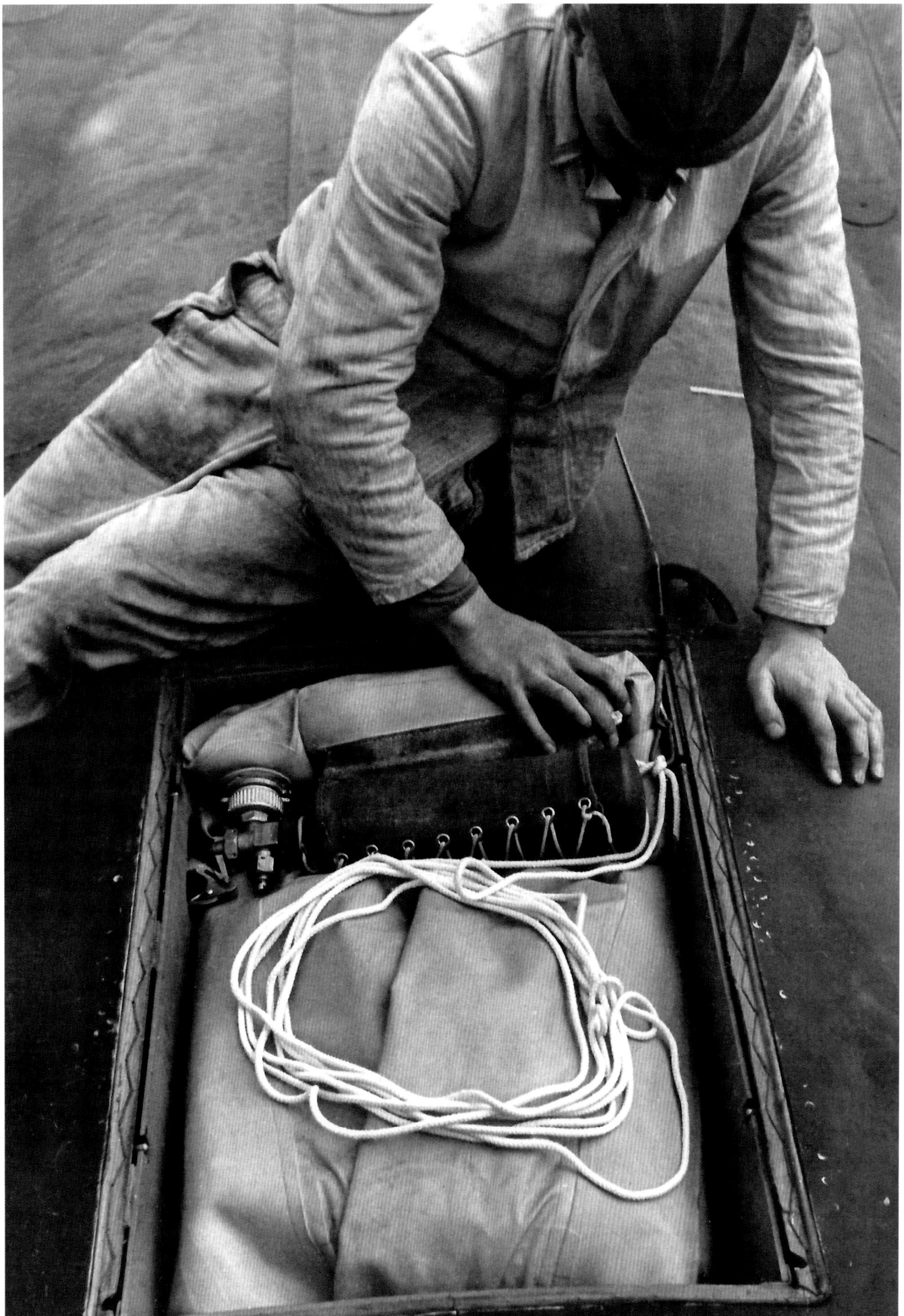

This ground crew member inspects the inflatable life raft mounted on the aircraft before a mission. Notice the compressed air bottle attached to the raft.

been badly hit by heavy losses, they were pulled out of the battlefield to be built again and refitted with new crews and new aircraft, keeping the men in the same outfits. This allowed German airmen to renew the bonds between those who would fly and fight together and who would depend on each other for survival.

The failure of the *Luftwaffe* was symbolic of the fate of the Third Reich. Germany's leaders wanted to reach goals that were well beyond the capabilities of the nation. The tremendous but misleading success in the first years of the war should not disguise the lack of professionalism in the ranks of those who conducted the Third Reich operations. While there was undoubtedly a high degree of competence on the tactical and operational side, it is also true that the inability to coordinate the resources available and make them work on the level of grand strategy was also present. The structure of the *Luftwaffe* was a grand reflection of its commander, Hermann Göring. He was responsible of creating a personal army with responsibilities as far reaching as possible. The *Luftwaffe's* technical superiority was hampered by the continuous upgrade of existing aircraft. Instead of introducing new planes (with technological advances that might not be needed), it had to cope with a production program that failed to produce aircraft in sufficient numbers. This excessive commitment inevitably lead to a rate of attrition the *Luftwaffe* could not sustain and both quality of aircraft and aircrew gradually deteriorated. The loose of pace was also reflected in the technical development of their flight equipment, which was far superior to those of their enemies when the war broke, but dragged down during the war, contrary to the great improvements made in the personal flight equipment of allied pilots and crews in the last stages of the war. The particularly difficult operational and logistical difficulties that arose during the eastern campaign also reduced its fighting capability. By the end of the war the *Luftwaffe* was a shadow of its former self, gradually fighting a worsening battle of attrition, which it had no hope of winning. Between 1939 and 1945 more than 3,500,000 men and women served in the *Luftwaffe*. More than 165,000 were killed, over 192,000 were wounded and some 155,000 went missing. The *Luftwaffe* was officially disbanded in August of 1946 by the Allied Control commission.

ORGANIZATION AND CHAIN OF COMMAND

The *Luftwaffe* was one of three branches of the German armed forces *(Wehrmacht)* and was organized and administered independently of the Army and the Navy. The *Luftwaffe* itself was divided into three parts: air, air signal, and antiaircraft artillery. The majority of the *Luftwaffe* was formed by air units, and also had *Fallschirmjäger* or paratroop units, field divisions as well as many smaller anti-aircraft, engineer, communications, security units, medical corps and air police. It was organized on a territorial basis and with separated operational and administrative commands. This organization made it achieve a mobility and flexibility which was largely responsible for its initial success.

Luftwaffe *troops parade in front of a high-grade officer, while a field music band plays in the background. The bomber is a Ju 86. The photo was taken in a German airfield.*

High Command

The Third Reich had a single branch of the government known as the High Command of the Armed Forces (O.K.W. - *Oberkommando der Wehrmacht*), with Hitler as Commander-in-Chief and *Generalfeldmarschall* Keitel as Chief of Staff of the High Command and Commander-in-Chief of the German Army. Each branch of the German Armed Forces (Army, Navy and Air Force) had its own High Command: that of the Air Force was the *Oberkommando der Luftwaffe* (O.K.L). *Reichsmarschall* Göring was the Commander-in-Chief of the Air Force or *Oberbefehlshaber der Luftwaffe*, in charge of the administration and operations of the Air Force, and also the head of the Ministry of aviation or *Reichsluftfahrtministerium*, responsible for the coordination and supervision of civil aviation and the development and production of military aircraft.

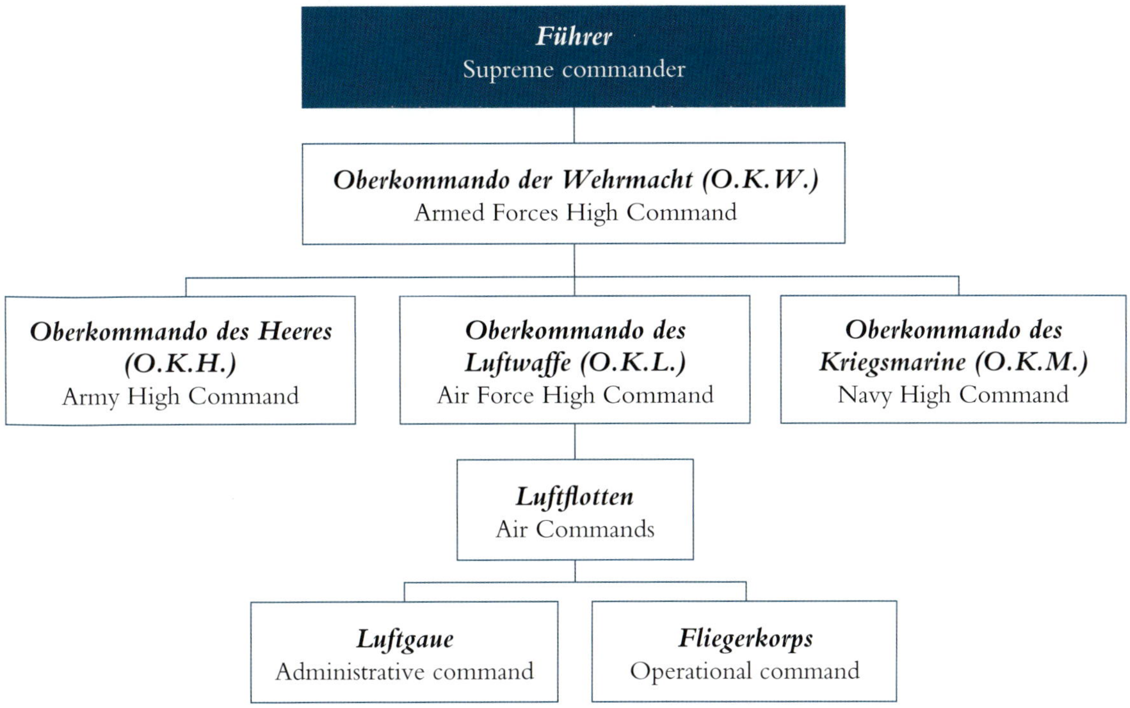

Luftflotten (Air commands)

The *Luftwaffe* was initially divided into four tactical and territorial air commands known as *Luftflotten*, each of which was assigned to a particular command area and controlled all air operations and activities in that area. When the war started and the German Army began occupying more territory, the air commands had to be expanded accordingly. What follows is the evolution of the *Luftflotten* during the course of the war:

1939	
Luftflotte 1	*Northeast Germany*
Luftflotte 2	*Northwest Germany*
Luftflotte 3	*Southwest Germany*
Luftflotte 4	*Southeast Germany*

1942	
Luftflotte 1	*Central front Russia*
Luftflotte 2	*North Africa, Italy and Greece*
Luftflotte 3	*France, Holland and Belgium*
Luftflotte 4	*Southern Russia*
Luftflotte 5	*Norway and Finland*
Luftwaffe befehlshaber Mitte	*Germany*

1944	
Luftflotte 1	*Baltic region*
Luftflotte 2	*Northern Italy*
Luftflotte 3	*France, Belgium and Holland*
Luftflotte 4	*Hungary, Yugoslavia, Romania and Bulgaria*
Luftflotte 5	*Norway and Finland*
Luftflotte 6	*Central front east*
Luftflotte Reich	*Germany*

1945	
Luftflotte 1	*Lithuania*
Luftflotte 2	*Northern Italy*
Luftflotte 3	*Western Germany, Holland*
Luftflotte 4	*Hungary and Yugoslavia*
Luftflotte 5	*Norway and Finland*
Luftflotte 6	*East Prussia*
Luftflotte Reich	*Central Germany*

Luftflotte administrative units

Luftgaue
Administrative commands

Flughafenbereichskommandaturen
Airfield Regional Commands

Einsatzflughafenkommandaturen
Operational Airfield Commands

Administration Supply Maintenance	Defense against air attacks	Operation of Signal units	Training of reserve personnel	Recruitment Mobilization Other training

The *Luftgaue* were the administrative and supply organizations of each Air Command or *Luftflotte*. They were stationary, and their authority was limited to well-defined geographical areas. They were relatively independent and responsible for the establishment and maintenance of all the airfields, workshops, fuel and weapons storage, active and passive defense against air attack, operations of signals units, recruiting, mobilizing, and training of reserve personnel, except for auxiliary units. They also had to provide the necessary administrative and supply personnel and their organization. The *Flughafenbereichskommandaturen* or regional commands were essentially administrative units and were not necessarily located at an airfield. They were mostly self-contained and only requested the assistance of the *Luftgau* when the units that had already been assigned to them proved inadequate. Meanwhile, the *Einsatzflughafenkommandaturen* or operational airfield commands had the mission of serving the flying units at their stations, so they were located on the airfields.

Generals Alfred Keller and Robert Ritter von Greim talk during a parade. Both were aces of the Great War and recipients of the prestigious Pour le Mérite *award.*

Luftflotte operational units

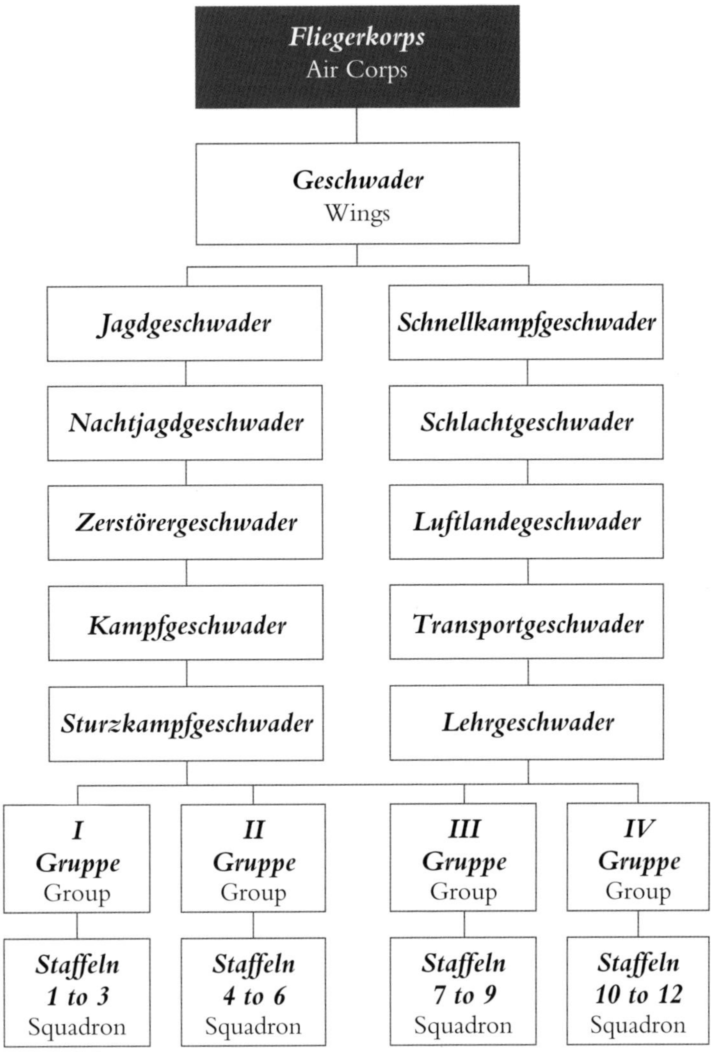

The *Luftflotte* had a series of subordinate operational commands known as *Fliegerkorps* or Air Corps. They were mobile commands that exercised control on the operations its own geographical area. Each *Luftflotte* could have one or several *Fliegerkorps* under its command, depending on the size of the command area and the nature of operations. Each *Fliegerkorp* was divided into different subordinate units or *Geschwader*.

The *Geschwader* was the equivalent of a Wing in the United States Army Air Forces. It was the largest homogeneous unit in the *Luftwaffe* and the largest to have a fixed nominal strength. The *Geschwaderkommodore* or *Kommodore* was the highest rank of the *Geschwader*. It was usually a *Major* or above in rank and also flew in combat operations with other airmen of his staff. A *Geschwader* had between eighty to one hundred and sixty aircraft, depending on the operational role. All aircraft within a *Geschwader* were of the same type, although the make and model may differ among other inferior-sized units. Initially the *Geschwader* was divided into three *Gruppen*, but occasionally would contain a fourth and sometimes a fifth, depending on the specific mission. Later in the war the fourth *Gruppe* was officially added. There were several types of *Geschwader* depending on the operational employment and the types of aircraft, bearing a prefix that indicated its role, as shown in the accompanying chart.

Geschwader		
Name	**Type**	**Abbreviation**
Jagdgeschwader	*Fighters*	*JG*
Nachtjagdgeschwader	*Night fighters*	*NJG*
Zerstörergeschwader	*Heavy fighters*	*ZG*
Kampfgeschwader	*Bombers*	*KG*
Sturzkampfgeschwader	*Dive bombers*	*StG*
Schnellkampfgeschwader	*Fast bombers*	*SKG*
Schlachtgeschwader	*Ground/tank attack*	*SchlG or SG*
Luftlandegeschwader	*Gliders*	*LLG*
Transportgeschwader	*Transport aircraft*	*TG*
Lehrgeschwader	*Experimental combat*	*LG*

The *Gruppe* was the basic combat unit for operational purposes. It was mobile and could operate separately in any command area. The *Gruppe* was led by a *Gruppenkommandeur*, which was an executive post held by an aircrew member whose rank could vary considerably. In the case of fighter units, it was usually held by a *Hauptmann*, while a *Major* was usually in charge of a bomber unit. The *Kommandeur* had his own operational and administrative staff, and also flew in combat operations. A *Gruppe* consisted of forty to fifty aircraft, and around five hundred ground personnel. At the beginning, the *Geschwader* comprised three *Gruppen* with a fourth which was usually the training unit or *Ergänzungsgruppe*. This *Gruppe* could also be used for a specific combat operation if required. Some *Geschwader* were using the fourth *gruppe* as a fully fledged combat formation as early as 1941. Even though initially it had been intended that the component *Gruppen* of each *Geschwader* should operate together from adjacent airfields, when the war started this was no longer materially sustainable and it became common for the *Gruppen* to be scattered over a wide area and even in different theatres of operations.

The *Staffel* was the smallest operational unit. It initially consisted of nine aircraft plus three additional planes held in reserve. The *Staffel* normally had between twelve and sixteen aircraft, with twenty to twenty five pilots and around eighty to one hundred and fifty ground crew. For tactical purposes it could be subdivided into *Schwärme* of five planes, into *Ketten* of three planes, or into *Rotten* of two planes.

In addition to the units mentioned above, there were other semi-autonomous units organized no higher than *Gruppen*. These include reconnaissance, coastal, army cooperation and naval cooperation aircraft. The *Jagdführer* were separate fighter commands which directed fighter operations in any particular theatre. The *Fliegerführer* were special commanders with control over highly specialized operations such as anti-shipping attacks.

Finally, it is worth making a brief comment about the system employed to designate the unit to which an aircraft belonged. It started with the *Gruppe*, designated with a Roman numeral, or the Staffel, designated with an Arabic number. The next segment was the abbreviation of the type of *Geschwader*, preceded by a slash symbol and followed by the number, using Arabic numerals. For example: An aircraft from IV./JG 1 belonged to the fourth *Gruppe* of *Jagdgeschwader* 1, while 3./JG 27 was an aircraft belonging to the third *Staffel* of *Jagdgeschwader* 27.

Hermann Göring on a visit to an air base. His Fliegerbluse *lacks the Eagle national emblem on the right breast. On his neck, he wears his Grand Cross to the Iron Cross and the* Pour le Mérite *award. In his left breast, he wears the pilot badge and an Imperial Iron Cross 1st Class with a 1939 Spange bar. His headgear is a summer peaked cap.*

The portrait photo of this Obergefreiter *shows the tunic and fittings of the* Schirmmütze *peaked cap for enlisted men. He probably belongs to an anti-aircraft unit.*

II. UNIFORMS

The uniforms, system of rank insignia and dress regulations of the *Luftwaffe* can be traced back to the organizations that existed before its official re-establishment in 1935. The uniforms and insignia were essentially a development of the principles established by the pre-Nazi German aviation organizations.

The First World War ended with the signing of the Treaty of Versailles in 1919. The successor of Imperial Germany, the Weimar Republic, was allowed to have only a small defensive military force, the *Reichswehr*. It's size and composition was controlled by the Allies in the hope that a future German military aggression could be prevented. The *Reichswehr* consisted of a small standing army called the *Reichsheer*, and a small defensive navy, the *Reichsmarine*. However, there was no provision for an air force of any sort.

In January 1933, Hitler rose to power as German Chancellor and soon recognized the potential propaganda value of sports flying. He gave orders to integrate the many private flying clubs throughout Germany into one unified organization, as well as the flying units of the SA and SS, designated as the DLV, Deutscher Luftsport Verband (German Air-sport Association). It was created with the task of promoting the interest in all aspects of aircraft and flight. The DLV especially encouraged the German youth to join by giving courses related to model planes, gliders, ballooning, and all aspects of flying. After 1935, when the secrecy regarding aerial re-armament was lifted, it served mostly as an Air force reserve and training ground for future members of the *Luftwaffe*.

The first regulations of DLV uniforms were established in November, 1933 and were applied to the regular members of the association, which had to be bought privately by each individual. Despite the fact that this was not a military organization, at least in theory, paramilitary styled ranks and insignia, together with civilian clothes with military cut were introduced. The 1933 regulation described the color of garments, which was blue-grey wool, as well as the different styles of Service dress, caps, belts, placement of the national emblem, and a rank system that included instructions on the use of rank insignia, collar badges and shoulder straps.

The German *Luftwaffe*, was formed in May of 1935 after the passing of the *"Law for the Reconstruction of the National Defense Forces"*. This law brought back into existence a free standing German army, navy and air force. The Treaty of Versailles was renounced and the Reichswehr became the *Wehrmacht* (German Armed Forces). The newly formed *Wehrmacht* would still consist of an army and a navy, designated as *Heer* and *Kriegsmarine*. The *Reichsluftwaffe* was officially established on February 26th 1935 and constituted a branch of the *Wehrmacht*. Less than a month later, conscription was reintroduced for all three branches of service. On May 21st 1935 the *Reichsluftwaffe* designation was altered to *Luftwaffe*.

This Unteroffizier *poses for the photograph wearing a* Fliegerbluse. *He is wearing a Radio Operator Badge on his blouse.*

The Regulations of the use of different forms of dress were prescribed in a Directive of April, 1935. They applied both to officials and soldiers. These regulations were modified several times during the war in the light of the experience of the front lines in the diverse theatres of operations and the limitation of supplies. Uniformity in dress by the *Luftwaffe* personnel, as with other branches of the German Armed Forces, was an objective that was never fully achieved, as suggested by contemporary photographs. The acquisition of clothes was the responsibility of the *Wehrmachtbeschaffungsamt* für *Bekleidung* und *Ausrüstung*, the Armed Forces Acquisition Clothes and Equipment Office. The storage and distribution depended on the *Heeresverwaltungsamt*, the Army Administrative Subjects Office. This Office had branches in every Region or Military District. However, officer and certain senior Non-commissioned officer ranks were responsible for purchasing their own uniforms and

This Oberfeldwebel *is wearing his shoulder boards on the shirt. Notice the machine-embroidered National emblem, sewn on a triangular cloth base, on his left breast.*

were allotted a clothing allowance through the *Luftwaffe's Verkaufsabteilung*, the Air Force Sales Department. They could also purchase their uniforms from the armed forces clothing depots, but privately purchased uniforms were obviously made of a higher quality.

Luftwaffe Ranks and insignia

The ranks of the *Luftwaffe* were influenced by the German Air Service of the First World War. However, the DLV attempted to develop a new rank system that would serve for two purposes. The first was to disguise the military-sounding rank names and thus conceal the true intent of the association in a time when Germany was subject of strict restrictions on behalf of the Treaty of Versailles. After the restrictions were denounced by Hitler, new rank terms were introduced. Ranks were grouped in different rank classes, each of them composed of several ranks. The same rank could have a different designation depending on the branch or specialist career. Detailed information and description on branch color and ranks for special careers and formations, such as *Luftwaffe* field divisions and supplementary officers and officers of the reserves, are beyond the scope of this book.

The lowest grade personnel of the *Luftwaffe* were the Privates or *Mannschaften* ranks, as follows: *Flieger* or *Airman* (equivalent to Kanonier or Gunner, *Funker* or *Signaller*, Grenadier, Fusilier, *Schütze* or Rifleman, *Jäger* or *Mountain rifleman*, *Pionier* or Engineer and *Sanitätsoldat* for Medic), *Gefreiter* or Corporal, *Obergefreiter* or Leading Corporal and *Hauptgefreiter* or Staff Corporal, later renamed as *Stabsgefreiter*.

Non-Commissioned officers of Junior Rank class or *Unteroffiziere ohne Portepee* were as follows: *Oberjäger* or Senior rifleman, *Unteroffizier* or Lance-Sergeant, *Fähnrich* or Ensign and *Unterfeldwebel/Unterwachtmeister* or Sergeant. Non-commissioned officers of Senior Rank class or *Unteroffiziere mit Portepee* were as follows: *Feldwebel/Wachtmeister* or Company Sergeant-Major, *Oberfähnrich* or Senior Ensign, *Oberfeldwebel/Oberwachtmeister* or Squadron Sergeant-Major, *Hauptfeldwebel/Hauptwachtmeister* or Regimental Sergeant-Major and *Stabsfeldwebel/Stabsfeldmeister* or Staff Sergeant-Major. The rank compositions with *Wachtmeister* were issued for the Flak artillery and for artillery units of the *Luftwaffe* field divisions and Parachute divisions by a Regulation of 1943.

Officers of the Company grade were as follows: *Leutnant* or Lieutenant, *Oberleutnant* or Senior Lieutenant, and *Hauptmann/Rittmeister* or Captain. Officers of the Field grade were as follows: *Major* or Major, *Oberstleutnant* or Lieutenant-Colonel and *Oberst* or Colonel.

General Officers ranks were as follows: *Generalmajor* or Major-General, *Generalleutnant* or Lieutenant-General, *General der Flieger* or General of Flying Troops, *General der Flakartillerie* or General of Anti-Aircraft Artillery, *General der Luftnachrichtentruppen* or General of Air Signals communications Troops, *General der Fallschirmmjäger* or General of Parachute Forces, *Generaloberst* or Colonel-General, *Generalfeldmarschall* or General Field Marshal and finally *Reichsmarschall* or *Reich Marshall*, a rank introduced by Hitler for Hermann Göring on the 19th of July, 1940. He was the only man to hold the rank during the Second World War.

The German Armed Forces employed a color-coded system to indicate specialties within a given branch of service,

***Luftwaffe* Waffenfarbe arms colors regulations**		
Branch	**Color**	
Flak Artillery and Ordnance	*Bright Red (Hochrot)*	
Reich Air Ministry and subordinate units	*Black (Schwarz)*	
General Officers	*White (Weiss)*	
Flying Personnel and Paratroopers	*Golden Yellow (Goldgelb)*	
Signals	*Golden Brown (Goldbraun)*	
Engineers	*Rose Pink (Rosa)*	
Air Traffic Control	*Light Green (Hellgrün)*	
Administration	*Dark Green (Dunkelgrün)*	
Medical	*Dark Blue (Dunkelblau)*	

This photo of personnel of an air base posing with a Junkers Ju 86 bomber in the background shows a variety of uniform tunics, including several patterns of Fliegerbluse *and* Tuchrock *cloth tunics. (Militaria Arganzuela)*

called *Waffenfarbe*, or *"arms color"*. These colors were used on items of uniforms, insignia of rank and other accessories, mostly as piping to indicate the wearer's branch of service. The basic system was adopted by the DLV to identify the four branches of the organization. The *Luftwaffe* continued with the practice and expanded it upon the four initial colors. These early colors reflected the relatively simple initial organizational structure of the *Luftwaffe*. From 1935 on, there was a swift increase in the introduction of new colors to identify the new formations and functions. Numerous amendments and alterations in color were ordered in the following years and combined colors were used for different categories of specialist officers.

Collar and shoulder insignia

Collar tabs were adopted by the newly formed *Luftwaffe* on April 14th 1935 following the basic pattern that had been utilized by the DLV. The collar tabs were worn in matching pairs in a mirror image on the right and left collars and indicated the branch of service and rank of the wearer. They had a rhomboid shape, were made of cloth in the specific *Waffenfarbe* branch color of the wearer and placed on stiffening cardboard or sackboard inlay. The cloth was folded to the reverse and glued or sewn.

Shoulder straps and boards were, together with the collar tabs, the most visible means of indicating the rank in the *Luftwaffe*. They were made of blue-grey cloth and had a lining of basic cloth. They were either sewn into the shoulder seam or removable. They had a rounded edge on the collar end, measured 4.5 cm wide and the length usually extended from the shoulder seam to a distance of 2 cm from the collar.

The collar rank insignia of privates from *Flieger* to *Stabsgefreiter* consisted of plain oval collar tabs that were made of cloth in the specific *Waffenfarbe* branch color of the wearer and a cord piping in the same branch color sewn on the edge of the collar. Inside the tabs, aluminum wings were consecutively added for each rank upgrade, from one wing in the rank of *Flieger* to four wings in the rank of *Stabsgefreiter*. All ranks of privates wore the same type of shoulder board; the only differencing feature was the branch piping, reflected in the cloth base underlay construction of the board. Additionally, ranks from *Gefreiter* to *Stabsgefreiter* used sleeve insignia consisting of *"V"* shaped chevrons made of a triangular basic cloth to which of strips of Tresse were consecutively added for each rank upgrade. Chevrons were worn centered on the upper left sleeve.

Non-commissioned officers from *Unteroffizier* to *Stabsfeldwebel* collar rank consisted of a 1 cm wide cloth braid or Tresse with a checkerboard pattern for the trimming of collars. It was made of bright aluminum thread, but due to the visual prominence, new subdued versions were made in gray. It was sewn around in the front edge of the collar of the tunics and flight blouses of all NCOs with certain exceptions. Certain appointments wore cord piping in the specific *Waffenfarbe* branch color or the officer silver color sewn on the edge of the collar. The oval collar tabs were sewn without any space between them and the Tresse. They were made in the specific *Waffenfarbe* branch color of the wearer and had no piping surrounding them. The wings were made of pressed aluminum and were attached to the tab by prongs. They were consecutively added for each rank upgrade, from one wing in the rank of *Unteroffizier* to four wings in the rank of *Stabsfeldwebel*. Shoulder straps for junior NCOs had a Tresse placed around the edge forming a *"U"* and leaving a space on 1 mm on the edges to expose the cloth underlay with the branch *Waffenfarbe* underneath. Senior NCOs had the Tress surrounding the entire outer edge of the shoulder strap and also aluminum-colored metal pips attached by prongs. Pips were

Ranks of the Luftwaffe *(Fliegertruppe)* and approximate UK/US equivalents

Luftwaffe	*Translation*	*R.A.F.*	*U.S.A.A.F.*
Enlisted men (Mannschaften)			
Flieger	*Airman*	*Aircraftsman 2nd Class*	*Private*
Gefreiter	*Corporal*	*Aircraftsman 1st Class*	*Private 1st Class*
Obergefreiter	*Leading Corporal*	*Leading Aircraftsman*	-
Hauptgefreiter	*Staff Corporal*	-	-
Junior Non-Commissioned officers (Unteroffiziere ohne Portepee)			
Unteroffizier	*Lance-Sergeant*	*Corporal*	*Corporal*
Unterfeldwebel	*Sergeant*	-	*Sergeant*
Senior Non-Commissioned officers (Unteroffiziere mit Portepee)			
Feldwebel	*Company Sergeant-Major*	*Sergeant*	*Technical Sergeant*
Oberfeldwebel	*Squadron Sergeant-Major*	*Flight Sergeant*	*Master Sergeant*
Hauptfeldwebel	*Regimental Sergeant-Major*	-	*Senior M. Sergeant*
Stabsfeldwebel	*Staff Sergeant-Major*	*Warrant Officer*	*Chief M. Sergeant*
Officers (Company grade)			
Leutnant	*Lieutenant*	*Pilot Officer*	*2nd Lieutenant*
Oberleutnant	*Senior Lieutenant*	*Flying Officer*	*Lieutenant*
Hauptmann	*Captain*	*Flight Lieutenant*	*Captain*
Officers (Field grade)			
Major	*Major*	*Squadron Leader*	*Major*
Oberstleutnant	*Lieutenant-Colonel*	*Wing Commander*	*Lt. Colonel*
Oberst	*Colonel*	*Group Captain*	*Colonel*
Officers (General grade)			
Generalmajor	*Major-General*	*Air Commodore*	*Brigadier General*
Generalleutnant	*Lieutenant-General*	*Air Vice Marshall*	*Major General*
General der Flieger	*General of Flying Troops*	*Air Marshall*	*Lieutenant General*
Generaloberst	*Colonel-General*	*Air Chief Marshall*	*General*
Generalfeldmarschall	*General Field Marshal*	*Marshall of the R.A.F.*	*General of the A.F.*
Reichsmarschall	*Reich Marshall*	-	-

consecutively added for each rank upgrade, from one pip in the rank of *Feldwebel* to three pips in the rank of *Stabsfeldwebel*.

The collar ranks for Company grade officers consisted in the oval tab in the wearer's *Waffenfarbe* and surrounded with silver piping on the edge. The tab had a silver embroidered wreath and a series of silver-embroidered wings consecutively added in the middle for each rank upgrade, from *Leutnant* to *Hauptmann*. Company grade officers had the shoulder boards made with five bright silver soutache parallel braids that were rounded in one edge to form a button loop. The underlay was made of cloth in the wearer's rank color. The rank pips were made of gold-colored metal, one pip was added for an *Oberleutnant* and two for a *Hauptmann*.

The collar ranks for Field grade officers was displayed with the oval tab in the wearer's *Waffenfarbe* and surrounded with silver piping on the edge. The tab had additional leaves in the silver-embroidered wreaths that extended upwards and encircled the silver-embroidered wings, consecutively added for each rank upgrade from *Major* to *Oberst*. The shoulder boards were made with two bright silver soutache parallel braids with five bends on either side, including the button loop, and two bends on the base. The rank pips were made of gold-colored metal. One pip was added for an *Oberstleutnant* and two for an *Oberst*.

The individual's *General officer* collar rank was displayed on an oval white cloth tab surrounded with a golden braid, with a gold embroidered wreath and a series of embroidered wings consecutively added in the middle for each rank upgrade from *Generalmajor* through *General der Flieger*. The *Generaloberst* and *Generalfeldmarschall* ranks had a flying eagle clutching a swastika overlaying the base wreath. The rank of *Generalfeldmarschall* had the addition of two silver crossed batons on the left collar, and later in both of them. Shoulder boards consisted of three bright golden soutache parallel braids with four bends on either side, including the button loop, and two bends on the base. The two outer braiding cords were made of a gold thread while the center cord was made of aluminum thread. The rank pips were made of gold-colored metal. One pip was added for a *Generalleutnant*, two for a *General der Flieger*, etc. and three for a *Generaloberst*, positioned one above and two at the base. The rank of *Generalfeldmarschall* had the three braids made of gold, but *General officer* pattern braids were also used, and two crossed silver batons in the center.

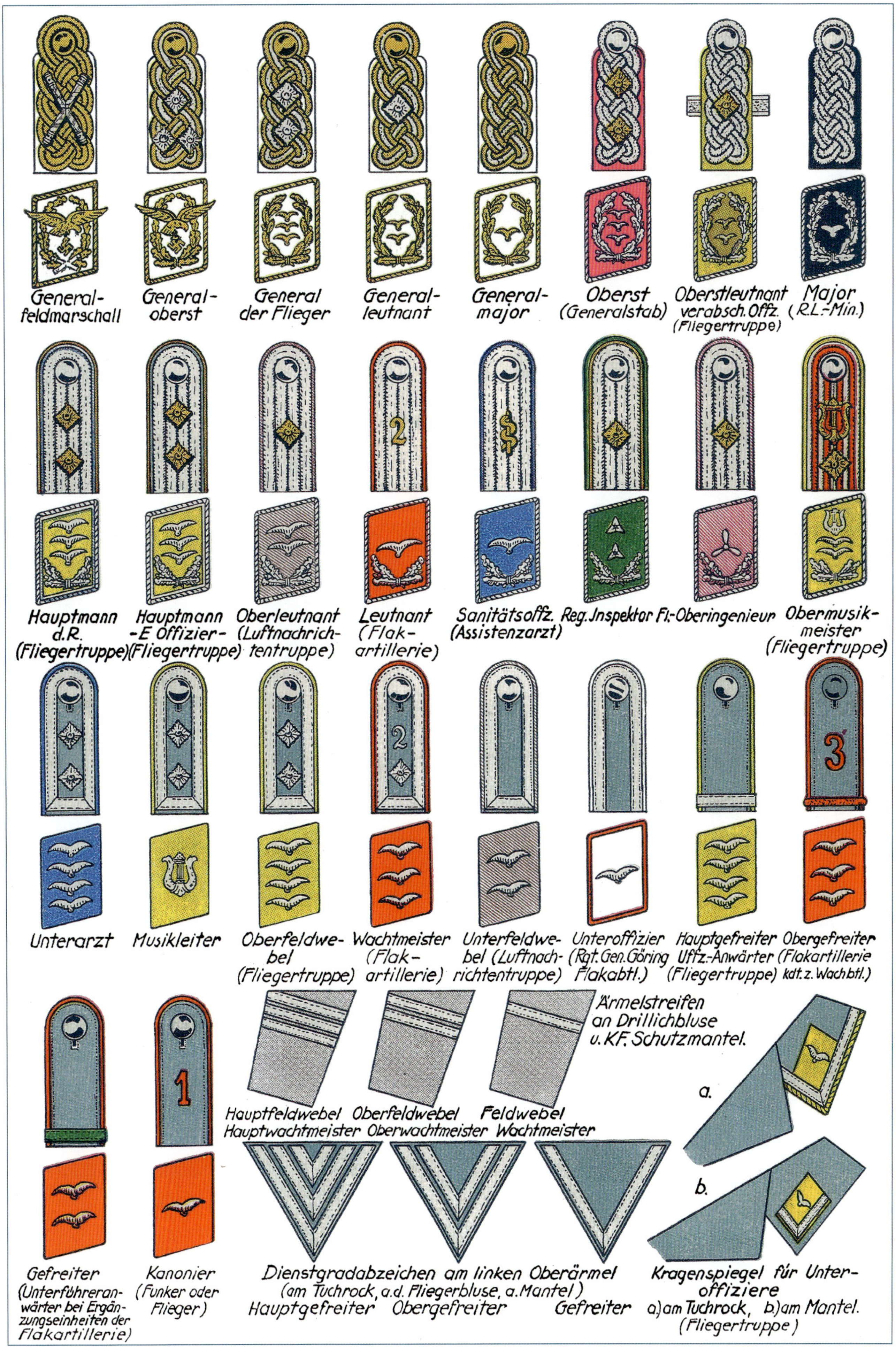

A rank chart found in the famous Reibert *manual. It shows the collar, shoulder and sleeve rank insignia of the* Luftwaffe.

A group of Luftwaffe ground troops stand at ease as the Generalmajor *in the foreground delivers an encouraging speech. He has chosen to wear riding breeches adorned with double white stripes and a pair of privately purchased non-regulation riding boots.*

This Oberfeldwebel *is wearing the two sleeve rings made of flat-aluminum braiding, indicating he was appointed for troop service and employed in the war establishment of a unit.*

This Hauptmann *is wearing a* Tuchrock *service tunic. Notice the braided collar patches and the* Luftwaffe *national emblem on his right chest pocket, which overlaps the flap.*

This Feldwebel *wears his* Fliegerbluse *as part of his walk-out dress. Notice his dagger, suspended from under the tunic.*

1. Headgear

When the *Luftwaffe* was formed in 1935, it adopted most of the headgear of the earlier *Deutscher Luftsport Verband,* the German Air Sports League. Regulations dictated for the national eagle emblem to be worn on almost all the headgear. The original first pattern national eagle, slightly smaller and with a drooped tail, was utilized until a modified, second pattern national eagle was introduced in late 1936 or early 1937. Along with the introduction of the peaked cap, a new winged wreath and a national tri-color cockade was also introduced and utilized by all ranks until the end of the war.

The early peaked caps had a saucer shape or *Tellerform* that was replaced with a new *Sattelform* saddle-shape, which featured a higher peak and a top with an oval shape. Visor caps were a standard item for all military personnel and regulations dictated the form of dress they were to be worn depending on the individuals rank. The peaked cap was worn by all ranks of all branches, including administrative officials. Officers and non commissioned officers were allowed to wear it with the service dress, the undress uniform and the walking-out dress. Officers could also wear

An Unteroffizier *wearing the* Fliegermützen *cap inclined to the right, as per regulations.*

the peaked cap with the parade dress if they were not part of the parade, together with the dress uniform. The company and Field grade officers' caps were distinguished from the enlisted men and NCO's caps by bright silver-aluminum piping and a silver-aluminum chin cord, which was gold colored in the case of general officers. They featured an embroidered *Luftwaffe* eagle and an embroidered winged wreath and cockade both mounted on a cut-out black wool base which was hand stitched in the front.

The caps for Enlisted men and NCO ranks visor caps had the appropriate *Waffenfarbe* Branch of service piping and featured a blackened leather chinstrap. Both the national emblem and the winged oak leaf wreath were made of an aluminum light metal alloy. Non-commissioned officers with the ranks of *Oberfähnrich*, *Unterärzte*, and *Oberfeuerwerker* were allowed to use the officer quality cap with officer fittings and insignia. Officers, NCO's and enlisted men could choose to purchase their caps from the armed forces clothing depots or to privately purchase higher quality versions from tailors.

The *Luftwaffe* used a *Schiffchenform* or Boat form overseas field cap, originally developed by the DLV in 1933 and adopted by the *Luftwaffe* after its official establishment on February 1935. The cap featured the *Luftwaffe* emblem and the national tri-color cockade. After the army decided to upgrade their field cap, the *Luftwaffe* followed with the introduction of the *Enheitsfliegermütze* flight cap on September 1943 as the new form of head-dress. The design of the field cap was based on the army *Feldmütze*, and the *Luftwaffe* version of the Mountain Trooper's *Bergmütze,* with minor variations. The new cap was intended to replace the *Fliegermütze* flying cap and the *Luftwaffe* version of the bergmütze mountain caps. The *Luftwaffe Enheitsfliegermütze* was made of a blue-grey cloth and had the *Luftwaffe* national emblem and cockade. Caps for officers and other ranks with grades equivalent to officials had a silver-aluminum piping running along the seam of the crown.

Other forms of headgear were also used by the *Luftwaffe,* such as the *Stahlhelm,* as well as other protective headgear specifically designed for cold weather. During the early days of the *Luftwaffe*, men wore the First World War M17 versions of the steel helmet for military training, parades and other ceremonies. When the M35 helmet was introduced, the *Luftwaffe* was among the first to receive it in large numbers. The later M40 and M42 helmet models were also used extensively by personnel of all branches of the *Luftwaffe*.

An impeccably dressed Major wearing the white Sommermütze *peaked cap. Interestingly, he has kept the inner metal ring of the cap, an element that was often discarded.*

Peaked caps

Schirmmützen

Peaked cap for officers

In March 1935, a new oval shaped peaked cap with a higher front peak than the previous model was distributed to company and field grade officers. Caps worn by officers, regardless of branch of service, featured a bright silver-aluminum piping and a silver-aluminum chin cord, except for generals, which used gold colored fittings. The top was made of a wool-rayon blue blend construction. The front center of the cap had a hand embroidered *Luftwaffe* eagle in silver-aluminum wire threads with bright silver-aluminum bullion accent threads on a cut-out, *Luftwaffe* blue-grey wool base. The black, horizontally interwoven mohair center band had a hand embroidered, winged, oak-leaf wreath together with a surrounding hand embroidered national tri-color cockade. The national tri-color cockade was usually manufactured in black and silver-aluminum wire threads with a central dot made in red colored wool. The winged wreath and cockade were both mounted on a cut-out black wool base which was hand stitched in place.

2

2. Certain non-commissioned officer ranks were authorized to wear officer's aluminum chin cords and hand embroidered insignia in their service caps, as the case of the NCO Officer candidate of the photo. However, the piping on the crown and the top were of the user´s appropriate *Waffenfarbe*.

1

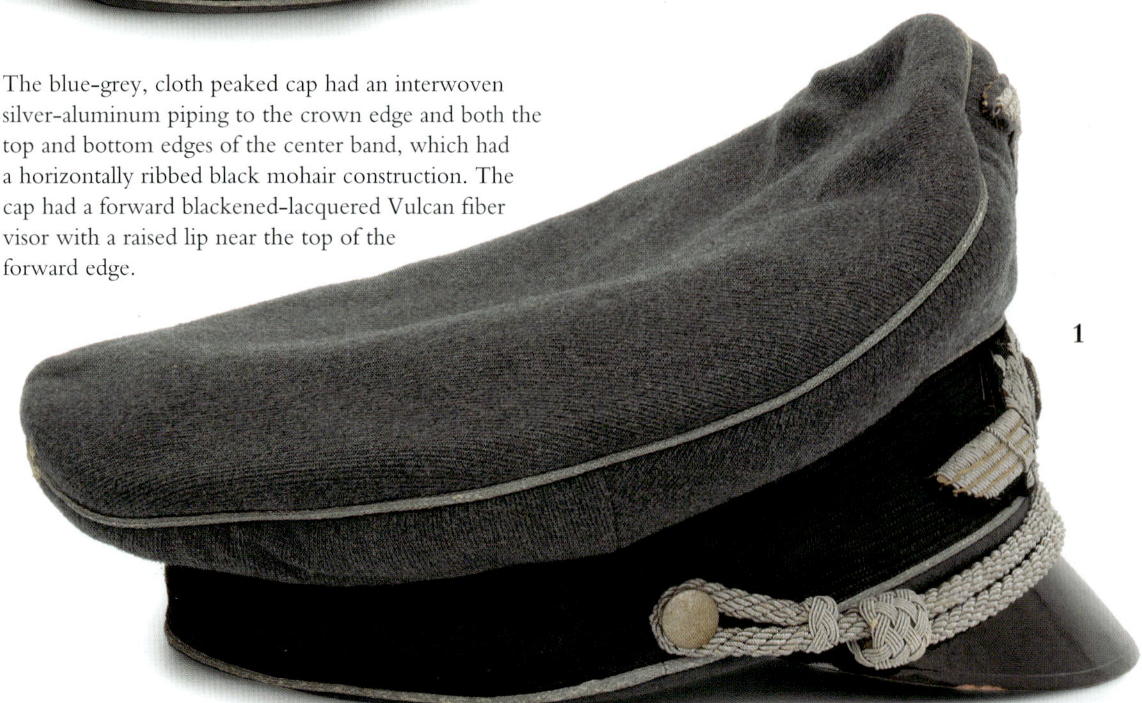

1

1. The blue-grey, cloth peaked cap had an interwoven silver-aluminum piping to the crown edge and both the top and bottom edges of the center band, which had a horizontally ribbed black mohair construction. The cap had a forward blackened-lacquered Vulcan fiber visor with a raised lip near the top of the forward edge.

3

4

3. *Above:* The internal cap crown stiffening wire has been removed but a vertical stiffener to the front center and internal padding gives the cap a *Sattelform* saddle shape with overlapping side panels and a high, central, forward peak. *Below:* The winged wreath and cockade were both mounted on a cut-out black wool base which was hand stitched in place.

4. The visor's underside featured a standard green color. It had a tan sweatband and it was fully lined with a satin material with a rhomboid moisture shield of clear celluloid material.

Peaked cap for EM/NCO

The peaked cap for enlisted men and NCOs was worn by all branches. It had the same basic construction of the officer's cap, with some notable differences. The caps utilized the appropriate *Waffenfarbe* piping, they were issued with blackened leather chinstraps and finally the National emblem and the winged oak leaf wreath were made of an aluminum light metal alloy. NCOs' and enlisted men had the possibility to privately purchase their caps, which were manufactured with higher quality materials, or obtain them from armed forces depots. Although enlisted personnel had their caps issued from the armed forces clothing depots.

6

6. The photo shows an *Obergefreiter* with an army depot issued peaked cap. Notice the shoulder sleeve insignia, worn by *Luftwaffe* ranks from *Gefreiter* to *Stabsgefreiter*.

5

5. The top of the cap was made of blue-grey cloth and had a *Waffenfarbe* band of piping cord around the crown and the top and bottom edges of the black mohair band. The cap of the photos has the yellow piping issued to personnel serving with all flight units.

7. The black leather chinstrap consisted of three sections. Two small straps with buttonholes at the end were fixed to the cap band with smooth black lacquered metal buttons. The central large strap had rectangular metal loops at either end to connect the side straps as well as two sliding adjustment buckles. All the loops and buckles were painted black.

7

8. Close-up photo of the National emblem insignia. It had a stamped aluminum construction, stylized *Luftwaffe* eagle in flight, clutching a canted swastika in one talon. It was affixed by means of prongs in the reverse. Two emblem patterns of the emblem existed, the earlier being slightly smaller than the second pattern, shown in the photo.

9. The oak leaf wreath with cockade was made of pressed aluminum metal. The wreath was painted in a silver color, while the cockade had the roundels hand painted. It was worn centered in the front of the cap band.

10. *Top:* Detail of the makers markings found in the sweatband. *Bottom:* The sweatband was made of brown leather, while the inside lining was manufactured in a light tan or brownish yellow cotton fabric. The sewn diamond-shaped moisture shield was made of stiff clear celluloid.

Summer peaked caps

Sommermützen

Summer peaked cap for officers

The use of the white summer peaked cap was permitted during the warmer months of the year (from April through October). It had the same basic construction and features as the blue-grey peaked cap, but was made of a white cotton fabric with a mixture of wool. However, other similar white fabrics were used in private purchase caps. The white top was removable for cleaning purposes and was fixed to the frame by a system with a press stud on the front. The summer caps lacked the aluminum piping around the white top, per regulations.

12

12

11

12. The removable *Luftwaffe* eagle insignia was made with silver-aluminum bullion wire with the background in white felt and affixed to the crown via prongs through stitched loops. The wreath and cockade were also made using aluminum bullion wire with bright silver highlights over a black felt background.

13. The officer´s style chin cord was made of two twisted web cords, with an eye sewn into a narrow web knot on each end. Two other larger movable knots were placed on either inner edge to adjust the cord tension. It was affixed to the cap by two silver pebbled aluminum buttons.

13

11. He Vulcan fiber visor was either matte or glossy in appearance, with a simulated machine stitched, leather trim to the rim. The raised seam on the cloth top is frequently mistaken for a white piping.

14

14. The bottom edge of the top had a sewn band of white fabric, which had an eyelet in the front to be fixed through a fastening split-pin on the frame. The frame had a protruding ring with a press button on the front to adjust the top in place.

15

15. Photo-postcard of *Leutnant* Albert Scheidig wearing the summer peaked cap.

16. The celluloid sweat diamond in the private purchase cap of the photos is marked *"Max Lindner, München"*.

16

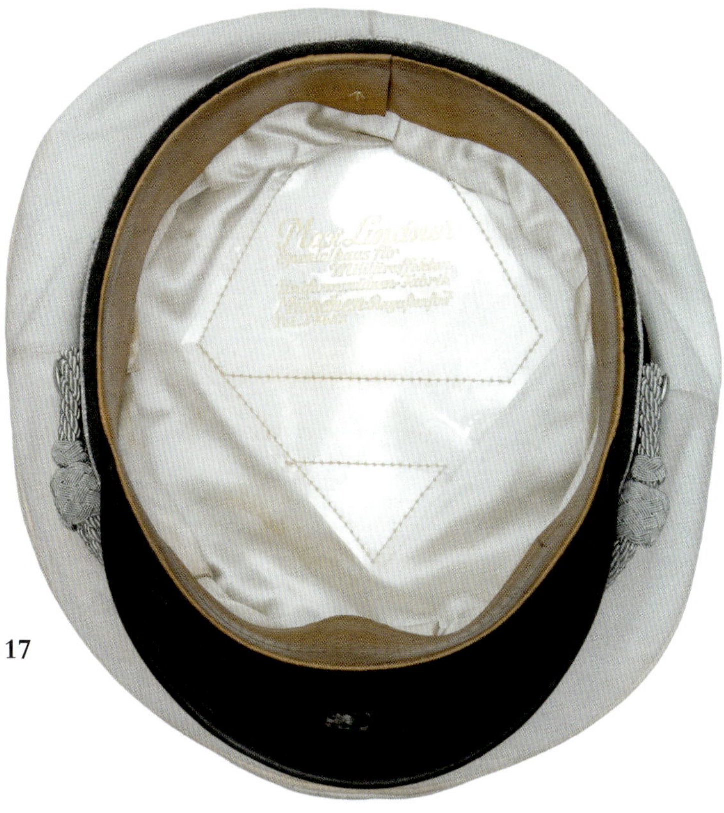

17

17. The interior had a light brown sweatband and was lined with satin cloth. The cap was made by a private firm, marked in the rhomboid moisture shield of clear celluloid material.

Summer peaked cap for EM/NCO

The *Sommermütze* summer cap was available to wear by all ranks. It had the same construction style for both officers or enlisted men and Non-Commissioned officers. The cap was allowed to be used in the months of summer as part of the white summer uniform. It featured a removable top made of a diagonally patterned cotton drill until 1937, when they changed to a double twill of white cotton pattern. According to regulations, the summer caps for enlisted men and NCO were required to have a *Waffenfarbe* band of piping cord around the top and bottom edges of the black mohair band.

18

18. The national emblem pin-on badge was centered on the upper front portion of the top, and was manufactured in a white or silver-colored embroidered aluminum metal. It could be removed in order to allow the white top to be cleaned in an efficient manner.

20

19

19. Detail of the cockade and surrounding winged oak leaf wreath for enlisted personnel. It was made of a pressed aluminum alloy and consisted of five leaves and two acorns on both sides. The wings were made of four horizontal layers with the ends set in a 45 degree angle. The wingspan was about 14.5 cm on the upper edge. The roundels of the cockade were hand painted.

20

20. Front and back views of the summer cap. The front view shows the correct location of the Eagle National emblem and the cockade. The photo above shows the summer peaked cap in wear.

21

21

21. This private purchase specimen was manufactured by the Karl Igel Company, a maker from the town of *Fürstenwalde*. The lining was made of artificial silk and had the sewn diamond shaped celluloid moisture shield in the center.

22

22. The summer cap for enlisted men and NCO had a 2mm *Waffenfarbe* band of piping cord around the top and bottom edges of the black mohair band. The visor was made of either leather or Vulcan fiber that was lined on the underside by black artificial leather until 1936, when an order prescribed visors to have a green underside. It was black-lacquered and had a sewn-on edging of black lacquered oilcloth on the rim.

Flyer´s caps

Fliegermützen

Early manufacture flyer´s cap for officers

The flyer´s cap was adopted by the Luftwaffe shortly after its official establishment on February 26, 1935. The original, short winged, first pattern national eagle of the specimen of the photos, popularly known as *"drop"* or *"drooped"* tail eagle, was utilized until a slightly modified second pattern eagle was introduced in late 1936. Flying caps for officers were usually adorned with the National emblem and cockade using hand embroidered silver-aluminum wire threads.

24

23

23. Who has more rings? These two pilots count the rings of their "Mission canes". A new ring is painted after a safe return to the base. Fighter pilots also used these type of wooden canes to mark their air victories. Both pilots are wearing flyer´s caps.

24. This early war flyer´s cap features fold down side and back panels with sloping, downward scallops to the front and forward sides. It is made of a better quality blue-grey cloth than the cap for enlisted men and NCOs.

25

25. The interior of the cap was lined in grey rayon. The sweatband has been omitted on the cap of the photos, which was a common occurrence. A cane was affixed to the longitudinal center between the cloth and the lining for stiffening purposes.

26

27

27 The cap for officers was adorned with a silver piping, the national emblem and the national cockade made in hand-embroidered silver wire. The piping and insignia for generals was made of gold thread or wire.

26. The embroidered national emblem was positioned on the upper front, with the swastika positioned above the upper edge of the flap. The tri-color cockade was placed in the front center of the flap. The silver piping was made of 3mm aluminum cord.

26

Mid war manufacture flyer´s cap for officers

The use of the flyer´s cap dates back to the DLV, the German Air Sports League. It was used by all ranks throughout the war, even though it was replaced in 1943 with the introduction of the new field cap. It was intended to be used on occasions where other form of head-dress was not required by regulations. The flyer´s cap for officers was made of better quality material than the cap issued for NCOs and other ranks.

28

28. *Above and Left:* The flyer´s cap for officers was made of a fine quality cloth. It had a Schiffchen or boat shape. Below: Some officer caps featured a machine embroidered *Luftwaffe* eagle constructed with pale silver cotton threads and mounted on a cut-out, blue-grey wool base. The national cockade could also be machine embroidered using black, white and red rayon threads. Both the eagle and the cockade are hand stitched in place.

29. The inside had a blue-grey cotton twill lining. The sweat band, when present, was sewn to the lower inner edge and was made of grey leather. The size and makers name were ink marked.

28

29

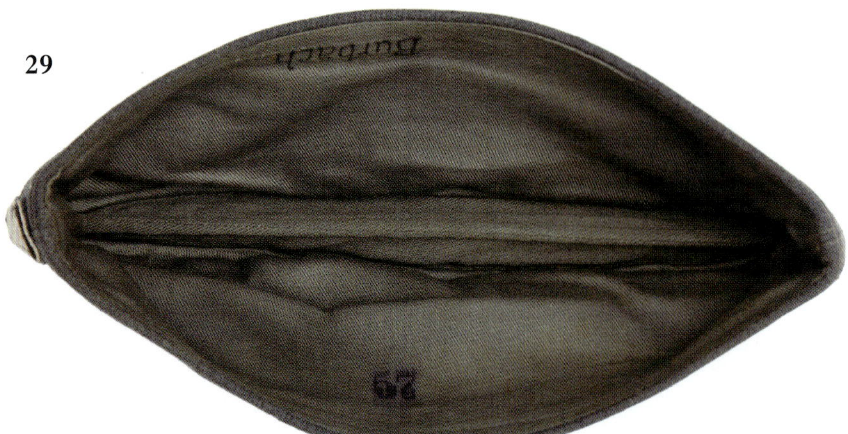

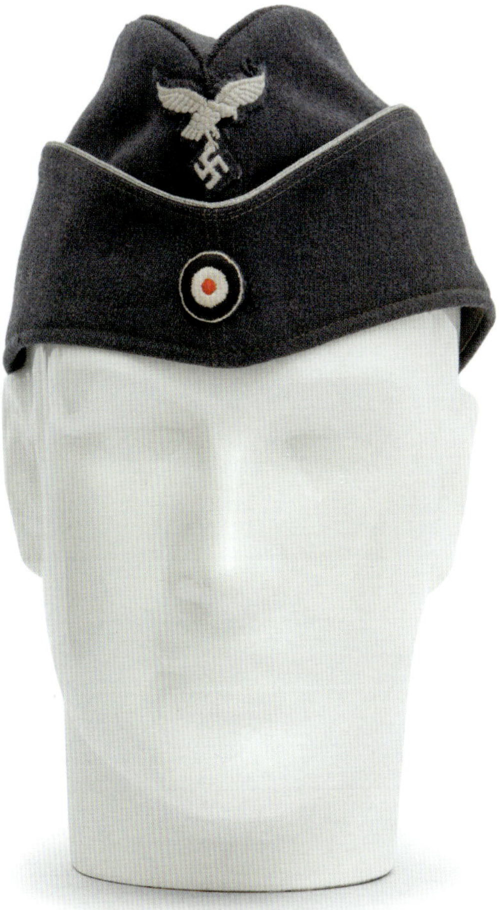

30

30. *Above: Oberst* Günther Lützow wearing the officer's version of the flyer´s cap. This famous German ace is credited with 110 victories during his service in the Spanish Civil War, and the Western and Eastern fronts during the Second World War. *Left and Below:* The so-called *Schiffchen* or boat shape of the cap is evident in the photos. The silver piping was sewn along the upper edge of the flap.

Flyer´s cap for EM/NCO

Enlisted personnel received their caps from government supplies, even though they were authorized to purchase them privately. The quality of the issued caps was lower than the private purchase and officer caps. According to regulations the flyer´s cap had to be worn in an inclined position to the right, within a finger's width above the ear and the right eyebrow. At the same time, the national emblem and cockade had to be positioned in the center of the face.

31

31

32

32

31. Caps for enlisted men and NCOs usually had no piping on the upper flap, but some senior officer candidates, such as *Oberfänhrich*, *Unterarzt* and *Oberfeuerwerker* were granted permission to use the silver piping of the officers in their flyer´s caps. In the photo, an enlisted man is cleaning an artillery shell. He wears an EM cap.

32. The inside of the cap was lined in ribbed, blue-grey cotton twill. The sweatband was frequently omitted in wartime caps. The photo shows the size markings of the cap.

33

33. The *Luftwaffe* national emblem was made of grey cotton machine-embroidered wool with a backing of blue-grey fabric. The front center of the flap has a machine-embroidered, national cockade made in black, white and red rayon threads.

Replacement caps

Einheitsfliegermützen

Replacement cap for officers

The *Luftwaffe* replacement flyer's cap was issued in September of 1943 as a new form of head-dress to replace both the *Fliegermütze* flying cap and the *Luftwaffe* version of the *Bergmütze* mountain cap. The style was similar to the army replacement field cap, but it was made of a blue-grey cloth and had the national emblem and cockade. The caps for officers and some NCO ranks featured a silver-aluminum piping running along the seam of the crown.

35

34

34. The interior of the cap was fully lined in grey rayon. The specimen of the photos has a tan leather band in the front forehead section.

35

35. The cap had a short, fabric covered forward visor with a cardboard internal stiffener, with a slightly raised lip to the bottom of the forward edge. The silver-aluminum cord along the crown of the cap indicates it belonged to an officer.

36

36

36. The front center of the cap had a machine embroidered, national emblem placed above a separate, machine woven cockade in black, red and white rayon threads. It was not unusual that officer used the standard pattern cap with machine-embroidered insignia instead of the hand-embroidered version. The photo shows the replacement cap in wear by the officer that has been awarded with the Iron Cross.

37. The back and side panels were designed to be folded down to protect the wearer´s ears and neck and the scalloped front section could be secured with the buttons closed under the wearers chin. When folded, the top edges were buttoned with one or two small buttons on the left edge and a loophole on the right edge. Buttons were made of various materials, including blue-grey plastic, pebbled silver aluminum, or soft, blue painted metal.

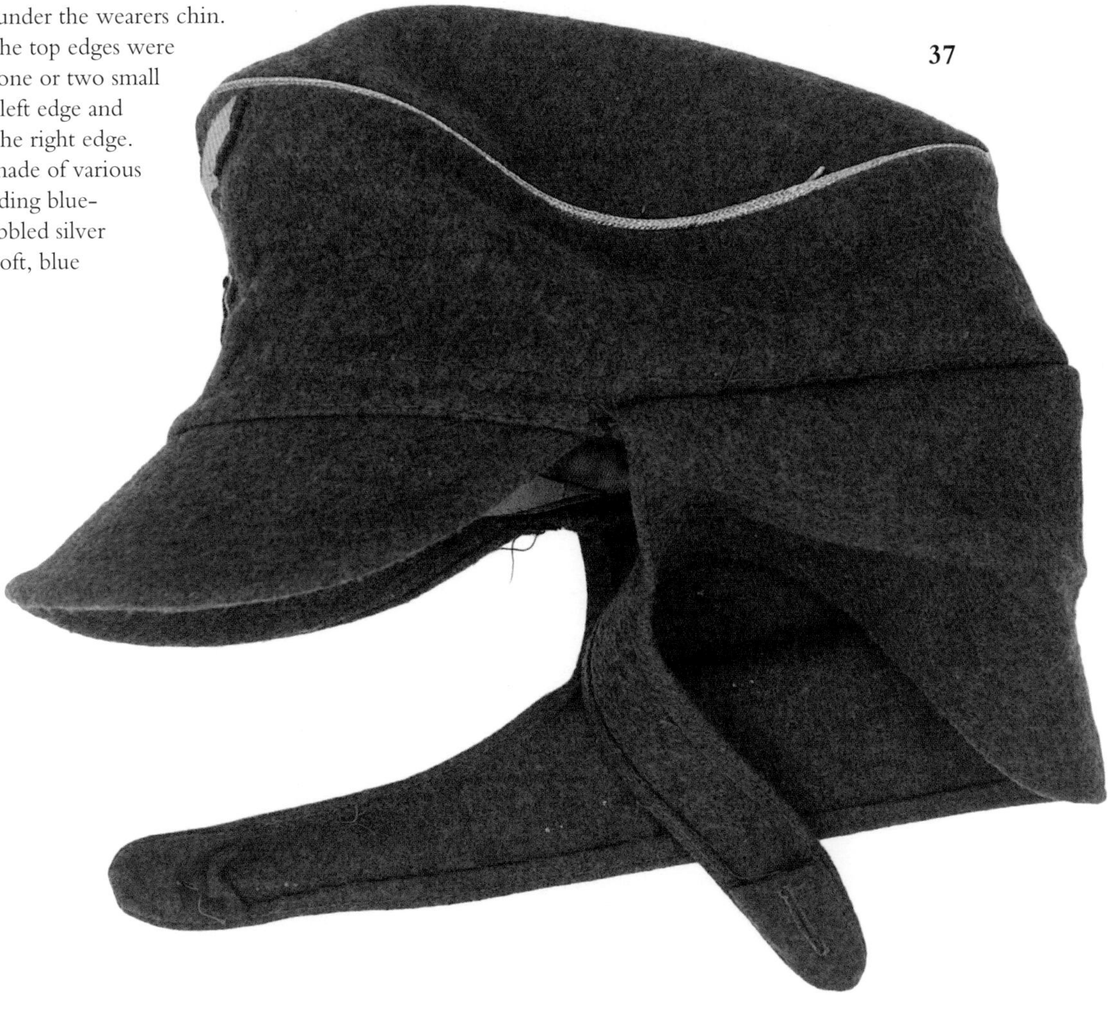

37

Replacement cap for EM/NCO

The *Luftwaffe* replacement cap was made of a blue-grey cloth and featured fold down side and back panels. The bottom edges were sewn to the body. It had a scalloped front with a single closure button stitched to the right side and a loop on the left side. When folded, the button was positioned at the front center. The back and side panels were designed to be folded down to protect the ears and neck and could be secured with the button closed under the user's chin.

38

38. Studio photo of a *Flieger* wearing the *Einheitsfliegermütze* flyer's cap. Regulations prescribed the cap to be worn horizontally, with the front center edge of the visor in line with the eyebrows. Period photos suggest that a more slanted position was preferred.

39

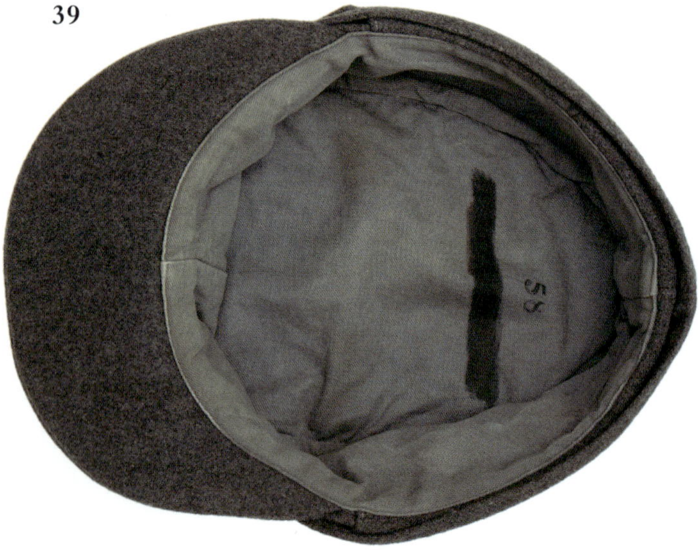

39. The visor was made with a flexible pad of plastic or cardboard, covered by the same fabric of the body. The liner was made of blue-grey twill fabric. The visor of the photos has an ink-stamped size *"58"*.

39

40

41

41. Close-up of the machine-embroidered national emblem on a one-piece backing of blue-grey woven fabric. Below the *Luftwaffe* eagle was a separate, sewn machine-woven cockade. Other caps had the national emblem and cockade machine-embroidered on a single piece backing of cloth forming an inverted triangle.

40. The folded panels were cut in two parts, with the seam joining at the back. The bottom edge was sewn to the body. When the panels were unfolded, the button secured them under the chinstrap. The buttons of the cap of the photos are made of blue-grey painted metal.

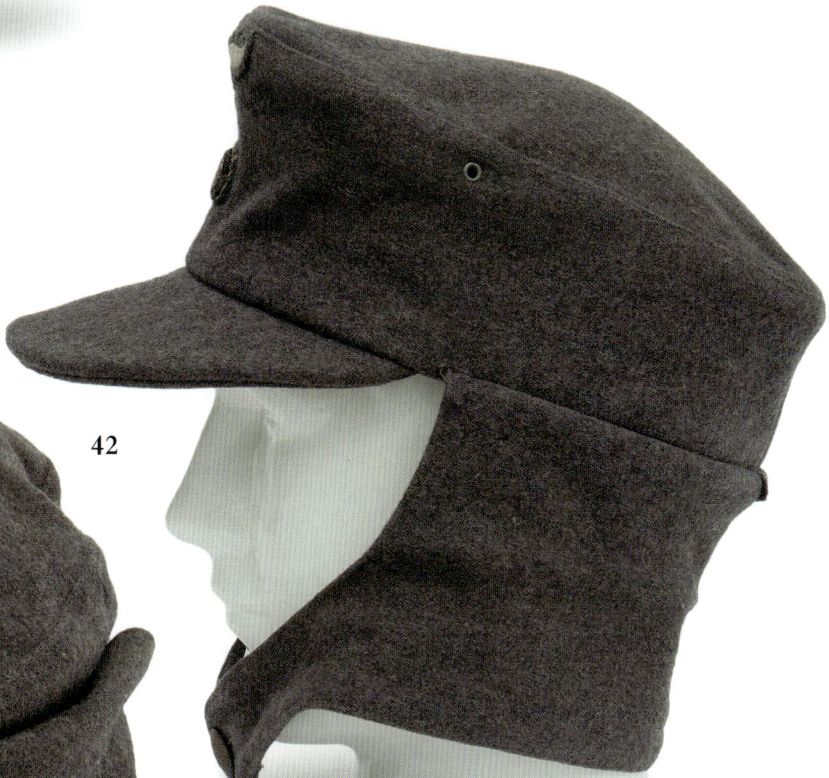

42

42. The replacement cap was sometimes manufactured with two ventilation holes at both sides of the body, placed at approximately 1 cm below the crown seam.

Winter Fur cap

Pelzmütze

The extremely cold temperatures of the Russian front in the winter found the Germans completely unprepared, and without proper cold weather garments. After the winter of 1941 to 1942, the High Command gave orders for the development of suitable winter garments. No official standard issue pattern fur cap apparently existed. Photographic evidence shows that one of the most commonly type used by *Luftwaffe* personnel was a model briefly based on the pattern of both the Mountain *Bergmütze* and *Einheitsfliegermütze* caps, including fold down back and side panels designed to protect the wearer's ears and neck.

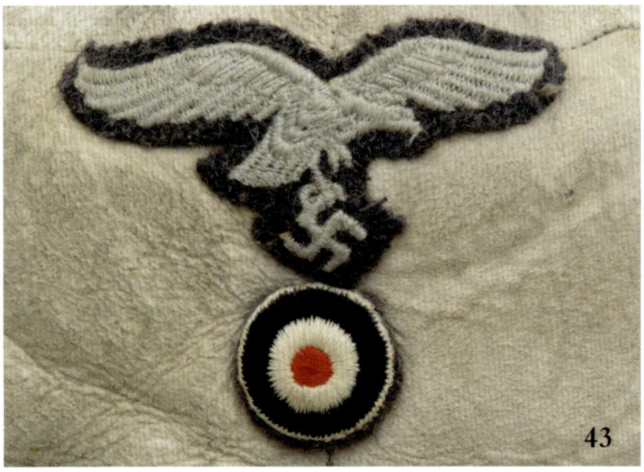

43

43. The machine embroidered national emblem constructed in silver-grey rayon threads on a cut-out *Luftwaffe* blue-grey wool base is positioned in the front center of the cap. A machine embroidered, national cockade in black, white and red rayon is placed just below the national Adler. Both the eagle and the cockade are sewn to the cap.

44

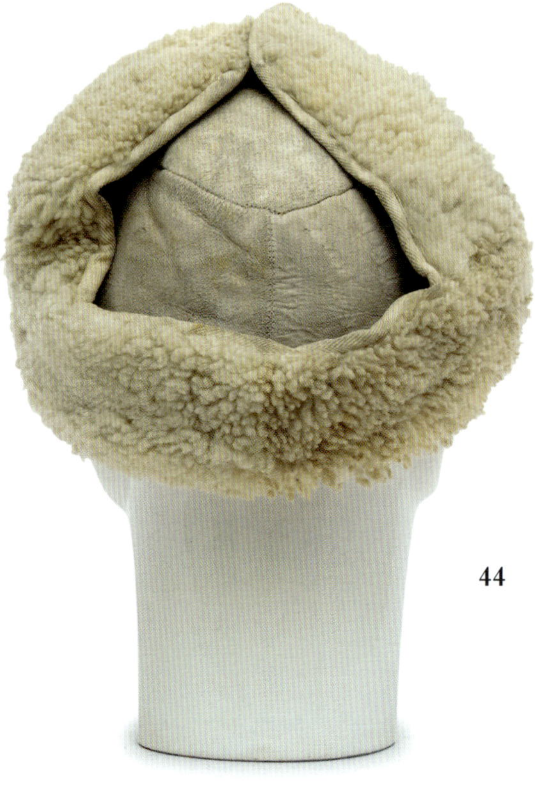

44

44. The whitened sheepskin winter cap had the hide to the exterior and sheep wool to the interior. It featured fold down side and back flaps. They were held in position at the top of the cap by a thread loop and a grey Bakelite button. When the side and back flaps were in the upright position the sheep's wool was visible to the exterior.

45

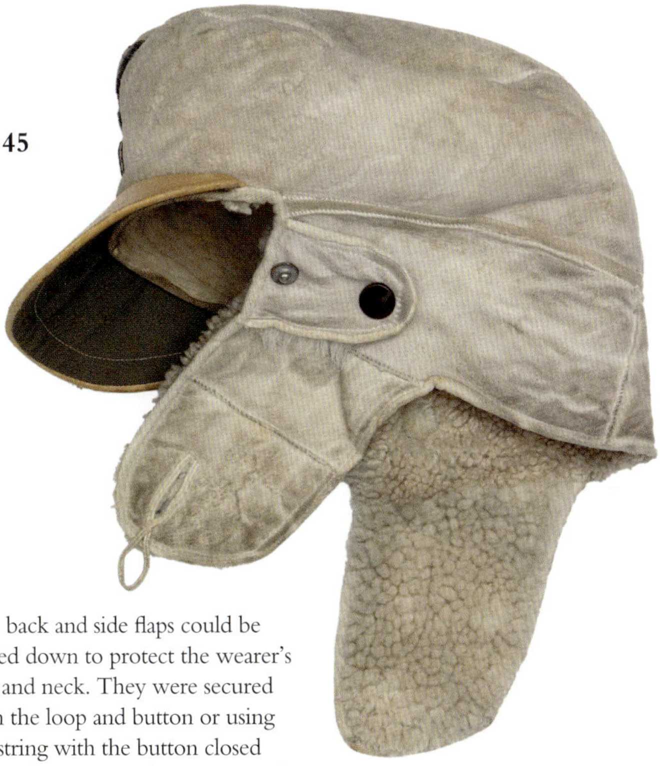

45. The back and side flaps could be folded down to protect the wearer's ears and neck. They were secured with the loop and button or using the string with the button closed under the wearer's chin as required.

46

46. On both sides of the fold-down panels was a small circular cut-out with overlapping, horizontal ear coverings with a single snap closure. The side panels also had an additional male snap which enabled the coverings to be held in the open position to expose the ear holes or in the closed position, as required.

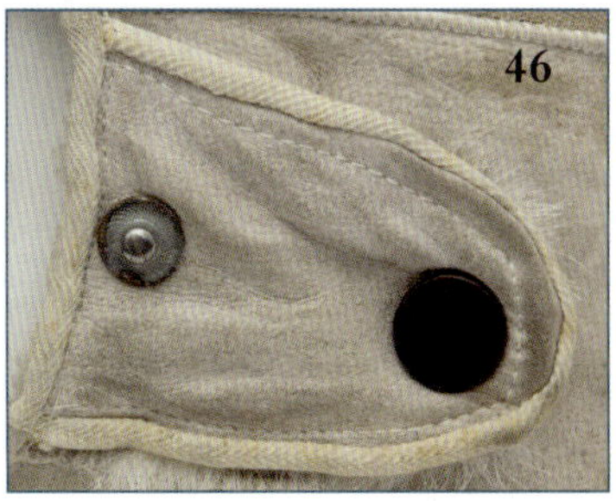

46

47

46

47. The interior of the cap was fully lined in white sheep wool. It had a machine sewn fabric tag with an ink-stamped date *"1943"*, and the *Reichsbetriebsnummer*, (National factory code numbers) a system introduced in 1942 and intended to replace the previous manufacturer markings on garments and equipment and thus prevent bombing raids on German factories.

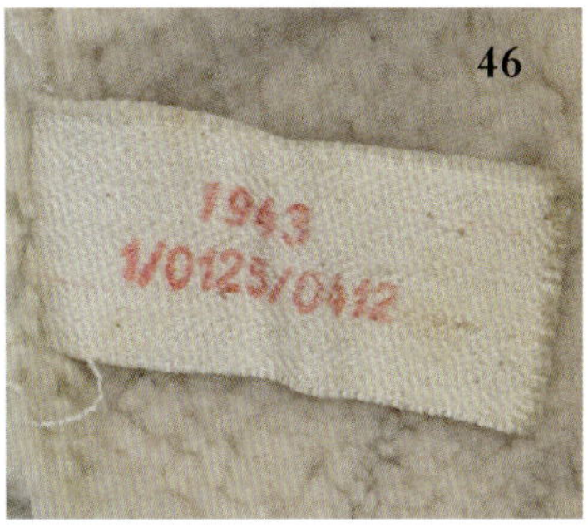

46

Helmets

Stahlhelme

M35 helmet

During the early days of the *Luftwaffe*, the First World War M16 and M17 helmets were worn during basic military training and ceremonial events. These pre-war models were used until the development of the smaller, lighter M35 helmet model in June 1935, and introduced into the *Luftwaffe* in limited numbers in 1936. It was painted both internally and externally with a satin blue-grey finish. The *Luftwaffe* pattern national eagle decal was placed on the left side, while the national tri-color shield decal was placed on the right side of the helmet. The M35 helmet was produced and distributed until 1940, when a new version was issued.

49

48

48. The M35 helmet had the entire rim crimped inwardly to a width of about 5 mm. It had three holes to accommodate the liner rivets, located at the rear center of the helmet and on each forward side, slightly ahead of each temple. Openings for the insertion of the ventilation lugs were found on each side.

49

49. Detailed photo of the national tri-color helmet decal. In March, 1940, prior to the invasion of France, an order was given to discontinue the use of the tri-color decal on helmets in production and to remove those from the existing helmets, especially those used in combat. However, the order was often ignored. *Above*: Studio photo of a *Leutnant* wearing the M35 helmet.

50

50. Detailed view of the second pattern *Luftwaffe* national emblem eagle decal which began to appear in 1937, at a moment when *Luftwaffe* insignia was being standardized for large-scale production. This type of decal is typical of helmets used from 1937 to 1945.

51

51. The chinstrap buckle was made of aluminum or steel. It had a single pronged type construction with a slight curvature. The tip of the prong was flattened and rested against the lower bar of the buckle.

52. The M31 liner system consisted of an outer ring made of light a metal alloy and an inner ring also made of metal. The light metal hanging loops with rings were attached to the outer ring. The liner was fixed to the steel helmet by three rivets and attachment pins made of aluminum-silicon-magnesium alloy. A leather lining with eight *"fingers"* made of sheep or goat leather was attached between the inner and outer rings and tied together with a string.

52

53

53. The helmet had a two-piece chinstrap made of natural leather. One end of both straps ends had tear drop-shaped eyelets to insert double-ended buttons, which secured it to the hanging loop of the helmet liner.

M40 helmet

The M35 design was slightly modified in 1940 in an effort to simplify its construction and reduce labour costs. The manufacturing process now incorporated additional automated stamping methods. The principal change was to stamp the air vent mounts directly onto the shell, rather than utilizing separate fittings. This relatively straightforward step helped to improve wartime manufacturing process, but required a new shell mould to be made. As a result, the shape of the M40 became slightly more rounded than the M35 and also heavier, as it had a slightly thicker steel shell. Also, the practice of placing the national tri-color shield on the helmet was discontinued.

54

54

54. The helmet of the photos has an unusual matt field-grey color, which suggests it was either used by *Luftwaffe* ground troops or it was a re-issue Heer helmet.

55. Detailed photo of the National emblem and the air ventilation hole into the side of the shell. The vent was no longer made from a separate piece, but simply pressed into the steel of the helmet shell.

54

56. Close-up photo of the split rivets. From 1940 the liner band was made zinc coated steel. The quality of the leather lining also changed. Sheep skin continued to be used, but goat and pig skin were also introduced.

2. Tunics

The *Luftwaffe* was formed through a combination of several paramilitary, police, political, and air sport organizations that eventually merged and turned into Germany's newest branch of service. With the formation of the German Air Force, most of the uniforms were developed from the designs that had already been established by these organizations. The groups which had the greatest influence on the Luftwaffe uniform design included the Deutsche Luftsport-Verband, the Nationalsozialistisches Flieger Korps, the Polizeigruppe, and the Landespolizeigruppe *"Wecke Zbv"* and *"General Göring"*.

The Dress regulations were prescribed by an order of April, 1935 and applied for officers and enlisted men. Commanding officers had the prerogative to alter these regulations on the field. A uniform appearance was never achieved during the war, due to several factors, being the first and most important one the difficulty of production and supply of raw materials. On the other hand, flying personnel seldom followed strict observance of Dress regulations, especially front line soldiers and pilots who preferred a smart appearance regardless of orders. Dress regulations were modified and adapted to the situation in several occasions during the war. Most of the modifications were focused on the simplification of the garments, due to combat experience and availability of raw materials.

The Gefreiter *of the photo is wearing the flying blouse for enlisted men and the* Einheitsfliegermütze *flight cap. Even though the photo was taken 1943, the soldier is still wearing the collar cord piping, discontinued by regulations since 1940.*

During the war, several types of uniforms were issued. The standard service uniform tunic at the beginning of the war was the *Tuchrock*. The standard pattern service uniform was adopted by the *Luftwaffe* in March 1935, and was based on the uniform worn by personnel of the previous sports clubs as early as 1933. Other popular garment was the *Fliegerbluse* or flight blouse. It remained in service throughout the war with minor modifications. Originally flight blouses for enlisted men and NCO's were without external pockets until regulations of May 6th 1940 when the second pattern flight blouse with external hip pockets was introduced.

An new type of uniform tunic, the *Waffenrock*, was introduced in November 1938 with the intention of replacing both the Flight blouse *(Fliegerbluse)* and the cloth tunic *(Tuchrock)*. However, the *Tuchrock* production continued after the introduction of the new garment, while the *Fliegerbluse* continued to be manufactured until the end of the war. It was single-breasted with five metal buttons and could be worn with the opened or closed collar. The material of issued tunics was twill fabric. As it occurred with other garments, officers and certain senior NCO's could choose to purchase their uniforms from the armed forces clothing depots or to privately purchase garments of higher quality from tailors. These were generally made of tricot, a fine quality woven fabric, which could be of two basic weights; a summer and a winter weight.

The photo shows Hans-Ulrich Rudel on the right, shortly after being awarded with the Diamonds for his Knight's Cross, Oak leaves and Swords. He is wearing the Tuchrock tunic, while the man on the left wears a private purchase Fliegerbluse. The photo was taken in April, 1944.

Dress tunic

Gesellschaftsanzug

Evening Dress tunic

The Evening Dress was issued for wear by all officers of the *Luftwaffe*. It consisted of a jacket, vest and trousers with a Tresse on the side. The front of the jacket had two rows of four buttons on each side. Collar tabs were not used. The uniform was worn with a white shirt that had stiff breast without folds and stiff wing collar. The jacket and trousers were made of blue-grey tricot or similar cloth. The jacket was lined with artificial silk. The formal uniform dress required a white colored vest and tie, while the blue vest and black tie was used for the informal dress. White vests were made of quilting fabric and usually had mother-of-pearl buttons.

2

1

1

1

1. The photos show a fine set of rounded cufflinks with the *Luftwaffe* Eagle emblem, to be used with the evening dress uniform. They were made by the famous jeweller and silversmith H.J. Wilm of Berlin. The lid of the rectangular box has the National emblem printed on the center.

1

2. The jacket had two buttonholes on the front, beneath the end of the lapels. Two pebbled metal buttons joined by a 7 cm chain of the same color was fixed to the buttonholes. The buttons were silver for officers and gold for general officers.

2

3. The Dress Aiguillette was worn with the parade dress and dress uniforms. The photos show the pattern worn by officers up to and including the rank of *Oberst*, and also for officials with officer ranks. It consisted of a flat braiding measuring 40 cm long and a double sling of cord at both ends of the braiding than measured some 39 cm long.

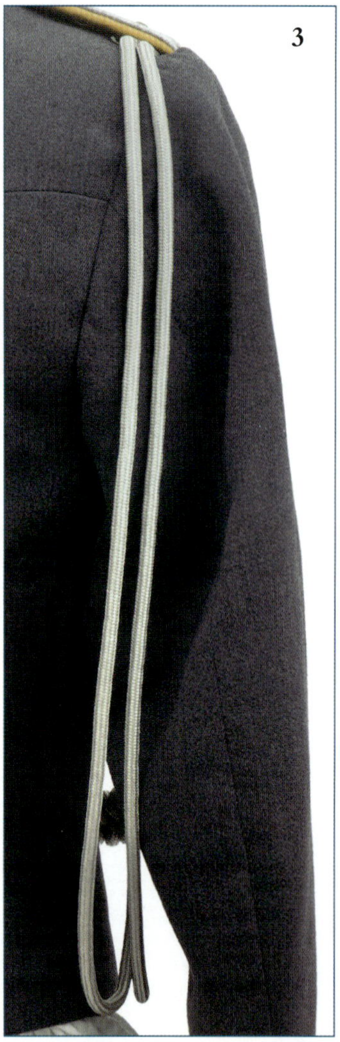

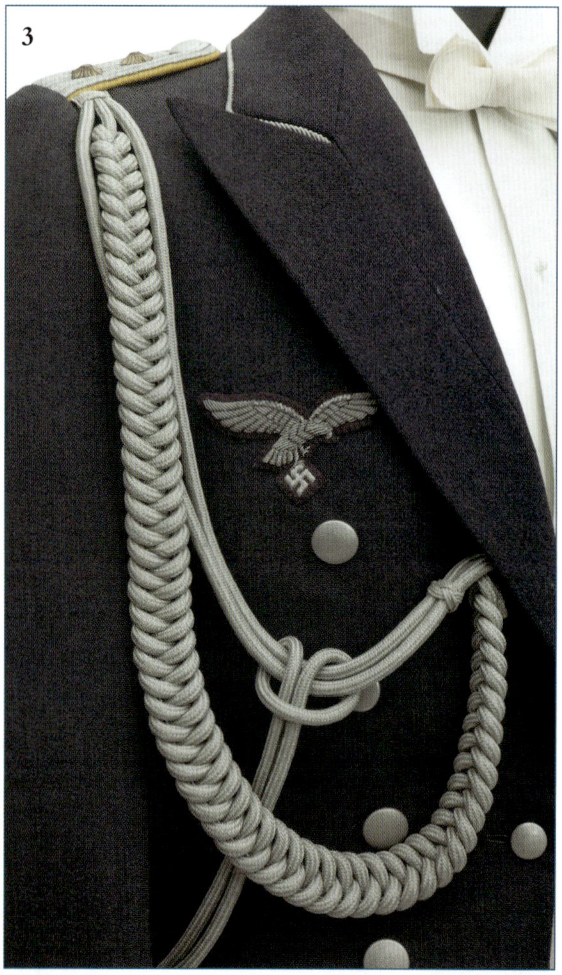

4. A thin cord with an eyelet at one end of the braiding was passed through the loop of the short cods and then secured to a button beneath the right lapel. On the other end of the braiding, the cords passed through a rectangular band of tress with a buttonhole. The band was fastened to a small horn button placed beneath the right shoulder board. The braid was placed around the right shoulder and across the right breast.

5. The bright silver aluminum aiguillettes were introduced in April, 1935, when the Evening dress was issued. The previous pattern was made of matt aluminum cording.

6

6

6. This private purchase jacket was made by Willhelm Kreutzer, a well-known tailor from Würzburg. The white cloth label sewn to the jacket indicates the name of the officer and the date of manufacture.

7. The body of the jacket was lined with blue-grey artificial silk, while the sleeves were lined with white fabric. One or sometimes two inner pockets were inserted in the lining of the breasts. The shoulder boards were sewn into the head of the sleeve seams.

7

Flyer blouse

Fliegerbluse

Flyer blouse for officers

The flight blouse was introduced in March 1935 and its design was influenced by the Imperial 1915 pattern blouse. Although specifically designed to be used for flying duties, it was such a successful design that it became a popular garment with all personnel and used for many other functions. The officer version was made of a finer quality blue-grey gabardine or similar fabric. It had two slightly curved hip pockets without flaps. The national emblem was placed on the right breast and the collar had an aluminum cord (golden for general officers) surrounding the edge.

8. *Above:* Detailed view of the *Leutnant* collar tab. Notice the twisted silver cord piping surrounding the rhomboid tab.
Right: Officer shoulder boards were made of two bright silver parallel braids, forming a loophole in the upper end which was used to secure it to the tunic. The base was made of cloth in the wearer's rank color.

9. Blouses for officer's ranks differed from the enlisted men's first type in the presence of external hip pockets. Designed for flying duties, it became so popular with the airmen that it was used in many other instances.

10. Detail of the machine-woven Eagle national emblem on a blue-grey backing. These variations are of the type worn in private purchase tunics.

11. Commemorative honor cuff titles were worn by personnel to denote the assignment to certain elite units. The *Jagdgeschwader Richthofen* title was instituted in 1935. The title was made of a 3.3 cm wide dark blue cloth with the inscription embroidered in gothic letters.

er Richthofen

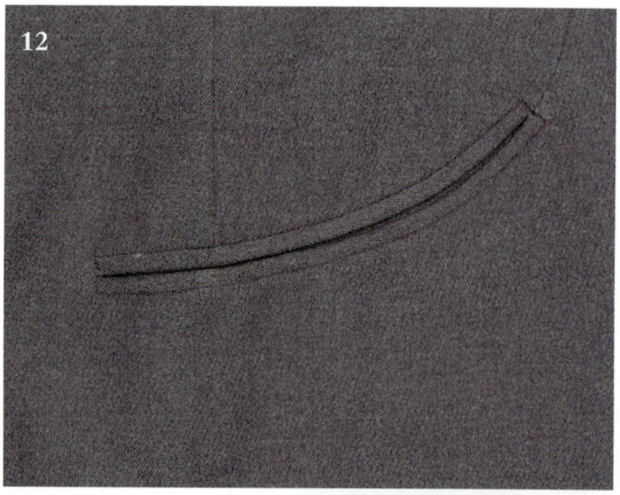

12. View of the officer´s blouse hip pockets, slightly curved and with no flaps. They measured 16 cm.

13. The lining was made of blue-grey twill fabric. It was closed by four buttons. The national emblem was sewn to the right breast.

13

These two Croatian officers are wearing Fliegerbluse *tunics. They are both wearing the* Znak Hrvatske Zrakoplovne Legije *(Croatian Airforce Legion badge). The pilots used a cloth embroidered version of the badge. Croatians volunteered to fight alongside Germany during the campaign against the Soviet Union. The pilots were allowed to wear these badges on their uniforms.*

Flyer blouse for EM/NCO

The pre-war version of the jacket had no hip pockets. In December 1940, as a result of requests from enlisted men and NCO personnel, regulations introduced external, hip pockets that closed with buttoned rounded flaps. This pattern remained in use and production during the war. It was made of blue-grey wool rayon and had a vertical front closure consisting of five buttons on the right front panels and hidden buttonholes on the left panel. The *Fliegerbluse* was generally worn with the neck open and without a shirt and tie by all ranks for service dress and open-necked with a shirt and black tie as walking out dress.

14. Collar insignia and shoulder straps of a *Feldwebel*. The Tresse braid has the typical checkerboard pattern.

15. The *Flieger* on the photo wears his *Fliegerbluse* without the *Luftwaffe* Adler on the right breast. Its use was required for NCOs and other ranks by an order of October, 1940. The regulation was issued to make the personnel more easily identifiable in the field.

16. Detail of the Flight Technical Personnel's trade badge. NCOs and enlisted men were assigned and received training for a specific military function. On successful completion of the appropriate training, they were issued a distinctive trade specialty badge to be worn on the lower left sleeve of the service tunic and the flight and field blouses as identifying insignia.

ESPAÑA

17

17. The *Fliegerbluse* of the pictures belonged to a Spanish volunteer of the 15. *Spanische Staffel*, known in Spain as *"Escuadrilla azul"*. It was a unit of the *Luftwaffe* formed by Spanish pilots and ground personnel that fought in the Eastern front during the war. The armshield was machine weaved and had the Spanish colors and the name *"España"* on the top. It was authorized to be worn on uniforms on July, 1941 by an order of the German Army High Command.

18

18. A cloth strap with a buttonhole on one side was inserted in the rear seam of the sleeves at a distance of 3 cm above the edge. It was secured to a small black button on the other side of the sleeve. A second button placed close to the front seam allowed the sleeve to be narrowed.

18

The photo shows a mechanic Unteroffizier *of the 15.* Spanische Staffel *ready to board the train that would bring him back to Spain after fighting on the Easter Front. He is wearing a* Fliegerbluse *with several decorations and badges. On his chest, he is wearing a German* War Merit Cross *2nd Class with swords, while on his left breast, above the Spanish Falangist badge, he is wearing the Spanish* Medal for Suffering, *awarded to wounded or captive personnel. The blue color of the badge, together with the Spanish ex-captive cloth badge on his left sleeve, indicates he was he was captive in republican zone during the Spanish Civil War. On his right chest, above the* Luftwaffe *National emblem, he is wearing the Spanish Air force mechanic cloth badge.*

19

20

19. The sleeves of the blouse were slightly curved and tapered from the elbow down. The rear seam ran along the elbow.

20. Uniform pieces were generally factory marked on the inside, usually stamped in black ink. The purpose of the stamping was to show the origin of production and the size of the uniform piece. The photo shows the marking number sequence, from top to bottom and from left to right: Length of the tunic back, collar size, chest size, overall length and sleeve length.

21. The lining was made of blue-grey artificial silk. It consisted of patches sewn on the inside of the back panels, around the sleeve seams and on the shoulders.

21

22. View of the hip pocket used to store the first-aid kit. It was made of strong fabric and closed with a button.

23. The tunic had breast pockets made of lining fabric at either side, which closed with a button and loop. The lower pockets had slanted openings and a buttoned flap. The right hand hip had a pocket used by pilots for the first-aid kit storage.

24. The waistline side seams had three, vertically aligned, stitched eyelets for the belt support hooks on either side. A strap of lining fabric was sewn on the inner side as reinforcement. Another strap with six eyelets to attach the belt hooks and support the weight was sewn above the first, at the same level. Once the hook was attached to the inner strap, the point was inserted through the eyelets and was the only part of the hook to remain visible to the outside.

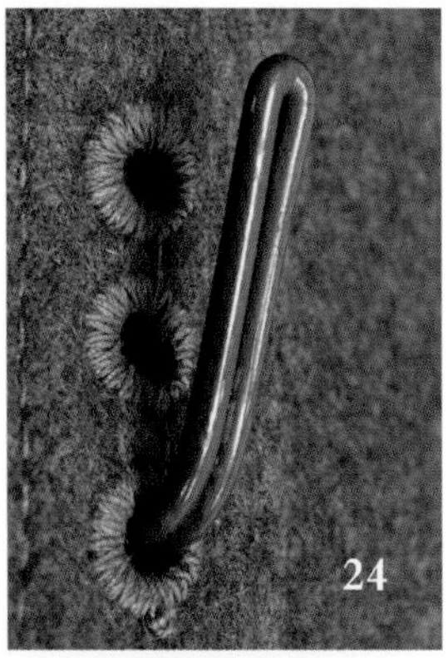

Service tunic

Tuchrock

Service tunic for officers

The standard pattern service uniform was adopted by the *Luftwaffe* in March 1935, and was based on the uniform worn as early as 1933 by personnel in the civilian organizations. The 1935 pattern uniform tunic was designated as *Tuchrock*, (Cloth tunic) and was worn open at the neck. The tunic closed with four buttons and had four pockets with buttoned flaps. Custom-made tunics for officers were made of a fine quality cloth. The Insignia worn in the tunic consisted of the collar tabs, the silver or gold piping around the lower edge of the collar according to rank, the shoulder straps and the hand-embroidered national emblem worn on the right breast.

25

25

25. *Above:* Detailed view of the *Hauptmann* collar tab. Notice the twisted silver cord piping surrounding the rhomboid tab. *Right:* Officer shoulder boards were made of two bright silver soutache parallel braids, in *"V"* shaped threads, forming a loop in the upper end which was used as a buttonhole. The underlay was made of cloth in the wearer's rank color. The rank pips for officers up to and including *Oberst* were made of gold-colored metal.

26

26. This *Leutnant* is wearing the *Tuchrock* service tunic with the officer Dress Aiguillette. Visible on his left chest pocket are the Civil Gliding proficiency cloth badge and the DRL *(Deutscher Reichsbund für Leibesübungen)* Sports Badge.

27

27. Detail of the hand-embroidered officer breast emblem made of metallic wire. The version for officers was made in silver-aluminum wire, while the general officer version used gold threads. The backing was made of wool and it was handsewn to the tunic, above the right breast pocket.

The photo shows Generaloberst *Alexander Löhr (in the foreground), and his aide during a field visit. Both officers are wearing the* Tuchrock *service tunic. Notice the officer's breeches, adorned with a white double stripe on the sides. The use of the stripes was reserved to general officers.*

28

28

28. The tunic was completely lined with blue-grey artificial silk or satin. The sleeves were usually lined with white striped lining fabric. The jacket incorporated inner belts and buckles fitted on each side of the waist, designed for a tight fit.

28

Service tunic for EM/NCO

The *Tuchrock* for enlisted men and NCOs was constructed with a blue-grey wool-rayon mix. It was a single-breasted tunic that was worn with the opened neck. It had four patch pockets with rectangular buttoned flaps. The cut of the sleeves had a small curve and slightly tapered down from the elbow. The end of the sleeves was turned upwards about 16 cm to form the cuffs. The closed with four metal buttons.

29. Close-up view of the collar tab and shoulder board of an *Unteroffizier* of the Flight branch, as indicated by the yellow collar tab and piping on the edge of the collar.

30. Detail of the embroidered breast national emblem. The droop tail of the eagle indicates it is a 1st pattern emblem.

31. The *Gefreiter* on the photo wears the *Tuchrock* cloth tunic with white shirt and black tie. Notice the pointed flaps of the tunic pockets. The cross straps and lack of sleeve rank insignia suggest that the photo was probably taken in the early days of the creation of the *Luftwaffe*. On his left sleeve, he is wearing the Flying Technical Personnel specialty badge.

32. A band of Tresse, the distinctive insignia of an NCO was sewn on the lower edge of the collar. The shoulder straps had the Tresse around the outer edge except at the base and had a branch piping.

33

33. The *Tuchrock* tunic had two breast pockets and two hip pockets. It could only be worn with open collar. The eagle national emblem was sewn above the right breast pocket with the swastika covering part of the buttonhole and just above the flap button.

34

34. According to Regulations, belt hooks with their openings were required, a feature that was actually never incorporated in cloth tunics. It was worn by all ranks as a full-dress uniform in the early years of the war and was primarily used as a service dress by officers during the war years.

35. This *Unteroffizier* is wearing the *Tuchrock* Service tunic with a white shirt and black tie.

36. The tunic is a privately purchased garment made by Traugot Rahne of Hannover. The maker's label was sewn to the inner neck area of the lining. The name of the owner of the jacket and the date of manufacture is found on a second cloth label.

37. The lining was made of blue-grey twill fabric. The tunic featured an horizontal slash pocket on the left breast panel and a small, wool reinforced horizontal slash to the reverse of the exterior left hip pocket with a sewn, nickel-silver plated, *"D"* ring intended for the sword or dagger hanger.

This Feldwebel *wears the* Tuchrock *cloth tunic with white shirt and black tie. He wears the second model Flak Artillery personnel badge on the his sleeve.*

Uniform tunic

Waffenrock

Uniform tunic for officers

The *Waffenrock* was introduced in November 1938 and intended to replace both the flight blouse and the service tunic. However, the *Tuchrock* production continued after the introduction of the new garment, while the manufacturing of the *Fliegerbluse* only ceased with the end of the war. The *Waffenrock* was a single-breasted tunic with five metal buttons and could be worn with the opened or closed collar. The material was generally tricot, a fine quality woven fabric. Officers ordered their *Waffenrock* tunics in both a summer and a winter weight, the difference being in the thickness of the fabric.

38. Detailed view of the collar insignia and shoulder boards for a *Generalmajor*. The yellow shoulder board and shoulder underlay belongs to the flight branch.

41. The eagle national emblem was hand-embroidered with silver wire thread. The backing was made with a cut-out blue-grey cloth. It is sewn to the right breast pocket, just above the flap button.

39. Photo of *Oberst* Hannes Trautloft, an Ace who served from 1932 until the end of the war. He flew 560 combat sorties and was credited with 58 victories. He wears the *Waffenrock* uniform tunic closed at the neck.

40. The ribbon on the second button hole in the tunic indicates the wearer was awarded with the *Winterschlacht Im Osten* or Eastern Front Medal. It was instituted on May 26, 1942 to recognize those who participated in the first winter of Operation Barbarossa, the invasion of the Soviet Union.

42. Photo of Adolf Galland during a ceremony. He is wearing the *Waffenrock* tunic with the collar in the closed position. Worth noting is the Spanish Cross in both pilots´ tunics, awarded to those members of the German Air Force who fought in the Condor Legion during the Spanish Civil War.

43. The jacket was lined with artificial silk and had an inner pocket. Two inner belts made of cloth with adjusting buckles in the edges were fitted on each side of the waist. They closed in the front and were designed for a tight adjustment to the waist.

44. When the collar was closed, it was fixed with a cloth tab sewn on the right underside of the collar, and a small plastic button hidden beneath the left lapel. When worn with the opened collar, the cloth tab was buttoned to the rear.

45. When the tunic was worn with the opened collar, it was closed using four buttons. The upper fifth button and its corresponding buttonhole remained hidden beneath the lapels.

Uniform tunic for EM/NCO

The *Waffenrock* for enlisted men and NCOs was made of woven fabric and the cut was the same of the officer tunic. When worn with the open collar, it closed with four buttons, but when worn with the closed collar, it was secured with five buttons. The jacket was lined with blue-grey twill fabric and had a pocket of lining fabric sewn to the inside of the left front side, used for first-aid pack stowage. Certain elements, such as the pockets of the first-aid kits, the belt hooks supports and the eyelets were frequently omitted. The hook and eye of the collar was also omitted by an order of 1939.

46

46

46. View of the collar and shoulder strap insignia of a *Flieger* of the flight branch as denoted by the yellow cloth collar patch and the shoulder strap piping.

47

47. Detail of the standard enlisted machine-embroidered breast Adler emblem with blue-grey backing. The swastika overlaps the pocket flap of the tunic.

48

48. These two men riding on the train wagon are wearing *Waffenrock* tunics. The *Unteroffizier* facing the camera is wearing it with the open collar. The belt hooks protruding from the sides of the tunic of the man with his back to the camera are clearly visible. (Militaria Arganzuela)

49. The *Kanonier* of the portrait is wearing a *Waffenrock* tunic and a service belt with an aluminum buckle. Notice the bayonet hanging from his left waist.

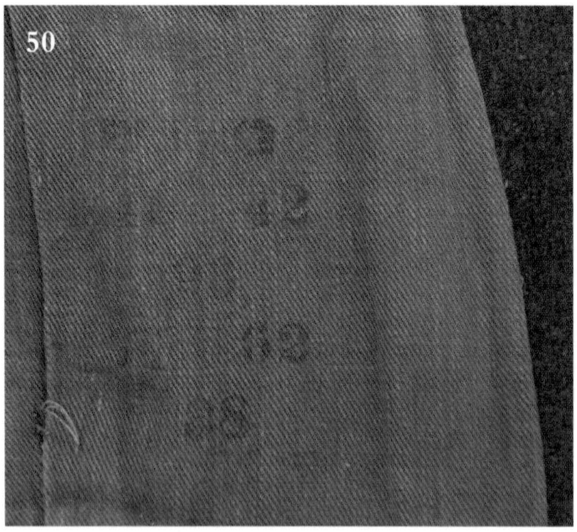

50. Detailed view of the factory markings, stamped in black ink. This jacket had a cloth label with the name of the soldier sewn to one of the inner pockets.

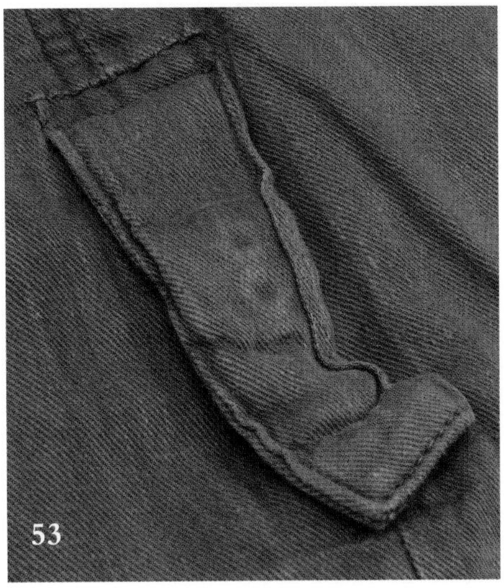

51. The jacket was lined with blue-grey twill material and had an inner breast pocket to store the first-aid kits. The center back seam had a 22 cm long slash on the bottom. The left edge reached for the left bottom to a distance of 3cm. The jacket closed with five buttons positioned on the right front panel and the corresponding five buttonholes of the left panel.

52. Two hooks were located on both sides of the jacket at waist level, whose function was to support the belt and help to distribute the weight of the field equipment fixed to it. A strap of lining fabric was sewn on the inner side as reinforcement. Another strap with eyelets to attach the belt hooks and support the weight was sewn above the first, at the same level.

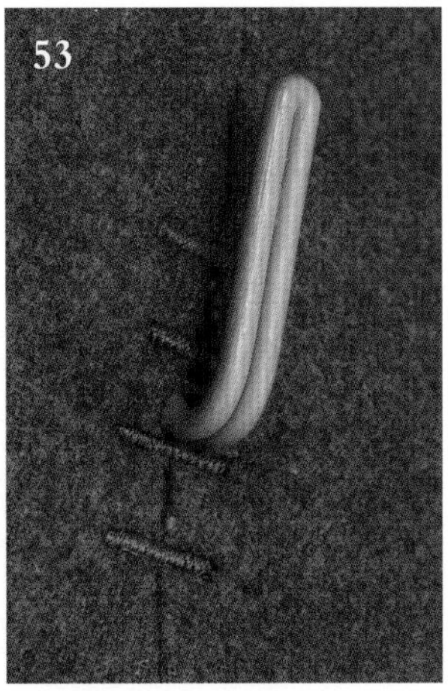

53. Once the hook was attached to the inner strap, the tip was inserted through openings on the seams of both sides of the tunic, being the only part of the hook to remain visible to the outside. Visible in the photo are the reinforcement stitching on the seam between each opening.

Summer tunic

Sommerrock

During the summer months of continental Europe, officers were authorized to wear the white uniform on appropriate occasions. The white tunic for officers had the same design and cut of the *Tuchrock* cloth tunic. It was made of white gabardine, linen or cotton cloth. The tunic was single-breasted and closed with four pebbled metal buttons. It had two breast pockets and two hip pockets with pleats and buttoned flaps. It was worn opened at the collar with a white shirt and black tie.

54

54

54. View of the *Hauptmann* collar tab and shoulder boards. The rhomboid tab was surrounded by a twisted silver cord piping. Officer shoulder boards were constructed with two bright silver soutache parallel braids forming a loop which was used as a buttonhole. The underlay was made of cloth in the wearer's rank color. The rank pips for officers up to and including Oberst were made of gold-colored metal.

55

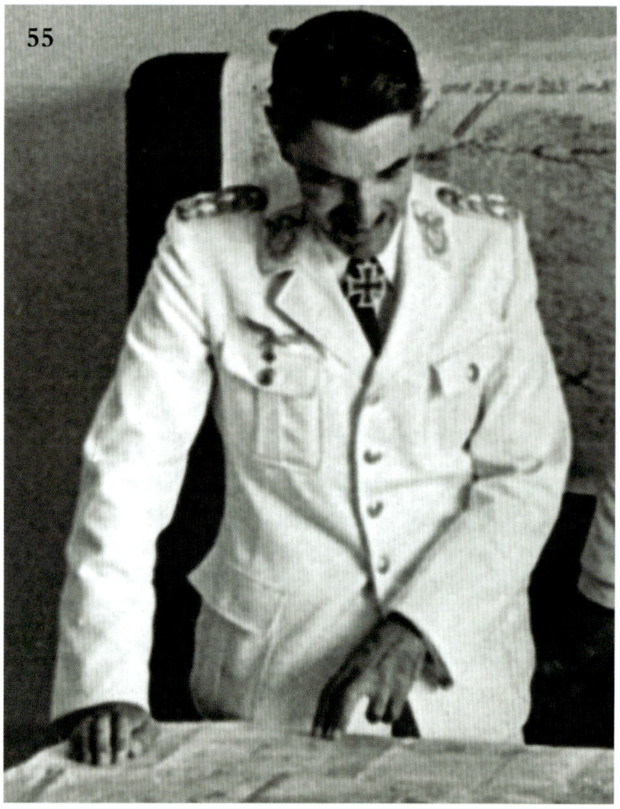

55

55

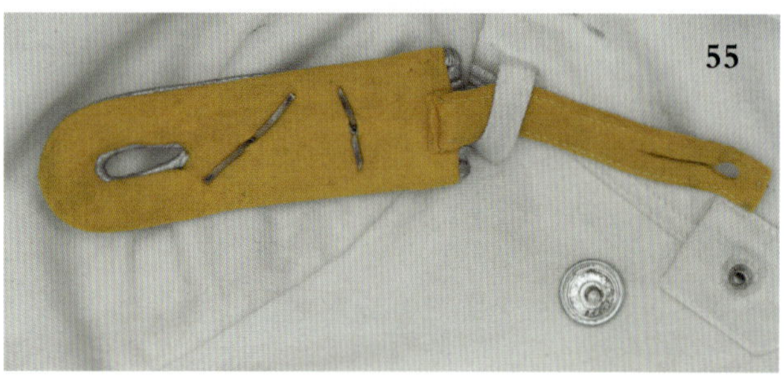

55

55

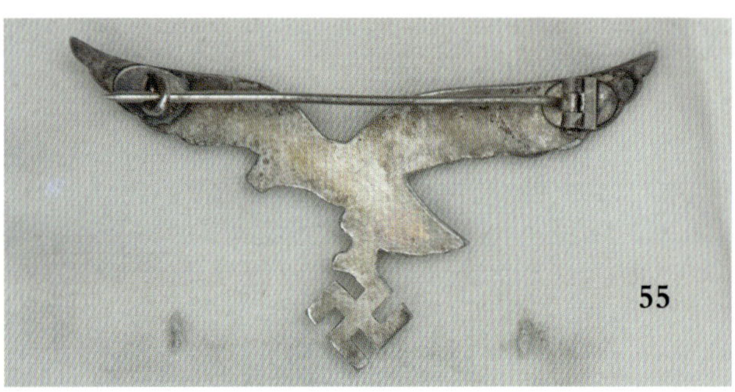

55. All the insignia of the tunic was removable in order to facilitate an easier cleaning. The national emblem was made of pressed metal and fixed to the tunic by a horizontal pin on the back of the insignia. The collar tab was fixed with four press studs. Removable shoulder boards had a tongue that extended the length of the underside and had a buttonhole in the edge. The tongue passed through a cloth loop sewn to the shoulder of the jacket and was fixed to the special screw-in button, used with thick shoulder straps.

56. The piping cord on the collar was omitted. The tunic could be worn without the collar patches within military installations and for office duties and could be used with the blue-grey trousers. In this case, the use of the white summer or the blue-grey visor caps was optional.

56

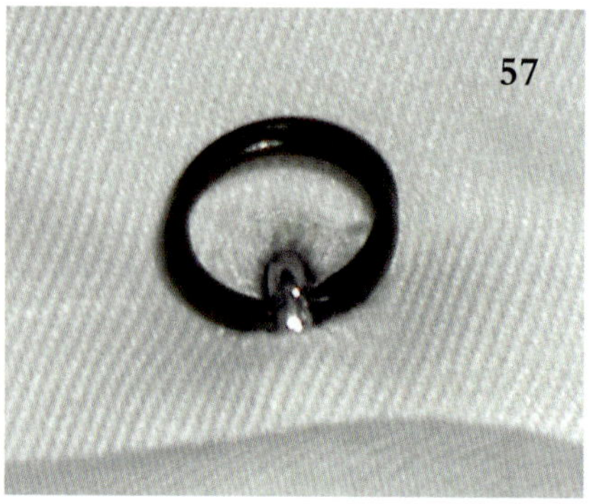

57. The lining was made of white fabric and was only present at below the armpits and at the back, from the shoulder and collar seams downwards to approximately 10 cm. No collar cording was used in the summer tunics. Buttons were removable by an eyelet and split-ring system.

Drill tunic

Drillichrock

The drill *Luftwaffe* tunic was intended for field by officers during the summer months. The cut was the same of the *Tuchrock* cloth tunic. It was made of a strong cotton twill fabric. The breast and hip pockets had a center pleat that was omitted in later production versions with rectangular buttoned flaps. The front had four metal pebbled buttons that were sewn or removable by eyelets and spring rings. Collar patched and shoulder boards were removable, as well as the metal eagle national emblem.

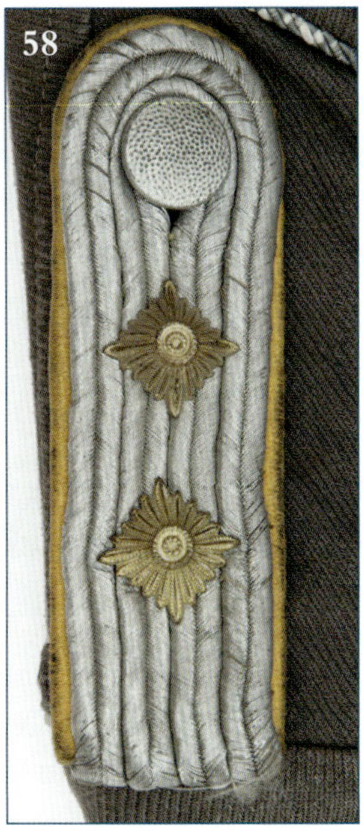

58. View of the removable collar tab of a *Hauptmann*.The rhomboid tab is surrounded by a twisted silver cord piping and presents an aluminum embroidered oak leave wreath. The embroidered wings were centered above the oak leaves.

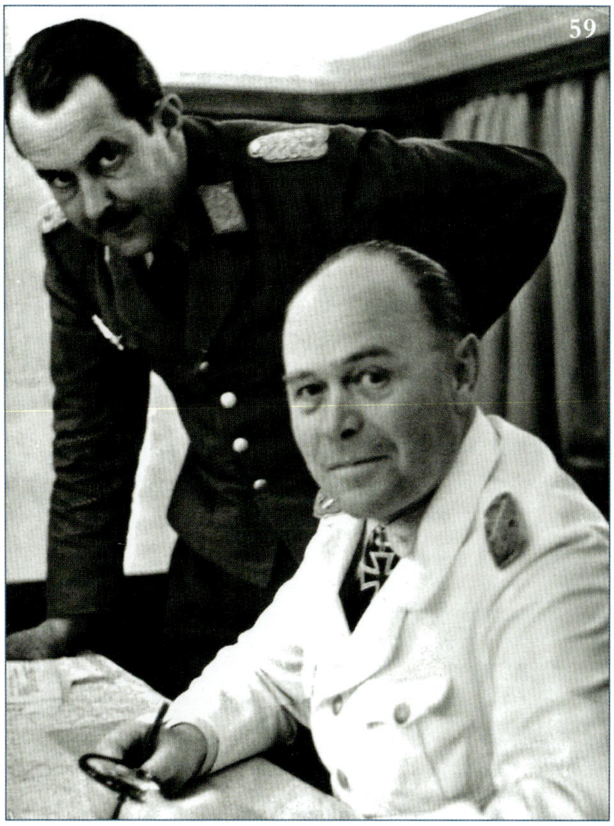

59. Two officers discuss in front of a map during a briefing. The one standing up is wearing a drill tunic.

60. The insignia was removable for ease of cleaning. The collar tab was fixed with four press studs. The removable shoulder straps had a tongue that extended the length of the underside and had a buttonhole in the edge. The tongue passed through a cloth loop sewn to the shoulder of the jacket and was fixed to the removable collar button.

61

61. The national emblem was made of pressed metal and fixed to the tunic by a pin on the back of the insignia. Regulations prescribed the emblem to be placed on the right breast, with the swastika covering the buttonhole of the flap, which often made it difficult to open it.

62

62. The drill jacket had a lining consisting of a patch of fabric covering the shoulder area and a semicircular patch of fabric which surrounded the armpit seams.

3. Greatcoats

The photo shows Generaloberst *Ernst Udet with* Major *Mölders on his left and* Major *Galland on his right. Both Galland and Udet are wearing leather greatcoats.*

The Greatcoat constituted an essential uniform item of clothing and was worn by all ranks during cold or inclement weather. The basis of the design was the Imperial German army's greatcoat. The *Luftwaffe* version of the greatcoat was initially introduced by the DLV, and was later adopted by the *Luftwaffe*. The color of the greatcoat was blue-grey and the cut was the same for all ranks. Several minor design modifications took place during the war. Early production greatcoats were equipped with button holes on both front closure panels, which allowed the coat to be buttoned up on the left or right hand. The buttons on the greatcoats for the ranks from *Flieger* to *Oberst* had a silver finish, while those of the ranks from *Generalmajor* to *Reichsmarschall* were gilt finished. Before the end of the war, the buttons for the ranks of *Flieger* to *Stabsfeldwebel* were changed to a blue-grey finish. An order of March, 1940 ordered all shoulder boards of greatcoats to be of the detachable type. A regulation of May 1942 abolished the use of the collar tabs for enlisted men and non commissioned officers NCOs stipulating that they had to be removed by October 1942 the latest. Additional regulations of January 1943 reinstated the use of collar tabs by enlisted men and NCOs of the Guard Regiment Berlin and the *Führer Flak Battalions*. Finally, an order of June, 1942 prescribed the use of open back pleats, so the greatcoats could be worn with an unbuttoned back half-belt over the buckled leather service belt with field gear attached. Besides the standard greatcoat, the *Luftwaffe* also introduced a rubberized coat for personnel of motorcycle units and drivers of open-cab vehicles. Even though they were initially intended to be used only by enlisted men, they ended up being worn by all ranks in the field. In addition to the cloth greatcoat pattern, officers were permitted to purchase leather greatcoats at their own expense. These were made of blue-grey dyed fine grain quality leather. The design and construction was similar to the standard greatcoat, but it had no collar insignia and featured removable shoulder boards. They were to be worn only for service. Buttons were initially made in blue-grey plastic and later of lightweight pebbled metal, as per regulations. Officials of middle grades of the fire fighter branch were the only ones allowed to have their leather greatcoats made of black leather instead of the usual blue-gray tone.

This Portrait photo shows an enlisted man wearing the standard pattern greatcoat with the closed neck.
Collar patches of enlisted men were omitted on new manufactured coats and were to be removed from the existing ones from October 1942 onwards.

Service greatcoats

Tuchmäntel

Service greatcoat for officers

Even though officers were allowed to buy their greatcoats from a tailor, they often used greatcoats supplied by *Luftwaffe* clothing depots in the field, as in the case of the specimen shown in the photos. Greatcoats were made of blue-grey wool and featured a double breasted front formed by two panels which went beyond the front center of the garment. Both panels had two vertical rows of six buttons on either side, from waist to the top corner of the lapels. The right buttons were fixed to the buttonholes positioned on the edge of the left panel, while the right panel was fixed with a single black button on the waist of the left panel. Two slash pockets with rounded flaps were located on each side at waist level.

1

1. The greatcoat was partially lined on the breast and the upper back areas with blue-grey cotton twill. The sleeves were also lined with cloth. The black button for the closure of the right front panel is visible on the photo, as well as the inner hip pockets bags.

2

2. This Non-commissioned officer is wearing a high quality tailor made greatcoat in his marriage ceremony. It was common to wear the garment with the lapels turned down and only three buttons attached.

3. Detail of the ink stamp found in the left side lining of the greatcoat. The numbers indicate, from left to right and top to bottom, the length of the back, the collar size, the chest size, the greatcoat length and the sleeve length. The name of the manufacturer has also been ink-stamped on the garment.

4. The collar closed with a hook and eye system. In case of foul weather, the user could wear the collar in an upward position. The right collar had a sewn cloth strap with two button holes on the reverse, while the left side had two corresponding buttons, to which the strap was fixed. A third button on the left side of the collar secured the strap in place when the collar was in the downward position.

Leather greatcoat for officers

The leather greatcoat was a garment intended for use exclusively by officers and officials of officer ranks and was not available in army depots; the officers who chose to wear it had to buy them from private tailors. Production was forbidden in 1944 to save raw material. It was made of different shades of heavy blue-grey leather, and the cut and style were similar to the cloth greatcoat, but usually had a separately made skirt that was sewn at the waist area. The shoulder boards were fixed using a slip-on system and the buttons were detachable to allow a better cleaning.

5

5. The greatcoat was fully lined in brownish-blue twill, but it was not uncommon to have a detachable buttoned liner made of wool or fur. The skirt was made of several panels of leather according to regulations, made for economy reasons. The back featured a horizontal half-waist belt with two buttons to the waistline. The skirt featured hooks and eyelets on the iside to hold it to the back when it was folded upwards.

6

6. The greatcoat of the photos features an inner belt to allow a better fit. A leather belt was sewn horintonally to the left panel of the greatcoat, just below the armpit. A female pressure stud was located on the end of the belt, while a row of male press studs ran parallel to the belt along the center. For closure, the belt passed through a metal loop attached to the edge of the right front panel and was secured with one of the press studs.

7. Photo of the cloth label found inside the pocket. The greatcoat was made by *Felwa lederbekleidung*, a well known maker of leather garments.

8. The greatcoat featured detachable aluminum pebbled buttons and slip-on shoulder boards to ease the cleaning of the garment. The slightly slanted hip pockets on either side of the greatcoat had rectangular flaps.

9

9

9. The collar could be worn in an upward position by means of a leather strap sewn on the obverse of the left collar with a female press stud on the end, and a male press stud on the right collar. When not used, the strap was folded and secured on the left collar. General officers were not required to wear collar patches on the leather greatcoats.

8

Raincoat for officers and NCO

Wettermäntel

Regulations allowed officers and certain NCOs to purchase several garments which were prohibited for enlisted ranks. One of these items was the rubberized raincoat. It was athorised to be worn on the same occasions when the cloth greatcoat was worn, except for parades. The raincoat followed the basic pattern of the fabric greatcoats. Early models featured a double breast with two vertical rows of six aluminum pebbled buttons, two hip pockets with flaps, a vertical tail skirt opening and a horizontal half waist belt with a two button closure at waist level on the back.

10

10. Early raincoat models were fully lined with twill cloth. The center back of the raincoat had an overlapping vertical slash which closed with buttons. It featured two vertical rows of six buttons on the front, and a similar row of button holes on both front panels, which enabled the raincoat to be buttoned either with the left or the right panel overlapping in front.

11

11. A vertical slash located below the left hip pocket allowed the dagger to be hanged to the inside, by means of a ring and strap sewn below the armpit. The height of the ring could be adjusted with three bakelite buttons placed in a row along the cloth strap.

12. Detailed view of the size the ink stamp found on the inside of left pocket bag.

13. The raincoat featured two large, outer unpleated hip pockets which were placed with a small angle and had unbuttoned flaps.

14. The raincoat was made of twill fabric and was rubberized on the inside. The sleeves were non-adjustable and had large seams. It was designed to be used without the addition of a belt and always over the standard service uniform.

15. Detail of the detachable shoulder board of an *Oberleutnant*. An order of August, 1937 required the use of buttons of the detachable type and the shoulder boards of the slip-in variety.

Protective coat for motorcyclists

Kradschützenmäntel

The *Kradmäntel* was a protective coat designed specifically to be used by *Kradschützen* or motorcycle and motorcycle rifle units. It became so popular that it ended up being worn by all types of personnel of the *Wehrmacht*, especially drivers and passengers of open cabin vehicles. The coat was introduced in 1936 and was made of heavy rubberized blue-grey twill on the outside. The rank insignia was indicated by the addition of insignia on the forearms and upper sleeves, instead of the more common shoulder straps or boards.

16

16. The protective coat was made using two front panels and a back panel, sewn together in the sides and shoulders. The edges of the panels were reinforced with fabric stripes. Both front panels overlapped in the center front of the coat and closed with four upper buttons. The back panel had a vertical slash in the center that ran from the bottom edge to the waist.

17

17

17. When riding a motorcycle, the driver could strap the skirt to his legs. Two buttons were located on the inside of the coat, over the pocket bags, to which the back panel corners were buttoned. At the same time, the corners of the front panes were wrapped around the back of the legs and buttoned using one of the two buttons located on the outside, at both sides of the coat.

18. Detail of the ink stamp, indicating the name of the manufacturer, the size and the date.

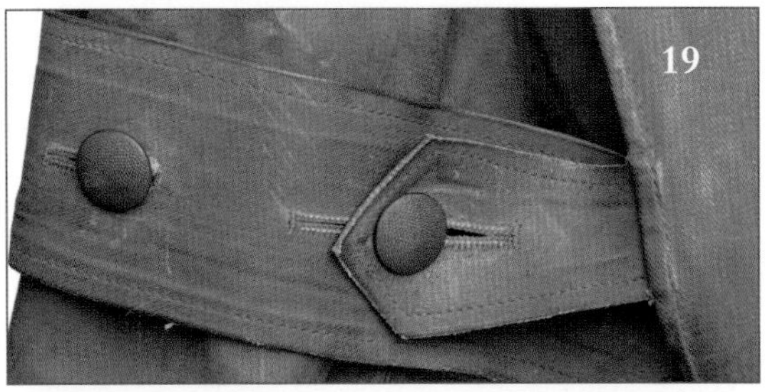

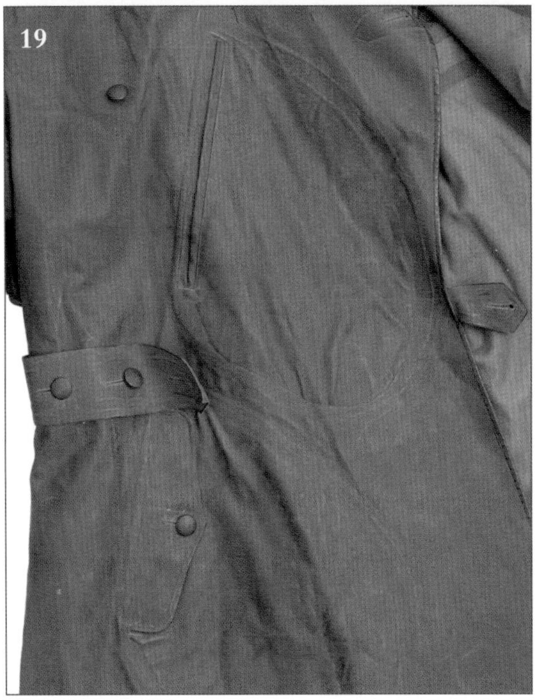

19. The coat had two slant hip pockets secured with buttoned flaps on either side and a breast pocket on the right side without flaps. The waist closure was achieved by a belt that was sewn on the left side seam, ran along the back of the waist, passed through a fabric loop and buttoned to one of the three buttons fixed to the right side of the jacket. An additional buttoned cloth strap on the edge of the left panel secured a tight fit.

20. The collar was lined with blue-grey cloth. When used in an upward position, a sewn strap and buttons sewn on the underside secured the collar in place. The coat closed in the front by means of two rows of buttons located on either side of the front panels.

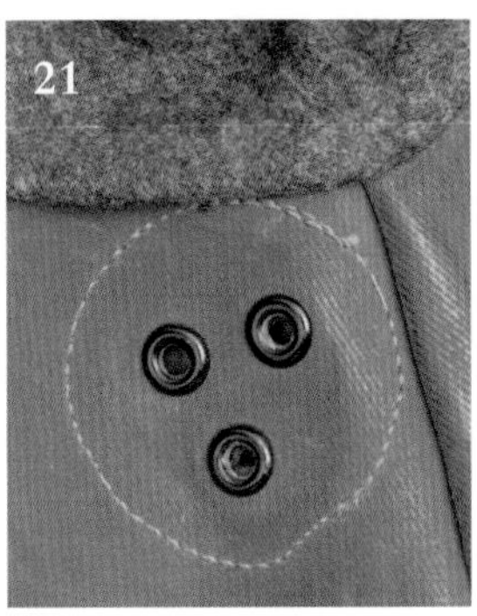

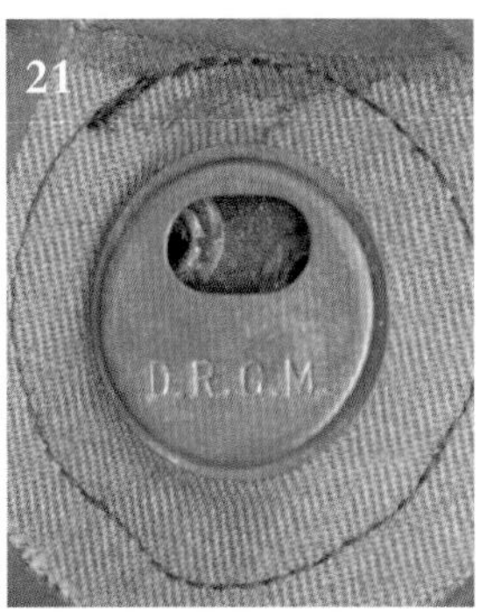

21. Three ventilation holes were present below the armpits. The system consisted of a circular metal box which was sewn to the area below the armpits and reinforced with a cloth strap. The acronym D.R.G.M. stands for *Deutsches Reichsgebrauchsmuster*, indicating the method was a registered patent.

4. Trousers

This Gefreiter *returning home on leave is wearing the short lace-up ankle boots without gaiters and long straight trousers.*

The *Luftwaffe* had several models of trousers which were worn according to regulations. Long trousers were worn by all personnel and could be used with marching boots, low quarter shoes and lace-up shoes. When they were used with marching boots or ankle boots with gaiters, regulations prescribed that they were to be tucked under them. To achieve a better fit, the folds were secured with a rubber band or by adjusting the socks over the trouser legs. Soldiers preferred to fold the legs forward, which allowed better leg movement. This non-regulation habit was officially recognized by an order of February 1942, which prescribed that the legs had to be folded forward to allow sufficient freedom of movement of the knees. Generals and officers of the general staff corps were authorized to wear adornment stripes in their trousers of their branch color. The lateral seam had a piping cord and two stripes of badge cloth stitched to the sides. The flying trousers were used by personnel when on flight duty. The style and cut was basically the same as the long trousers, with light differences. The adornment stripes were not used, and the trousers could be used either with a belt or issue suspenders. In 1939, production of the flying trousers was discontinued to conserve raw material. However, in 1940 a new model of flying trousers, designed after the ski trousers, was introduced. Riding breeches for enlisted men and NCOs were authorized only for mounted personnel, being strictly forbidden for non-mounted troops. They were made of blue-grey cloth. The leg portion was cut with a pronounced flare through the thighs that allowed freedom of movement, while the part from the knee down had a tight fit. Officer's breeches were made of a blue-grey tricot or similar quality cloth. The cut was the same as the enlisted men breeches, but personal preferences, fashion and other factors made the privately purchased breeches to be designed with a wide range of variations. Adornment stripes could be added to the breeches in the same manner of the long trousers.

The officer of the photo is wearing private-purchased breeches with riding boots. The flare of the thighs is not as pronounced as in other models. Notice the belt with crosstraps.

Riding trousers

Stiefelhose

The Stiefelhose were intended to be worn by officers, which had to purchase them privatlely. Regulations prescribed that the style and cut was to be similar to the enlisted men issue breeches. However, a wide range of variations can be found in several aspects of the garment, generally influenced by fashion and personal preferences of the officers or the tailors. The most notable differences were found in the shape of the thigh area and the leg closure area, which could be closed using buttons, straps or a combination of both. The breeches were made of grey/blue wool tricot or other similar high quality cloth. Officer´s breeches sometimes featured leather reinforcements on the seat area, usually limited to those used for horseback riding.

1. Detailed view of the ring fixed by a cloth cord above the watch pocket found on the right front of the trousers. The internal watch pocket was slightly slanted with a 7 cm opening. The ring was used to attach the watch keychain when keeping the watch on the pocket to allow an easy access.

1

2

2. The fly closed with concealed buttonholes. The inner pockets were made of white cloth. The officer has added a leather reinforcement to his breeches. This practice was done by officers for riding horses while on uniform and occasionally for fashion.

3. The legs were covered by the riding boots and were sometimes made of a fabric that could withstand the friction of the boots. They showed a wide variety of closing methods, such as the cord and button combination of the specimen of the photos.

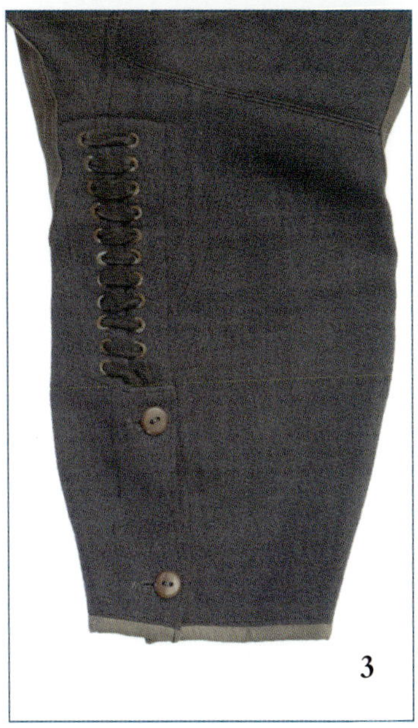

3

Breeches

Reithose

The issue riding breeches were distributed exclusively to mounted enlisted personnel of *Luftwaffe* field Divisions. They were manufactured with a blue-grey cloth. The fly area had five buttons on one side and four concealed buttonholes with a reinforcement strap on the other. The upper button was larger than the others, being the only one that was not concealed. The back of the waist was higher than the front and featured a V-shaped cutout. At both sides, there were two horizontally sewn cloth stripes with a pronge buckle, made for a perfect waist adjustment. The breeches had two slanted side pockets that closed with a button, a rear button on the right back side, and finally a watch pocket on the front right, just below the waistline.

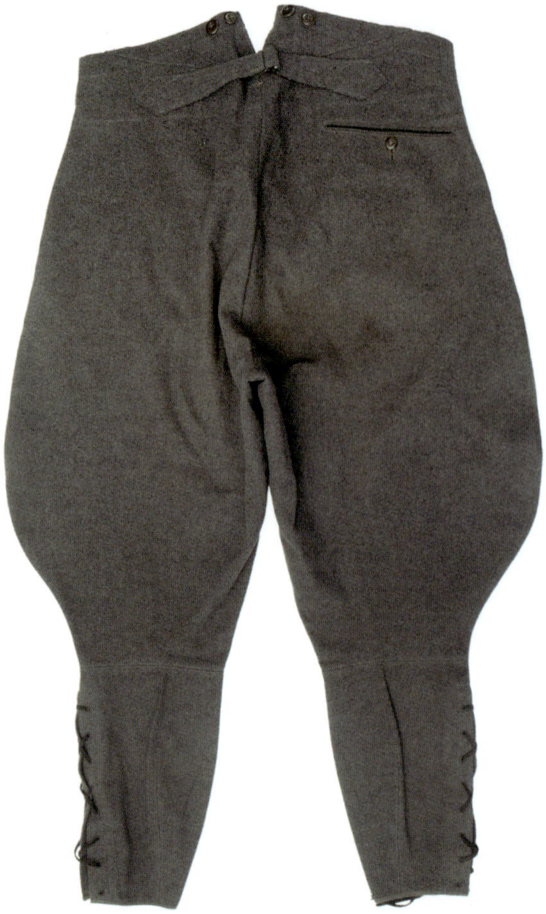

4. Close-up of the ink marking of the issue trousers, showing the name of the manufacturer, and other relevant information.

5. The waist was lined blue-gray or white twill cloth. All the pockets were internal and made of basic white cloth. Additional buttons were sewn to the outside of the front and back of the waist to secure the suspenders.

6. Close-up view of the back of the trouser´s waist. The two cloth stripes sewn on either side joined with a pronged buckle and were used to narrow the waist for a better fit.

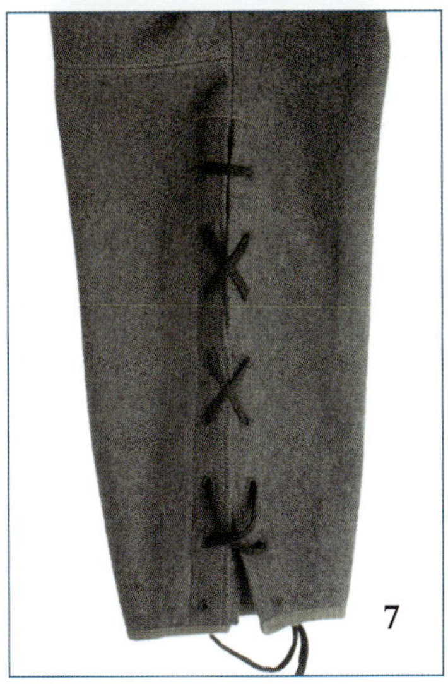

7. The end of legs had a vertical slash on the outer side. Each of the edges of the slash had a vertical row of eyelets to which a string was adjusted, effectively tying the legs.

Long trousers

Lange Hose

The *Luftwaffe* uniform long trousers or *Tuchhose* were made in blue-grey wool fabric and were cut straight. Regulations allowed them to be used by Officers, NCOs and enlisted personnel. The cut and style was similar to the riding breeches, except for the straight legs. The leg openings were folded inwards and had a sewn strap of cloth on the inside as reinforcement. The center front of the leg opening was slightly higher than the back to avoid contact with the shoes and prevent them from wrinkling and deteriorating. Trousers could be privately purchased, and usually presented non-regulation features, such as two side waist adjustment straps instead of a single strap on the back, the addition or substraction of external waist buttons and a different style of front closure.

8. The trousers on the photo were tailor made. The label can be found inside the back pocket and indicates the name of the maker, and has a provision for the name of the officer, the date of manufacture and a control number.

10. The private purchased trousers on the photos have a different design of the waist and front closure. All the fly buttons are concealed. The the upper button has been moved to the inside, and closes with an additional cloth strip with an eyelet. The front suspender buttons are placed inside the waist and the back adjustment strap has been replaced by two side straps.

9. The photo shows two *Obergefreiters* and an *Oberfeldwebel*, all of them wearing long trousers.

5. Belts and buckles

The use of military belts and their corresponding buckles can be traced back to several centuries. Throughout history soldiers have have often worn belts, usually made of leather, to carry weapons and secure their tunics. Daggers would be concealed inside the belts, and swords attached to them with hangers. A new innovative box buckle with a quick-release catch and its corresponding belt was invented in 1847 by a Prussian military man, which included shoulder straps to support most of the weight of the equipment hanging from the belt.

During the Third Reich there was a prescribed form of wear of the belt and buckle with the buckle being positioned on the right side and the corresponding buckle catch on the left side. First introduced in May 1935, the *Luftwaffe* enlisted men/NCO's belt buckle underwent minor modifications in late 1937 or early 1938 with a new pattern eagle and again in 1940 with a slight difference in construction.

Luftwaffe personnel initially utilized brown leather accoutrements but during the war the leather items were generally blackened. Originally military buckles produced under government contract had the addition of a leather tabs which were designed to help support the ammunition pouches and prevent slippage but regulations in 1942 discontinued the tabs to preserve leather although the directive was not completely adhered to.

Two officers are flanking the color bearer Non-commissioned officer during a parade. They are both wearing the brocade waist belt. (Intaria)

A group of bomber crew members are being briefed before a mission. Most of the men are wearing service belts with their flight one-piece flight suits.

The Feldwebel *of the photo is wearing the enlisted men belt with the flight blouse as his service uniform.*
The Spanienkreuz *on the right of his tunic indicates he is a veteran of the Condor Legion during the Spanish Civil War.*

Belts for officers

Leibriemen

Belt for officers

The officer's belt was made of light brown leather, with a thickness of 3.5 mm and a width of 6 cm, which was reduced during the war to save raw materials. Pre-war belts had a 1mm wide groove stamped in both edges; a feature discarded in most wartime production belts. The rectangular buckle was made of pebbled matt-white metal and had two prongs. It was buckled from right to left and covered the bottom button of the tunic.

1

1. The officers on the photo are all wearing breeches and riding boots. The *Hauptmann* on the left has added a cross strap to his belt, while the officer holding the map has opted not to use it. He is also sporting a first pattern dagger on his left hip.

2

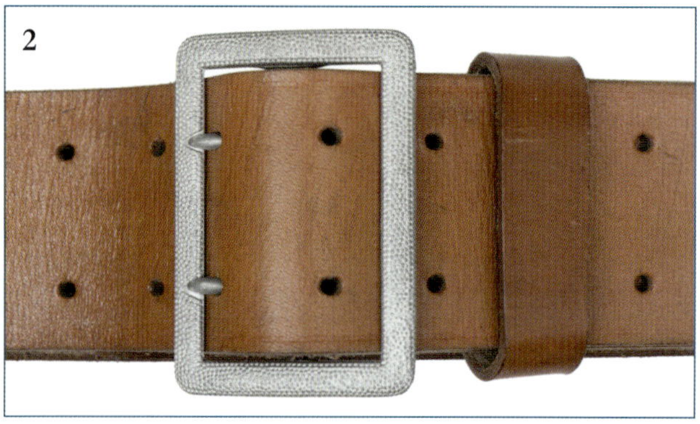

2. Detailed view of the rectangular buckle with two open prongs. The surface was pebbled and the corners were slightly rounded. A leather loop was placed near the buckle to secure the end of the belt when adjusted. The belt was worn with the buckle on the left and the running end on the right, passing through the buckle and ending in the wearer's left.

2

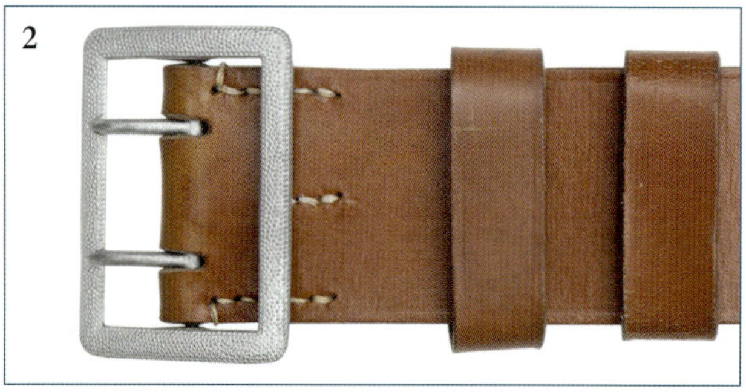

3. The end of the belt was rounded and had six or seven pairs of holes to secure the prongs of the buckle. The width of the belt was reduced due to wartime shortage of leather.

3

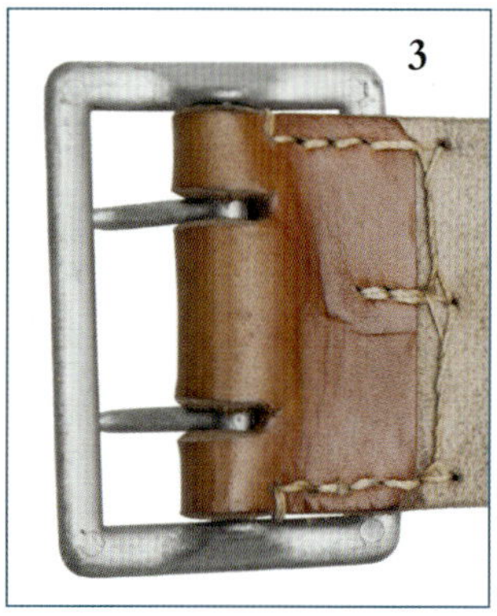

Cross strap for officers

Originally the officer belt was intended to be used in conjunction with the cross strap. It was intended for wear as an optional item by officers, officials with equivalent officer ranks, bandmasters and music superintendents. The use of the cross strap was abolished by an order of February, 1940. The cross strap was made of the same brown leather material of the belt and had metal fittings. It was worn around the right shoulder, passing beneath the shoulder boards.

5
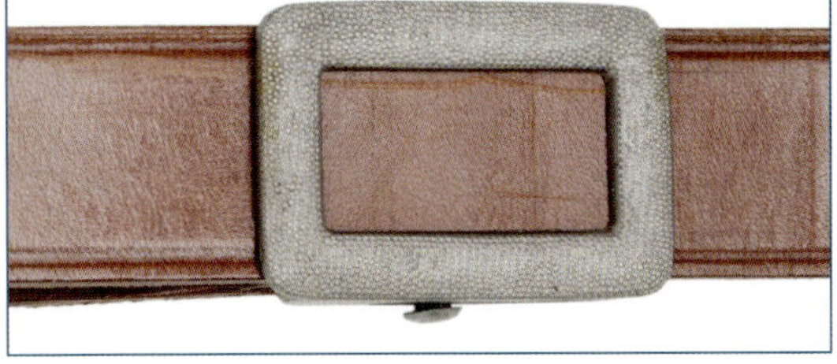

5
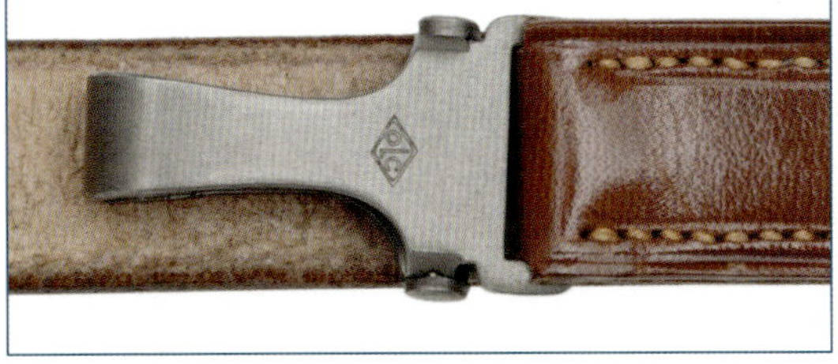

5. The cross strap was 2.4 cm wide and featured a clip with a friction bar to adjust the size. The front end had a carbine hook sewn to the inside that was fixed to a leather loop with a metal ring that was adjusted to the left front of officer belt.

5
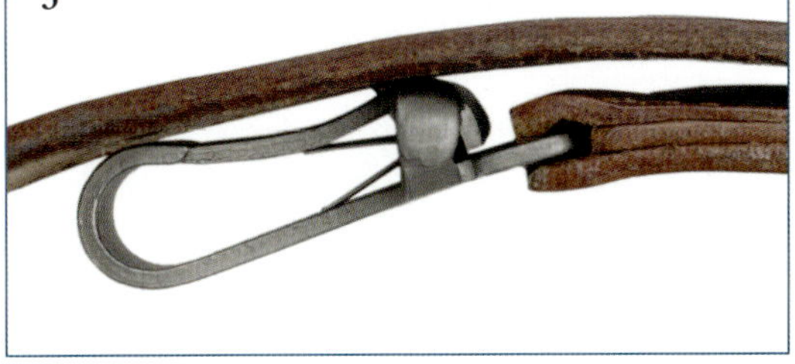

4
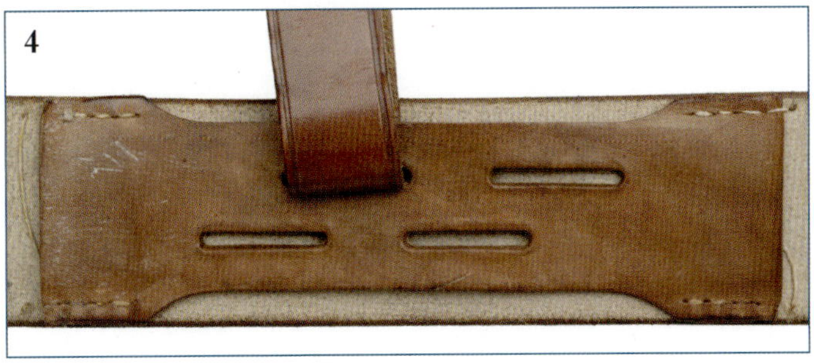

4. The belt had two leather strips sewn to the inside of the belt, with horizontal eyelets to adjust the cross strap leather loops. The loops were made of a brown leather strip with pear-shaped eyelets on both ends that closed with a two-sided metal stud. The back end of the cross strap had a leather strap with a D-ring sewn on the inside, to which the loop was attached.

5
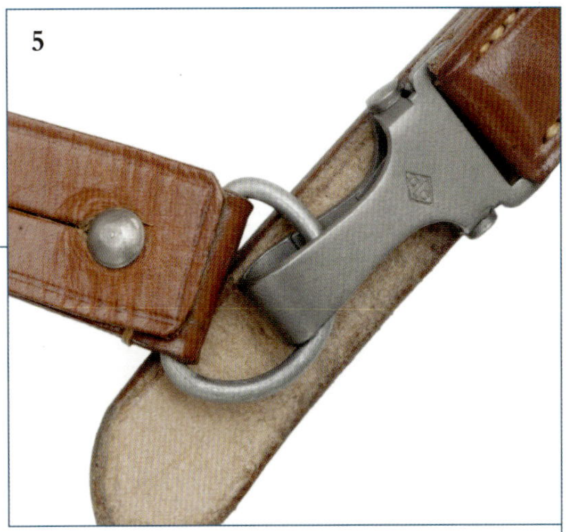

4

4
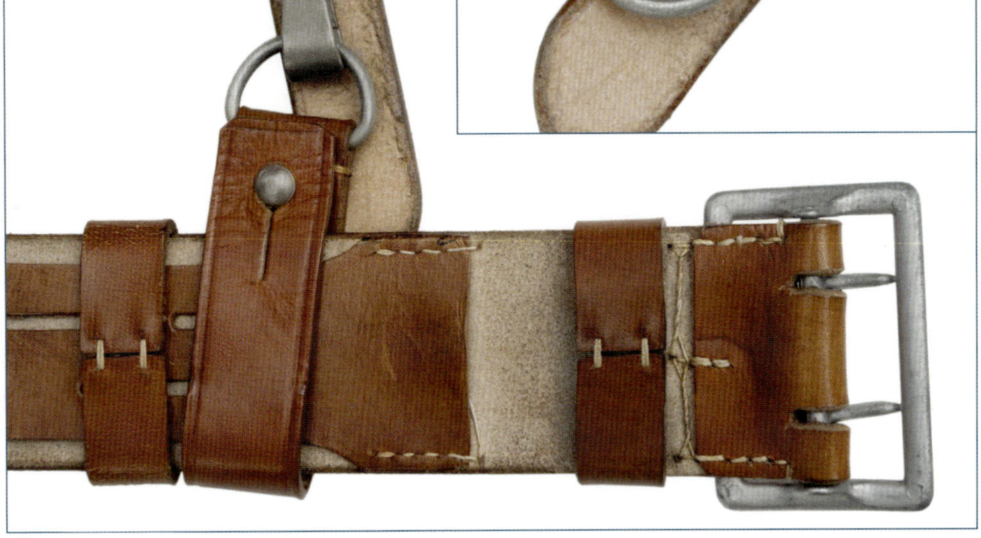

Belts and buckles for EM/NCO

Koppel und Koppelschlösser

Belt and buckle for EM/NCO in aluminum

The belt for NCOs and enlisted personnel consisted of a leather black belt and a metal buckle with the *Luftwaffe* national emblem. The belt measured about 4.5 cms wide. The buckle was initially made of aluminum and usually presented a pebbled surface. The *Luftwaffe* eagle emblem was engraved in the center, surrounded by a laurel wreath forming an oval shape.

6. This *Flieger* wears the aluminum buckle on his service black leather belt.

7. The *Unteroffiziers* on the front row are all wearing black leather belts with aluminum buckles, while the *Oberleutnant* on the left wears the officer´s belt.

8

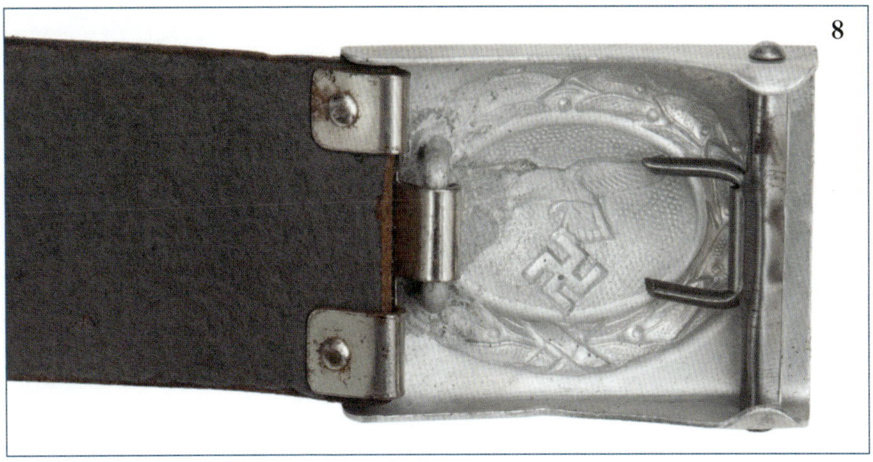

8

8

8. The belt of the photos was made of black leather. Belts and buckles were issued by army depots or privately purchased in specialized shops, as is the case of the specimen of the photos. These belts had a higher quality workmanship; the exterior featured a high-gloss finish and often included a cloth strip fixed on the inside to protect the uniform.

8

Belt and buckle for EM/NCO in steel

The pattern of the belt buckle changed slightly around 1940. The buckle was made of stamped steel and painted with a blue-gray dull paint. The surface of the buckle was smooth, except for the area inside of the oval laurel thread, which remained with the pebbled surface of the previous pattern. Buckles were often marked on the obverse with the manufacturer's name and always date-stamped on the brown leather tongue. In 1942, an order was issued to suppress the leather tongue of all buckles due to wartime shortages.

9

9

9. *Above:* A soldier wearing the steel belt buckle. *Left:* The photo clearly shows the difference between both buckle patterns. The aluminum buckle is being worn by the *Unteroffizier* on the left, while the man looking at the camera uses the steel pattern.

10

10. The catch of the buckle had many different variations. The variation of the photo includes two extra support braces on the welded sides. The buckle had two prongs which were attached to a metal cylinder that allowed a 180 degree rotation, which eased the attachment of the buckle to the belt. The inner right end of the belt had a strap of leather sewn with heavy duty cotton thread that featured several pairs of holes that were used to fix the buckle in place.

11. Detailed view of the stamp found on the buckle leather tongue, dated in 1941.

10

10

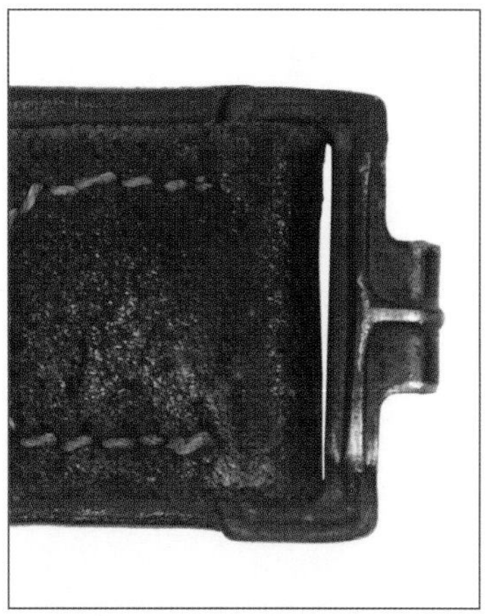

6. Footwear

Officer wearing his ankle boots with gaiters. Notice the NCO/EM pattern *fliegerbluse*.

This officer is wearing private-purchased riding boots, while the crew member of the photo below prefers to use service boots. Pilots opted to wear private purchased boots during combat missions, especially in the first part of the war.

The leather marching boot is one of the most recognizable items of the German military. They date back to the late 17th century, when European nobles started to wear them over their dress shoes while riding and hunting. Several European nations adopted the jackboot as part of their military uniforms through the 20th century.

Luftwaffe enlisted men and NCOs used the same marching boots than the rest of the branches of the armed forces. Despite being issued in a natural brown color, servicemen were required to maintain a black finish on their boots by applying bootblack. To make them more durable, the leather soles were reinforced with round hobnails nailed into them. In an attempt to conserve leather, the leg part of the marching was shortened in 1939. Finally, a new short ankle boot was issued in 1941 to all troops. Officers and NCOs were allowed to buy their own footwear, which were usually of a higher quality. Officers and some NCOs favored the use of riding boots when wearing breeches or riding trousers. In the opening stages of the war, many fighter pilots preferred to use these high boots during combat missions, but after several injuries suffered in which the difficulty to take them off for treatment aggravated the wounds, they were ordered to use exclusively flight boots.

Ground crew personnel servicing an aircraft for the next mission. The man on the left is wearing marching boots, while the other has lace-up shoes.

Officers high boots

Hohe Stiefel

The use of high boots was authorized to officers wearing riding breeches. During the early stages of the war, some fighter pilots favored the use of the high boots during combat missions instead of the flight boots. Most of them had the boots made by private shoemakers, usually manufactured with higher quality leather and with a superior craftsmanship. Most boots were based on civilian designs and showed features that were against regulations, a fact that was often overlooked by their superiors due to the special status that fighter pilots enjoyed in the *Luftwaffe*.

1

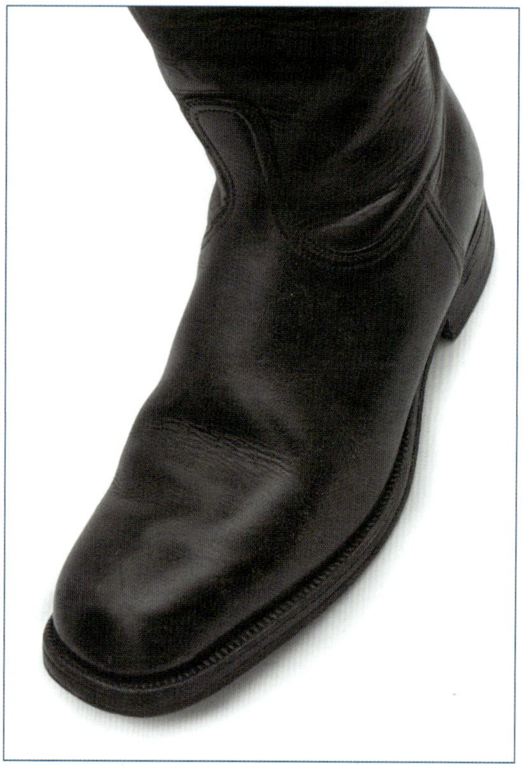

1. The length of the leg portion of the boots varied depending on the manufacturer, even though it was generally higher than the marching boots.

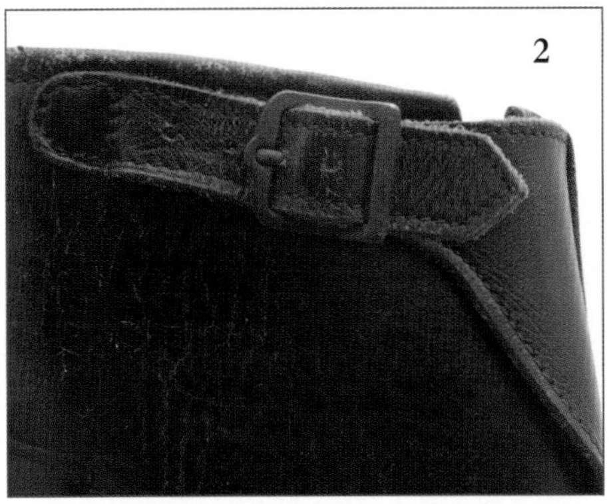

2

2. Privately purchased riding boots were often based on civilian models and generally featured elements that were clearly against regulation, such as the buckle and straps on the upper edge of the shafts as shown in the specimen of the photos.

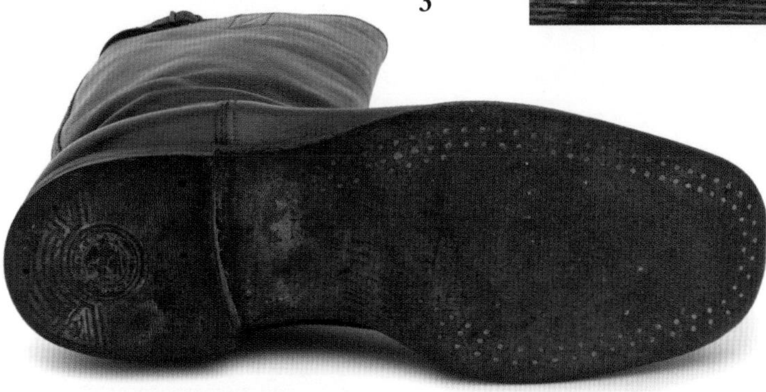

3

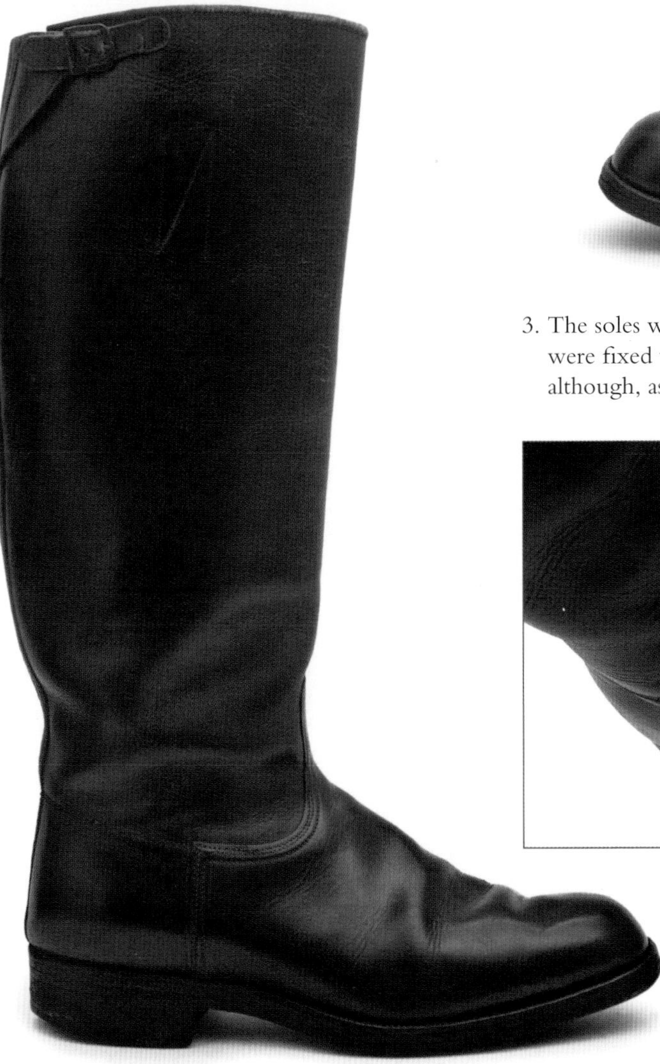

3. The soles were made of thick leather, to which a rubber or leather heels were fixed with nails. They usually featured leather or rubber half-soles although, as the case of the boots of the photos, no half-soles at all.

4

4. The construction of the high boots used by pilots was similar to the marching boots, but showed a narrower cut, a high quality workmanship and were usually made of smooth-surfaced soft leather.

Marching boots

Marschstiefel

Marching boots were issued for use by enlisted men and NCOs. They were made of blackened leather. The concern with leather shortages led to a directive issued in September 1939 when the use of tall leather marching boot was restricted to personnel serving in the field. Another regulation in November 1939 shortened the marching boot in an attempt to conserve leather. Increased leather shortages led to an order of 1943 by which the production of the tall marching boots was discontinued altogether.

5. This group of enlisted men and Non-commissioned officers are all wearing marching boots.

6. The foot part of the boots was constructed of two leather panels. The large forward panel had the form of a tongue and reached the instep. It was connected to the smaller rear panel covering the heel area by lateral double seams.

7. The leg portion of the boots measured approximately 40 cm from the upper edge to the heel. To the inside of both sides were pull straps of black webbing reaching 5 cm above the upper edge. The straps were double laid and sewn on about 3cm below the upper edge.

8. This *Oberfeldwebel* is wearing a pair of marching boots. (Militaria Arganzuela)

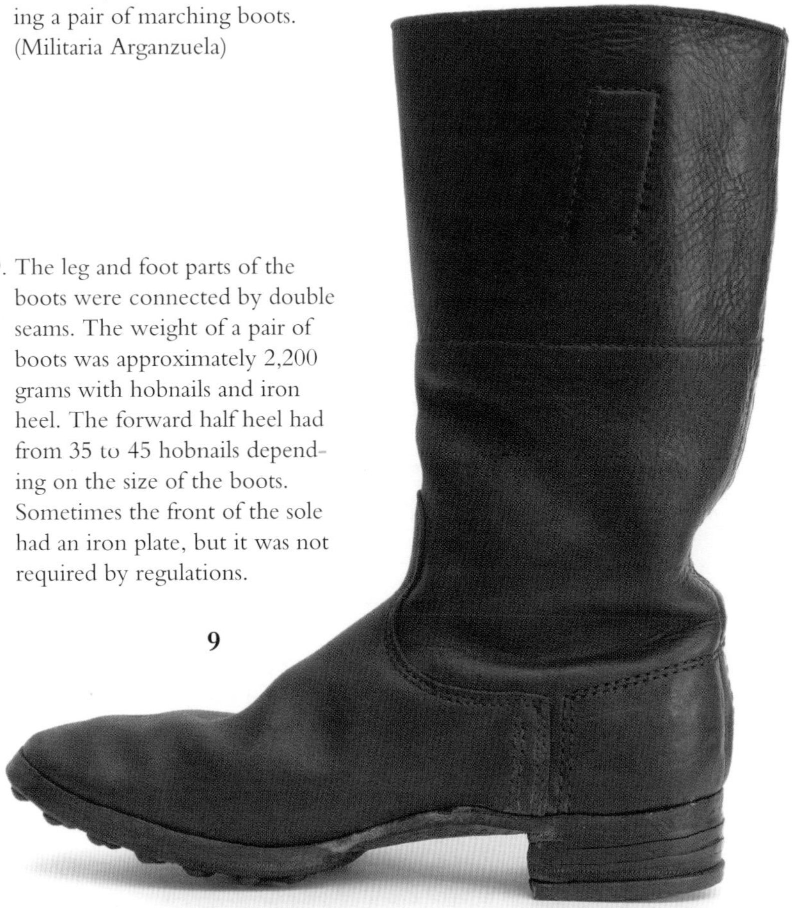

9

9. The leg and foot parts of the boots were connected by double seams. The weight of a pair of boots was approximately 2,200 grams with hobnails and iron heel. The forward half heel had from 35 to 45 hobnails depending on the size of the boots. Sometimes the front of the sole had an iron plate, but it was not required by regulations.

10

10. The leather heel consisted of three layers of leather and was about 3 cm high, depending on the size. It was reinforced by an iron heel plate round the outer rim.

7. Swords and daggers

The leather greatcoat in use by a grinning Major.

Edged weapons with decorative portepees were a tradition originally introduced in the Prussian army at the beginning of the Nineteenth century. This tradition was kept throughout the rest of the century as well as the beginning of the Twentieth century, and continued during the Third Reich. In 1934, the *Reichminister der Luftfahrt* ordered the introduction of an officer dagger. Non-commissioned officers and enlisted ranks were authorized to wear a knife. On July of 1937, the *Luftwaffe* introduced a second pattern dagger together with a new hanger for wear by officers and officials with the equivalent of officer's ranks, which was extended to senior NCOs in 1940. The production of the first pattern dagger was consequently discontinued.

In 1944, orders restricting the wear of daggers began to be issued in the face of the deteriorating war situation and the imminence of the entrance of the allied armies in German territory. This made the use of firearms as side weapons more practical than wearing daggers. These regulations were first issued in occupied countries, and finally a regulation of December 23, 1944 discontinued the use of daggers for all *Luftwaffe* personnel. As with the rest of the clothing and accouterments, officers and officials with equivalent ranks were required to privately purchase their daggers and hangers. Officers bought their daggers in special shops, which usually upgraded their daggers and hangers with the addition of more luxurious materials such as ivory and including ornamental patterns in the metallic parts. These accouterments were generally manufactured by subcontracted specialty firms and not by the mayor arms factories.

Just married. Oberleutnant *Walter Baumbach wears a private purchased greatcoat in his marriage ceremony. The dagger is on his left side and the hanger is fixed to a ring located inside the coat through a slash below the pocket flap. Baumbach was a famous bomber pilot, was awarded with the Knight's Cross of the Iron Cross with Oak Leaves and Swords.*

Flyer´s sword

Fliegerschwert

The officer sword was introduced in 1934, to be used by officer personnel of the *Fliegerschaft* on the occasions when its wear was required as per regulations. The sword was retained when the *Luftwaffe* was formed, and new orders were issued to regulate its use. The first of them was issued in 1936, and indicated that the sword could be worn by all officers and senior officer candidates with certain forms of dress. Later, the use was granted to senior NCOs and officers of equal ranks. The first model of sword had silver-plated fittings but in 1940 they started to be made of aluminum, due to shortages of raw material.

2

2. The photo shows an *Oberst* with a greatcoat holding his flyer sword during a ceremony.

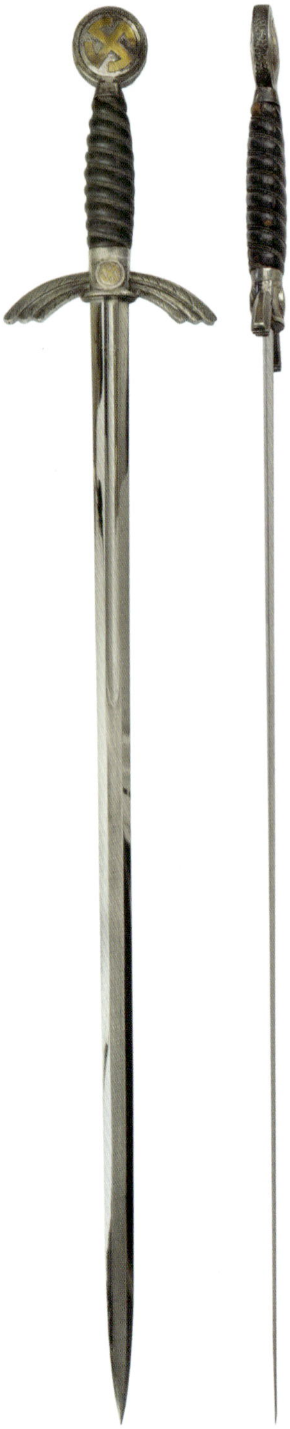

1

1. Detailed view of the finely chiselled oak leaves found on the sides of the flattened silver disk pommel with a sun wheel swastika.

3

3

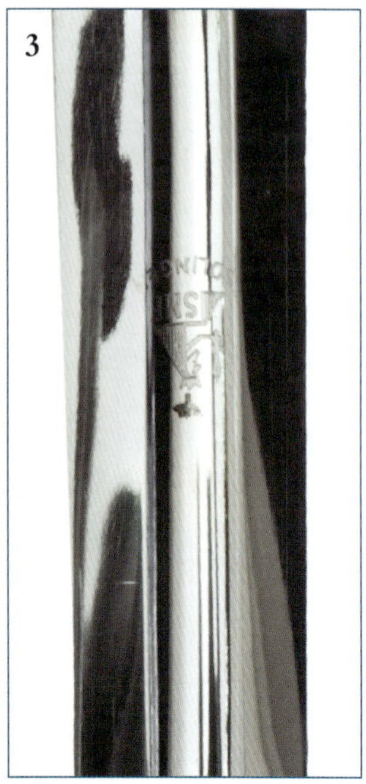

3. The nickel-plated blade features the SMF manufacturer's trademark. The king is sitting on the firm's initials *"SMF"*, while holding a sword in an upward position. Below the king is the location, Solingen.

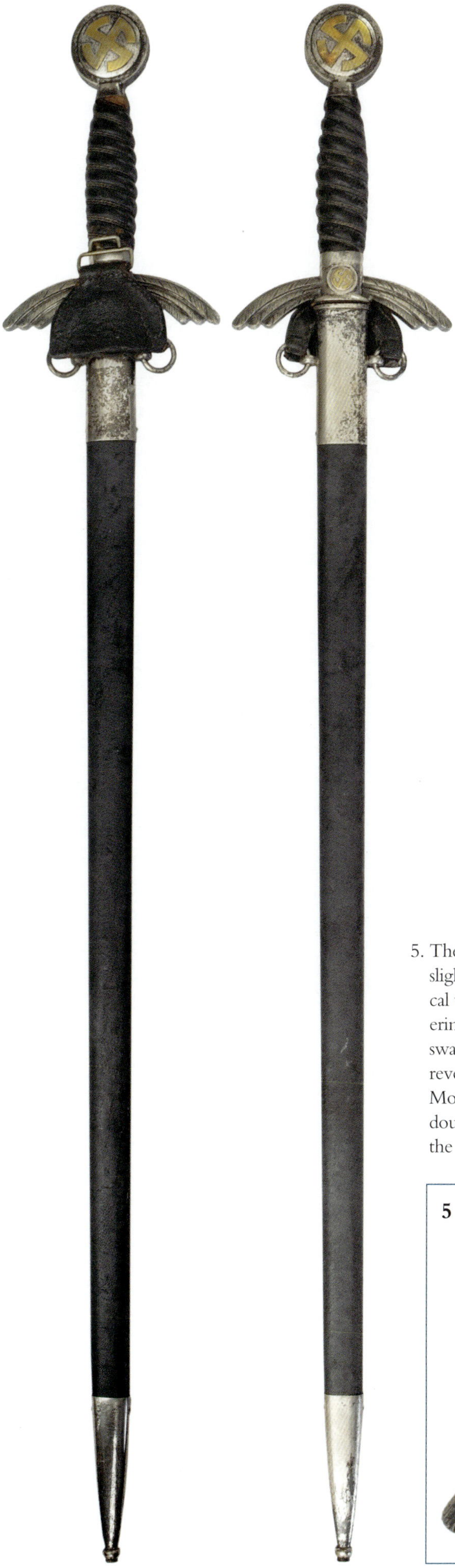

4

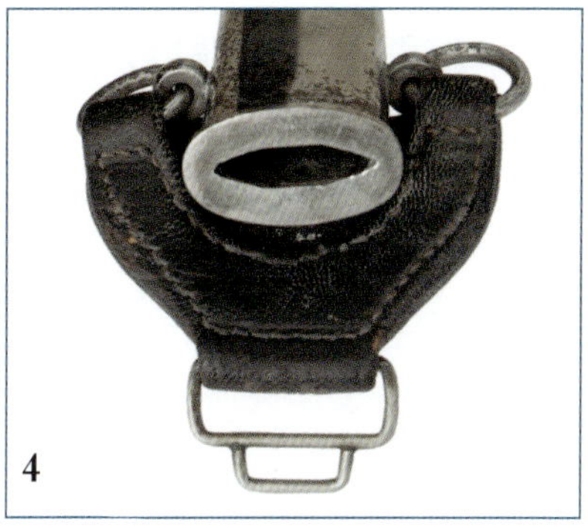

4

4

4

4. Details of the nickel-silver upper scabbard fitting, fixed to the scabbard with four headless retaining screws. A blue leather sword hanger was attached to the two-sided suspension rings soldered to the scabbard fitting. The sword was worn above the tunic and greatcoat. The upper loop of the hangers was attached to the inside belt.

5. The cross guard consisted of two slightly downward-curved symmetrical wings with detailed chiselled feathering. The center had a sun wheel swastika both in the obverse and reverse. The grip was covered with Moroccan blue leather, with a twisted double wire spiralling in grooves along the surface, from top to bottom.

5

Flyer's daggers

Fliegerdolch

Flyer's dagger for officers and NCO (first model)

The flyer's dagger or *Fliegerdolch* was introduced by an order of the *Reichsminister der Luftfahrt* in February, 1934 for wear by *Fliegerschaft* officers and NCOs, as well as privates who were in possession of the pilot badge. The dagger was adopted by the *Luftwaffe* in 1936, together with a series of regulations by virtue of which the use was extended first to all Senior NCOs and subsequently to junior NCOs and privates with the right to wear one of the flyers badges, except parachutists. The *Fliegerdolch* could be worn in walking-out dress and dress uniform. Officers, senior NCOs and junior officer candidates used the dagger with the portepee, while Junior NCOs and privates wore it unadorned.

6

6. The nickel circular pommel featured an inserted brass disk with a sun wheel swastika, also found in the obverse and reverse on the center of the cross guard. The disk and pommel were both silver plated, and the swastika was further gold plated.

6

7

7. An *Obergefreiter* poses for the camera in walk-out dress. He is wearing the *Fliegerdolch* on his left hip according to regulations.

8

8. The Portepee was worn by officers, senior NCOs and junior officer candidates. The hanger consisted of a double chain made of aluminum or nickel-plate, attached to the rings of the scabbards' upper and mid metal fittings.

9. The dagger had a polished double blade with a fuller. The crossguard featured two symmetrical wings at each side which were slightly curved downwards. The center was adorned with a sunwheel swastika on both the obverse and reverse. The scabbard was made of a tube covered in blue leather and incorporated three fittings.

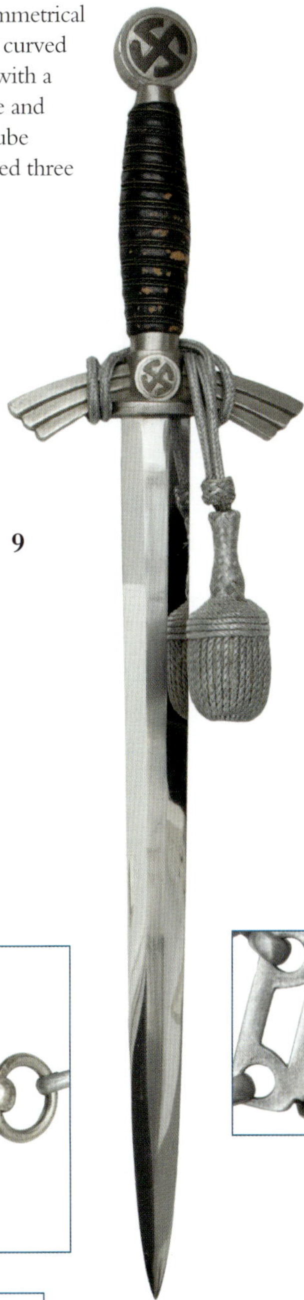

9

10

10. The hanger upper carbine spring hook was fixed to a loop sewn inside the tunic. The top and center fittings included movable metal rings that were attached to the chains of the hanger. The marking on the reads *"GES. GESCH."*, which stands for *"Legally Protected"*, over the initials *"OLC"* in a diamond, the trademark of *Overhoff & Co.*

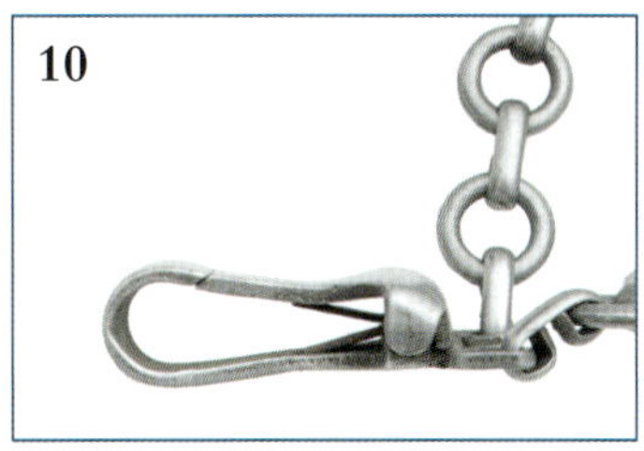

10

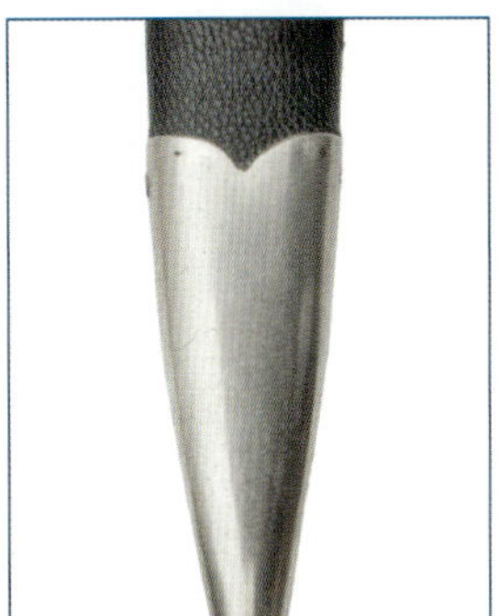

Flyer´s dagger for officers and NCO (second model)

The second type of the *Luftwaffe* dagger was introduced in 1937 to be worn by officers and senior officer candidates, and later expanded to senior NCOs, senior NCOs on the reserve and officials of NCO ranks. It was cheaper and easier to produce and differed from the first type in several aspects. The handle was constructed of solid plastic or made of wood and covered with celluloid. The colors ranged from orange to white. The crossguard had the shape of the national Adler with the head turned to the right and clutching a swastika with both legs. The pommel was screwed to the grip to secure the handle in place. The use of all type of daggers was discontinued from dress wear in December 1944.

11. This *Feldwebel* poses with his second type dagger with portepee. The dagger was worn over the tunic. The upper hook of the hanger passed through a horizontal opening under the flap of the left pocket and hooked either on the inside belt or to a loop sewn inside the tunic.

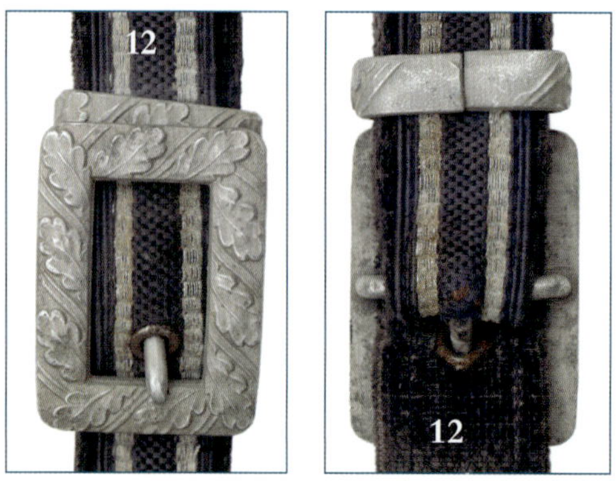

12. Hanger buckles were square with oak leaf ornaments around the edges. Apart from being an ornamental piece, they permitted the length of the hanger to be adjusted.

13. The design of the dagger consisted of a bulbous-shaped pommel with oak leaf ornaments covering the sides and the swastika displayed on the face on both the obverse and reverse. The pommel screwed onto the blade tang to secure the grip, cross guard and blade.

14. View of the upper clasp, which was secured to a loop sewn to the inside of the tunic. Some clasps were adorned with oak leaf patterns. The front section of the hanger featured suspension bands made of blue-grey tresse with two aluminum stripes running to each side. The rear of the hanger was made of dark velvet.

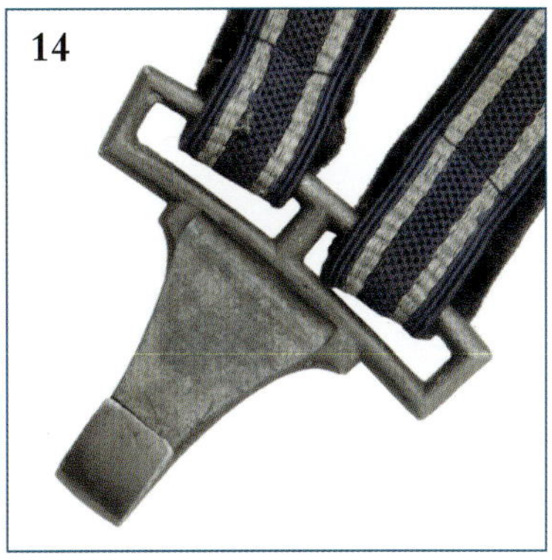

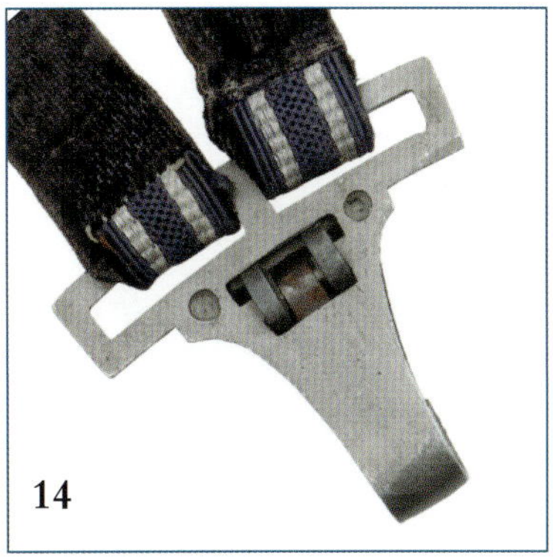

15. The dagger was worn with a cloth hanger which attached to the scabbard's two movable rings with carbine spring hooks.

16. The lower section of the scabbard was adorned with three oak leaves in a vertical row on both the obverse and reverse. The tip featured three grooves and culminated in a rounded point.

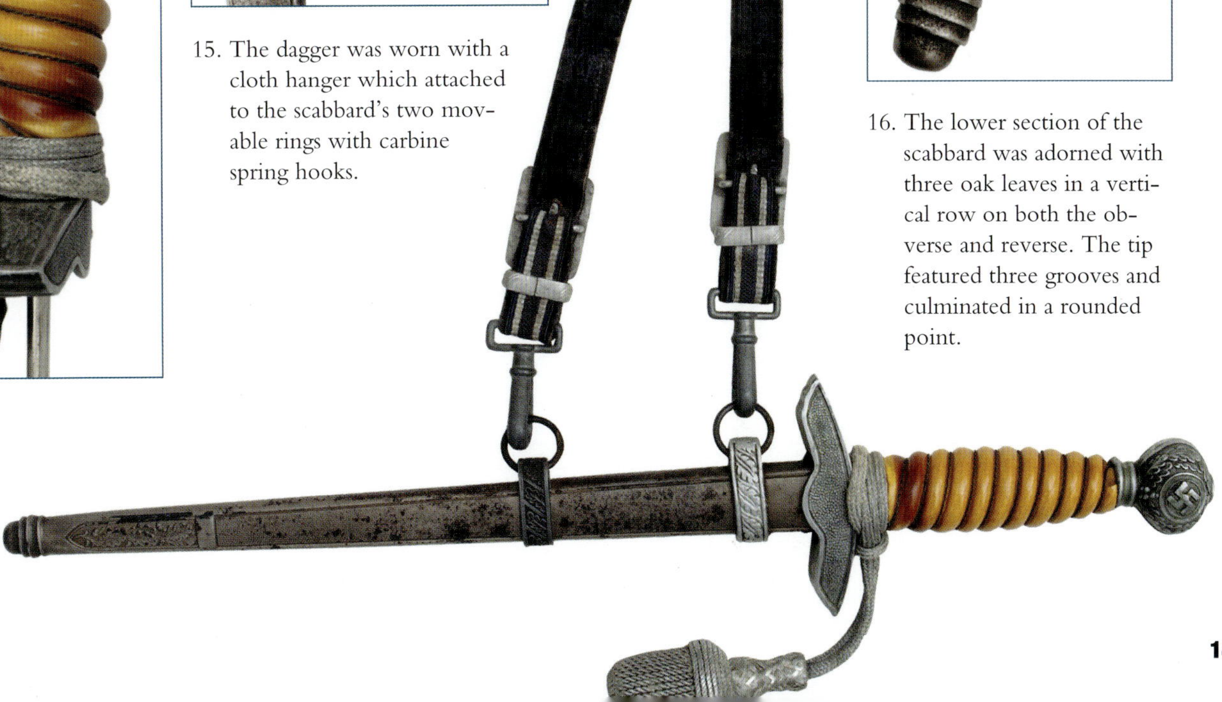

Oberstleutnant Erich Leie, a famous German fighter ace with 118 victories in 500 combat missions.

III. FLIGHT CLOTHING AND EQUIPMENT

When the Wright brothers made the first flight using a heavier-than-air machine-powered airplane in 1903, few people would imagine how decisive aircraft would become as a war weapon only a few years later.

The clothing and equipment used in that first flight was basically the same used when riding a bicycle. Nobody thought at that time that special clothing and equipment would be needed to ride those new wonder machines. Inventors continued to improve airplanes after the Wright Brothers, and soon clothing and equipment factories were forced to catch up with the technical advances in aviation. With airplanes being increasingly faster and flying at higher altitudes, pilots demanded clothing and equipment that would make them feel more comfortable and secure in the open cockpits of the early machines.

But it was not until the new invention caught the eye of the military, which understood the potential role of the aircraft as a powerful weapon of war, when the development of special clothing and equipment for flight started to gain momentum in the hands army research bureaus. When the First World War ended, some highly innovative ideas had been tried and tested, such as electrically heated flight suits, but never fully developed.

The end of the war caused a shift in the development of clothing and equipment back to private commercial firms, which designed and sold their products to the civilian market. Army budgets destined to research and development abruptly declined. The German air force had been disbanded after the Treaty of Versailles, while allied nations had doubts about the real effectiveness of aerial warfare. The tenacity of some committed military men prevented the complete disappearance of the air force in other countries, a possibility favored by a sector of the population that had suffered the rigours of the war and also by some members of the government who thought another branch of the army was not needed after such a devastating war.

The rebirth of air power was slow. Operating on minimal budgets that did not include resources for development of special gear and clothing, most pilots used obsolete WWI clothing and equipment, as well as commercial flight gear. For Germany, the turning point in the research and development of flight clothing was the rise to power of Hitler's Nazi party. Tired of the sanctions imposed to them after the First World War, they rallied together under Hitler's doctrine to bring the German armed forces back on their feet again. Huge budgets were destined for development of flight clothing and equipment. German military designers gained experience by testing their models during the development of glider clubs boosted by the government at a time when the use of engine-powered aircraft was forbidden by the Treaty of Versailles after World War I, as well as by the personnel pilot training exchange between the Soviet Union and Germany. But perhaps the most important testing ground for the German clothing and equipment was their involvement in the Spanish Civil War.

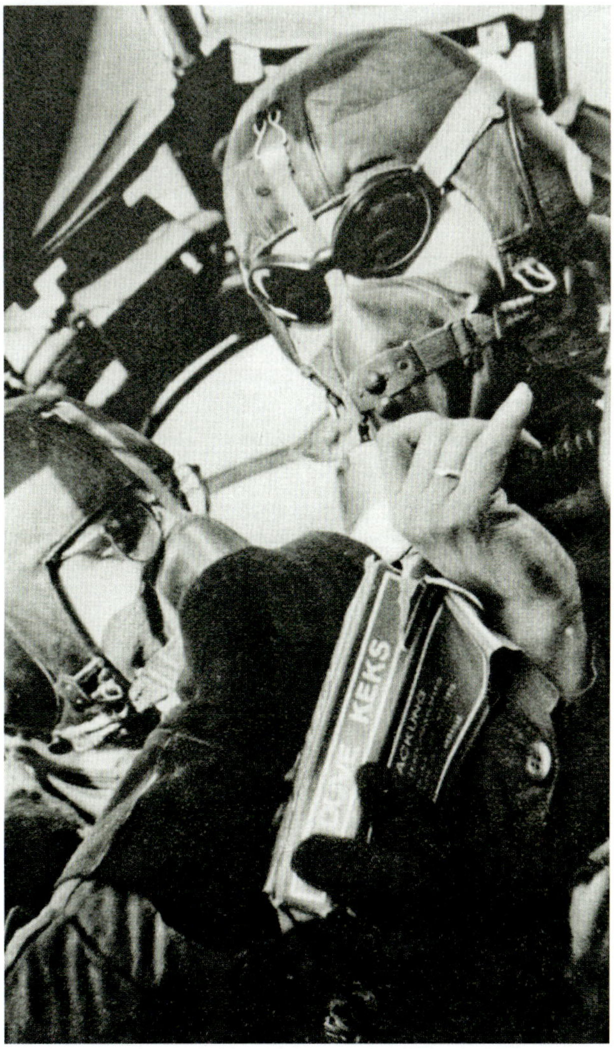

A crew member wearing the 10-67 three-strap oxygen mask and anti-splinter goggles during a high altitude flight over enemy territory. (Der Adler)

When the war in Europe started in 1939, the German *Luftwaffe* had an advantage of six years over her enemies, having developed a highly trained and morally confident fighting force capable of defeating any opposing force. The men behind the machines had the latest technology in flight equipment available at the time at their disposal, to the point that some technical solutions were copied by allied engineers. However, this initial advantage in development and design of flight clothing and equipment would eventually disappear, and further development lagged behind those of their allied counterparts.

The following pages will focus in the most important and recognizable pieces of flight clothing and equipment used throughout the war by the German *Luftwaffe*. What follows is a brief overview.

Flight clothing and equipment

Ground mechanics servicing a JG.54 Bf 109 G-2 from of the 9 Staffel, *III* Gruppe, "Green Heart" *after returning from a combat mission.*

The *Luftwaffe* had three basic one-piece flight suits to be used for specific climatic conditions: A light flight suit for summer use, a winter flight suit for maritime use and a winter flight suit for use over land. Later in the war, a two-piece flight suit was introduced during the war. Unofficially known as *"Kanal"* or *"Channel"* suit because it was first used in bombing missions which required the aircraft to cross the English Channel, they were more comfortable and easy to fit than the one-piece suits, and soon became popular with pilots and flight crews. Electrically heated suits were introduced later in the war. The system comprised an internal cabling that passed through a number of insulating elements installed between the lining and the outer shell of the suit, supplying warmth to the crewman's body, hands and feet. Some fine specimens of private purchase leather flight jackets will also be mentioned in the corresponding section. The use of privately purchased jackets by air force pilots is an almost unique occurrence during the war, with jackets as unique as their wearers.

The basic design of the German flight helmet dates back to the pre-war years and remained almost unchanged throughout the war. Three basic types of flight helmets existed. The first was intended to be used during the winter and was made of leather with fleece lining. The second type was designed to be used during the summer and was manufactured with fabric and lined with satin. Finally, a third type of helmet with a net covering the skull area was designed during the war to be used in temperate theaters of operations. Each of these helmets suffered slight variations during the war, mostly in the electric components, as well as in the provision for the adjustment of other pieces of equipment, such as flight goggles and oxygen masks.

As far as flying goggles are concerned, two basic configurations will be discussed. The first consisted of individual face pads that surrounded each of the eyepieces, while the second type used a single face pad to mount the two lenses. The first type had adjustable nose bridges that allowed the distance between each lens to be adjusted. On the other hand, the single cushion, though more comfortable to wear, had the drawback of the impossibility of adjusting the distance between each lens, making it necessary to have several sizes.

Germany began the research and development of oxygen breathing systems for their pilots in the early twenties. Several models of oxygen masks were manufactured during the war, some with two attachment straps and others with three straps. German oxygen masks were usually smaller and lighter than their allied counterparts, due to the fact that they had no provision for built-in microphones systems.

The use of gloves by *Luftwaffe* pilots depended basically on the type of plane they flew. Designs changed little throughout the war. Some fighter pilots preferred not to wear gloves or used private purchased or issue dress gloves. Thick leather gauntlets with fleece lining were mainly used by crew members of heavier aircraft for high altitude missions. Electrically heated gauntlets will also be mentioned.

Flight boots will also be mentioned. At the beginning of the war, many pilots preferred to use their leather top boots or normal shoes, depending on the trousers they used. Flight boots underwent little change in the basic design. The most significant changes in the design of flight footwear were the electrically heated boots. Initially, flight boots were fitted with double zip fastener closures, but as the war progressed, one of the zip fasteners was dropped, basically due to war shortages. Quality of raw materials and craftsmanship declined noticeably near the end of the war.

Luftwaffe life preservers were mainly used as flotation devices. Two main variations were used, both of which will be covered in this section. The first was the inflatable type, inflated with carbon dioxide bottles, and the Kapok filled type.

In addition to the flight gear and equipment intended for pilots and crew members, a group of basic tools were used for different tasks, being the correct navigation towards the target of utter importance for the success of a mission. Flight instruments and navigation tools including watches, flight computers and wrist compasses will be covered in detail.

Finally, this section will cover the most recognizable sidearms used by crew members and fighter pilots for their protection. Fighter pilots in particular used very small weapons due to the restricted space of their cockpits, such as the Hungarian Femaru M37 pistol. Others preferred to use the P-08, being the *"Krieghoff"* firm the primary supplier to the *Luftwaffe* during WWII and making these Luger pistols prized for their fine fit and finish.

A ground crewman helps the Me 109G-6 pilot adjust his parachute before riding his aircraft for a mission over Germany. The external disposable fuel tank is visible below the plane.

Flight clothing label system

The most noticeable aspect when attempting to study German flight clothing and equipment is the inconsistency in the labelling of the items. While some labels indicate little more than the name of the maker, the subcontractor and the size, others include a complete listing of data, including model designation, model number, equipment number, work/order number, *Luftwaffe* contract/requisition number and the manufacturer's code. Measures were taken later in the war to prevent identification of production areas. In 1943, most of the labelling information of the contract and the city in which they were located was replaced with an RB number formed by three series of numbers separated with bars preceded by the letters RBNr, the abbreviation of *Reichsbetriebsnummer*. Later, two or three character codes were also used identify suppliers and contractors.

To add more confusion, most articles suffered many variants during the war, mostly related to material, color, pattern and different production methods which altered production regulations. Many items suffered non regulation field modifications made to fit personal peculiarities of the wearer. A list and description of all possible variations is impossible to achieve.

In one form or another, German *Luftwaffe* labels included the following information: Article number *(Gerätenummer)*, order reference *(Anforderungszeichen)*, work number *(Werksnummer)*, manufacturer number *(Herstellernummer)*, size *(Grösse)*, date of manufacture *(Tag der Herstellung)*, and finally weight *(Gewicht)* and style *(Bauart)* if applicable. All relevant codes and numbers, as well as detailed views of labels, will be listed and illustrated.

8. Flight helmets

The use of flight helmets goes back to the early days of flight, especially after the development of military aviation that took place during the First World War. The need to protect the pilot's head against the cold, windy conditions of open cockpit airplanes of the time and the subsequent addition of communications and breathing equipment, made the use of protective head gear an essential part of the flying clothing of the pilots and crew members of military aircraft. The German military flight helmet designers had the advantage of the experience acquired by the testing of their models during the development of glider clubs by the German government at a time when the use of motorized aircraft was forbidden by the Treaty of Versailles after World War I, as well as the personnel pilot training exchange between the Soviet Union and Germany. But perhaps the most important testing ground for the German equipment was the involvement in the Spanish Civil War. During the conflict, the Germans tried a vast array of clothing and equipment that was designed in the previous years in battle conditions and took very valuable information that was used for further development and improvement.

But despite the technical advantage gained before the outburst of the war, the German flight helmet designs hardly evolved once it started, contrary to the allied flight gear design, which was improved and modernized greatly during the conflict. The basic design pattern of German flight helmets, established in the thirties, suffered no significant modifications or improvement throughout the war. This basic pattern consisted of five leather or fabric segments sewn together to cover the skull, with the addition of metal or rubber elements at both sides to house the communications equipment and protect the ears. The lion's share of the research and development of flight helmets for the *Luftwaffe* was given to the Siemens company, who designed and manufactured most of the communications systems. The production of garment itself was spread amongst a wide array of factories in German territory and occupied countries.

The Gefreiter *of this portrait photo is wearing the LKp S 101 flight helmet. The concealed adjustable strap and eyelet for the three-strap oxygen mask located in the top center of the helmet is clearly visible. The other two adjustment hooks are placed on the sides of the helmet.*

The *Luftwaffe* flight helmets had three basic types : Winter helmets, made of leather or fabric; summer helmets, manufactured with fabric and lined with satin, and finally net helmets. Each of these models had a great number of variations, depending on several factors, such as the need to install communications equipment, or the theatre of operations intended to be used. Another element which influenced the design of flight helmets was the adjustment of other pieces of equipment, such as flight goggles and oxygen masks. Several configurations were produced, fitted with attachment points for fixing of two or three strap oxygen masks.

Furthermore, the most important difference between the summer and the winter flight helmet was the manufacturing materials. The outer shell of winter helmets was made of leather and were lined with sheepskin for comfort and protection against cold weather. Summer helmets were made, as mentioned previously, with the same basic pattern, but were manufactured in a brownish cotton fabric and were lined with satin. Both types of helmets were designed with or without communications systems, which suffered minor modifications during the war. Throat microphones were either the rounded magnetic type, designated as Mi4, the oval carbon type, designated as Mi4b, or an improved model called Mi4c. Several types of closures were designed and used during the war, which had to fit tightly in the pilot's neck to ensure a correct pick-up of the vibration from the larynx, but not too uncomfortable to bother the neck of the pilot. Early systems comprised a single throat microphone fitted in one of the chinstraps, evolving to a system which combined snap fasteners to fit and quick release buckles which proved acceptable. Flight helmets had earphone receivers mounted on the helmet housing, which were made of metal or rubber, and wired internally between the shell and the lining.

Perhaps the most popular flight helmet of the *Luftwaffe* was the net or mesh helmet. It was much more comfortable to wear and could be used in all but the most extreme cold weathers. It was a very light helmet composed of the same segments in the skull area, but made of mesh instead of fabric or leather.

This Me 109 pilot is wearing the LKp N 101 net flying helmet together with hinged rigid-framed Splitterschutzbrille *goggles model FL. 30550, manufactured by* Nitsche & Günther. *The photo was taken somewhere in the Mediterranean, probably in Italy.*

Winter flight helmets

Winterkopfhauben

K33 flight helmet

The K33 helmet was designed for pilots or crew members who did not require radio communications. The garment was meant to be used in cold weather. It was developed at the beginning of the thirties, and was made of five segments of goatskin leather and with a fleece lining. A bandanna was sewn in the inner forehead area to protect the helmet from the sweat. It was fitted with double leather chinstraps, which were lined with chamois, crossed each other in the neck and bucked to a metal buckle placed at either side, secured by an horizontal leather loop above the buckle. The oxygen mask fastening system consisted of two metal hooks located at both sides of the helmet and an adjustable band on the upper center of the helmet which ended in a metal loop

1

1. The inside of the helmet was lined with fleece to protect the pilot's head of the low winter temperature. The photo shows the sweat shield placed in the internal forehead area, as well as the two leather chinstraps lined with chamois for extra comfort.

2

2. The woven spec label was sewn to the inside of the garment and showed the maker's name and size. The helmet was made by the known maker Karl Heisler and the size is a 54.

3. The top front fitting for the three-strap oxygen mask was achieved by an adjustable strap that was sewn vertically across the upper center of the helmet. The strap ended in a metal loop to adjust the mask hook. The other end of the band was fixed to a metal loop and secured by a metal friction buckle.

3

4

4. The helmet was void of communications equipment and lacked side apertures in the ears. Two flat metal hooks placed at either side of the helmet allowed the adjustment of the oxygen mask. The buckles next to the hooks secured both leather chinstraps.

K33 flight helmet (modified)

The basic design of this helmet dates back to the thirties, and had no provision for communications equipment. It was made of five segments of calf leather and was lined with fleece. A leather band was sewn in the inside forehead area. It was secured by two chinstraps that started at either side of the helmet and crossed and adjusted to metal buckles located on both sides. The specimen shown in the photos is one of the many variations of the standard model, which was made without the side hooks for attaching an oxygen mask. In the place of the earpads, the helmet has two apertures to adjust the primitive communications systems between pilots. When not in use, it closed by means of a leather earflap with pressure studs.

5

5. The back of the helmet did not include the standard vertical small strips of leather to hold the goggle fastening band in place and prevent them from blowing away during flight.

6

6. One of the side buckles to adjust the chinstrap. This model lacks the flat hooks to adjust the two-strap oxygen mask.

7. The leather earflaps located at both sides could retract and were fixed by a press button. Under the flaps, a round aperture allowed the fitting of the early communication systems for the crew members to talk to each other in open-cockpit aircraft. This feature was not standard in the K33 model, as it was manufactured to be used by crews which did not need to use communications equipment. During the war, it was not uncommon for a garment to suffer many manufacturing variants, which never appeared in the official quartermaster manuals.

7

8

8. The helmet was lined with five panels of fleece or rabbit fur. The long chinstraps were adjusted with two buckles placed on both sides of the helmet. They had a chamois lining to provide additional comfort to the wearer. The basic design of this helmet was the pattern for the rest of *Luftwaffe* flight helmets that followed.

8

LKp W 53 flight helmet

This model was intended to be used during the winter, and was internally wired with radio communication equipment. The Lkp W 53 was manufactured using the same basic design of the rest of the flight helmets; the outer shell was manufactured using five panels of goatskin leather lined with fleece or lamb fur. A leather band was sewn to the fur lining in the forehead area. The communication system consisted of a microphone and receivers in both earcups. A single rounded throat type microphone was inserted immediately above the chin strap, on the right hand side of the helmet. When the strap was adjusted to the pilot's neck, the throat microphone was tightly adjusted against the neck, near the larynx, allowing the sound waves to be picked up by the microphone. The helmet included flat hooks on either side for attaching the side straps of an oxygen mask, as well as vertical tabs in the rear to fix the straps of flight goggles.

9

9. The two-pin plug connected the flight helmet to the aircraft radio control box. The black plastic plug housing had moulded letters indicating the type of plug. This was a very early type of connector that was extensively used during the Spanish civil war, but it was deemed as obsolete at the outburst of the Second World War.

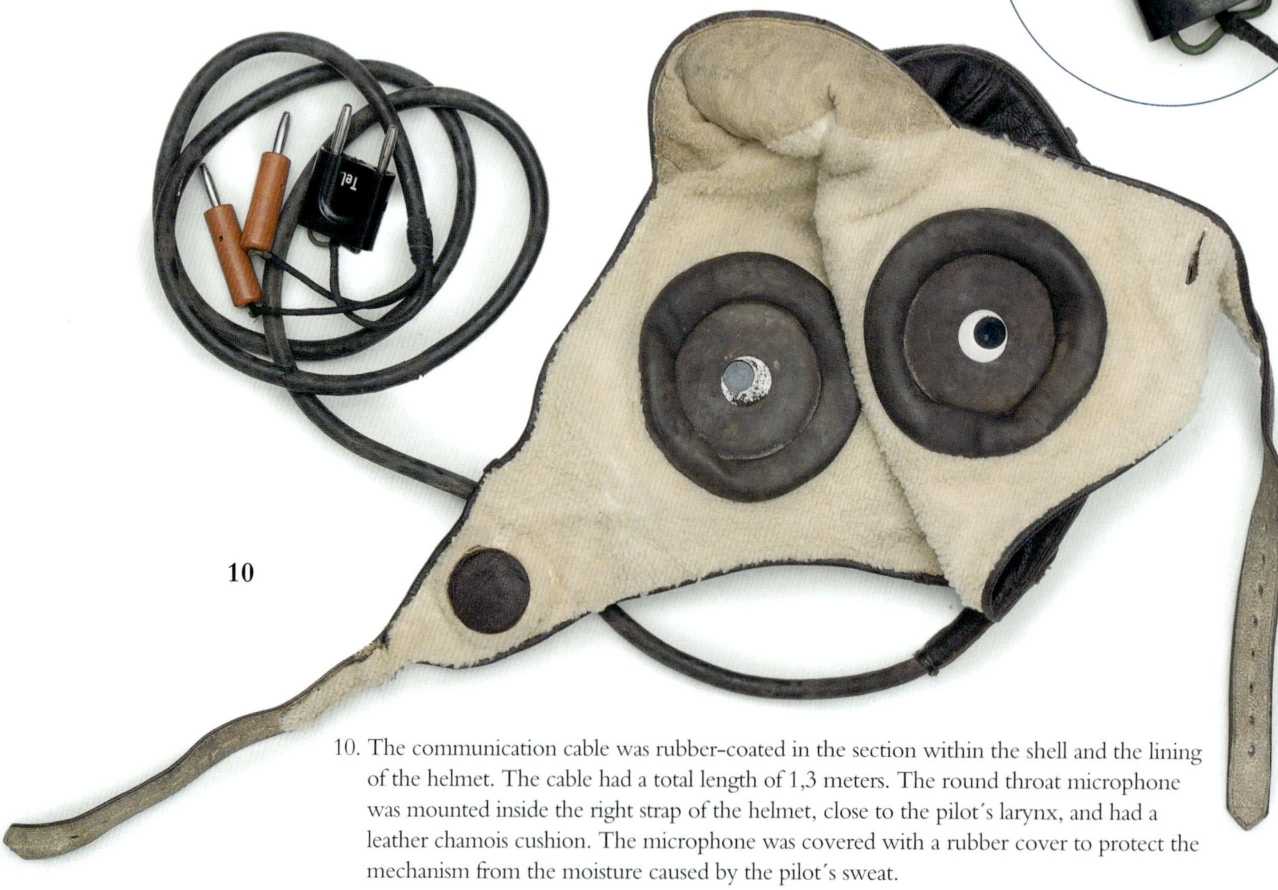

10

10. The communication cable was rubber-coated in the section within the shell and the lining of the helmet. The cable had a total length of 1,3 meters. The round throat microphone was mounted inside the right strap of the helmet, close to the pilot´s larynx, and had a leather chamois cushion. The microphone was covered with a rubber cover to protect the mechanism from the moisture caused by the pilot´s sweat.

11. The helmet had two small vertical straps which closed with pressure buttons on either side of the back of the helmet. They were used to secure the goggle straps.

11

12

12. This early woven label was sewn in the inside of the helmet, and showed information about the manufacturer of the communications system and the helmet model. The labelling information became progressively more detailed during the conflict.

13

13. A second label indicated the name of the helmet maker and the size, which is 58 in the case of this helmet.

14. The earphones were housed in black-painted aluminum rounded domes, which were later replaced by hard rubber moulded earcups painted in black or brown.

14

LKp W 100 flight helmet

The LKp W 100 was introduced in 1936 and improved in 1938. It had a simple but innovative design and was used throughout the war with minor modifications in the communication system. The outer shell was manufactured with goatskin leather and the lining was either of rabbit fur or lamb skin fleece.

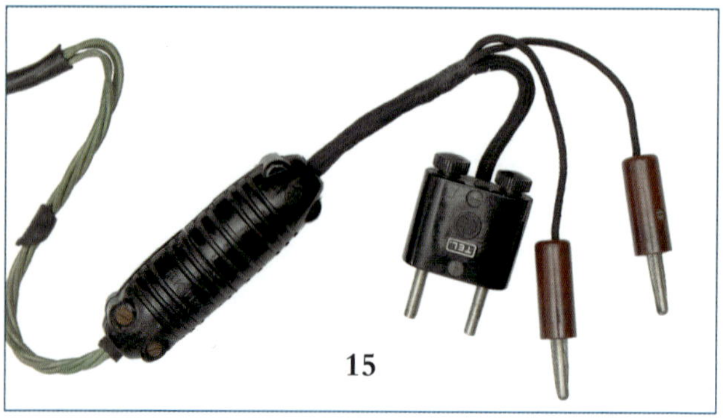

15

15. The cord had a length of approximately 1 meter and ended in a standard DIN-4 bee-hive pin plug which connected to the communication control box of the aircraft. An extension cable with the earlier type lugs has been connected to the DIN-4 plug of this helmet.

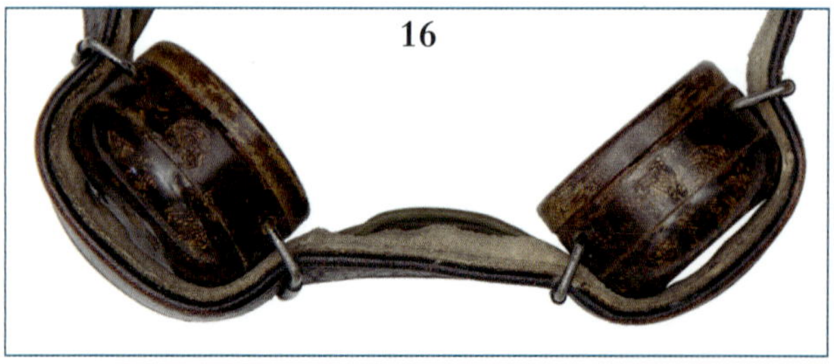

16

16

16. The helmet was fitted with two model Mi4 throat microphones that were attached to a leather chinstrap by means of two metal rings which emerged on both sides of the bakelite housings.

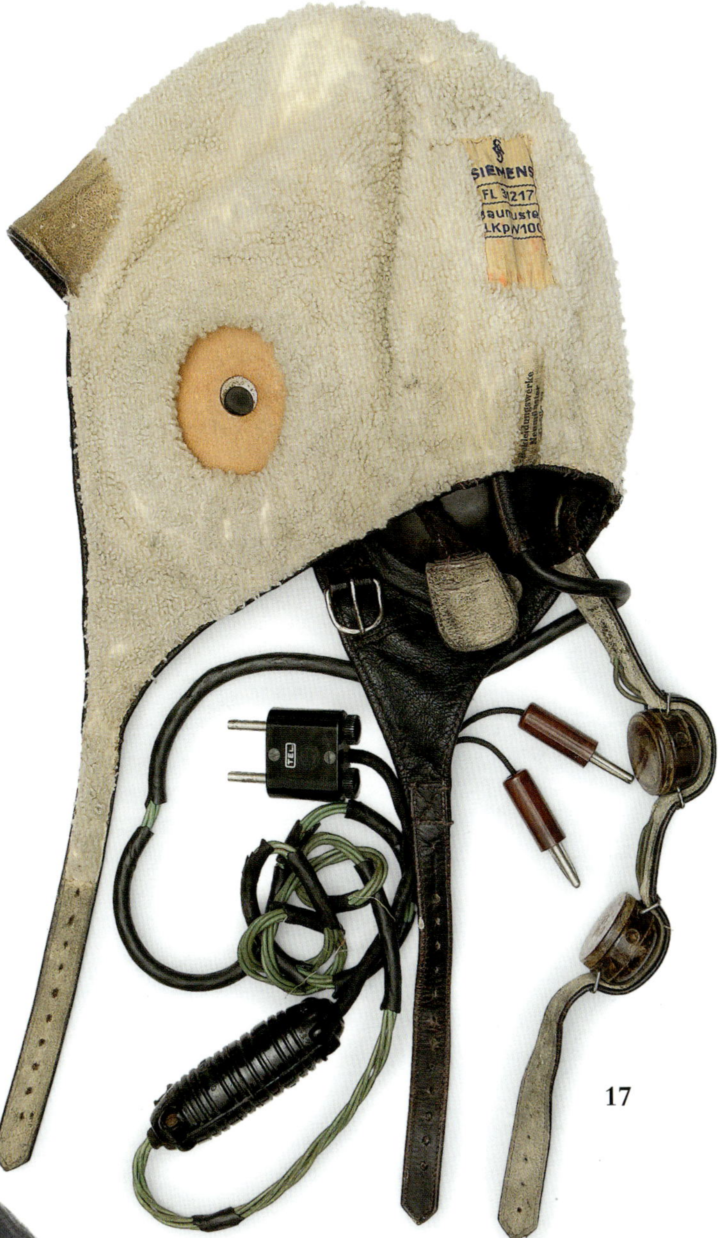

17

17. The lining of the helmet was made of rabbit fur or lambskin fleece. The inside of the earcups was lined with cushioned chamois earpads to provide comfort to the wearer.

18

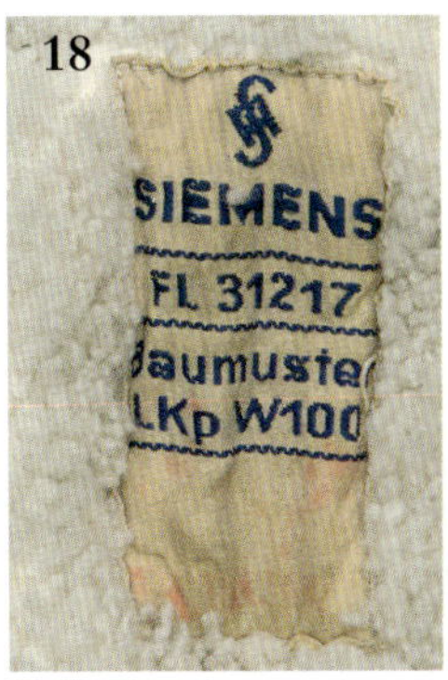

19

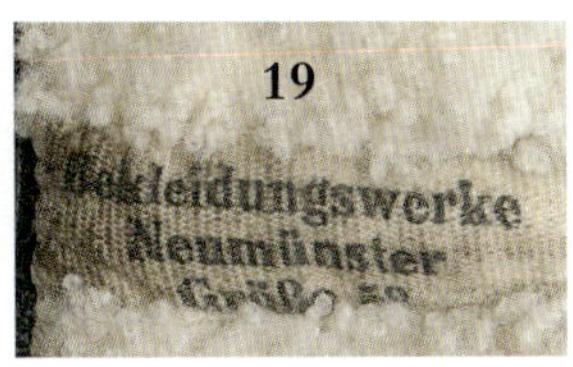

18. The helmet label is typical of early production models.

19. The name and address of the manufacturer was later replaced in spec labels with three letter codes to conceal information about location of production factories and prevent bombing by the allied air forces.

LKp W 101 flight helmet

Introduced in 1938, the LKp W 101 winter flying helmet was actually an improvement of the previous model with new communication systems made by Siemens. The earphones were encapsulated in a hard rubber cup, instead of the metal or plastic used in the previous model, and was covered with leather. A recess was added at the top to allow the goggle straps to rest securely in place and prevent them from falling from the pilot's head. The new elements provided pilots with improved insulation. Changes were also made to the throat microphones housing and the straps to make them more comfortable for the pilots. The helmet had the same hooks on either side, and a new concealed adjustable strap located in the forehead with an eyelet at the end for adjusting the three-strap oxygen masks.

20. Detailed view of the improved model Mi4b throat microphones. They were fixed to the neck by two straps with buckles at the nape of the helmet, and joined together at the front of the throat by means of a two-snap fastener, which could be quickly joined together or taken off by the pilot.

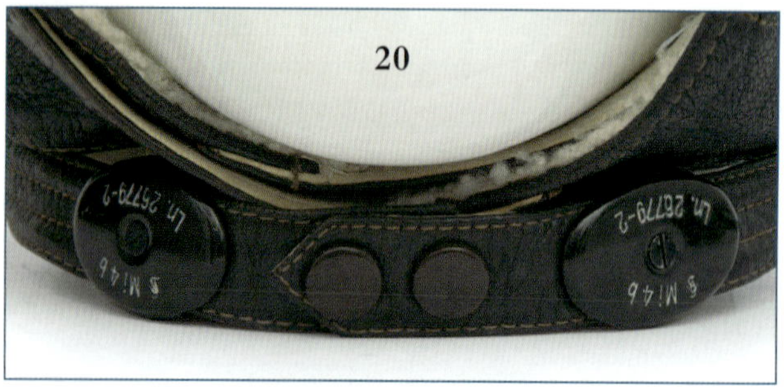

21. The two straps containing the microphones could be adjusted with buckles, joining at the nape by a large *"T"* shaped leather piece that was sewn to the back of the flight helmet. The cable ended up in a standard 4-pin DIN plug.

22. The pilot is checking his fighter on-board communication equipment using his Lkp W 101 flight helmet. The forehead strap and eyelet to adjust a three-strap oxygen mask is clearly visible.

22

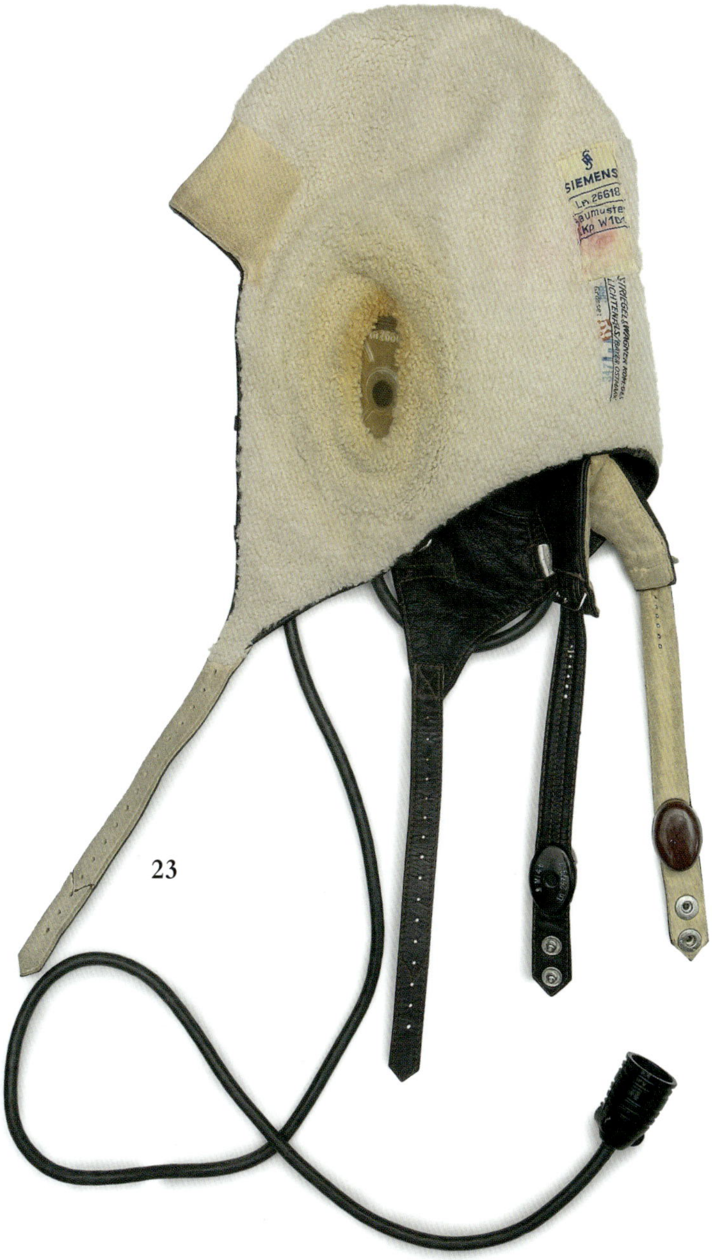

23

23. The helmet was lined with fleece. The information of the communication equipment manufacturer and other relevant data was consigned on different woven labels in early war specimens.

23

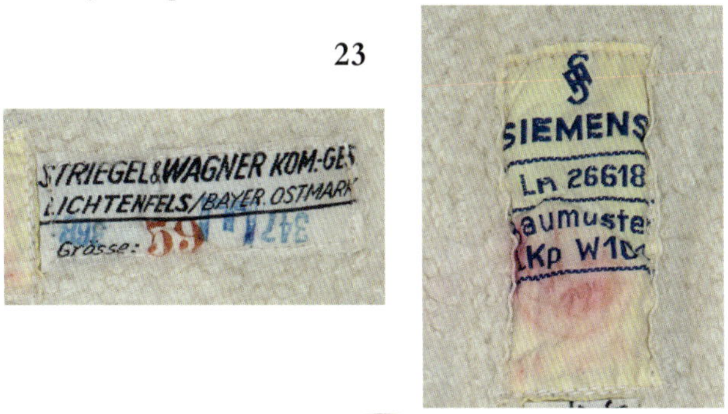

LKp W 101 flight helmet (modified)

This helmet is a modified version of the LKp W 101 winter helmet described in the previous pages which has been stripped from its communications system. These type of modifications were made for several reasons, such as the usage for glider planes or open-cockpit aircraft, in which communications were not a priority. The earcups of the helmet have been removed and replaced by leather segments to cover the aperture. In the center, an earflap has been added with two press buttons to keep it in an open or closed position. Below the earflap, an aperture was left in order for the pilot to hear the surroundings when not in flight and also to use the primitive communications system to talk with other crew members, which consisted of a rubber hose setup. In the nape of the helmet, a segment of leather was used to cover the hole where the cable came out of the helmet and an leather neck piece has been added.

24

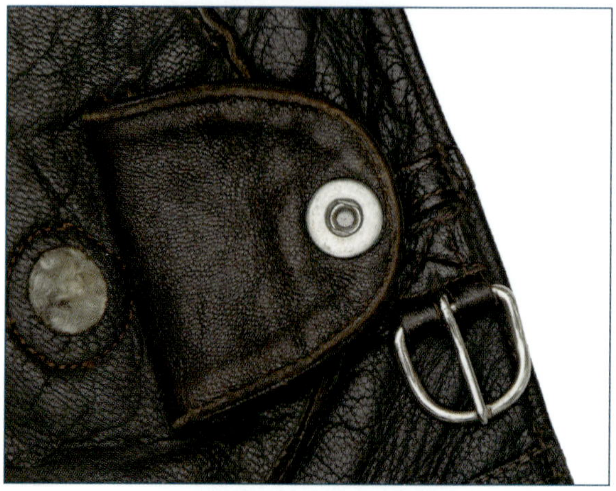

24. Detailed photo of the communications system modification. The prominent exterior earcup has disappeared and has been replaced by two earflaps which could be opened to reveal a small rounded aperture. A second press button holds the earflap in the open position when an external communication equipment is used.

25. The back of the helmet has retained the two vertical leather strips which are closed by a press button. They were used to secure the goggle straps and prevent them from falling during violent air manoeuvres or strong wind when flying in open-cockpit aircraft.

25

26. The helmet was lined with fleece. The inside of the earcup area was cushioned for extra comfort. All the communications equipment have been removed from the helmet, while the ear apertures have been retained to allow the fitting of an archaic communication system between crew members. Notice the earflaps with a pressure button, which could be used to keep it both in an opened or closed position.

26

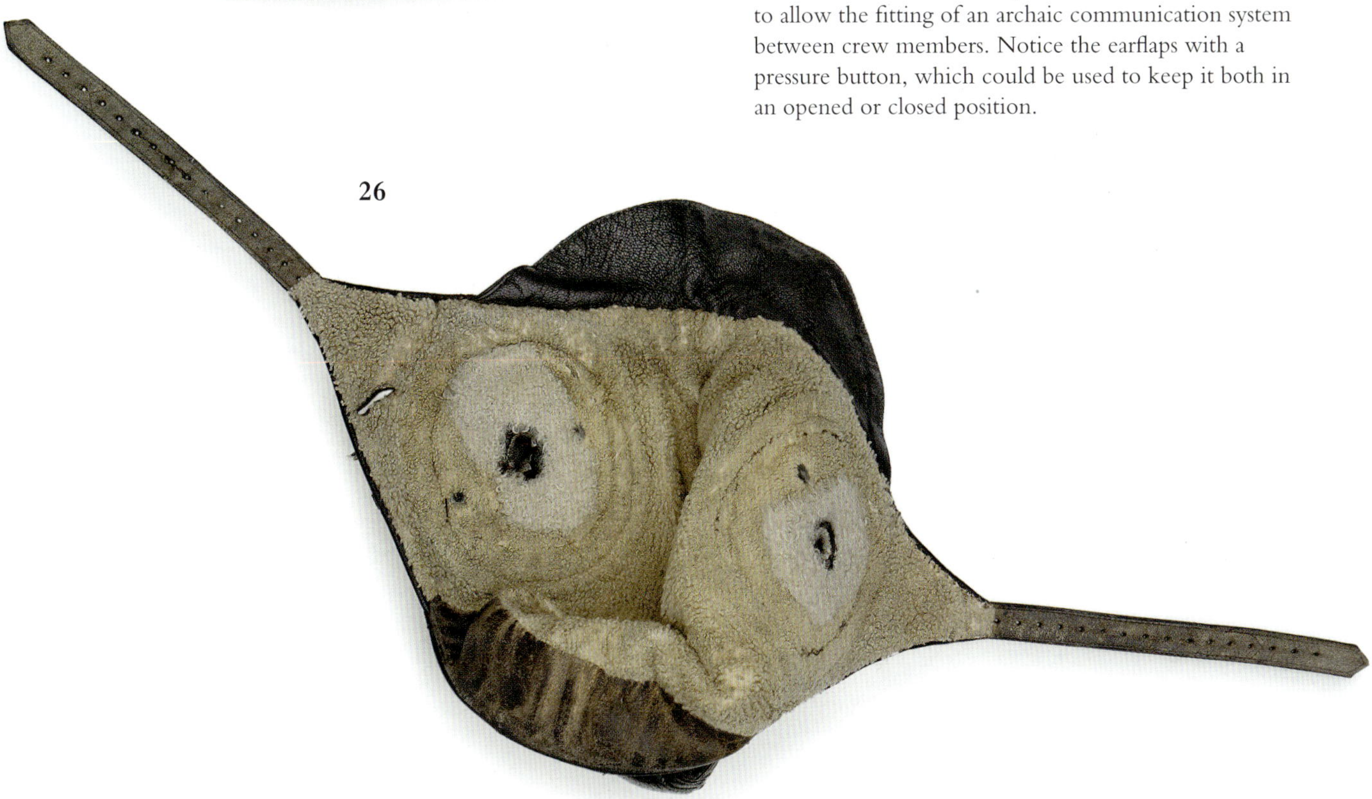

Summer flight helmets

Sommerkopfhauben

FK 34 flight helmet

The summer flight helmet model Fk 34 was introduced in 1936. It was intended for use in the summer by crew members who did not require communication equipment, such as training airplane crews, some gunner positions in bombers or even for fighter pilots flying obsolete aircraft. Production of the helmet ceased in 1943, even though it was declared obsolete after the introduction of the more advanced Lkp S 100 and Lkp S 101 models, both fitted with radio communications. It was manufactured with a fine brown cotton fabric and was lined in olive green cotton satin. The chinstrap consisted of two separate straps at either side of the helmet which crossed in the chin and were adjusted with a buckle located at both sides.

27. *Above:* Each strap was adjusted to the opposite side passing through an eyelet in the helmet and was secured by metal buckles. *Below:* The metal loop located on the helmet forehead for the three-point oxygen mask is visible in the photo below. The adjustable strap was sewn vertically across the upper center of the helmet.

28. The interior of the helmet was lined with grey satin. The chamois lining of the chinstraps are clearly visible. The woven label was hand sewn on the inside of the garment and shows the maker's name, Karl Heisler of Berlin.

28

29

29. One of the standard features of German flight helmets were the two straps which were intended to hold the goggle fastening band. They were made of leather and placed vertically at both sides of the back of the helmet . One of the sides was sewn on the helmet, while the other had a brown snap button. The photo also shows the strap that was sewn across the center of the helmet, which, together with two other flat hooks placed at either side of the helmet, was used to fit the three-point oxygen mask.

LKp S 100 flight helmet

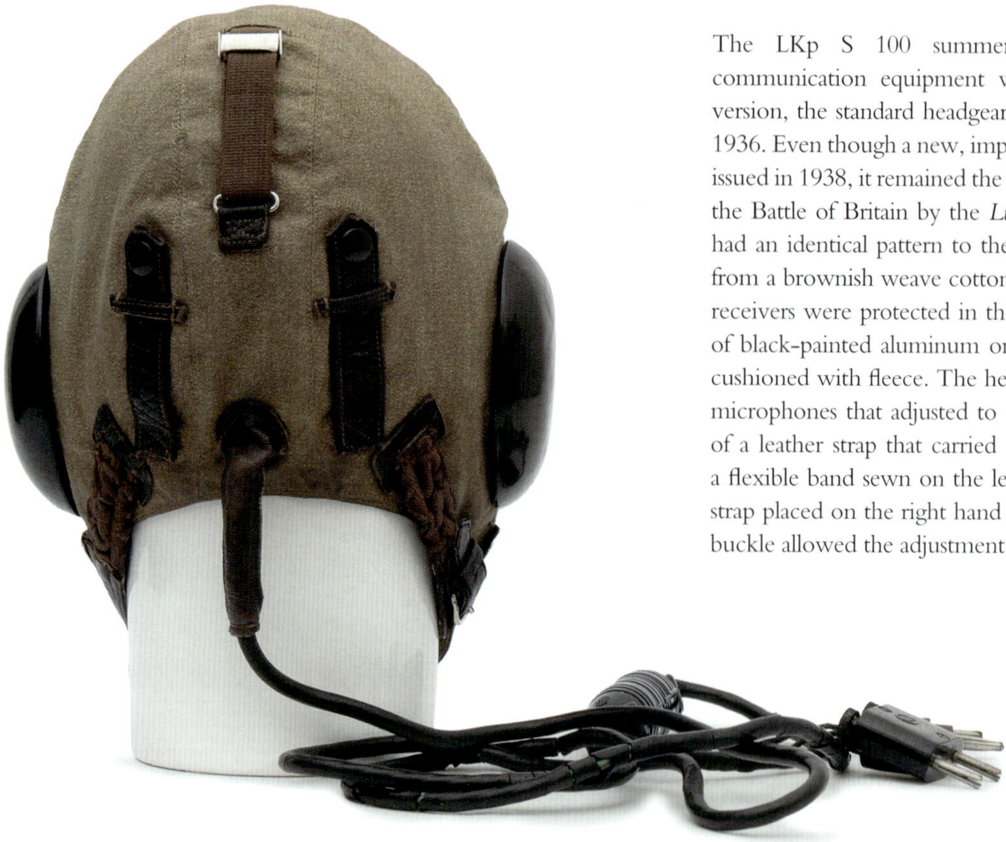

The LKp S 100 summer flying helmet with radio communication equipment was, together with the winter version, the standard headgear of the German air forces since 1936. Even though a new, improved version of this helmet was issued in 1938, it remained the most widely used helmet during the Battle of Britain by the *Luftwaffe* pilots. The construction had an identical pattern to the winter version, but was made from a brownish weave cotton and lined with grey satin. The receivers were protected in the outside by oval earcups made of black-painted aluminum or bakelite, while the inside was cushioned with fleece. The helmet was fitted with two throat microphones that adjusted to the neck of the pilot by means of a leather strap that carried the microphones and ended in a flexible band sewn on the left side of the helmet. A second strap placed on the right hand side of the helmet with a metal buckle allowed the adjustment of the strap.

30

30. The two labels found on the inside. The larger one reflects the radio communications maker's name, Siemens, while the other shows the manufacturer of the garment, Striegel & Wagner, G.M.B.H. as well as the size, a 56. Siemens obtained the lion's share of the contracts for the manufacture of the german flight helmet communication equipment.

31. The inside of the earcups were cushioned with fleece, while the chinstraps were lined with chamois. The maker's woven labels were found in the inside of the garment.

32. The earphone and microphone cables were wired internally, between the outer shell and the liner and reached the nape of the helmet, where a short leather junction was sewn and brought the cables together to the exterior into a cord. The leather junction allowed the cable to absorb the strain in case the cable was pulled. The insulated cord ended in a "beehive"-shaped DIN-4 connector which plugged in the aircraft's radio communication box.

31

32

LKp S 101 flight helmet

This flight helmet was intended to be used in the summer by those pilots who required radio communications. It was introduced in 1938 and was designed to replace the previous Lkp S 100 series. The winter and summer versions were identical, except for the manufacturing material, which was a brownish cotton weave. Two straps on either side of the helmet that closed on the opposite side by means of metal buckles secured the helmet in place. The receivers had outer oval rubber earcups that were covered with brown leather, while the inside was fitted with fleece cushions. The communication equipment cables emerged from the nape of the helmet. It was manufactured in four sizes.

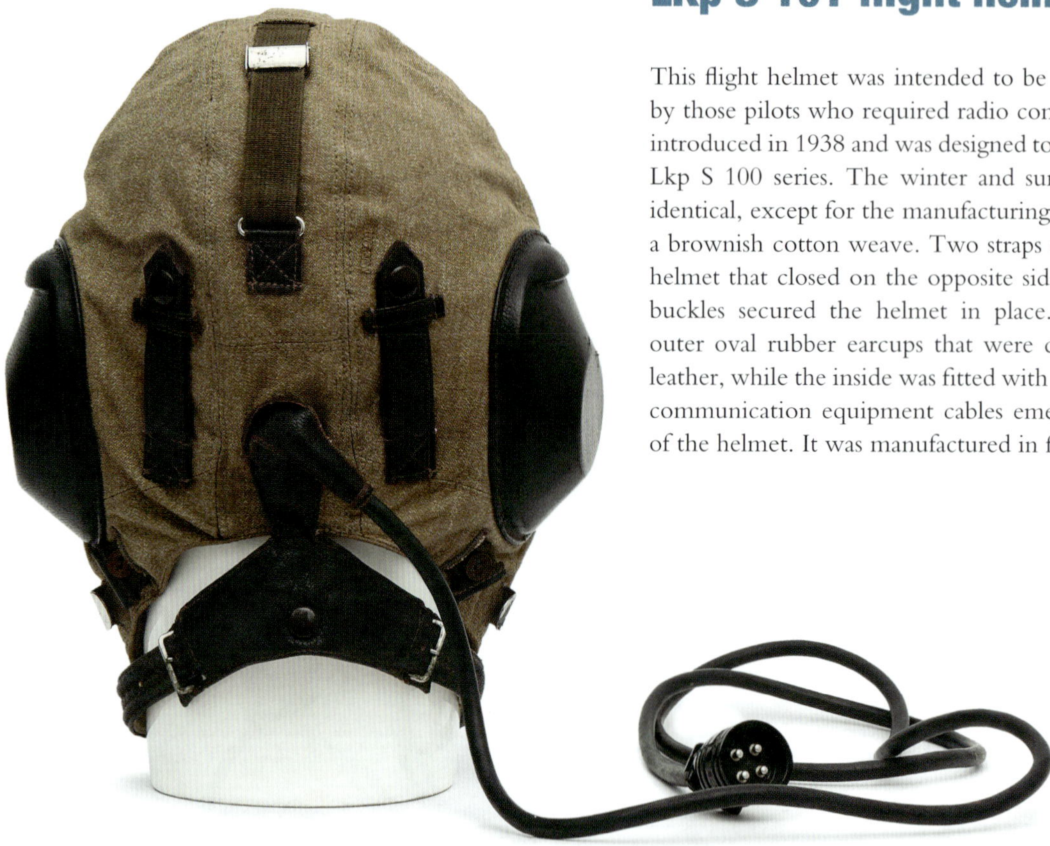

33. Detailed view of the typical early labels, the first one shows the maker of the garment, while the other indicates the name of the manufacturer of the communication equipment, Siemens, as well as other relevant data.

33

34

34. The Lkp S 101 in wear. One of the throat microphones is lying on the pilot's left shoulder. (Signal)

35

35. The throat microphones joined the helmet by means of a triangular leather segment sewn on the nape, which also had two horizontally extended leather straps with dual pronged adjustment buckles. The straps were designed to fit snugly around the pilot´s neck with the throat microphones placed to rest against the larynx. The improved carbon Mi4b throat microphones with bakelite housings were fitted in both leather straps, which connected at the front by means of a press button. The receiver and microphone cables emerged from the nape in the form of a single 1 meter long insulated cable and connected both the microphones and the receivers to the aircraft radio control box. As with most flight helmets, it had two vertical leather strap with a single metal closure snap on the back designed to secure the goggle fastening band.

Net flight helmets

Netzkopfhauben

LKp N 101 flight helmet (first version)

This net flight helmet was intended for use in temperate theatres of war. It was manufactured using mesh segments and inner leather reinforcements. The main difference between this model and the summer and winter flight helmets is the lack of chinstrap. The mission of securing the helmet in place relied on the oxygen mask straps. This extremely comfortable garment was introduced in 1941 and became the most popular flight helmet and the headgear of choice for many German fighter pilots. It was an improved design from the previous Lkp N 100 model and was fitted with the same communication equipment as its predecessor. The exterior earcups were covered with brown or black leather. The inside was fitted with a translucent membrane that served for filtering excess noise and keeping the delicate mechanism free of dirt and moisture. Several variants were made during the war, two of which are shown in the following pages.

36

36. Detailed view of the *"beehive"* DIN plug with four pins that connected to the aircraft's radio control system. It had a black or brown bakelite housing and had the spec numerals moulded on the outer surface.

37

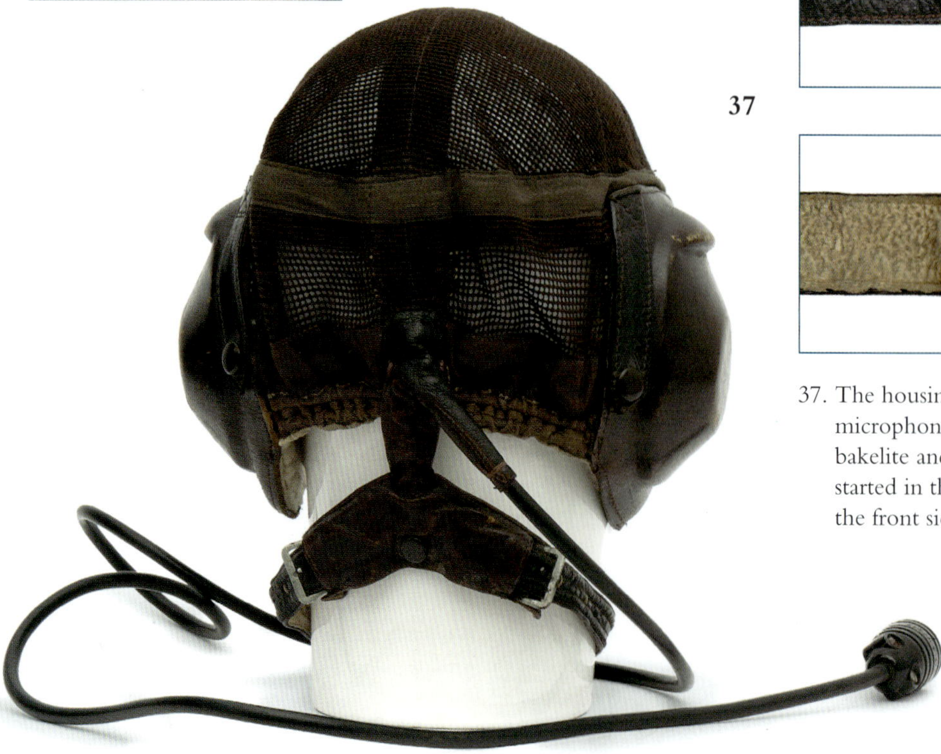

37. The housing of model Mi4c throat microphone was manufactured in plastic or bakelite and was fitted into the chinstrap that started in the nape of the helmet, closing on the front side by a press button.

38. Captain Juan Enrique de Frutos Rubio, a Spanish pilot of the *15. Spanische Staffel* or *"Escuadrilla Azul"* smiles for the camera. He is wearing the version of the Lkp N 101 net flight helmet with hooks for attaching the two-strap oxygen mask. The bakelite model Mi4b throat microphones are visible in the pilot's neck.

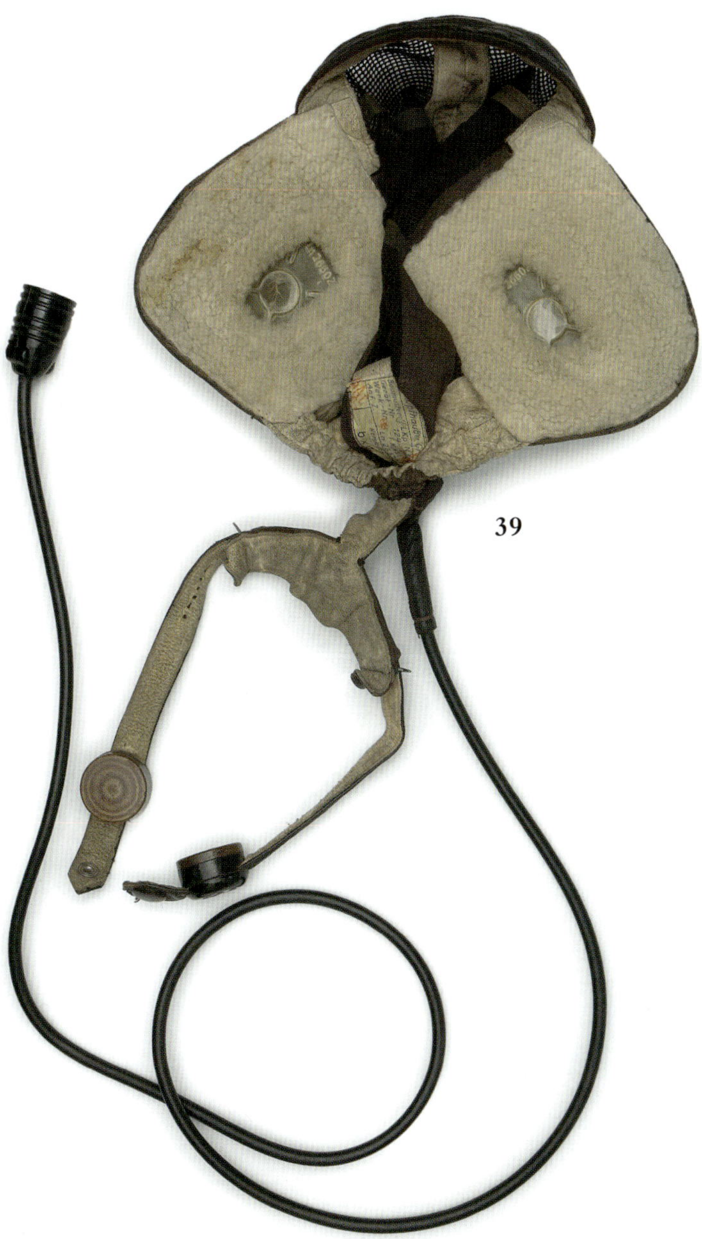

39. The first version had a 1 meter insulated cord which emerged from the nape. The helmet was configured to attack the two-strap oxygen mask and included two studs and two flat hooks on either side. Visible is the typical mid-war label, in which the name of the maker has been replaced by a three-letter code to prevent the factory being located and bombed by the allied air force.

LKp N 101 flight helmet (second version)

The second version of the Lkp N 101 helmet was identical to the first version, but was fitted with a metal loop attached to a semi-hidden strap that crossed the top of the helmet vertically for adjusting the three-strap oxygen mask. Other subtle difference was the much shorter communication cable that emerged from the nape and ended in a DIN-4 plug. The sides of the helmet were lined with fleece and the mesh segments had inner reinforcements made of leather and lined with chamois. The helmet had different design variations of the throat microphones straps as well as on the material and color of the mesh.

40. Mid-war woven labels typically contained the following information: Model designation: *"Netzkopfhaube"*, model number: *"Baumuster Lkp N 101"*, equipment number, work/order number , *Luftwaffe* contract/requisition number and finally the manufacturer´s three letter code, in this case *"bxo"*, which stands for *"Deutsche Telephonwerke und Kabel Industrie A.G"*. of Berlin.

41. In the inside of the helmet, a large leather strap lined with chamois crossed the top center from back to front and was sewn to the mesh panels that formed the shape of the garment.

42. The helmet consisted of a structure formed by six mesh segments in the skull and nape areas, sewn together with machine-woven fabric straps in the borders. The outer shell was reinforced in the forehead with a leather strip. At either side, the receiver housings were sewn to the helmet and lined in the inside with fleece or wool. Another leather portion sewn at the back of the helmet held the radio cables that emerged from the helmet.

42

43

43. Side view of the Lkp N 101 helmet. The sides were fitted with lugs and flat hooks to attach different oxygen mask models.

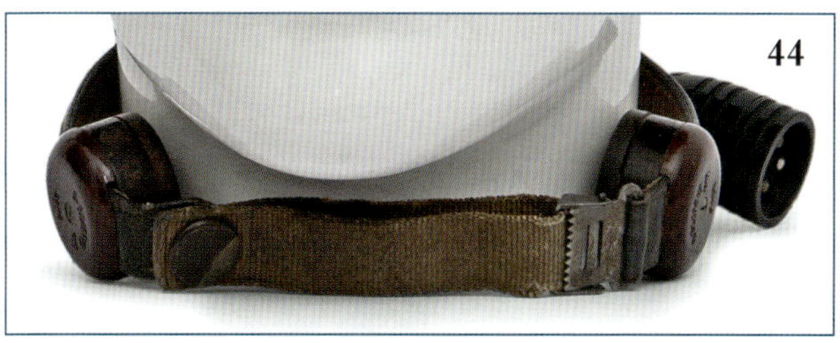

44

44. The throat microphones model Mi4b were fixed to the pilot's neck by two leather straps that adjusted by means of two metal buckles at one end and joined at the front with a press stud.

Helmet cover

Tarnbezüge für Kopfhauben

The cover was used by pilots flying daytime missions and was adjusted to cover the top of the flight helmet. It was manufactured in a pale yellow or white fabric and had a double function. The color reflected the sun rays and kept the helmet within a tolerable temperature range and protected the pilot's head against the sun, and at the same time helped the rescue teams to locate pilots that were shot down in the water. Helmet covers were constructed of several fabric panels and were issued in several patterns, depending on the flight helmet and the theatre of operations where it was intended for use. Some were reversible, and usually adjusted to the helmets by several hooks placed in the four edges of the garment.

45

45. The protective covers usually left the sides of the helmet without protection. The shape of the cover was adapted to the front area of the helmet. The hooks were placed at the edges of the cover to adjust firmly to the flight helmet. The back portion of the protective cover had an inner elastic band in the border to adapt its shape to the helmets fitted with communication equipment.

46

46. The cover was constructed using several fabric segments. The pale yellow color reflected light, thus protecting the pilot's head from direct sunlight, and helped the air rescue teams locate those pilots that were shot down above the sea.

47

47. The inner part of the cover was made of a brown cotton weave. The specimen of the photos is reversible, as it is fitted with double sided hooks.

48

48. Detail of the retaining hooks located on the edges of the cover to adjust it to the flight helmets. The base of the hook is sewn between the inner and the outer layers.

9. Protective goggles

Since the early days of aviation, the need to protect the eyes of the pilot from wind and all types of flying debris was considered essential, and became one of the most important parts of the flying gear. There were many factors to consider when using goggles, apart from the most common ones: protection against rain, wind, cold, dust, airborne objects and insects. Tinted glasses were necessary to diminish the infra-red and ultra-violet radiations of the sun. In case of fire in the cockpit, goggles had to protect the eyes from the flash and even provide certain protection against flames. Finally, some models offered relative protection against small shrapnel fragments that could hit the eye of the pilot during a dogfight.

The German flight goggles were the result of extensive research and development made by optical laboratories of private companies and scientists of the *Luftwaffe*. Other countries had a large array of goggles, mostly based in civilian models, that were tested on the basis of trial and error. On the contrary, the few goggle models used by the German aircrews were quite efficient and fulfilled their purpose from the beginning of the war. After a long period of research and trials, it was determined that flight goggles required to have large and slightly curved lenses to allow an optimum peripheral vision, but they could not be too curved as to distort the images. At the same time, the lenses had to be convex enough and not too large to provide a relative protection against small airborne objects that could make impact on them, but also had to allow conventional corrective spectacles to be used below them if necessary. With these parameters in mind, special glasses were developed which could deflect small pieces of shrapnel without shattering the lens and hurting the eyes of the pilot with pieces of broken glass. In addition to the military goggles, period photos show that German pilots and crew members also used a great variety of commercial models, found in the civilian market and designed in the twenties and thirties.

The pilot of this studio portrait is wearing a winter flight helmet and the Auer model 295 goggles. The priority of the pilots during the early days of aviation was the protection of the eyes, which was solved by the use of flight goggles offering protection from wind and objects while being at the same time comfortable to use.

Flying goggles had two basic configurations. The first type consisted of individual face pads that surrounded each of the eyepieces, while the second type used a single face pad to mount the two lenses. The first type had an adjustable bridge that allowed the distance between each lens to be adjusted, thus better suited to adapt to different types of user. The flexible bridge also allowed the goggles to be folded and tucked inside a metal tin which occupied little space in a tight aircraft cockpit. On the other hand, the single cushion goggles were more comfortable to use and offered more protection to the pilot's face, but the distance between each lens could not be adjusted, making it necessary to have several manufacting sizes.

One of the hardest problems to solve by the laboratories in charge of designing flight goggles was the way of holding them tight to the face and prevent them from blowing away. During tight air manoeuvres at high speed or in open gunner position, the goggles had to suffer a tremendous stress and tended to blow away from the wearer´s face. The testing failed to find a definitive solution, but managed to design a system formed by two hooks on either side of the goggles to which an elastic strap was held as a chinstrap. The system was not of the liking of the aircrew members, which had to add a new strap to the already overloaded space in their faces,which had to hold the helmet chinstrap, the oxygen mask and the conventional goggle straps.

It is worth mentioning that several systems were developed to protect the pilot's vision from the sun. These systems consisted in spare tinted glasses that came in several tones which effectively blocked the light depending on the mission. The glasses were easily interchangeable. Several German optical companies also developed special filters for different functions, such as the *"Neophan"* system, used to provide special sharpness to search for downed pilots, or filters like *"Umbral"* or *"Ultrasin"*. Some of the most important German optical makers in charge of manufacturing flight goggles were the following: Auer, Cellowaro, Knothe, Lietz, Nitsche & Günther, Uvex, Vogler, Wagner and Winter.

Model 295 goggles in wear. The curved lenses allowed a large peripheral vision, a vital feature for combat pilots.

Flight goggles

Fliegerbrillen

Model 295 Windschutzbrille flight goggles

Developed in the early thirties, these goggles were- used throughout the war. They were designed only to protect the pilot's eyes from the wind. It was used in open cockpit aircraft as well as for flight crew positions that were exposed to the outside, such as machine-gunners in bombers. The lenses were oval-shaped, providing an excellent peripheral vision. Both frames were made of metal and were fixed to a single rubber cushion that covered most of the user's face. In addition to the adjusting elastic cloth strap, another strap made of the same material could be fitted to hooks placed at either side of the goggles and positioned as a chinstrap.

1

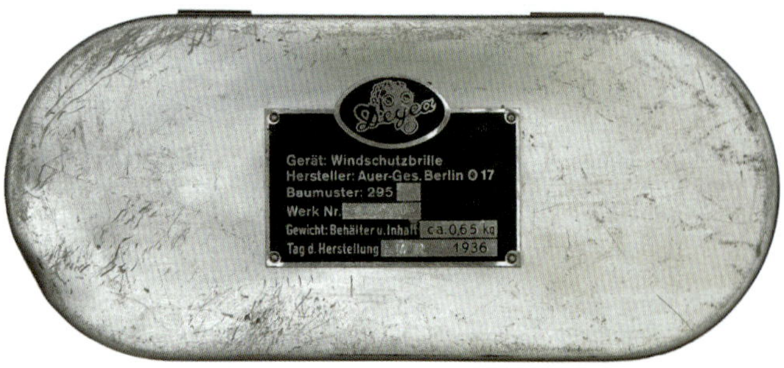

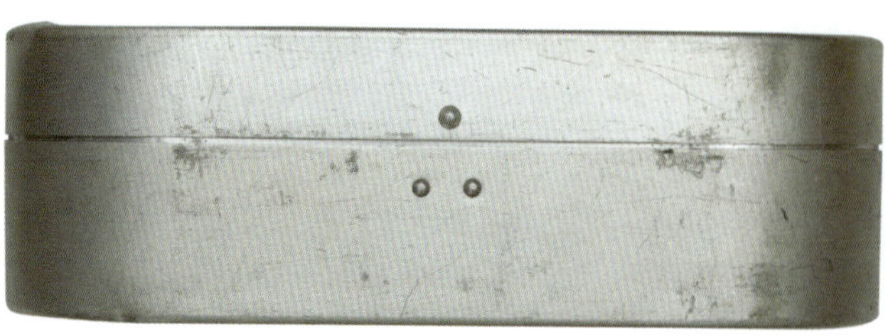

2

1. The goggles issued at the beginning of the war came in aluminum protective boxes. A small plate under the lid described the contents and the instructions for use. Another plate on the outside indicated the model number, the manufacturer as well as other relevant information.

2. A small aluminum container with an extra set of lenses and a chamois cleaning cloth was included in the box.

3

4

3. The elastic strap was made of grey cloth and had a built-in adjustment buckle for a precise fit. The flight helmet was fitted with two vertical leather straps at both sides of the back to hold the google elastic band and secure the goggles in place.

4

4. Detailed view of the hooks of the side metal loops, which accommodated an additional elastic band that was used as a chinstrap to prevent the goggles to blow away from the gunner´s face if caught in the slipstream. Notice the small pieces of paper on the sides of the lenses with printed letter *"L"* and *"R"*, indicating they were to be mounted on the corresponding frame.

Model 306 Fliegerbrille flight goggles

Model 306 flight goggles had very large curved lenses which provided a wide field of vision. This feature allowed the use of conventional corrective glasses below them. A separate rubber cushion was attached to each of the metal frames. It saw widespread use by *Luftwaffe* crewmen throughout the war. The goggles shown in the following pictures were manufactured by Georg Vogler.

6

6. A pilot dressed in winter gear. He is wearing his model 306 goggles over the Lkp W 101 flight helmet.

5

5. Detailed view of the elastic google band, fitted in the two leather vertical stripes of the flight helmet, which secured them in place.

7

7. The metal frames had small ventilation holes along the edges to prevent moisture from building in the lenses. It had two separate rubber cushions. Lenses could be either clear or tinted, which is the case of the specimen shown on the photos.

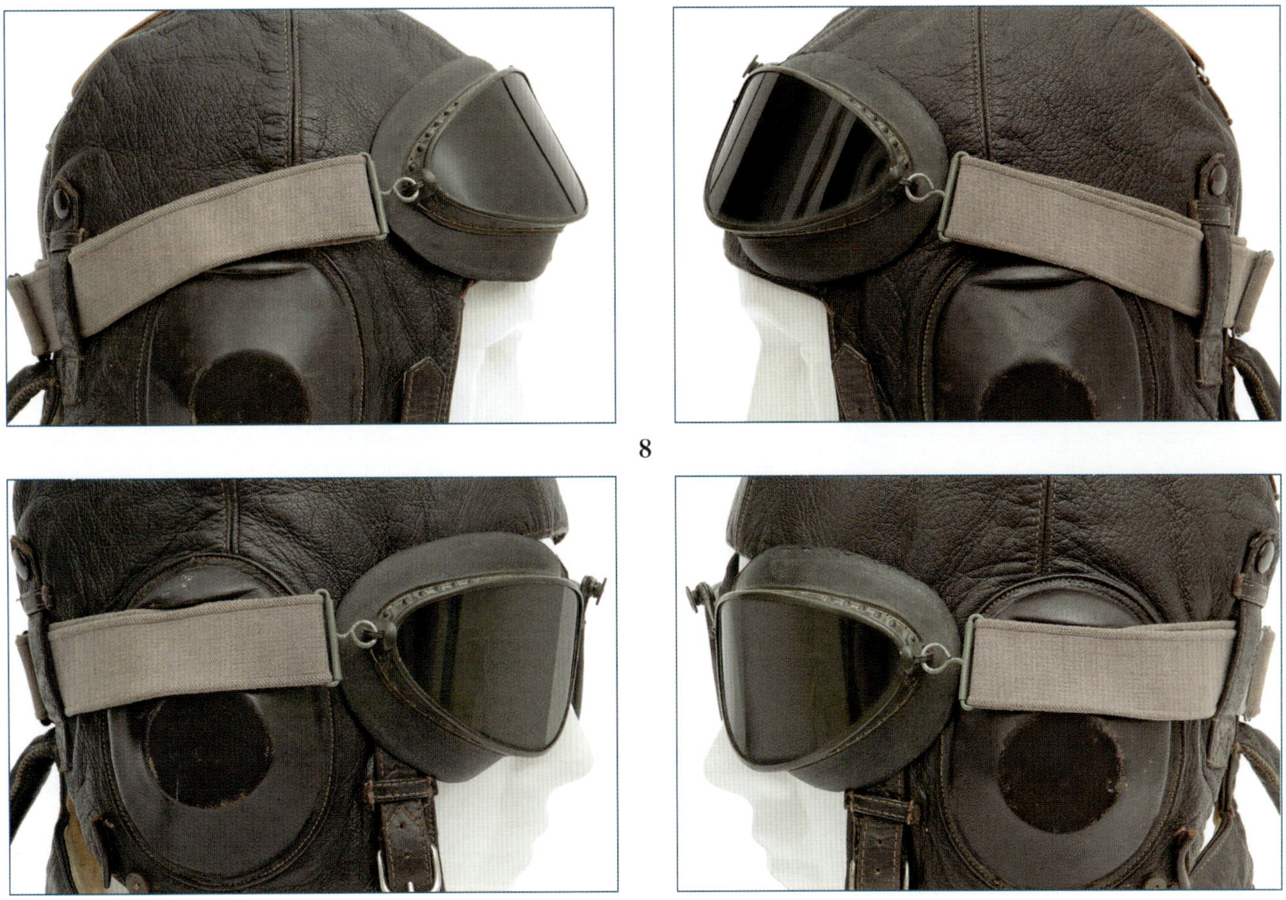

8

8. Some flight helmet models, such as the LkP W 100 of the photo, had a small recess on the top of the earcups to accommodate the goggle strap and secure them during tight aerial manoeuvres.

9

9. Spare lenses were clear and tinted. The upper border of the frames could be easily opened to replace the lenses. The nose bridge consisted of two metal pieces that overlapped one on top of the other and were secured by a screw that allowed a vertical movement and thus the regulation of the distance between both lenses.

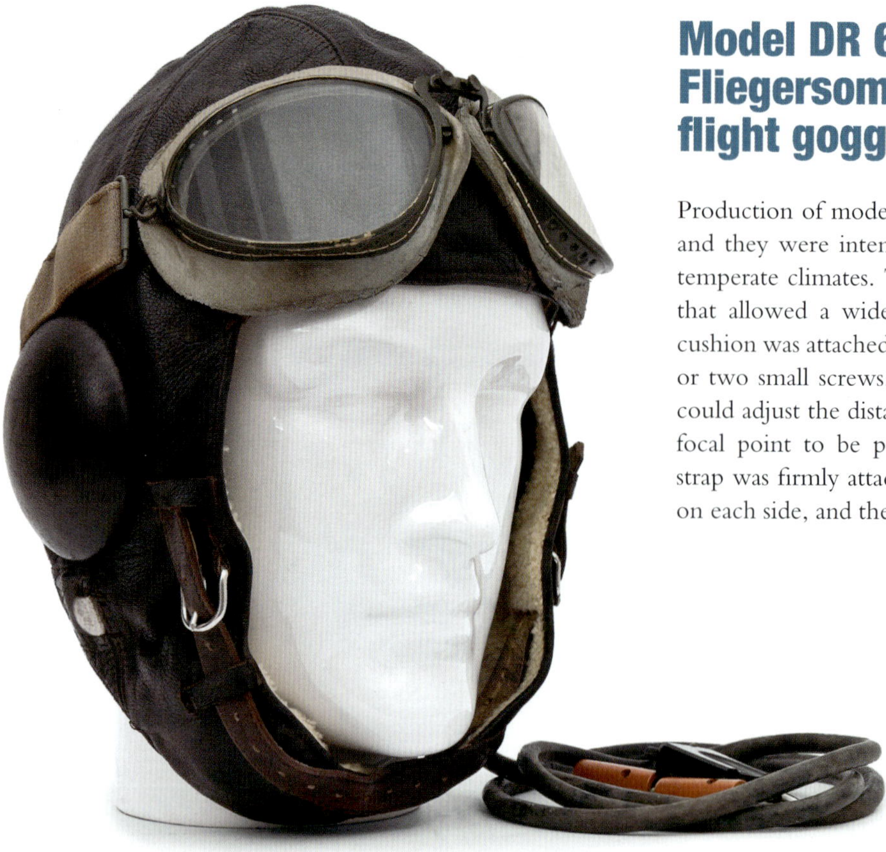

Model DR 652 Fliegersommerbrille flight goggles

Production of model Dr 652 flight goggles started in 1936 and they were intended to be used in low-level flights in temperate climates. They were fitted with two large lenses that allowed a wide peripheral vision. A separate rubber cushion was attached to each metal lens frame. By using one or two small screws, depending on the maker, the wearer could adjust the distance between lenses and thus allow the focal point to be positioned correctly. The elastic fabric strap was firmly attached to the goggles with a metal hook on each side, and the legth could be adjusted with a buckle.

10

11

10. The oval lenses had enough curvature to allow a wide field of vision.

11. The length of the straps could be adjusted with a built-in buckle. The goggle headband was attached to the flight helmet´s leather loops on the back to secure the goggles in place.

12. View of the side strap attachment. The ventilation holes are visible on the upper edge of the frame.

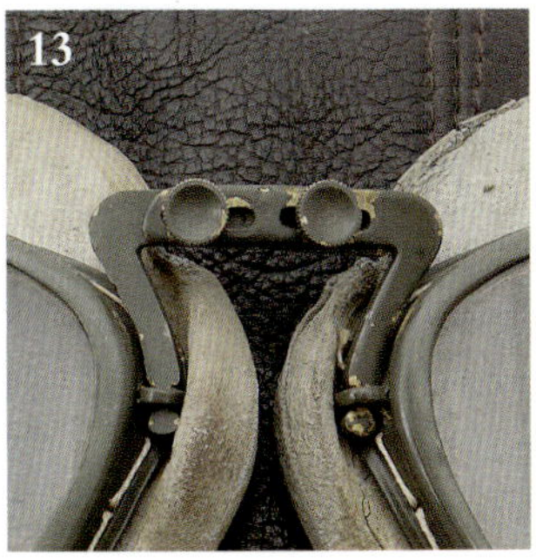

13. The nose bridge consisted in two glided metal pieces, each one attached to a frame, that overlapped one on top of the other and were secured by one or two small screws, allowing a vertical movement.

14

14. The elastic band was made of tan fabric. The rubber cushion surrounded each frame individually, which allowed the goggles to be folded.

15

15. The goggles were stored in a a small metal box, which was replaced by a crude cardboard box at the end of the war. The box also contained a set of tinted glasses in an individual metal container, as well as a replacement strap.

Model FL. 30550 Splitterschutzbrille flight goggles

These goggles were designed with a curvature that was capable of deflecting small shrapnel fragments and other flying debris. The official name is misleading, as they were not shatter-proof, as it seems to suggest: *Splitterschutzbrille*. They were initially designed as sun goggles and had conventional spectacle arms. Later, a second pattern was issued which replaced the arms with elastic straps. Two variants were produced, one with clear lenses and another with tinted lenses.

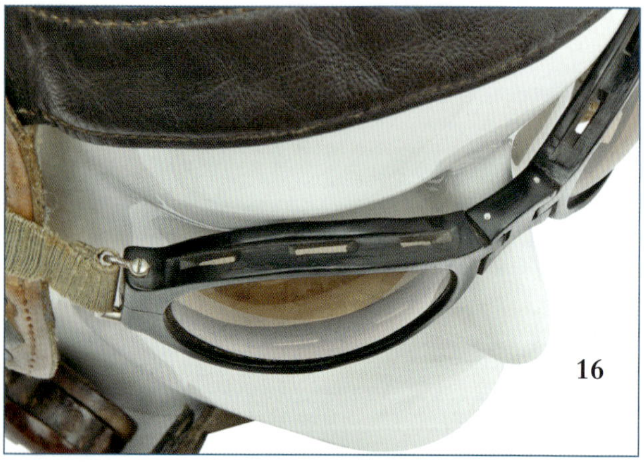

16

16. The oval thick lenses were fitted to a rigid moulded plastic frame in the first type and a three-section frame with a hinged bridge in the second. The frames had air vents on the top edge.

17

17. The grey cloth elastic band was secured on the sides of the frames with small metal hooks. a metal buckle allowed a precise adjustment of the band. The goggle band was secured to the flight helmet by the vertical leather straps placed at the back.

18

18. Hans-Ulrich Rudel, recipient of the Knight's Cross with Golden Oak Leaves, Swords and Diamonds. He is wearing the Lkp N 101 net flight helmet and the Nitsche & Günther Type *"D"* goggles with tinted lenses.

19

19. The optical maker Nitsche & Günther was in charge of the research and development of this goggle model, closely supervised by *Luftwaffe* medical experts. The company manufactured two variants. The first was Type *"A"*, with clear lenses and the second was Type *"D"*, with tinted lenses.

20

20. The goggles were issued in a cylindrical metal storage case with engraved specs in three lines. The first line indicated the model *(Flieger-Splitterschutzbrillen)*, the second line reflected the type of lens (Type *"A"* or *"D"*) while the number code (Fl.30550) was issued in the third line.

General purpose goggles

Brillen

Model 302 Kradbrille motorcycle goggles

This model, initially designed to be used by motorcycle drivers, saw widespread use by the *Luftwaffe* aircrews. The lenses were mounted into individual metal nickelled frames and each one cushioned with a leather pad. Both frames were joined by a leather nose bridge.

21. The frames had ventilation holes in the lower edge. The elastic band was made of grey cloth and incorporated a metal buckle for a precise adjustment. A hook was added in later models to provide a fast adjustment The leather cushions were sewn to each frame for a comfortable wear.

21

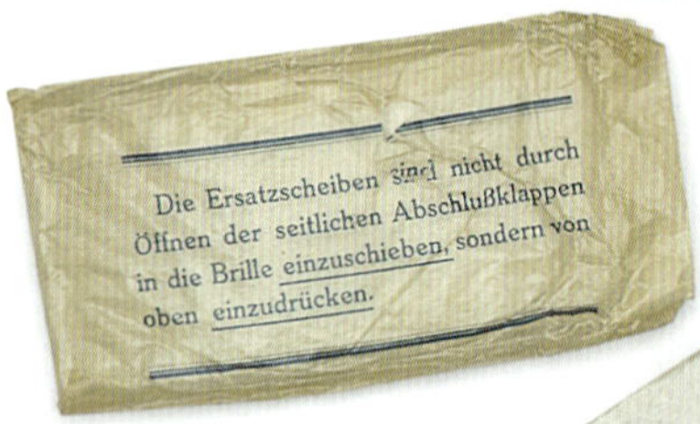

22

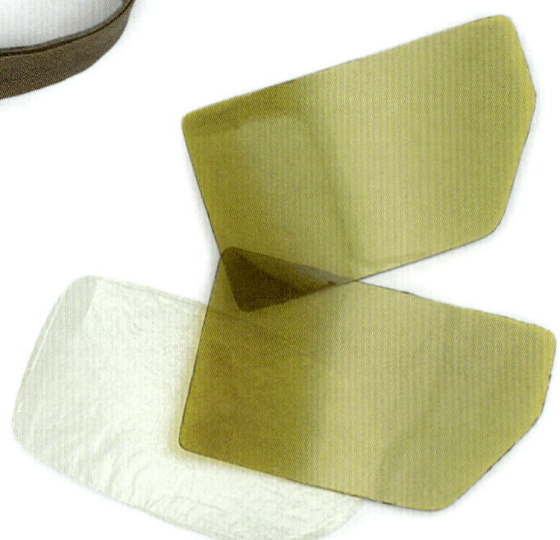

23

24

22. Spare lenses were issued in paper containers. The long curved lenses were made of plexiglass and allowed a wide field of vision.

23. The spare lenses were issued in different tones. Some were clear while others were tinted. The lenses could be easily replaced.

24. The goggles could be folded in half thanks to the leather bridge that joined both frames. The storage box was made of brown-lacquered metal and also contained the spare lenses.

Sun and dust protective goggles

These goggles were used to protect the eyes from dust particles and sun rays. The lenses had a rounded shape and a diameter of 5.8 cm and were mounted in an aluminum frame with ventilation holes at the edges. Both frames were mounted in a leather face mask and lined with chamois. Two leather tabs at either end of the mask with metal loops secured the goggle bands in place by means of a press stud located at the end of both left and right bands. The left band was made of leather and had a metal loop at the end. The right hand band had a 7 cm (2.7 inches) long section made of leather followed by an elastic band that ended in a metal hook. The goggles were issued in two sizes, with a different distance between lenses.

25

25. The metal storage box contained a black leather bag with the extra lenses and a small cleaning cloth. The lenses were easily replaced by removing small screws on the edges of the frames.

26

26. The aluminum frames had small ventilation holes. They prevented moisture from accumulating in the inner part of the lenses due to the weather conditions inside the aircraft.

27

27. The oval storage box contained the goggles and a bag with spare lenses. It was made of brown-colored lacquered metal and had a metal lid.

10. Masks

Germany began the research and development of oxygen breathing systems for their pilots in the early twenties. Contrary to other countries, the German scientists gave priority to the delivery system over the face piece itself. The pilots used extremely simple face masks not too different from those used in hospitals. Other even simpler systems were also tested. Until the beginning of the thirties, the delivery systems for pilots consisted basically of corrugated tubes connected to rubber mouthpieces which needed to be firmly clenched by the teeth of the user. This device presented significant problems, such as forcing the pilot to remove the breathing system from his mouth when talking to other crew members, or the fact that the moisture from exhaled air condensing in the tube was prone to freezing at low temperatures.

In 1935, German scientists took a giant quality leap towards the design of oxygen masks, creating innovative solutions that were much more advanced in comparison to the allies' equipment, to the point that they copied some of the technology from German captured specimens. Once the war started, German scientists continued developing fresh mask designs with the accent on reliability and security, while working on systems to attach the mask tightly to the flight helmet to prevent it from flying away from the face during tight air manoeuvres. Several models came out of the factories during the war, some with two attachment straps and others with three straps, which required the flight helmets to be modified. The material of the face pieces and hoses had many different colors. Examples in green, grey, brown, black and tan rubber have been seen.

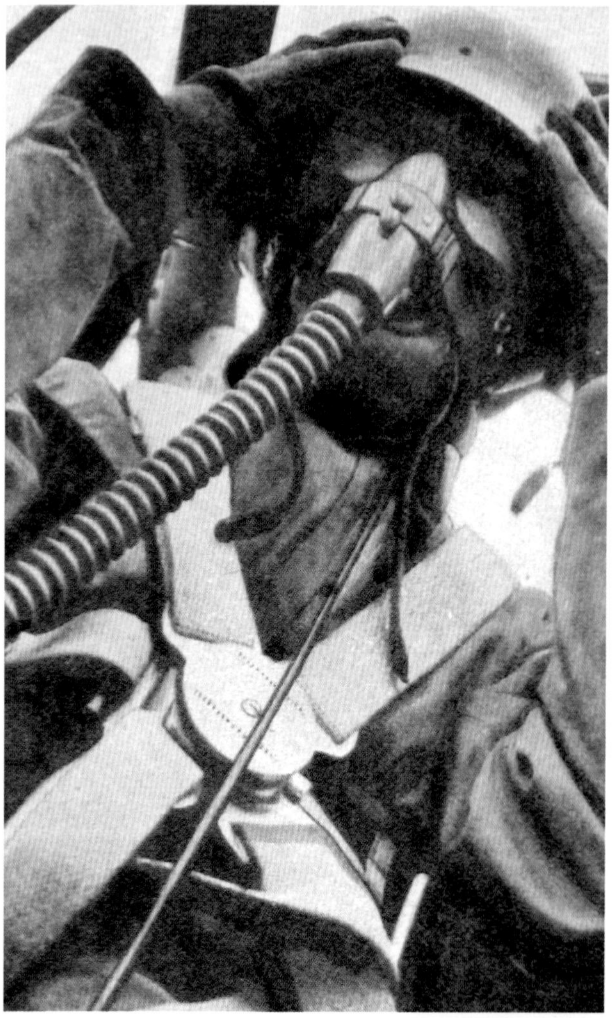

A bomber crew member gets ready for action. He is wearing full gear, including a special metal protective helmet. The clothing and equipment suggests he will be flying a high altitude mission. (Signal)

German masks were fitted with a quick disconnection device at the end of the hose, which allowed the mask to be separated from the aircraft's oxygen supply with a relatively soft pull. This method was intended to ease the mask disconnection in case the crew had to bail out of their aircraft. It is worth mentioning that German oxygen masks were usually smaller and lighter than their allied counterparts, due to the fact that they had no provision for microphone systems, a part of the communication equipment that was included in flight helmets.

One of the first oxygen masks in use by the German Air Force was the HM5 and HM15 series. Even though they were designed in 1935, they continued in use well into the Second World War. This model of mask had a moulded rubber face piece with a ribbed, flat trunk that stretched downward from the front of the mask. The ribs were designed to resist freezing. The trunk housed the exhalation valve and connected it to the breathing hose. The mask was held to the flight helmet by a three-point system, with two side straps, and a vertical strap on the front. This mask, though acceptable, had its shortcomings. The mask tended to freeze at high altitudes. The next model in the German mask arsenal was model 10-69. Introduced in 1937, it had basically the same mask body of the HM5/15 series, but was manufactured with two point straps. It was produced without an anti-frost shield, which made it lighter, and had a chamois lining around the edge. It was built in four sizes and even though it had the same freezing problems of its predecessor, it became popular because it was lighter and the two-strap attachment system provided more comfort.

The freezing problem was finally solved with the introduction of the model 10-67 mask. In this model, the exhalation valve was concealed inside the body of the mask, so the cold air did not come in contact with the exhaled air moisture and therefore prevented freezing. The mask was adopted in 1939, and even though the specimens manufactured by Drägerwerke received the name of Hm51, the official designation was finally modified for unification purposes. The *Luftwaffe* introduced another improvement, the 10-6701 mask, which is covered in the following pages.

Research and development of oxygen masks was carried out by several companies. The most important manufacturers were Drägerwerke, Drägergesellschaft and Auer.

Close-up of a pilot wearing the model 10-67 oxygen mask. Even though the mask had the official designation of 10-67, the designer and manufacturer of the first units, Drägerwerke, *initially named it as Hm 51. The photo belongs to the cover of the Spanish edition of the famous German magazine* Der Adler.

Oxygen masks

Höhenatemmaske

Model 10-67 oxygen mask

The 10-67 oxygen mask, initially named as *"HM-51"* by the designer Drägerwerke, but later renamed to the official designation, comprised a single molded rubber face mask with an attached leather frame to provide a tight fit and face protection against cold temperatures. The mask included an inner double cavity wall as an insulation method against freezing when used at high altitude. The exhalation valve was placed inside the mask rubber body, just above the hose. It was designed to be used with flight helmets that included two adjustment lugs on each side and an attachment ring on the upper front.

1

1

1. The 10-67 mask was secured with two bands with elastic sections at either side that ended in metal loops. Both bands were adjustable in size. The front band ran between the eyes and ended in a metal flat hook that attached to a metal loop located on the forehead of the flight helmet.

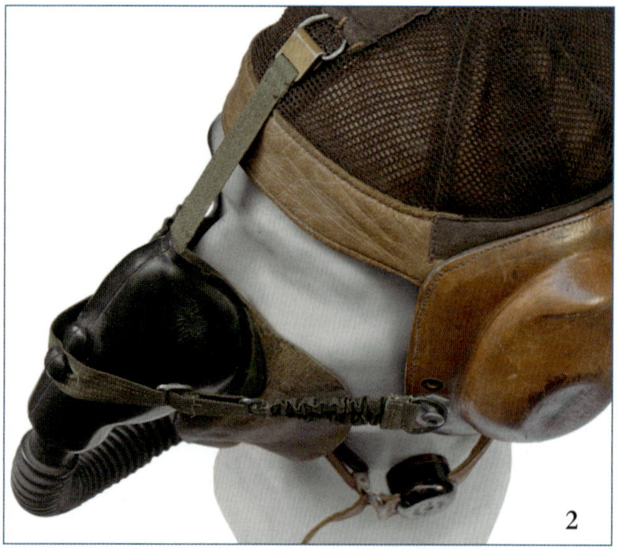

2

2

2. Detailed view of the upper attachment bands on the 10-67 oxygen mask. The forehead attachment point was omitted in later models, but it was eventually retrofitted after it was found that the masks did not hold firmly enough using only two points of attachment.

3

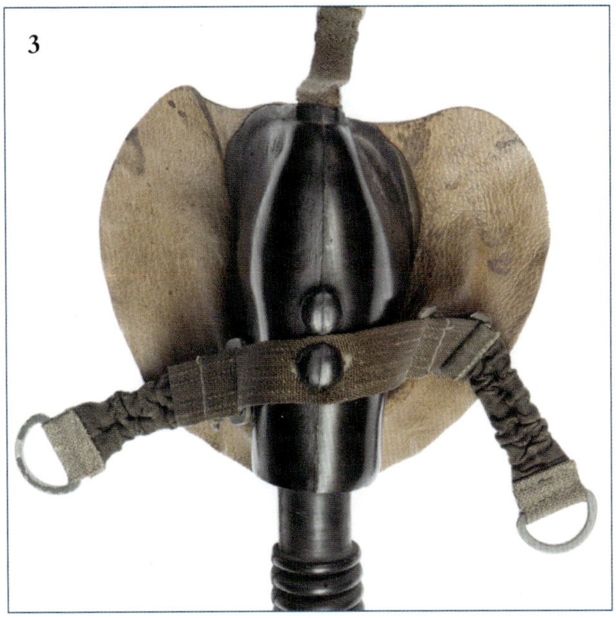

4

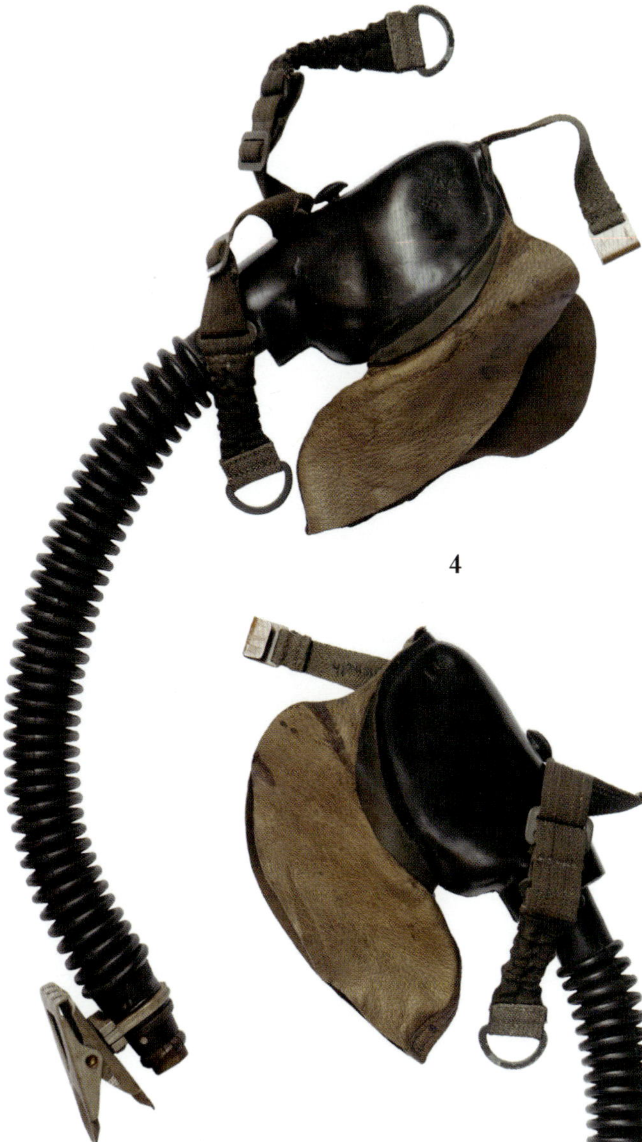

4

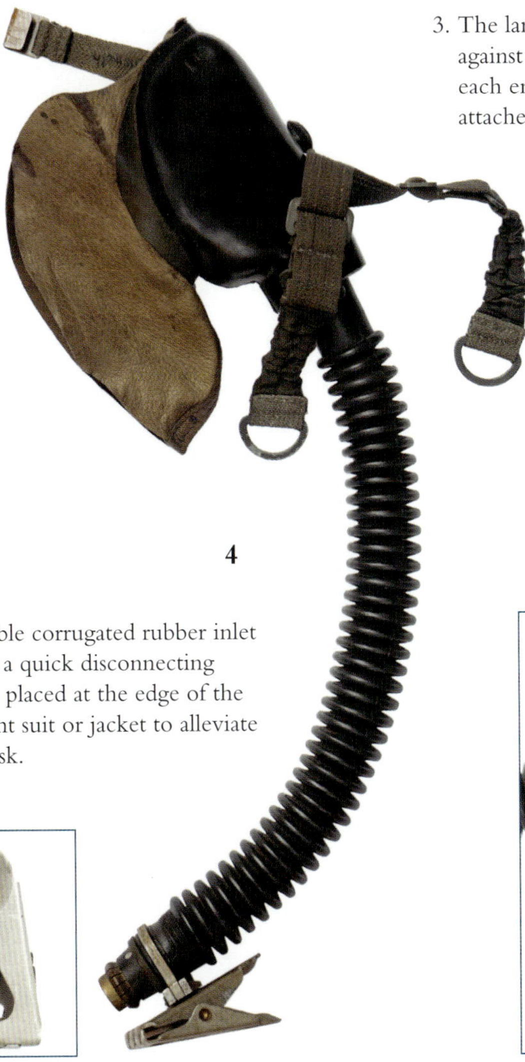

3. The large leather flap protected the cheeks and the chin against cold temperatures. The elastic strap with loops at each end was secured to the mouthpiece with an eyelet attached to a molded rubber button.

3

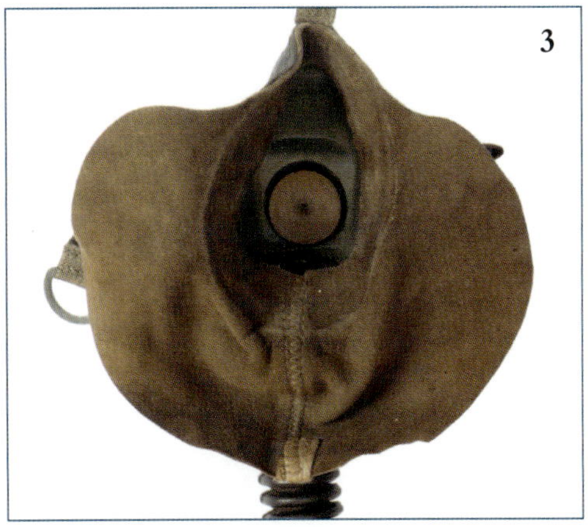

3

4. The mask had a flexible corrugated rubber inlet hose which ended in a quick disconnecting valve. The metal clip placed at the edge of the hose fixed to the flight suit or jacket to alleviate the weight of the mask.

4

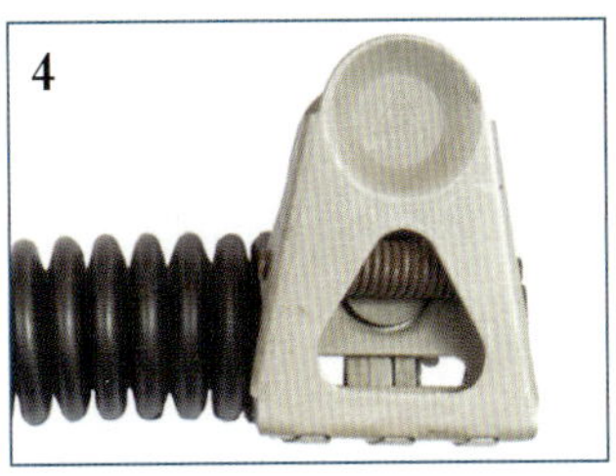

5

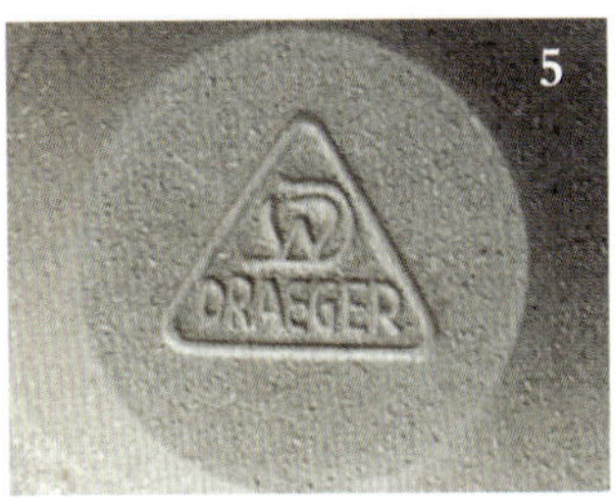

5. Detailed view of the markings found on the mask. The left photo shows the trademark of Drägerwerke A.G., the designer of the mask, stamped on the metal hose clip. The *"BWZ"* letter code molded marking found on the rubber mouthpiece corresponds to the Auer-Gesellschaft A.G. company, which manufactured the mask in their factory of Berlin. The official model designation is also present.

5

Model 10-6701 oxygen mask

The Dräger 10-6701 oxygen mask was designed to be used with helmets with two adjustment lugs, especially the Lkp N 101 helmet. It saw widespread use during the war by fighter and fighter-bomber pilots. It was an improved version of the previous model 10-67. The inner double cavity wall of the previous model, designed to prevent the mask from freezing at high altitudes, was omitted, making it lighter and cheaper to manufacture without compromising its performance. The attachment system was also modified, consisting of a new double strap system. Unfortunately, this improved adjustment system fell short of expectations. Many masks were modified to the previous three-strap configuration, by adding a third strap in the center of the rubber piece. This retrofitted third strap can be identified by the color of the cloth, which was in most cases orange.

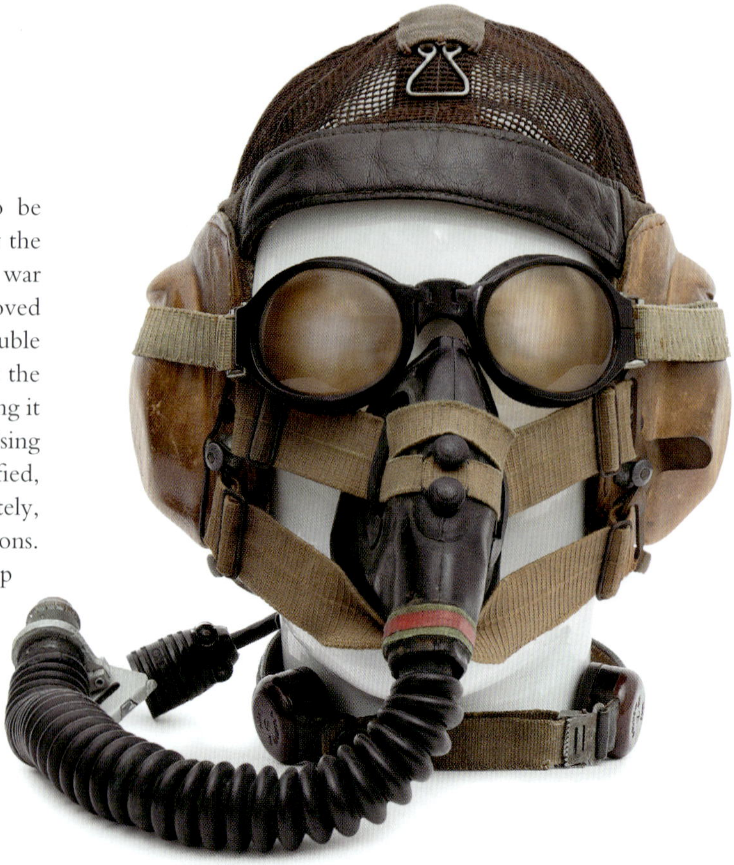

6. The 10-6701 mask adjusted to the Lkp N 101 flight helmet by means of two lugs placed at either side, below the earcups. The helmet also has hooks for three-strap masks. It is displayed with the Nitsche & Günther Type *"D"* anti-splinter goggles.

6

7

7

7. The improved attachment system consisted of a double metal hook and two parallel straps. The name of the maker and other specs were moulded into the rubber face piece.

8. The upper strap was fixed to the mouthpiece with a loop and rubber button located at the center. The lower strap crossed the chin of the mask , behind the hose.

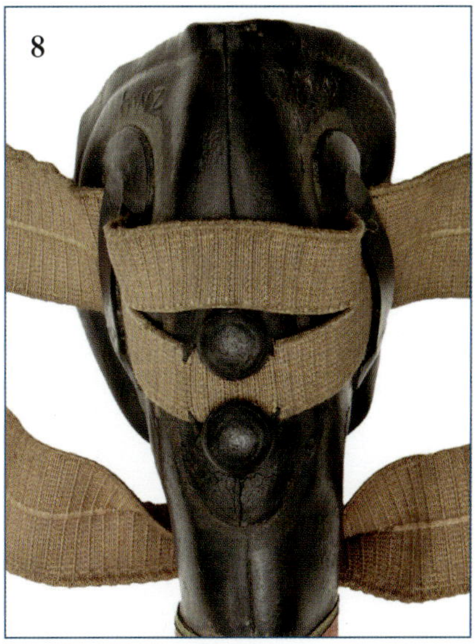

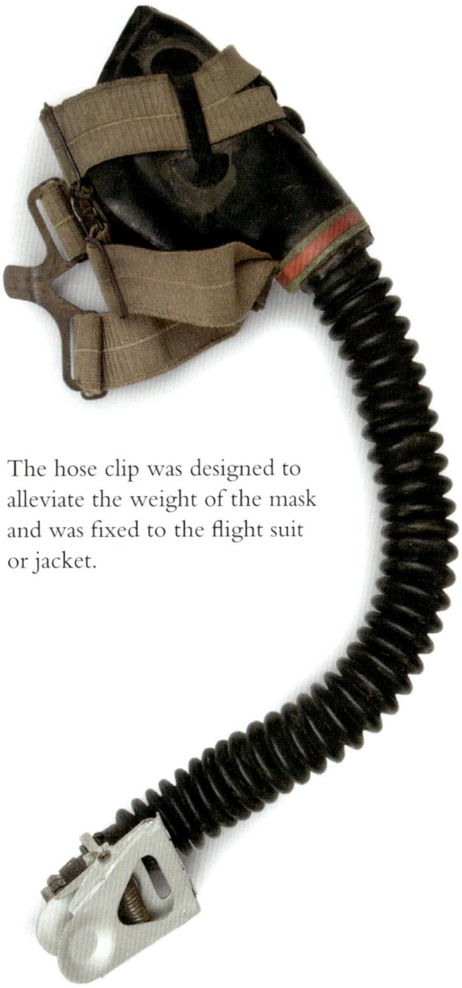

9. The hose clip was designed to alleviate the weight of the mask and was fixed to the flight suit or jacket.

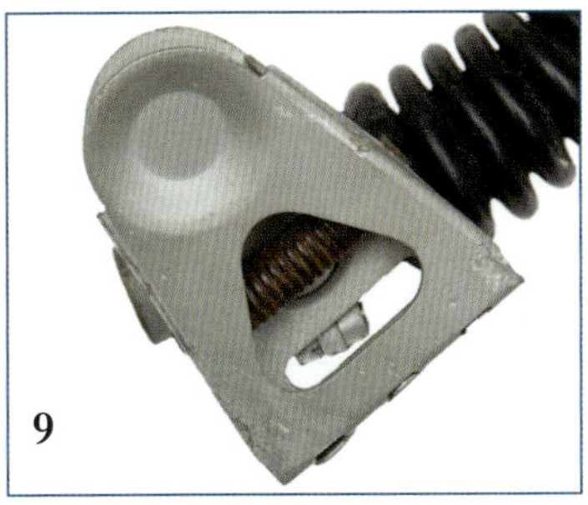

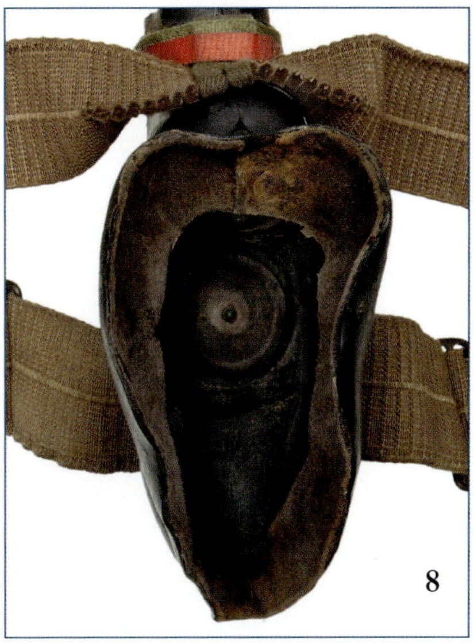

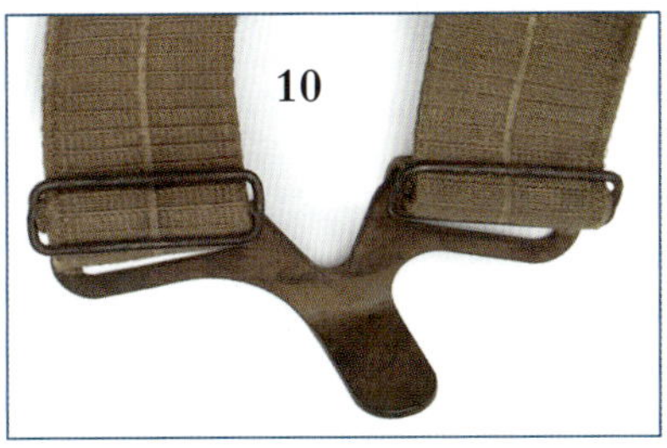

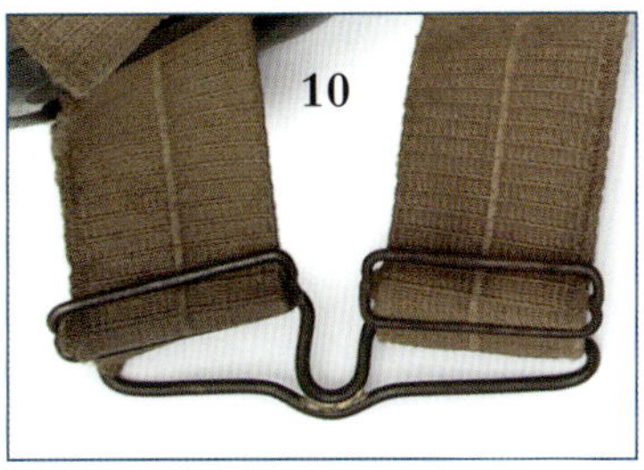

10. The mask was fixed to the flight helmet with metal hooks. The left hook had a quick release system, while the right one attached to the stud placed on the side of the helmet.

Face mask

Schutzmaske

In addition to the winter flight helmets, other methods were devised for protecting the crew members from the cold weather conditions during high altitude flights. The early war years saw the use of protective masks to cover the face. They were manufactured with soft leather and lined with suede, completely covering the pilot's face and offering protection against extreme cold weather in open cockpit aircraft or crew positions exposed to the elements. They were to be firmly tight against the face and used below the flight helmet and oxygen mask.

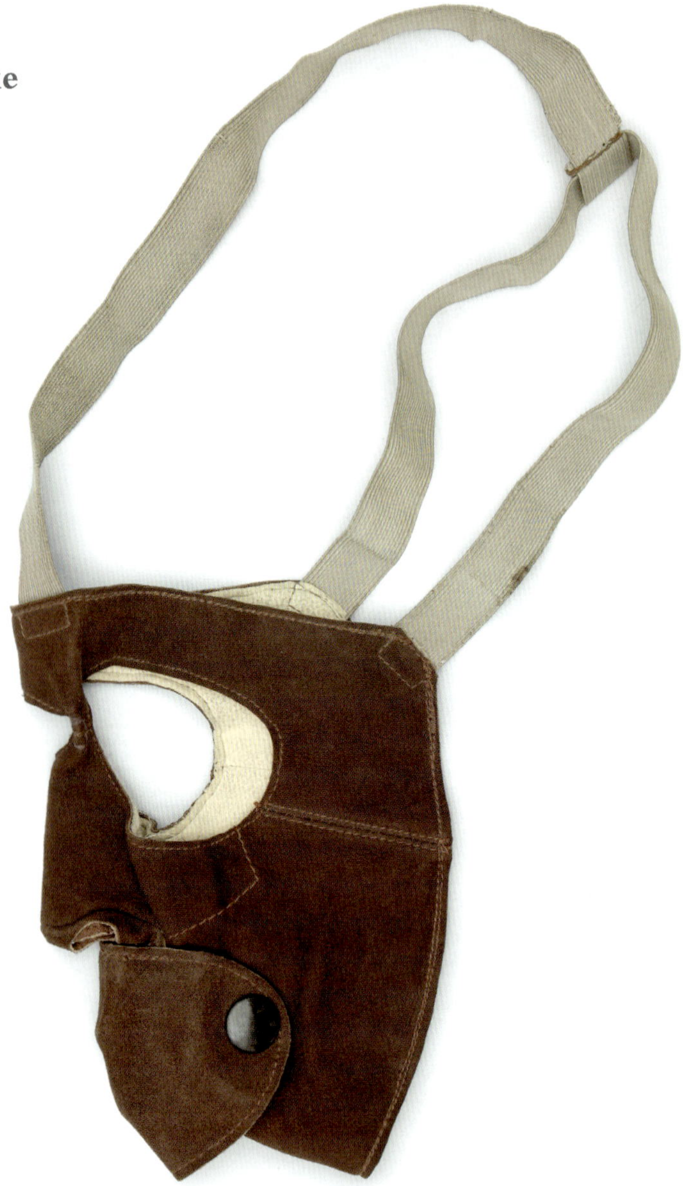

11

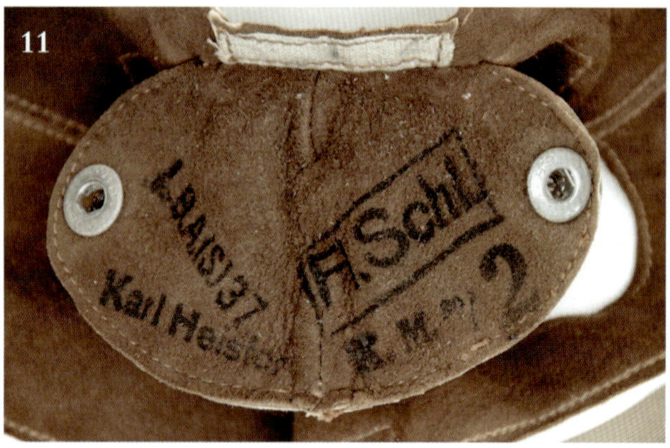

12

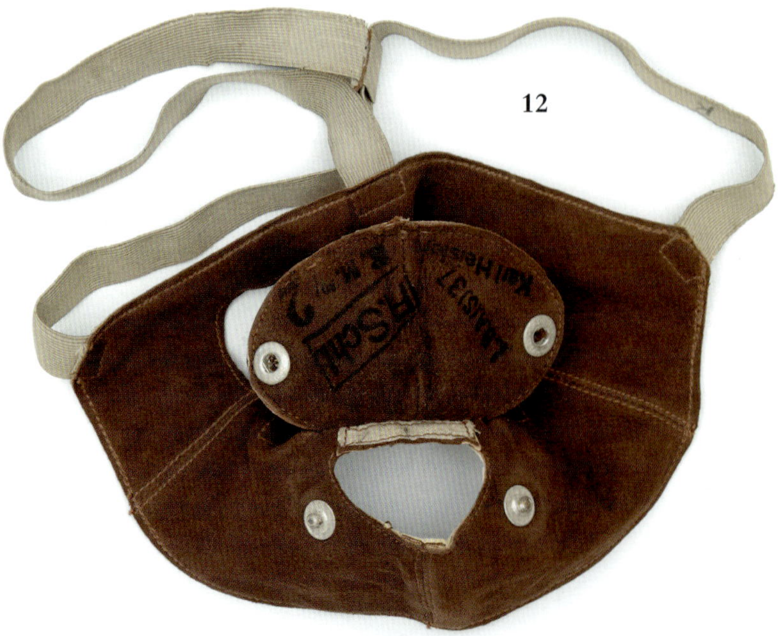

11. Ink markings found on the mouth flap. The information included the maker's name, Karl Heisler. The mask was made in three sizes reflected by numbers: small, medium and large. The specimen of the photo is a size 2 (medium).

12. The mouth was covered by a flap made of the same material than the mask, and could be used in an open or closed position by means of press studs. The aperture below allowed the mask to be used with conventional oxygen masks.

13. The protective mask was made with several soft leather panels and had large apertures in the eyes of the same size as the flight goggles. The nose was covered by a leather segment, with an opening on the bottom to allow normal breathing.

13

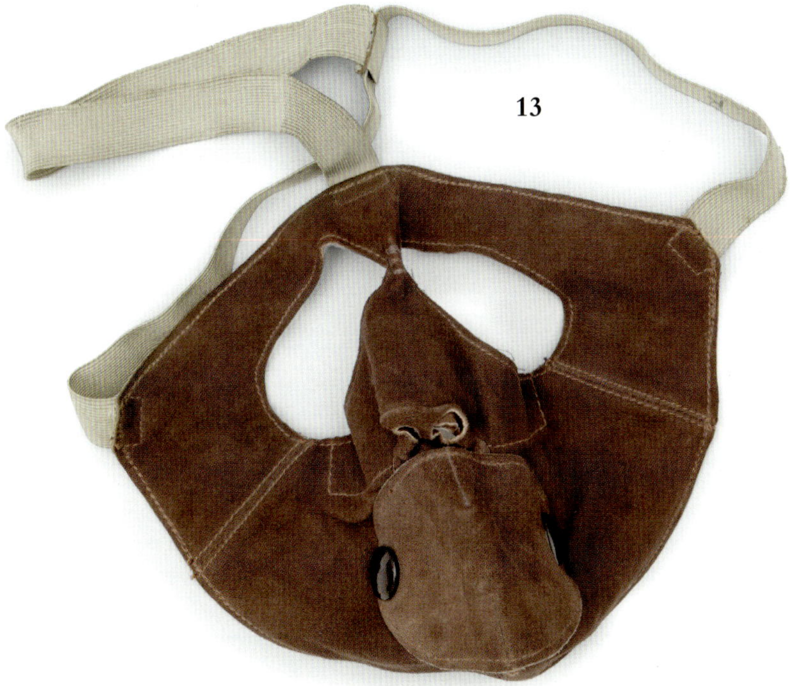

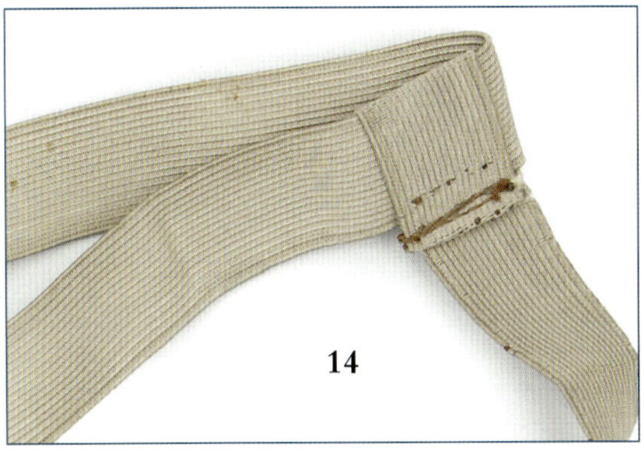

14

14. The mask adjusted tightly to the face with a strap system of grey elastic bands sewn between the leather and the lining. A vertical strap was sewn to either side of the mask, while a forehead band has one side looped over the horizontal strap at the neck and the other sewn to the center of the head.

15

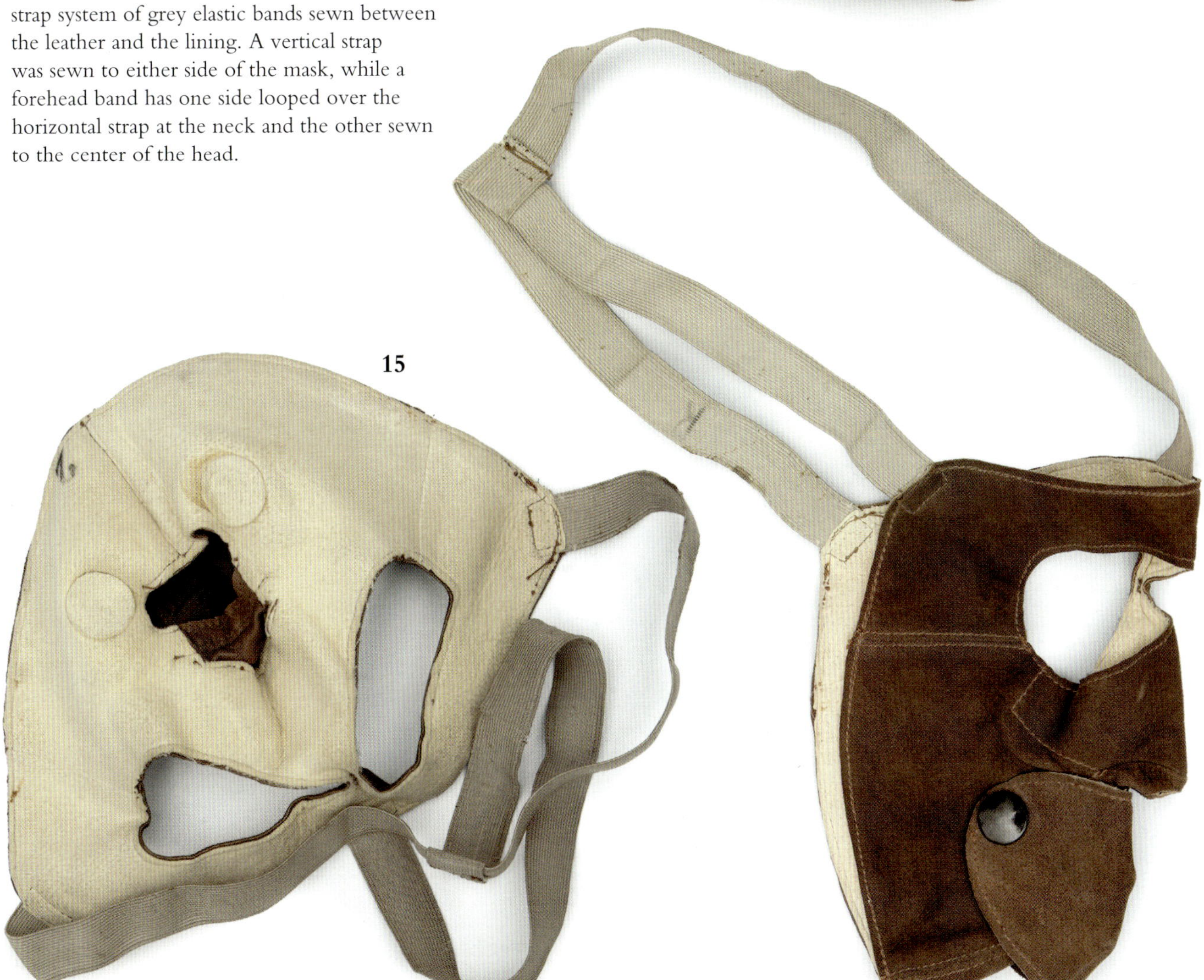

15. The lining covered the helmet, except for the mouth flap. It was made of chamois to provide a comfortable fit. The male press studs on the mask had an additional leather reinforcement.

11. Flight clothing

Since the early days of flight, one of the main consideration was to adapt the cold weather garments available in the market to the conditions of flight, especially from the low temperatures and airflow of early open cockpit aircraft. The initial designs were manufactured using materials that were extremely heavy and caused restrained movements inside the cockpit. The rapid development of aviation was always ahead of research and development of flight clothing and equipment. With aircraft reaching higher altitudes and cockpit spaces more constrained, the pilots faced new problems adapting their bulky and inadequate garments to the new aircraft models. Extremely cold weather during high altitude flights and the need of free movement in the cockpit without sacrificing protection lead to the design of increasingly sophisticated flight clothing, which solved most problems with ingenuity and brilliance, evidenced by the specimens which still remain nowadays.

The *Luftwaffe* had three basic one-piece flight suits in stock to be used for specific climatic conditions and used over different terrains: A light flight suit for summer use, a winter flight suit for maritime use and a winter flight suit for use over land. All flight coveralls were designed to be used over the service uniform. A two-piece flight suit was introduced during the war. It was unofficially known as *"Kanal"* or *"Channel"* suit because it was first used in bombing missions over Great Britain, which required the aircraft to cross the English Channel. They were more comfortable and easy to fit than the one-piece suits, and soon became popular with pilots and flight crews.

A pilot receives help to adjust his flight trousers from a ground crewman. He is wearing the "Channel" *flight trousers, easily identified by the large pockets on the front of the legs. (Signal)*

Electrically heated systems were introduced for one or two-piece suits and supplied additional warmth to the crewman's body, hands and feet. The system comprised an internal cabling that passed through a number of insulating elements installed between the lining and the outer shell of the suit. Both the cuff of the jackets and the legs of the trousers had connection studs to plug the gloves and boots, which were also wired with leads. The jacket and trousers of two-piece suits connected each other with a lead which ended in two studs, while a single external cable which emerged from the trousers connected the suit to the aircraft's electric system. The pilot had control of the temperature by means of a thermostat. The two-piece *"Channel"* suits were manufactured in a wide array array of materials and limitless number of color tones. These variations were due to several factors. During the German occupation of vast territories, many local factories began to manufacture garments for the Germans using a diversity of local raw materials. In the last stages of war, when German factories and other production facilities were being systematically bombed by allied forces, any material at hand was good for making news garments. Thus the need to use every available material meant that flight clothing was made with great diversity, although the quality of the craftsmanship was kept at reasonable levels regardless of the difficulties.

One of the most interesting aspects of the German flight clothing was the use of private purchased garments especially by elite fighter pilots. At the time when the *Luftwaffe* ruled the skies of Europe, fighter pilots created their own dressing style, encouraged by their new hero status. The standard issue flight clothing at their disposal was somehow uncomfortable and unattractive, and the pilots asked permission to their superiors to use comfortable, tailor-made garments which would set them apart from the rest, but were against the regulation. The feeling of belonging to an elite and their *"esprit de corps"* favored the tendency to use exclusive jackets. Pilots bought their leather jackets in Germany and occupied countries, such as France or Belgium. Most of them were sold as motorcycle jackets in the civilian market. Although many period photos showing groups of pilots using the same leather jacket can lead to the false impression that they are wearing officially issued models, the truth is that in some cases the commercial garments were bought collectively by the pilots of the same group. Others had their jackets tailor-made by Germans or professionals from occupied countries. Thus, the use of privately purchased jackets by air force pilots is an almost unique occurrence during the war, with jackets as unique as their wearers. It is possible, however, to establish a series of common features to all of them. Most of them were short waisted. They had a tight fit and were lined with light cloth, allowing the pilots unrestricted mobility in the fighter's cockpit. They were all made mostly of brown leather, and less often of black leather. They had breast and waist pockets which mostly closed with zip fasteners and sometimes with buttoned flaps. All of them were modified by adding shoulder boards.

A fighter pilot examines the damage in the rudder of his Messerschmitt Me109. He is wearing a summer "Channel" type two-piece suit and a life preserver. The flare pistol and signals flag pockets are visible on his right leg.

Private purchase leather flight jackets

Fliegerjacke

This private purchase civilian leather jacket was manufactured using two front and two back panels. Both front panels extended beyond the center of the jacket, the left hand panel overlapping the right one. It closed with two parallel rows of exterior buttons plus an additional row of inner buttons. The lining was made of mustard colored wool cloth. The jacket had four internal pockets. The breast pockets were slightly slanted and closed with snap-buttoned flaps.

1. View of the breast pocket flap. The slanted pockets allowed easier access to the contents. The breast eagle insignia above the pocket was manufactured in cloth.

2. The waist pockets closed with a zip fastener.

3. Werner Mölders wearing his Knight's Cross with Oak Leaves. He wears a civilian leather jacket with fur-lined collar. His shoulder straps have been sewn to the jacket.

Flight clothing

This private purchase civilian flight jacket has been adapted to suit the preferences of the pilot. It was manufactured using two front leather panels and a single back panel. A leather waistband with elastic sections closed at the front with press buttons. The front zip fastener closed from the waistband to the collar. It had two breast pockets and two waist pockets. The breast pockets were internal and closed with a pointed flap with a press stud closure. The waist slit pocket had no closure. The lining was made of mustard colored wool cloth. The end of the sleeves could be narrowed by a buttoned leather flap. The jacket has been fixed with *Oberleutnant* shoulder boards.

4. The metal pin-back emblem was usually fixed to the jacket by sewn loops of twisted thread. They were initially designed to be used in white cloth summer tunics, so they could be easily removed before washing the garment. Fighter pilots, however, used them extensively on leather jackets.

5. Fighter pilot Franz von Werra poses for the photographer. Notice the stick grenade ball and cord painted with the colors of the German flag that he has attached to the front zip fastener of his tailor-made jacket. (Signal)

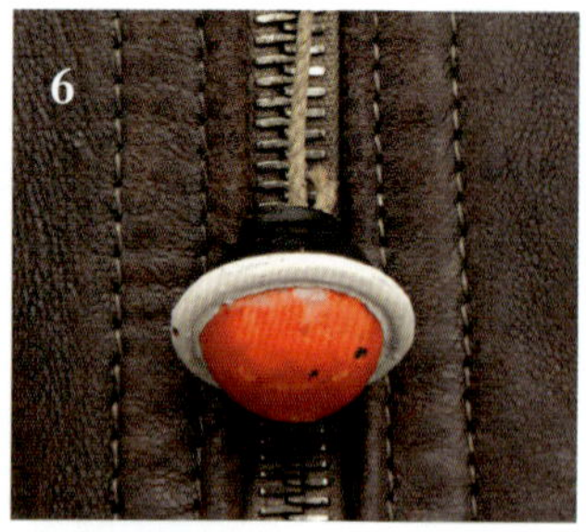

6. The slider of the jacket has a fitted piece of trench art. It comprises a fuze pull cap of a German stick grenade. The cap has been painted with the German flag colors. These add-ons to the jacket zip sliders seems to have been used to ease the opening of the zip fastener when using thick flight gloves, but some veteran pilots have noted that these type of decorations in service uniforms were simply a fad.

7. Detailed view of the zip fastener slider that closed the jacket. These motorcycle jackets were manufactured with metal zip fasteners to sustain the stress of strong movements made by the wearer while riding a motorcycle or flying an aircraft.

Flight clothing

This is a typical example of a civilian jacket used by combat pilots. Some famous fighter aces used this same jacket model, as period photos of pilots like Hartmann or Stumpf suggest. This model was apparently made in France. It was made using two front brown leather panels and a single back panel. The sleeves were also manufactured using a single piece of leather. The lining was made of wool. It closed by means of metal buckles in the waist and had an inner cord for an even tighter waist fit. A vertical front zip fastener running from the collar to the waistband closed the jacket on the front. The jacket had four inner pockets, all of them vertical. The upper breast pockets closed with zip fasteners, while the lower waist pockets had rectangular leather flaps which closed with a single plastic button. The cloth *Luftwaffe* emblem and the shoulder boards were sewn to the jacket.

8. Detailed view of the cloth *Luftwaffe* emblem, which was sewn to the jacket above the right breast pocket.

9. This photograph shows lieutenant colonel Joseph Priller wearing the same model of private purchase jacket pictured in these pages. He received the Knight's Cross in 1940, the Oak Leaves in 1941 and the Oak Leaves and Swords in 1944. The photo was taken on July 23, 1944.

10. The front waist metal buckle closure.

One-piece winter flight suits

Fliegerschutzanzug für Winter (Kombination)

11

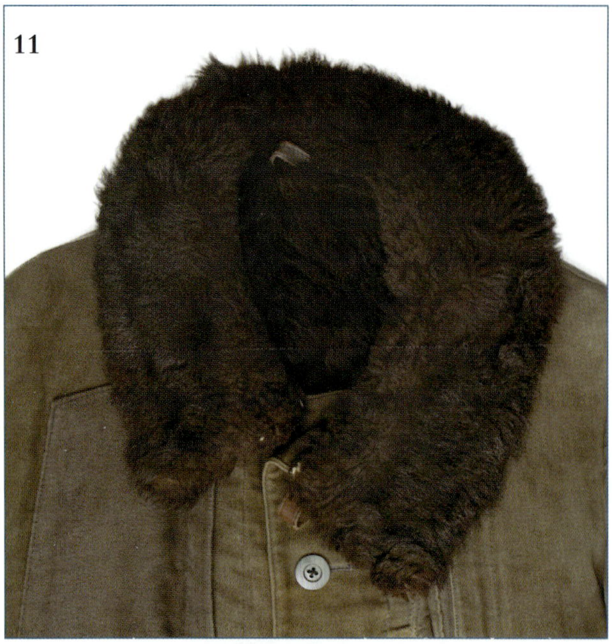

11

11

KW 33 one-piece winter flight suit

Officially designated as *Fliegerschutzanzug für Winter (Kombination) Baumuster KW 1/33*, this suit was designed for open-cockpit aircraft and high altitude flights. Designed in the early thirties, it was used at the beginning of the Second World War. The suit was manufactured in a type of fabric similar to suede leather, known as velveteen. The suit and collar were both lined throughout in thick fleece. It closed with a double row of plastic buttons in the center, running from the collar to the crotch.

11

11

11. The collar could be turned up and buckled with two leather straps. Two parallel leather tabs ending in metal rings were sewn to the right hand side of the collar. The left hand side was fitted with two leather straps each of them with two female press buttons on the edge, and a row of four male studs to secure the strap after passing it through the ring.

12

12. The suit had a front vertical aperture from the collar to the crotch, with a double button closing system. The left front edge had a row of buttons and a flap with eight buttonholes, while the right front edge had eight corresponding buttons as well as concealed buttonholes. The right front was buttoned to the wind flap, while the left front over the right front. The woven spec label and other ink markings were found on the inside of the garment. The label indicated the model, manufacturing code, the maker and the size.

12

13

13. A crew member fills the petrol tank of the aircraft. He is wearing the KW 1/33 winter one-piece flight suit. (Signal)

14. Close-up photo of the emergency aperture device and the spec label of the maker, Karl Heisler of Berlin. A concealed opening ran across the left front of the suit , from the collar to the waist. The opening was laced and kept closed by a length of cord which was attached to a pull ring, hidden beneath a triangular-shaped flap with a press stud. By pulling the ring, the lacing would come loose, and the suit would open could easily be removed without having to open any other button or zip fastener.

14

14

14

14

15. Three airmen wearing the KW 1/33 one-piece flight suit. The garment was designed on the early thirties, and was used well into World War Two.

16. Zip fasteners were made of metal, the slider was fitted with a leather tab to ease the opening while wearing the heavy winter gloves. The front of the slider had the maker's logo engraved.

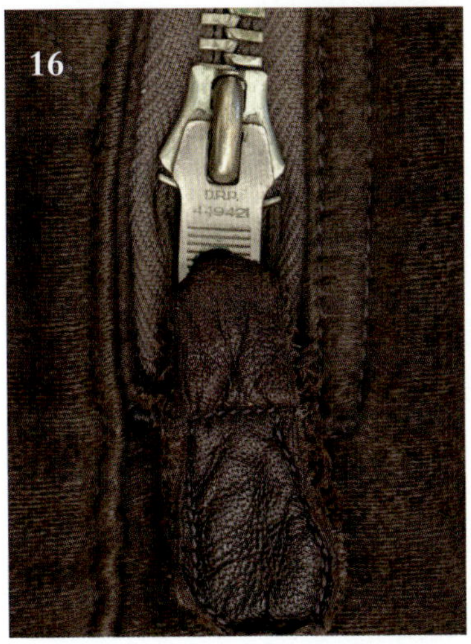

17. The sleeves had openings in the cuffs to help adjusting the suit. Two tabs with buttonholes placed on the edge of the opening and two plastic buttons placed in the other edge were used to close the openings. A third button in the cuffs allowed a tighter fit. An internal inner sleeve made ofv grey-colored twill with elastic seam was sewn to the inside of the sleeves. It was made to provide additional wind protection. The ends of the legs also had openings to facilitate adjustment of the garment and the flight boots. They closed with a zip fastener which closed downward. A cloth protection flap was sewn underneath the zip fastener, which also prevented wind from entering the suit.

18

K 3/34
one-piece winter flight suit

The KW 3/34 was a two-piece winter flight suit for flights over land. The official designation was *Fliegerschutzanzug für Winter (Kombination) Baumuster KW 3/34*, and was actually a variant of the one-piece suits, in which a thick cotton blue-grey colored fabric was used instead of the usual leather. This made the garment much lighter and comfortable to use. It was lined with blueish-purple velvet and was manufactured with the same aperture systems and pockets of the leather models.

18

19

19. *Leutnant* Demetrio Zorita, member of the 15. *Spanische Staffel*, poses with his Messerschmitt Bf 109 somewhere in the Eastern Front during the harsh winter of 1941-42. Incidentally, Zorita was the first Spanish pilot to brake the sound barrier.

18

18. The large collar was also lined with the same fabric used in the rest of the garment, a blueish-purple colored velvet. The collar could be closed using a ring sewn to the inner right of the collar and a leather strap sewn on the left hand side with two male press buttons on the edge and a row of four female studs sewn on the same side of the collar to adjust the strap.

20. *Above:* The main opening crossed the front of the suit from the right of the collar to the left hip. Underneath, a secondary opening broadened the first one and eased the adjustment of the suit. Both apertures closed with zip fasteners. It is worth mentioning that most pilots wore their service uniforms underneath the flight suit, so all systems aimed at facilitating the adjustment of these heavy flight suits were welcomed. *Left:* The woven spec label reflected the name of the maker, Karl Heisler of Berlin.

21. The suit was fitted with an emergency aperture device on the front left side. It opened with a metal ring. When the ring was pulled, the lacing would come loose and the suit would open and easily be removed without having to open any other button or zip fastener. This also allowed immediate access to survival equipment. The pull ring was concealed under a pointed flap with a press stud closure.

21

21

21

21

21

22. The cuffs had a wide aperture with zip fasteners and an inner cloth cuff to prevent wind from entering the suit. It closed with press buttons.

23. The legs also had wide slits with zip fasteners to help adjust the suit and the flight boots. The inner lining of blueish-purple velvet is visible in the photo.

24. The zip fasteners were manufactured by Rapid. The sliders had a leather tab to facilitate the unzipping while using flight gloves.

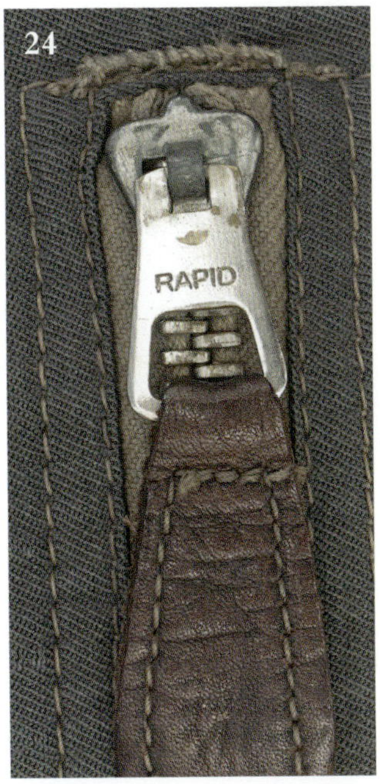

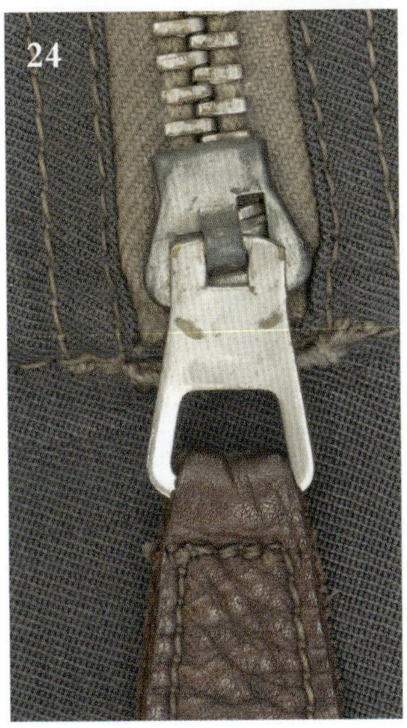

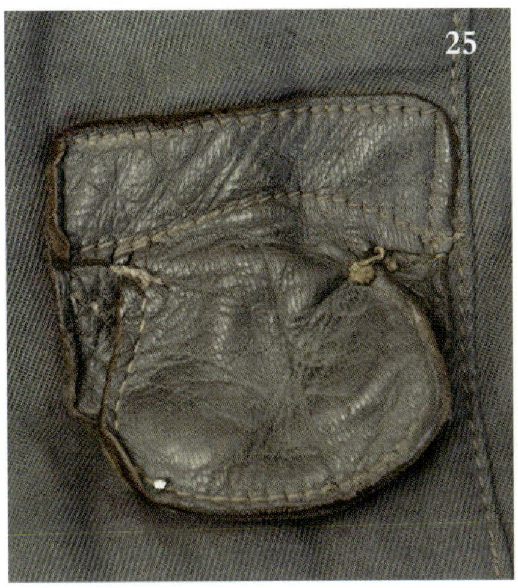

25. Electric connections were fitted on the cuffs and legs to plug the electrically heated gloves and boots. The inner electric wiring heated the back of the hands and the soles of the feet. The connecting system consisted of press studs, which were lined with leather.

One-piece summer flight suits

Fliegerschutzanzug für Sommer (Kombination)

K/So 34 one-piece summer flight suit (first version)

Officially designated as *Fliegerschutzanzug für Sommer (Kombination) So/34* it was introduced in 1934 for use in temperate climates. It was made of a brown cotton fabric with a twill lining. The first version had a horizontal zip fly opening, as well as a vertical map pocket in the chest that closed with a zip fastener. A vertical leather strap was sewn in the front center, designed to attach the oxygen mask hose clip and prevent it from swinging freely during tight combat manoeuvres. Production of this model ceased in 1941 in favor of the two-piece flight suits, but it remained in use throughout the war.

26. A pilot wearing the first version of the summer flight suit, with the vertical zip fly. He is wearing the flight boots over the suit.

27. The collar had large lapels. A metal loop held by a leather strap was sewn to the inner face of the right hand side of the collar, while the other side had a leather strap with press studs to adjust it when turned up for extra warmth around the neck. The base of the collar closed by a press stud.

28

28

29

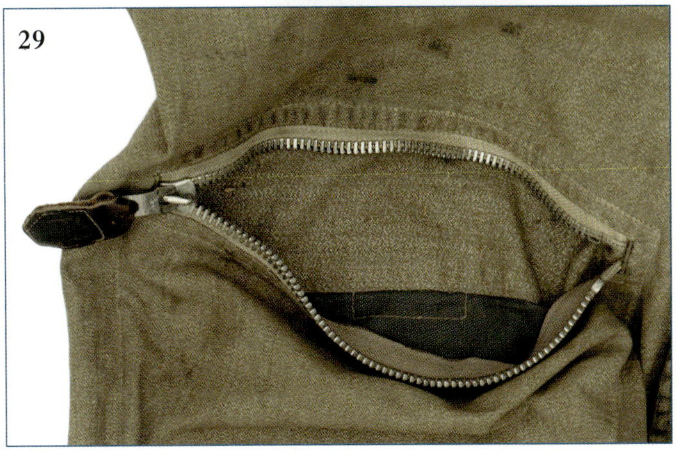

28. The suit featured several openings with zip fasteners, the main one running across the front, from the shoulder to the hip. A second slanted aperture on the right shoulder was concealed under a cloth segment made of twill cloth with a press button closure. The function of this cloth flap was to protect the apertures from the strong wind of open cockpits or exposed positions in bomber aircraft. A segment of twill cloth was sewn underneath along the zip fasteners.

29. The suit had two inner pockets on the front of the legs designed for survival equipment stowage which closed by zip fasteners. The inside of the pockets were lined with twill cloth.

30. A glider flight instructor demonstrates a dogfight air manoeuvre using his hands to represent fighters under the watchful eye of his pupils. He wears the first version of the K So/34 summer one-piece flight suit.

31. Detailed view of the metal zip sliders, with a leather tab sewn to the puller which helped the pilot unzip the pocket while wearing his gloves. The logo of the zip fastener maker is engraved on the sliders.

32. The inside of the sleeves was lined with twill cloth. The inner end of the sleeve was fitted with elasticized inner cuffs with snap closures. The large aperture had a zip fastener closure. To prevent the zip fastener from opening during flight, the edge of the cuffs had additional press buttons for a tight adjustment. The legs also had 35 cm long apertures that ran vertically along the seams. The photo shows the cloth flap under the closure to protect the legs from the wind.

33

K/So 34 one-piece summer flight suit (second version)

This is the second version of the summer suit. The most notorious differences were the position of the horizontal zip fly opening, which was placed in a vertical position, and the breast inner pocket, which was replaced by a larger secondary emergency aperture device. Furthermore, the second version retained the waist and leg pockets.

33

33

33

33

33. The collar had the same adjustment system as the first model when it was turned up for neck comfort, consisting in a metal loop on one side of the collar and a strap with press buttons on the other. A row of four female press buttons allowed a precise adjustment of the strap. The vertical leather strap located on the front center of the suit to attach the oxygen mask hose clip was also present in this second version.

34

34

34

34. All flight coveralls were designed to be used over the service uniform. The photo shows the main aperture, divided in two parts, each with a zip fastener. The main aperture crossed the front of the suit from the right of the collar to the left hip. Once the first zip fastener was open, a second, concealed aperture with another zip fastener widened the first aperture. Both closures were concealed by a large buttoned cloth flap placed on the right shoulder.

35. The inner front vertical pocket was replaced by a secondary emergency aperture device. The opening ran vertically on the left front of the suit from the collar to the waist. The pull ring was concealed under a pointed flap with a press stud closure. By pulling the ring, the lace would come loose, and the suit would open and could easily be removed without having to open any other button or zip fastener.

36. The label included information of the maker´s name, address, manufacture date and size. The manufacturer of the suit was Bekleidungsfabrik Habelt of Crailsheim, Baden-Württemberg.

37. The sleeves were lined with a grey twill cloth. They had inner cuffs with elasticized edges fastened with press buttons for additional protection against the wind. The cuffs had press button closures to prevent the zip fasteners from opening.

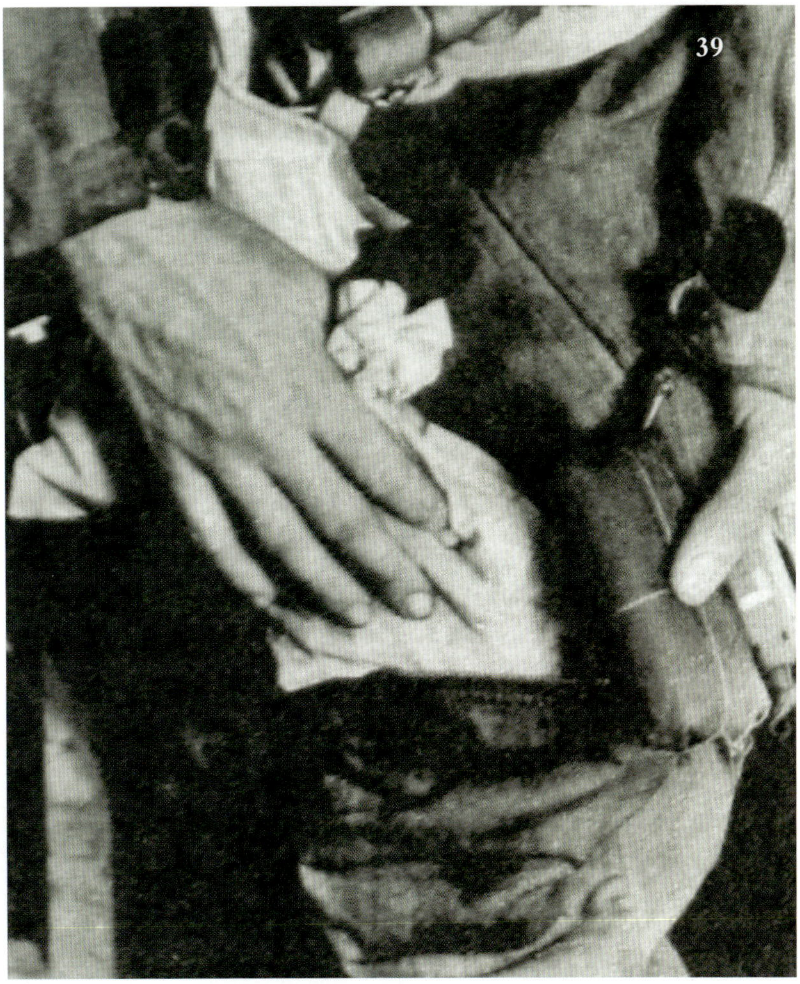

39. The leg pockets were designed to store survival equipment and other essential objects for the pilot, such as maps, chocolate bars or first-aid kits, as shown in this period photo. (Der Adler)

38. Detailed view of the zip fastener slider with the leather tab fitted in the puller. The zip fastener was manufactured by the Rapid company, a quite uncommon manufacturer.

Two-piece *"Kanal"* flight suits

"Kanal" Fliegerschutzanzug

40

40. *Oberst* Gotthard Handrick, a famous Olympic athlete and fighter pilot, chats with his comrades somewhere in Lapland during the winter of 1943. He wears an undyed soft leather flight jacket.

Two-piece *"Kanal"* natural leather flight suit

Flight suits were often manufactured in small factories located in occupied or German allied countries, using indigenous raw materials. This led to a wide variety of flight suit variations depending on the available local resources. The flight suit of the following photos was a variation made in a small Bulgarian factory. Bulgaria was a German ally well known for manufacturing many flight suits for the *Luftwaffe*. It was made using undyed soft leather sheepskin and canvas with a thick fleece liner. The suit was mostly issued in the Easter front, especially for pilots who had to fly obsolete open cockpit aircraft not provided with heating systems or without connectors for electrically heated flight suits.

41

41

41

41. The large collar was lined with fleece and had a zip fastener front closure system. The collar could be turned up for extra warmth and closed with a strap with press buttons and a ring placed at either side.

42

42. *Above:* The waist had a single vertical seam made of canvas which closed with press studs. The front opening was closed with a zip fastener. *Left:* Many flight suits were made in small local factories in occupied or German allied countries. In this case the jacket was made in Sofia, Bulgaria, as indicated by the maker's label.

43. Detail of the sleeves, which show the concealed cuffs with elastic and press button fastening. This was a common feature of most *Luftwaffe* flying suits and jackets.

43

44. *Hauptmann* Gavilán, member of the 15. *Spanische Staffel*, poses in front of his aircraft's damaged wing after landing from one of his missions. He wears an undyed leather jacket and grey cloth *"Channel"* trousers, a typical clothing configuration for a fighter pilot on the Eastern front. The photo was taken in 1943. He shot down nine Russian planes during the war.

45. The trousers were lined with thick fleece. The rest of the features were the same as with other *"Channel"* trousers, with two large leg pockets, a side pocket designed to hold the flare pistol, several side pockets with zip fasteners and long apertures in the legs with zip fasteners. This particular model has several side buttons and two buttoned tabs on the back of the waistband to adjust the issue suspenders.

46. The zip fasteners had white leather tabs on the sliders.

47. View of the flare pistol pocket, sewn to the right trouser leg. It closed with press buttons and a central leather tab for a more secure adjustment. The lower part of the pistol pocket was reinforced with a black leather segment to prevent the heavy pistol from tearing the cloth. A small loop was used to attach the pistol lanyard.

48. Below the pistol pocket, a long pocket was used to store the *Fahnentasche* or signal flag. The long thin pocket had two canvas reinforcements and closed with a flap with press buttons.

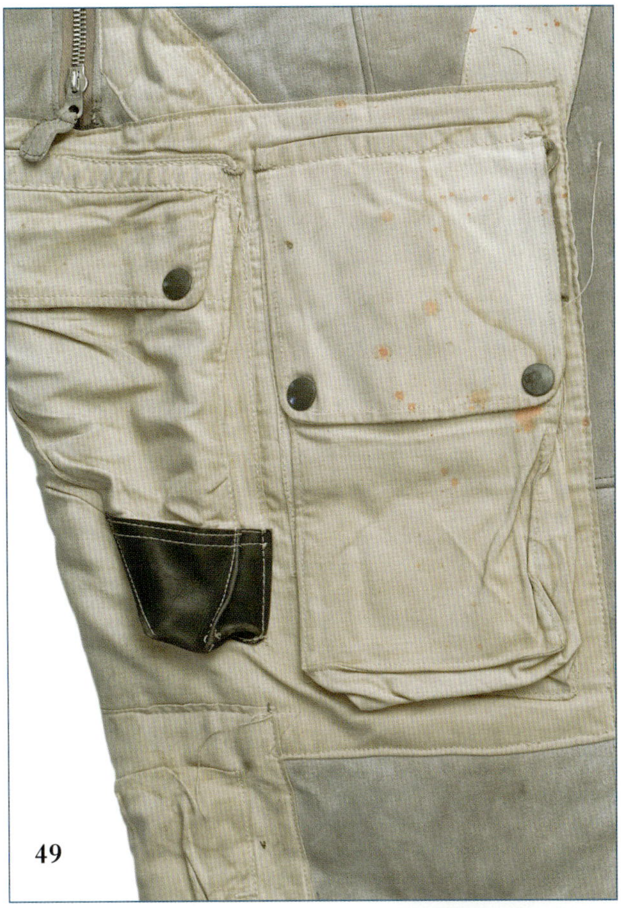

49

49

49. One of the large leg pockets, the most prominent feature of the *"Channel"* trousers, was placed alongside of the kampfpistole pocket . It was made from a segment of canvas cloth and sewn to the trousers. The bellowed pocket had a great storage capacity. It closed by two flaps on either side of the aperture with press buttons and a large front flap which closed either with large plastic buttons or, as in the case of this particular specimen, with press buttons The pilot used the pocket to store important equipment, such as flight instruments, or food and drink, such as water bottles, cookies or chocolate bars.

49

50. The left leg pocket was mainly used to store the flares for the pistol, secured in specially designed loops sewn on the inside of the pocket. The pocket was also used to keep several first-aid kits and a pocket knife, as well as any other object that the pilot considered relevant for his mission.

51

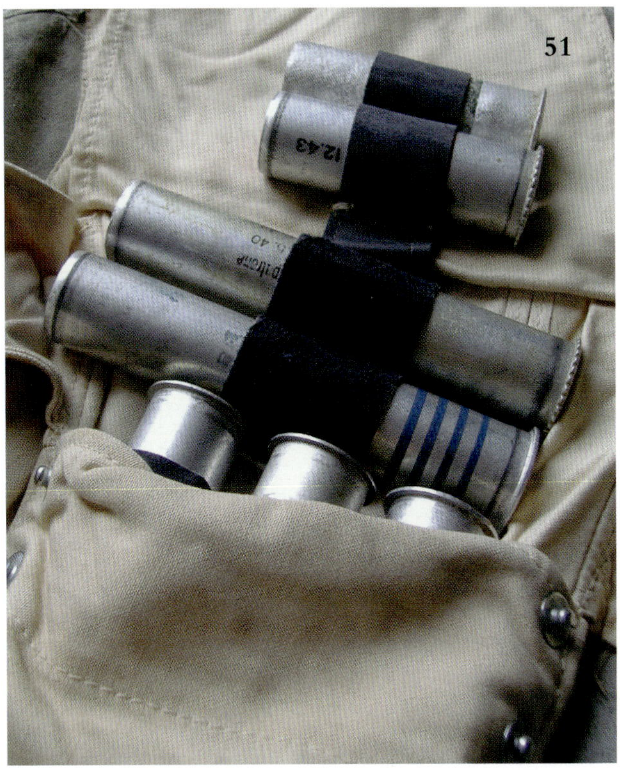
51

50

51. Detailed view of the loop sewn on the inside of the large leg pocket, to secure the flares for his *Kampfpistole*, and keep them within reach in case of an emergency.

Two-piece *"Kanal"* cloth flight suit

The two-piece fur-lined winter *"Channel"* flight suit was designed to fly over land and was manufactured in blue-grey cloth. The jacket was fully lined with fleece, including the long collar. It closed in the front with a vertical zip fastener and two press buttons on the waist. The trousers had identical design and features to the rest of the *"Channel"* models.

52. *Oberstleutnant* Hans Philip, recipient of the Knight's Cross with Oak leaves and Swords. He wears the blue-grey cloth *"Channel"* winter jacket. His headgear is the *Einheitsfliegermütze*, a campaign cap introduced in 1943 for use by all *Luftwaffe* personnel, which replaced both the *Fliegermütze* and the *Bergmütze*.

53. The large collar was lined with fleece and could be turned up and closed for extra warmth, with a ring and strap adjusting system.

54. The cuffs had long slits which closed by zip fasteners and a buttoned tab on the edge for a tight fit. The photo shows a detailed view of the the concealed cuffs with elastic and press button fastening. This was one of the features of German flight suits and jackets that were never dropped from production during the war.

55. The jacket had three pockets. The first one was a vertical breast pocket to store maps. The waist had two pockets at either side of the front. They were slightly slanted for an easier access to the inside in the confined aircraft cockpit, and closed with press buttoned tabs

56. Detail of the *Feldwebel* shoulder sleeve insignia. Regulations called for the insignia to be sewn to both sleeves of one-piece flight suits or jackets, half way between the shoulder and the elbow. The sleeve had a brown or dark blue cloth base to which the stylized birds and bars were sewn.

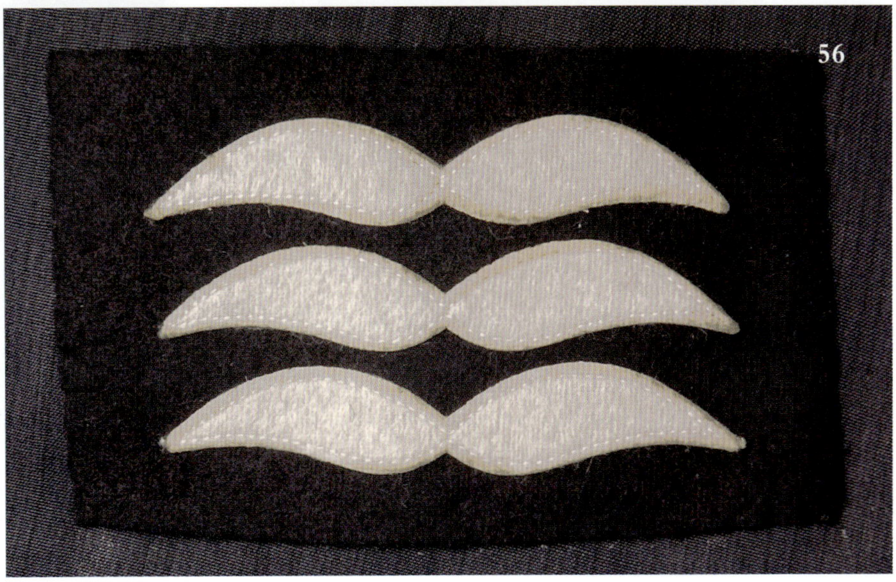

57. The trousers were lined with fleece. They had two large leg pockets, typical of the *"Channel"* trousers. Both pockets had large flaps with press buttons. The waist line had sewn buttons on the inside and straps at the sides, all of them designed to adjust the issue suspenders. In some cases the use of suspenders was essential, as they prevented the trousers from falling down due to excessive weight when the pockets were fully used.

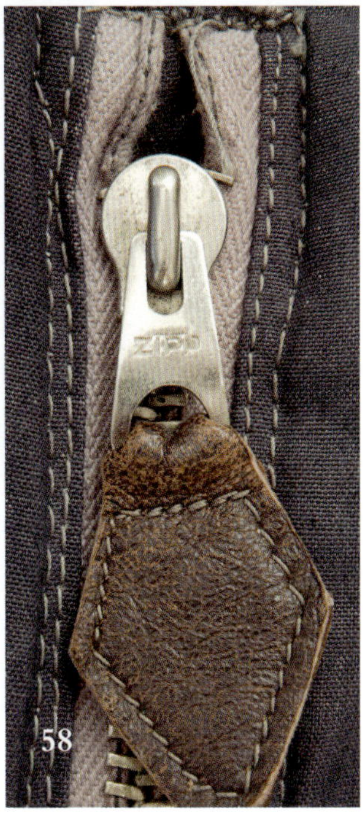

58. Detailed view of the zip sliders. The maker of the zip fastener was engraved in the puller.

59

59. Late-war zip fasteners were made of composite materials such as plastic, due to shortages of raw materials.

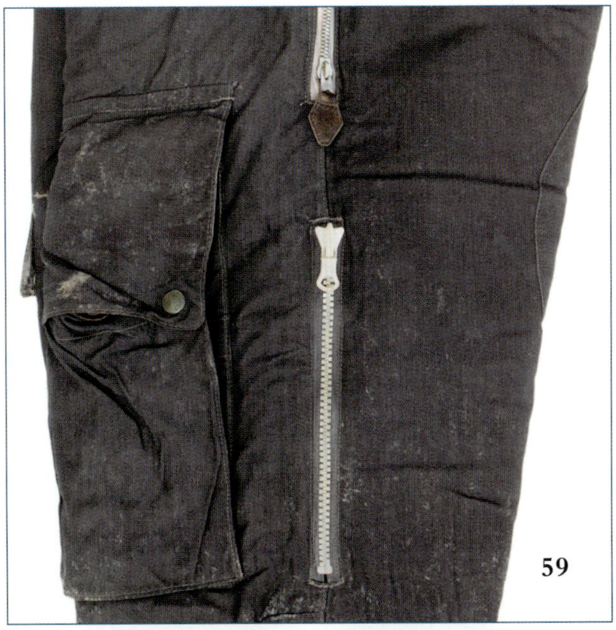

59

60

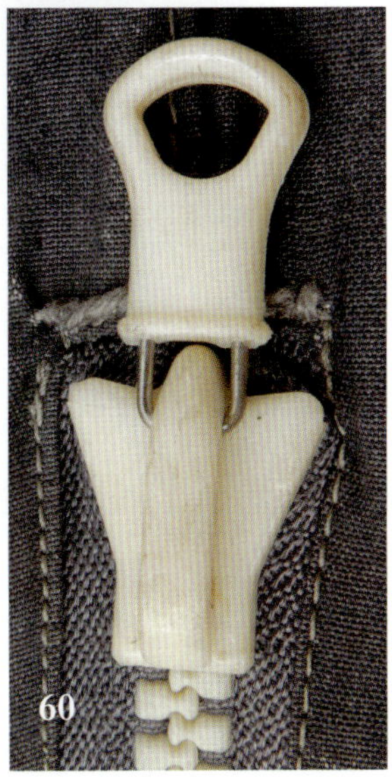

60

60. The flare pistol pocket was located on the right leg, while the signal flag pocket was placed just below the first. The signal flag pocket was included as a design feature later in the war, and some trousers were retrofitted with the pocket by field riggers. Reinforcement canvas straps were added to prevent the flag stick from ripping the cloth.

"Kanal" Leather flight jacket

Flight tunics used by fighter pilots and crew members were made with a limitless amount of materials and colors. When German resources became strained by the constant bombing of factories by the allies, any available material became good enough for the manufacturing of clothing and equipment. The jacket of the photos was manufactured following the basic features of the *"Channel"* type garments and was made from natural soft leather sheepskin, had a front zip fastener and a waist with a single vertical seam made of canvas with a front press stud closure.

61

61

61. The collar and front of this jacket has a brown fleece trimming, while the rest of the jacket has lamb's wool lining. The breast map pocket is made from a separate piece of leather.

62. Detail of the zip fastener at the end of the sleeves, which was secured by a horizontal flap with a press fastener. Also visible are the concealed inner cuffs with elastic fastenings.

63. The jacket had slash hip pockets on each side that closed with a tab press fasteners.

64. View of the cloth label of the jacket, showing the RBNr code.

62

63

64

Electrically heated two-piece *"Kanal"* flight suits

"Kanal" **Fliegerschutzanzug mit elektrischer Beheizung**

Electrically heated *"Kanal"* cloth two-piece flight suit

Before 1941, German winter flight clothing consisted of bulky one-piece flight suits designed several years before, that provided neither the comfort nor the protection from the weather that *Luftwaffe* pilots required. That year, a new, innovative flight suit was introduced. The most important feature was the fact that it was made of two elements, jacket and trousers, with a built-in modern electric heating system. As with the one-piece suits, several types of *"Channel"* suits existed, both for summer and for winter. The suits were connected to the aircraft electric system and delivered 24 volts for the heating filaments placed between the layers of fabric, providing the crew members with an effective protection against extremely low temperatures. This new flight suit was unofficially designated as *"Channel"* suit, as they were extensively used by pilots flying combat missions across the English Channel against Great Britain.

65

65. After a successful mission, a cigarette. *Leutnant* Gonzalo Hevia Álvarez-Quiñones, member of the Spanish voluntary 15. Spanische Staffel, wears a two-piece *"Channel"* type flight suit. The photo was taken somewhere in the Eastern front in February 1943.

66

66

66

66. The collar closed like the one-piece suits, and was adjusted by a metal loop on one side of the collar and a strap with press buttons on the other. A row of four female press buttons allowed a precise adjustment of the strap.

67. The zip fasteners of both legs and sleeves were made by the famous Rapid firm.

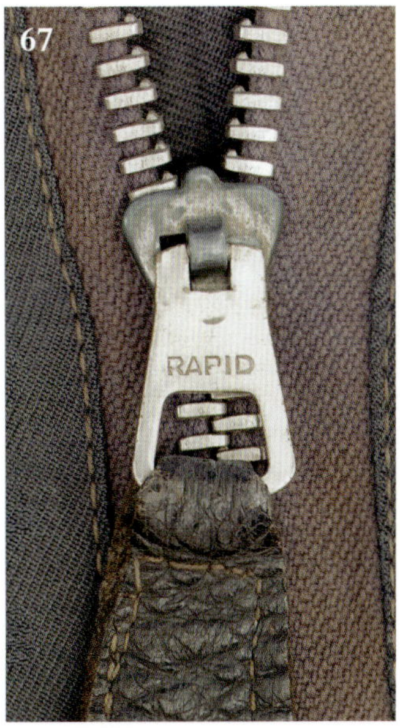

68. The cuffs had long apertures with a zip fastener for easy adjustment. Notice the concealed additional cloth cuffs with press buttons. The connectors to plug the electrically heated gloves were protected with a leather cover.

69. The jacket closed with a vertical center zip fastener and had a cloth tab with two press buttons for waist closure.

70

71

72
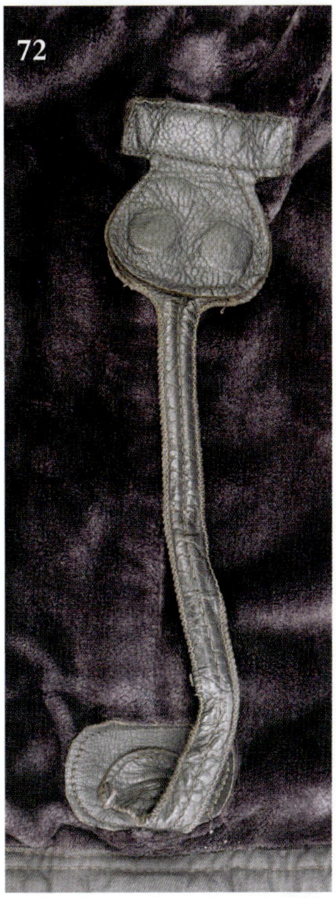

70. The label shows the name of the maker, the famous Karl Heisler. Later in the war, the names of flight gear manufacturers were replaced with three-letter codes to prevent them from being located and bombed by allied forces.

71. Detail of the inner belts and buckles fitted on the waist of the jacket, designed for a tight fit.

71

72

72
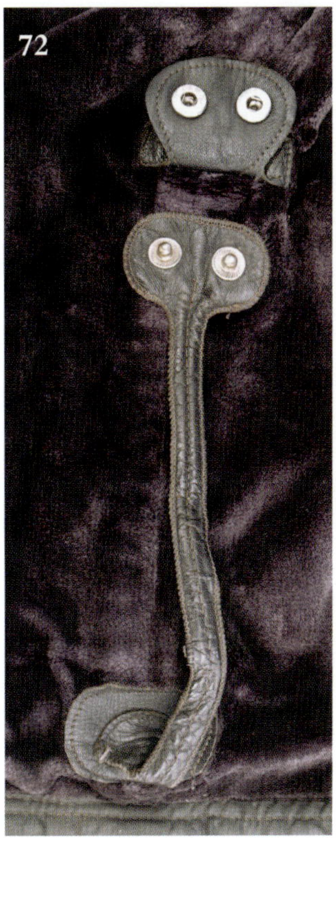

72. Inside the jacket, a long cable with an electric connector at the end, allowed the transmission of electricity from the trousers to the jacket. The cord had a stud connector and was covered with leather. When the connection was not used, it could be folded and secured with another tab inside the jacket.

72
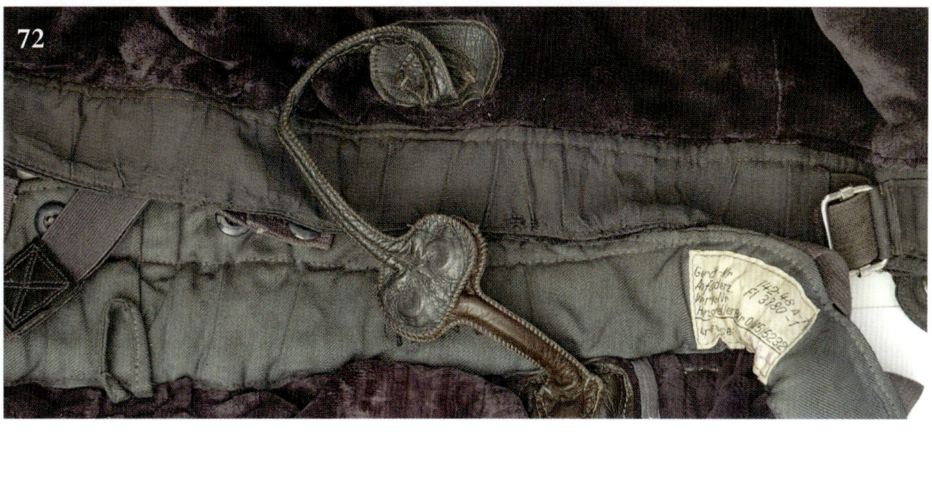

73

73. The trousers had several buttons in the waist area to adjust the suspenders. The waist could be adjusted with an inner belt with pressure buckles placed on either side of the front. The waist closed on the front with a cloth tab with eyelets and two buttons.

73

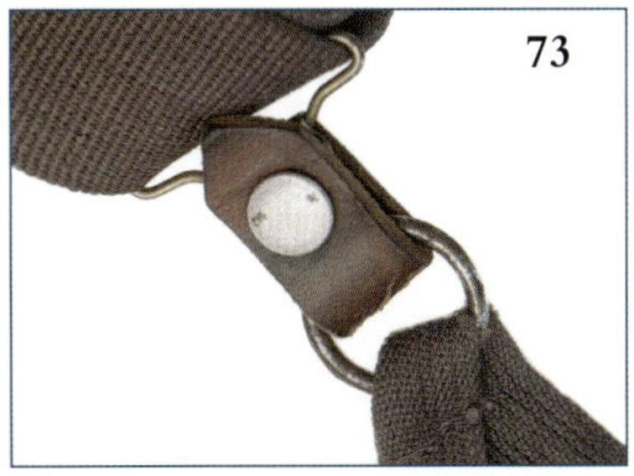

73

74. The inside of the trousers were lined with velvet. The label indicated the article number *(Gerät-Nr)*, the order reference *(Anforderungszeichen)*, the manufacturing code *(Werk-Nr)*, the manufacturer code *(Hersteller)* and the size *(Grösse)*.

74

74

75 

75. The trousers had large pleated pockets on the legs, with a front flap with two press studs and two smaller flaps on the side of the aperture which closed with a single press stud. Both flaps were lined with brown cloth. The photo shows the inside of the left pocket. It was used to store the pilot's survival equipment.

75 

75 

76 

76. The main electric cable that plugged to the aircraft's electric system and provided electricity to heat the suit emerged from the pocket. The lanyard of the flare pistol was tied to a loop inside the trousers to prevent it from getting out of reach in case of being accidentally dropped. The loops on the inner flap and inside of the pocket were designed to secure the flares and other survival equipment, such as a knife, first aid kits, etc.

77. The right leg pocket was somewhat smaller than the left one and was used to store an assortment of articles that the pilot deemed as necessary during a mission. It also had leather loops and other compartments. In addition to the side and front flaps, the pocket was also fitted with a leather strap in the center of the main flap with a male press button on the edge which could be adjusted to a female stud on the outer center of the pocket. These strap secured the contents of the pocket and prevented them from spilling out during tight air manoeuvres.

78. The loops placed on the inside of the leg pocket were designed to secure the flares for the flare gun or Kampfpistole, which was kept in a special pocket located on the right leg.

79. Close-up view of the pocket for the flare pistol, located in the side of the right leg. The lanyard was used in case the gun dropped accidentally from the hand of the user, keeping it always within the each.

80. The legs had long apertures with zip fasteners. They were designed to help the pilot adjust the trousers and the boots. The electric connectors for the electric flight boots are clearly visible on the sides of both legs.

81

81. Erich Hartmann was the top scoring fighter pilot of the Second World War. He flew 825 missions with 352 victories. The photo shows him wearing the *"Channel"* type jacket with lined collar.

Electrically heated *"Kanal"* leather two-piece flight suit

This winter weight two-piece leather variant of the *"Channel"* suit was introduced in the final stages of the war, especially to a number of fighter units assigned to the Defence of the Reich. The basic design was similar to other *"Channel"* type flight suits, but it was manufactured using leather as the basic material. In spite of the hard conditions that the German industry was enduring in the last months of the war due to the constant bombing of factories, these late war garments had the same or even higher craftsmanship of earlier uniforms.

82

83

83. The large collar was lined with purple velvet. The jacket had an inner vertical breast pocket on the front center to store maps and other objects. The cloth *Luftwaffe* emblem was sewn on the right breast.

82. It closed on the front, with five concealed buttons. The inside of the jacket was lined in a light grey cloth. Other variants of this jacket had a double closure by means of button and a zip fastener.

84. The cuff was adjusted with a tab with press buttons. The aperture had zip fasteners made of plastic instead of metal due to war shortages. The inner concealed elasticized cuffs were also present in these type of jackets. They were designed to prevent wind and cold from entering the jacket.

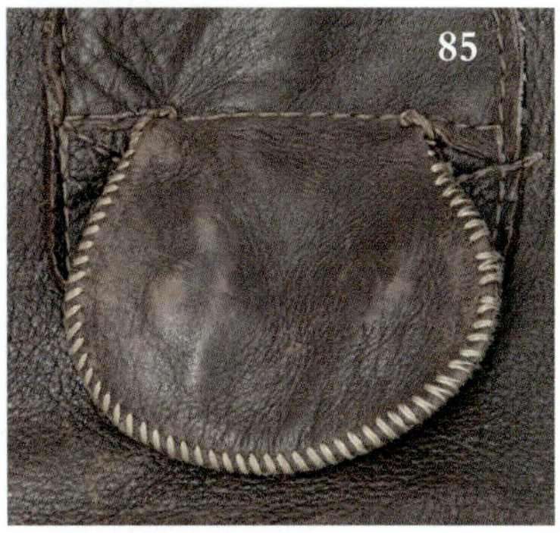

85. The electric system consisted of two press stud connectors which were attached to the gloves and flight boots. Leather tabs were fitted with press stud plugs. The connectors which transmitted the electricity to the trousers were located on the inside of the jacket.

86. The woven label contained detailed information of the garment, such as the size, the manufacturing date and the RBNr code.

87

87

87

87. The trousers had large pockets in the front of either leg, as well as side pockets for storing survival equipment and personal objects for the long missions.

88. *Above:* The inside of the trousers was lined with velvet.
Left: The label indicated the article code *(Gerät-Nr)*, the order reference number *(Anforderungszeichen)*, the manufacturing code *(Werk-Nr)*, the manufacturer number *(Hersteller-Nr)* and the size *(Grösse)*.

89. The trousers closed in the waist with a cloth tab with two buttons and were fitted with an inner elastic belt. On the front, the belt ended in two metal buckles for closure.

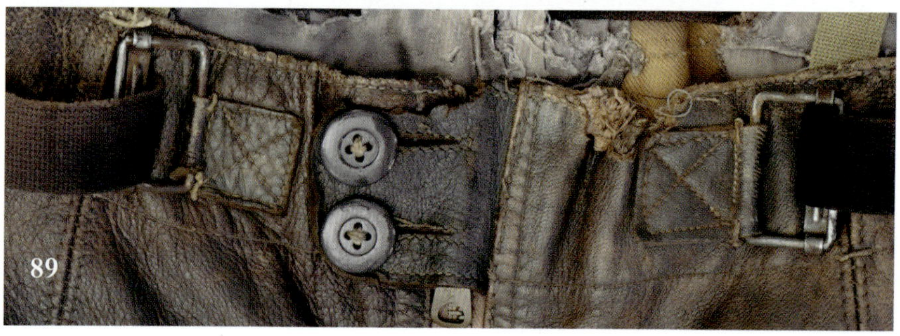

90

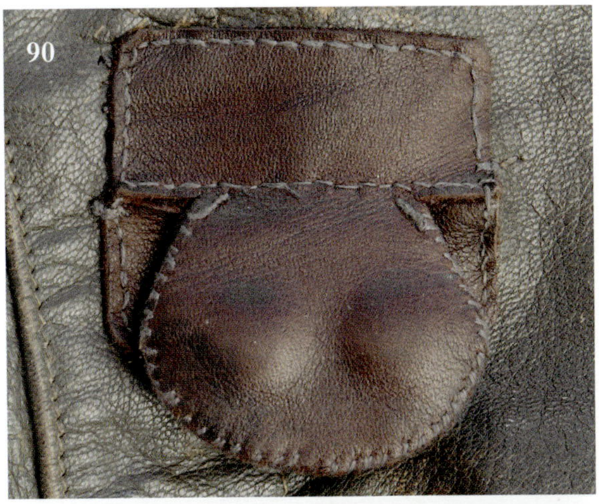

91

91

90

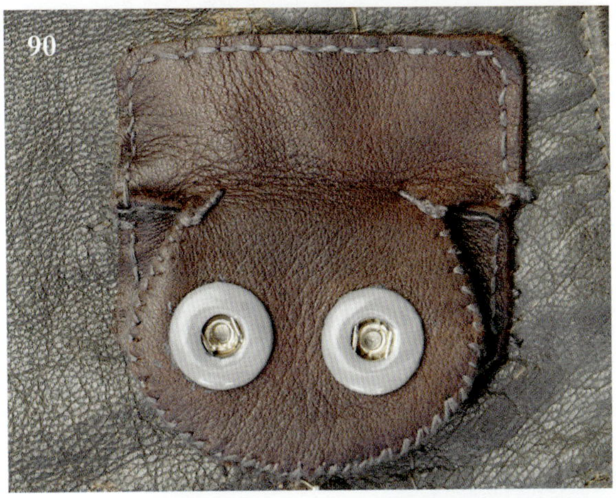

90. The press studs for electric connection were fitted into a leather tab and placed on both legs to connect the electrically heated boots.

91. Both legs had long vertical apertures that ran across the seams to help the pilots adjust the trousers and wear the flight boots inside. The sliders had a leather tab to facilitate the unzipping while using flight gloves.

91

92. The large leg pockets were bellowed for a higher capacity and had two side flaps which closed with a press button to keep the contents from spilling in case of a violent flight manoeuvre. The pocket had a main flap which closed with three plastic buttons.

93. The left leg had a pocket designed to hold the flare pistol or *Kampfpistole*, one of the most important equipment parts for crew members. Closure was made with a small tab in the center and a large with two plastic buttons.

Electrically heated *"Kanal"* leather flight jacket

This jacket is yet another variation of the winter weight *"Channel"* jacket, with an unlined leather collar instead of the more common velvet lining and a front closure consisting of five buttons. A cloth cord ran across the waist of the jacket between the outer layer and the lining, to allow a tighter waist fit. The rest of the features are the same as other jackets of this type, including long apertures with zip fasteners in both sleeves, and electric press studs to connect the electrically heated gloves.

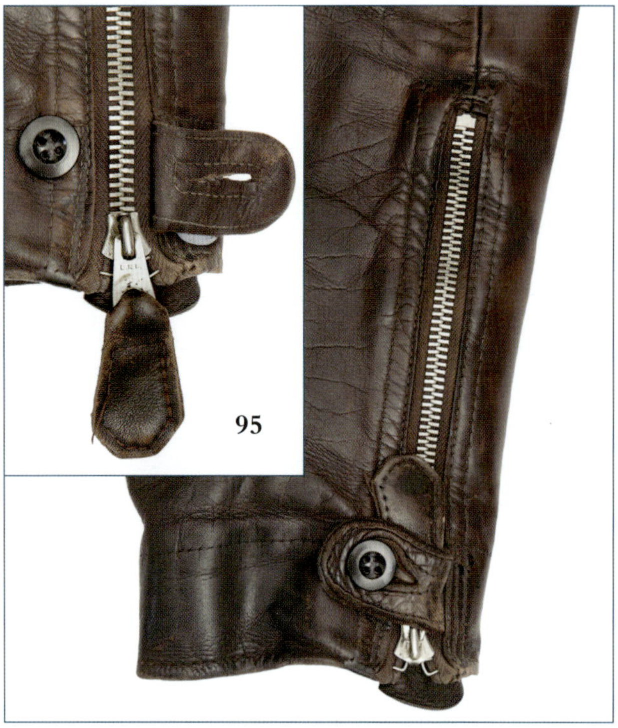

95. View of the sleeve apertures with zip fasteners. A buttoned leather tab on the cuffs allowed a tighter fit and prevented the zip fastener to open during flight.

94. The *Luftwaffe* emblem was made of cloth and sewn on the right hand breast of the jacket.

96. The jacket had an inner tightening cloth cord which ran vertically across the waist and emerged at either side for a tighter adjustment.

12. Flight gloves

Many hours of research and testing were conducted over the years to solve the problem of providing adequate gloves for airmen. Since the early years of flight, the need for a solution to the problem became evident, since the early aircraft had open cockpits and aviators at high altitudes regularly encountered extremely low temperatures. Researchers considered several factors in the development of gloves: heat insulation, dexterity requirements, size and construction and comfort provided by the gloves. Protection against cold by insulation was determined by thickness of clothing. The thickness of the insulating material could be decreased if there was a source of auxiliary heat. Electrically heated gloves, when they were finally perfected, offered an excellent solution to the problem for crewmen who were not required to move very far from their positions in an aircraft. The blast of air that came in through the windows of bombers at that temperature could freeze a gunner's hands after only a few seconds. Both heavy winter and light summer gloves also kept the wearer's hands clean and protected them from flash burn in the event of a fire.

The crew member of the photo checks his equipment for a high altitude mission. He is wearing heavy leather gloves with gauntlets. (Der Adler)

Glove designers and manufacturers were aware of the importance of several physiological considerations. If an aviator's body heat was to be maintained at an appropriate level, his hands had to be adequately protected. Normally the extremities, especially the hands, play an important part in the physical regulation of body temperature. When the hands feel cold, a person usually considers he is cold. On the other hand, if the extremities are too warm, the skin of the rest of the body is stimulated to lose heat more rapidly. Another problem for the researchers was finding a proper solution to warm the palms of the hands and most importantly the ends of the fingers without causing bulkiness that would interfere with dexterity. Mittens were better than gloves for warming but had a serious interference with dexterity, given that they allowed the fingers to touch each other. When the crew members needed a degree of manual dexterity, they had to remove their gloves, causing frostbite of the fingers. The size and construction of gloves had a direct effect on heat insulation, dexterity, and comfort, and also an indirect effect on the heat regulation and cold sensation of the body. If the gloves were too small, they not only decreased the manual dexterity, but also lessened the effectiveness of heat insulation. Gloves that were too large also reduced dexterity.

The comfort of gloves was a personal choice and most likely impossible to evaluate in an objective way. An individual's opinion of whether a pair of gloves was comfortable was, however, entirely influenced by the factors mentioned above and also the airman's confidence in his ability to do his job quickly with his gloves on when he was under stress and pressed for time. This was especially true in the case of *Luftwaffe* pilots, who often preferred to use no gloves or wear privately purchased dress gloves rather that the issue gloves intended for flying duties. The pilots resisted to wear gloves because they needed to feel the controls. This attitude caused many serious burns and other hand injuries. Bomber crew members, flying at higher altitudes for longer periods of time in cockpits or spaces subject to cold weather, were much more receptive in the use of gloves.

A variety of materials for both the outer shell and the lining of winter gloves can be found in *Luftwaffe* flight gloves, but no single material was completely satisfactory. Among the materials used for the outer shell were horsehide, calfskin, and pigskin. Linings were constructed first of a variety of furs and then of lamb's wool and wool fabrics. Once the war started, no change or dramatic modification in the design of gloves took place.

This smiling pilot, just landed from a seemingly successful mission, unbuckles his throat microphone. He is wearing leather gloves. (Der Adler)

Flight gloves with gauntlets

Flieger Lederhandschuhe

The official designation was flight summer gloves with gauntlet, unlined. They were made of brown high grade kid leather. The cuff or gauntlet was made of a single piece, seamed at the outer side and lined with suede leather. The method of adjusting was achieved by the addition of two straps. The first one was located on the upper edge of the cuff and the second one on the seam of the cuff, just over the wrist. Both straps were sewn on the outer seam and passed through a metal ring on the thumb side, then turned back and fixed with press buttons. The ends of the straps were slightly wider to prevent the strap from slipping through the ring.

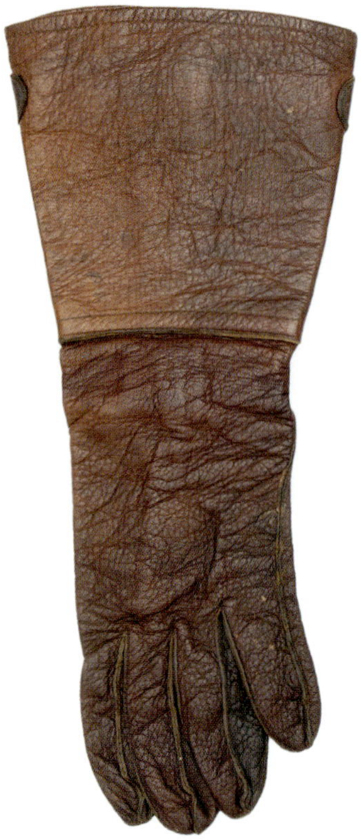

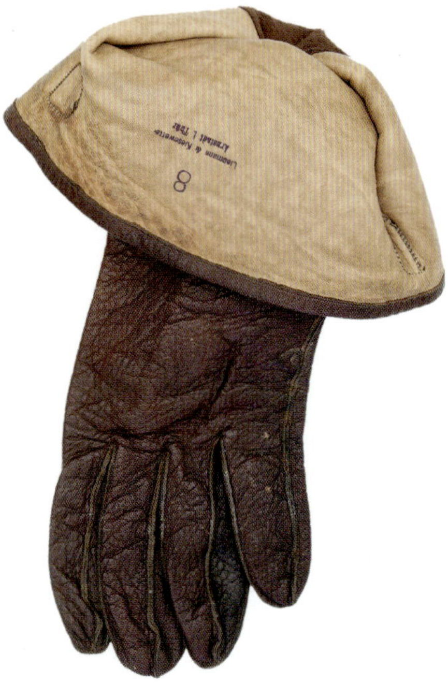

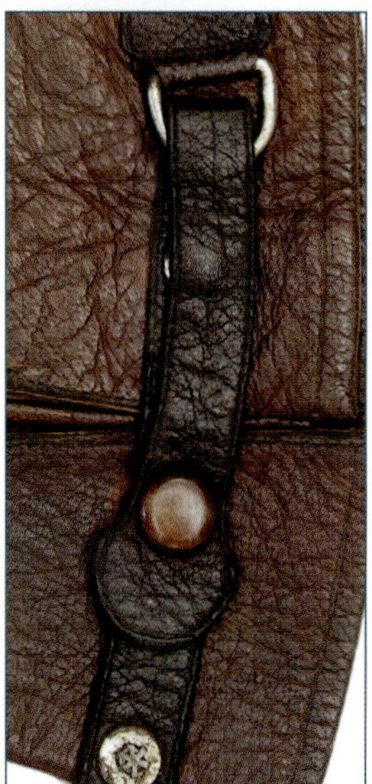

Electrically heated flight gloves with gauntlets

Flieger Lederhandschuhe mit elektrischer Beheizung

The FW m/ 40 gloves were developed to be used in conjunction with the electrically heated flight suits or jackets. They were made of soft blue-grey leather suede. The 8w/ 24v electrical heating wiring was inserted between the leather and the cloth lining of the glove. The oval-shaped plugs were placed at the edge of the gauntlet cuffs and connected to the sleeve fitting plugs. The inside of the gauntlet had a soft leather surface. The markings were ink-stamped on the interior, and included the size, the RB number, an LBA proof stamp and other technical data.

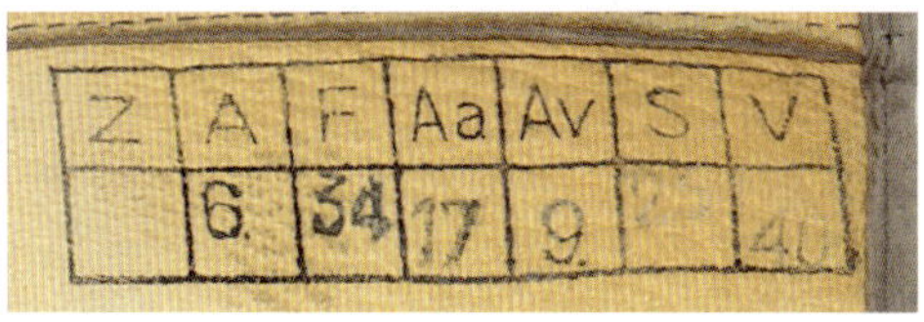

13. Flight fur boots

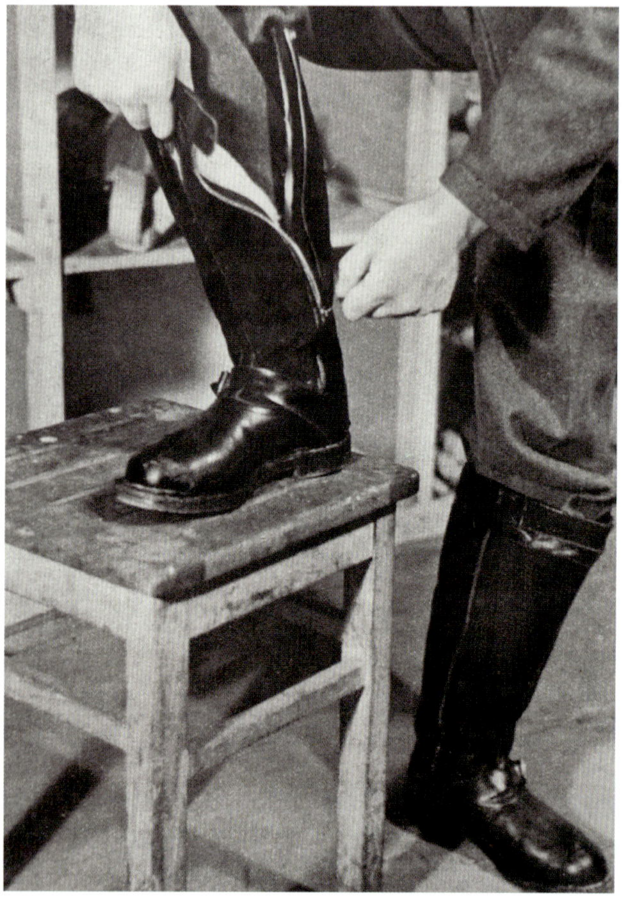

The pilot of the photo of the right is using a bench to put on his flying boots. The zip fasteners made the process easier, and also allowed a fast removal in case of a leg wound without aggravating it. Some pilots preferred to tuck their trousers or flying suits under the boots. However, veterans have commented that more experienced pilots preferred to wear the boots under their flight suits or trousers for a more firm attachment, which prevented them from blowing away by the parachute opening shock. (Left: Signal; Right: Der Adler)

Since the first years of flight, proper footwear proved to be a vital part of any outfit for any climate. In cold weather and at high altitudes, proper flying boots were essential in preventing the feet from becoming frostbitten. The feet constitute about 10 percent of the total body surface. Under hot conditions, approximately 13 percent of the body's heat can be lost through the feet. However, under cold conditions, when the heat loss might be expected to increase, reductions in the blood's flow and temperature may cause the portion of body heat lost through the feet to fall as low as 7 percent. Therefore, the need to have proper footwear was essential for pilots and crews.

In Germany, flight boots were developed well before the beginning of the war and, as with other pieces of equipment, remained in use until the end with minor modifications. Before the war started, German pilots preferred to use tight, officer dress boots when using breeches and normal shoes with long trousers. Other crew members preferred the issue marching jackboots. Both choices of boots were preferred over the standard flight boots because they offered a much sharper and stylish look. But as the war progressed, a growing number of injuries took place due to insufficient foot protection or the fact that wounds were aggravated due to the difficulty of extracting the boots when an injury occurred.

The standard issue fur lined winter flight boots were introduced 1935 followed by an improved model that was introduced in 1937. Both models proved to be suitable for flying but at the same time they were impractical when the pilot had bailed out or crash landed, as they were difficult to walk any distance. Also, the inside lining of fur would become easily matted down, which resulted in loss of heat retention. Many new patterns were tested and considered to overcome the shortcomings of the flight boots, but finally no suitable pattern was officially adopted and the flight boots, with minor manufacturing variations, continued to be utilized for the duration of the war. With the development electrically heated flight suits, intended for cold weather flights, the first electrically heated flight boots were introduced to complement the flight suit capabilities. The boots worked with the same technology as the suits, with built-in, insulated heating elements that drew their power by means of metal automatic buttons in the boots which connected to other connectors found in the flight suit legs.

Lunchtime at the airbase. The pilot in the center of the photo is wearing ankle boots instead of flight boots, a relatively common practice with pilots and flight crews. The connector for the electrically heated flight boots is clearly visible on the left leg of his "Channel" trousers.

Flight boots

Flieger-Pelzstiefel

Model Pst 3 flight boots

The *Pst 3* fur lined flight boots were introduced in November, 1936 and were designed to be worn together with the flight protective suits. They were made of chocolate brown leather, the shafts were made of suede and had a lamb skin lining. The boots closed with one or two metal zip fasteners running along the shaft. The upper end was secured by a leather tab with a press stud. The boots had two leather tightening straps with buckles intended to prevent the boots from blowing away during the bail-out and the parachute opening. The first was located on the top of the shaft and ran vertically across the front of the ankles. The second one reached over the instep and buckled at the outer side of the boot. Several boot companies manufactured high quality flight boots, with the model made by Paul Hoffman & Co, being one of the most popular in the early stages of the war.

1

1. The tightening straps were 2 cm wide and were placed on the instep and on the upper edge of the boot shaft. They prevented the boots from being lost from the parachute opening shock. Some pilots often found that the boots were still not tight enough and decided to wear their flight suits or trousers above the boots instead of tucking them inside to further secure them from being blown away in case of bail-out.

2

2. Flight boots had a sole made of two layers of leather and individual rubber soles and heels. The design of the boots proved to be unsuitable for walking any distance in case of bail-out and forced landing.

3

3. The cloth label indicates that the boots were manufactured by the famed clothier Paul Hoffman & Co of Berlin. Size and other relevant information is also found on the label.of tucking them inside to further secure them from being blown away in case of bail-out.

4

4. The shaft of the boots was made of suede leather, while the feet section had chromed leather. The front and back seams of the legs had a leather strap, to which a leather loop was placed on the upper part to hold the tightening strap. All the fittings were nickel-plated.

Model Pst 4004 flight boots

An improved version of the Pst 3 flight boots, designated as model *Pst 4004*, was introduced in September, 1937. The most notable difference was the presence of two zip fasteners, one on each side of the boot shaft, even though late war specimens are found with a single zip fastener. It was made of black leather with the leg part made of suede. The sole and heel were made of a single piece. Even though the quality of the material deteriorated during the war, the overall quality of the boots remained within high standards.

5

5

5. The boots had two tightening straps, one around the instep and another on the edge of the shaft. The shaft had a sewn-on leather tape which ran horizontally across the top edge with three leather loops to retain the tightening strap. The top edge of the inner part of the shaft also had a small closure strap with a black painted female press button. The corresponding male button was placed at the other side of the zipper closure.

6. The boots were lined with natural lamb skin and had metal zip fasteners on the inside and outside of the shafts. Mid and late war boots can be found with a single zip fastener due to restrictions of raw materials.

6

7. The label contained detailed information, such as the size, the manufacturing date and the RBNr code.

7

8

8. The insoles were made of leather. The outer soles and heels were made from a single piece of rubber with an anti-skid pattern and were sewn to the insole.

Electrically heated flight boots

Flieger-Pelzstiefel mit elektrischer Beheizung

Model Pst 4004 E flight boots

The electrically heated flight boots were a modification of the previous Pst 4004 flight boots. The designation of *Pst 4004 E stood for Pelzstiefel 4004, Elektrisch.* Even though the previous flying boots were well suited for cold weather, they suffered some disadvantages, the most important consisting in the flattening of the internal fur after usage for a long period of time, which resulted in the loss of insulating properties. The new model of electrically heated boots was introduced in February, 1940 and worked using the same principle of the electrically heated flight suits. The insulated heating filaments were placed between the leather and the fur lining of the boots and had a press button plug on the top edge of the shafts which connected to similar connectors on the legs of the flight trousers.

9

9. The top edge of the inner part of the shaft incorporated a small closure strap with a black painted female press button to prevent the zip fastener from opening. The dual press studs for the electric connection were fitted into a leather tab and placed on the top inside of both legs to allow the connection to the electrically heated *"Chan*nel" two-piece flight suits

10

10. The upper calf sections were constructed using black suede leather. They closed with vertical zip fasteners that ran along the inner seams of the shafts. They were lined with natural lamb fleece.

11. On the top inner part of the boot, between the underlying suede and the leather zip fastener was a machine-sewn spec cloth label. It indicated the name of the manufacturer, Paul Hoffman & Co, the size and the year of manufacture.

11

12

12. The foot portion of the boots was made using two leather panels; a large forward panel for the instep and a small rear panel that covered the heel area. The boots had stacked leather heels and insoles with sewn anti-skid, rubber outer soles and a glued rubber outer heel.

14. Life preservers

These crew members prepare for a mission plotting the route with the help of a flight navigation computer. Both are wearing the Kapok life preserver.

As soon as the man began to fly over water, the need for a floatation device that would save his life became evident. Life preserver vests for use in ships had been around for years. The modern life jacket probably originated with the invention of Captain Ward of the British Royal Navy in 1854. It was a cork vest designed to offer ship crews buoyancy and weather protection at the same time.

By 1861, cork became the main material for life jackets. Cork was replaced around the turn of the century with kapok, a fibrous and supple vegetable material that was much softer and offered improved buoyancy due to its fibres, filled with air-trapping honeycomb structures. The first commercial kapok-filled life vests were available as early as 1912. Kapok became the standard life vest material, and was welcomed on board of naval ships where sailors wore their life vests at all times, even while they were sleeping. For many years, cork and kapok coexisted in life vests. But some designers thought that the kapok-filled life preservers were too bulky, and studied several ways to solve the problem. Peter Markus came out with the first inflatable life preserver in 1928. It was nicknamed the *"Mae West"* in reference to the buxom entertainer, whom wearers of inflated vests were thought to resemble.

World War II brought a change in life jacket technology. Life jackets meant the difference between life and death for many flight personnel.

Although inflatable rubber life vests were available, kapok or cork vests were preferred by most airmen because they were considered foolproof, and did not require any action to provide buoyancy. However, concerns about reliability persisted, especially after the Battle of Britain, where many airmen died as a result of losing consciousness and floating head down. This lead to the development of life vests with buoyancy provided in the ring around the neck as well as to the chest area. Other vests were equipped with an automatic inflation system, using a small $C0_2$ cylinder. Wearers were encouraged to inspect the $C0_2$ cylinders regularly to see if the caps were punctured, and check frequently for leaks in the vests themselves. Unfortunately, these safety measures were not always followed. The reliability of this type of vest eventually quieted most of the sceptics. However, crewmen had the choice of using either the pneumatic or kapok-type life-preserver vests while flying over water, and the photographic evidence shows that both types were used by all crewmen without regard of the position or the type aircraft flown.

The famous pilot ace, Major Theodor Weissenberger wears an inflatable life vest.
Weissenberger flew more than 500 combat missions and claimed 208 victories. He survived the war, only to be killed in a car racing accident in 1950.

Kapok life preservers

Kapokschwimmwesten

Model 10-76 B-1 kapok life preserver

The Kapok-filled jackets were made of strong cotton fabric and consisted of tubular-shaped tubes in which the kapok material was inserted. The tubes were divided by seams across the front and back of the vest. A collar formed by several rows of kapok-filled tubes was sewn to the center of the breast area and ran along the edges of the front panels and around the neck. This collar could be laid down or pulled up if needed. A chin collar was also fitted to prevent the sliding of the head to the sides in case the wearer was unconscious. The first model (10-76 A) had more buoyancy on the back, making the wearer to rotate to a face down position and causing him to drown if unconscious. The 10-76 B-1 model was introduced in 1943 and solved the problem by removing the kapok *"sausages"* from the back and providing more buoyancy on the front.

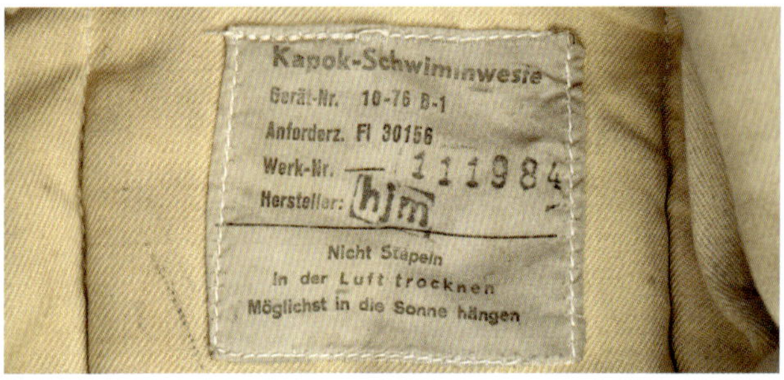

1

1. The 10-76 B-1 model had the kapok-filled tubes only present in the front part of the vest, which provided more buoyancy on that area. This allowed the face of the airman to remain above the water and prevented him from drowning.

2. Bomber crew members being briefed before a mission. They are all wearing the 10-76A *Schwimmweste*. Bomber crews often used the kapok life vests, unlike fighter pilots who preferred the less bulky inflatable life vests.

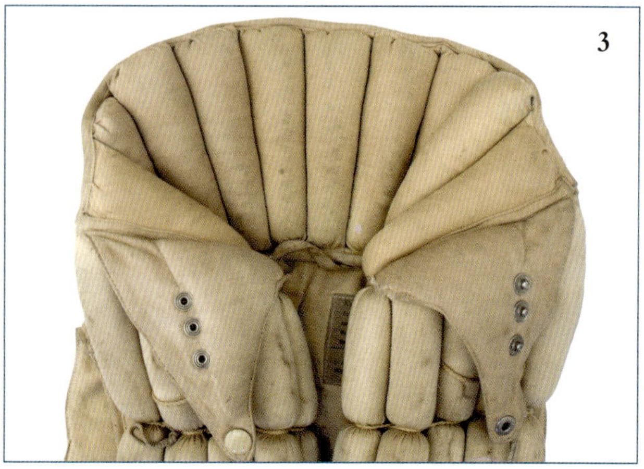

3. The neck had chin collars on the sides that adjusted with press buttons. They held the collar in the upward position and prevented the head of the user to slide to the sides and drown.

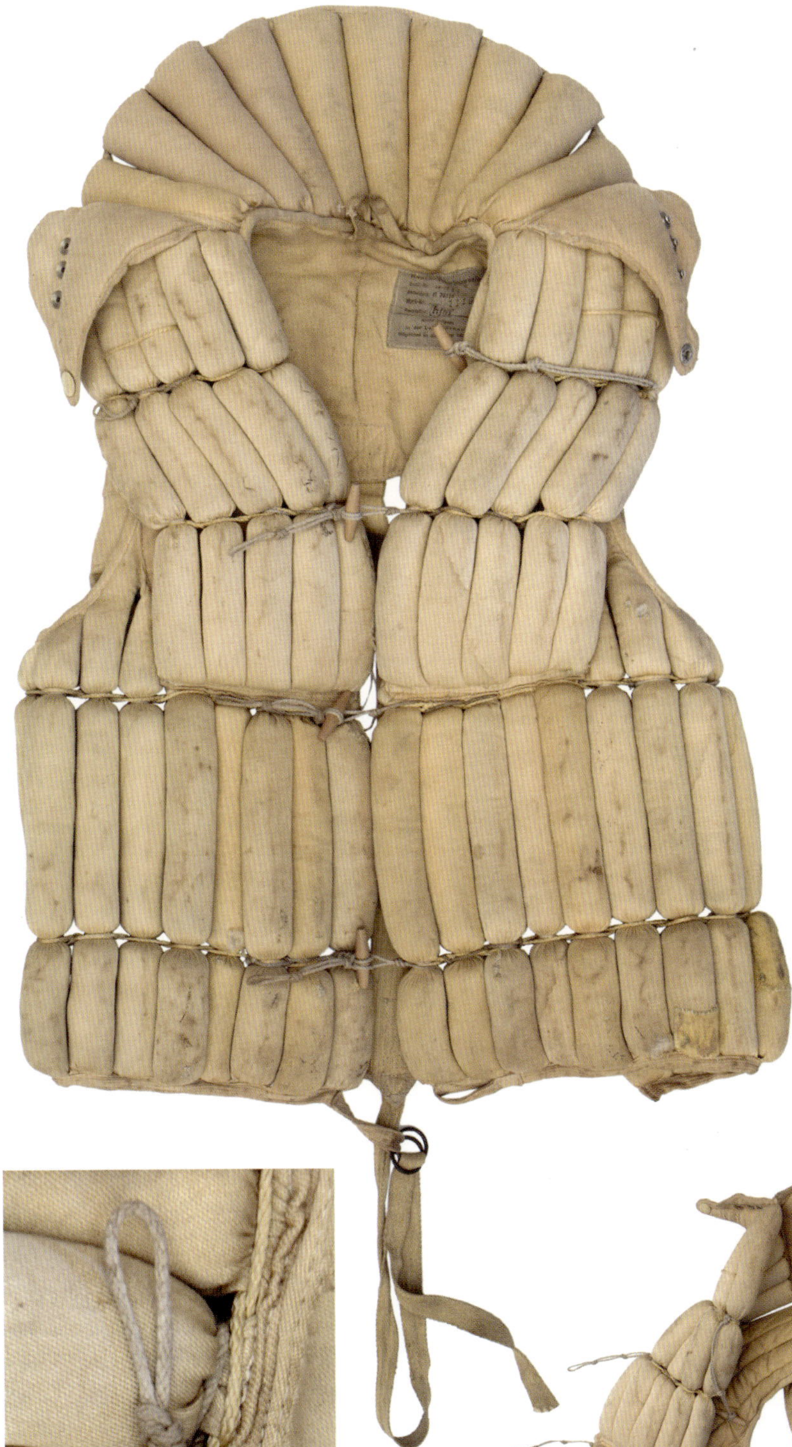

4. The vest was made of kapok material inserted in vertical tubes that were tied together with thick cord at 15 cm intervals, forming a sleeveless waistcoat. The collar was constructed of the same material and was sewn to the center front of the vest.

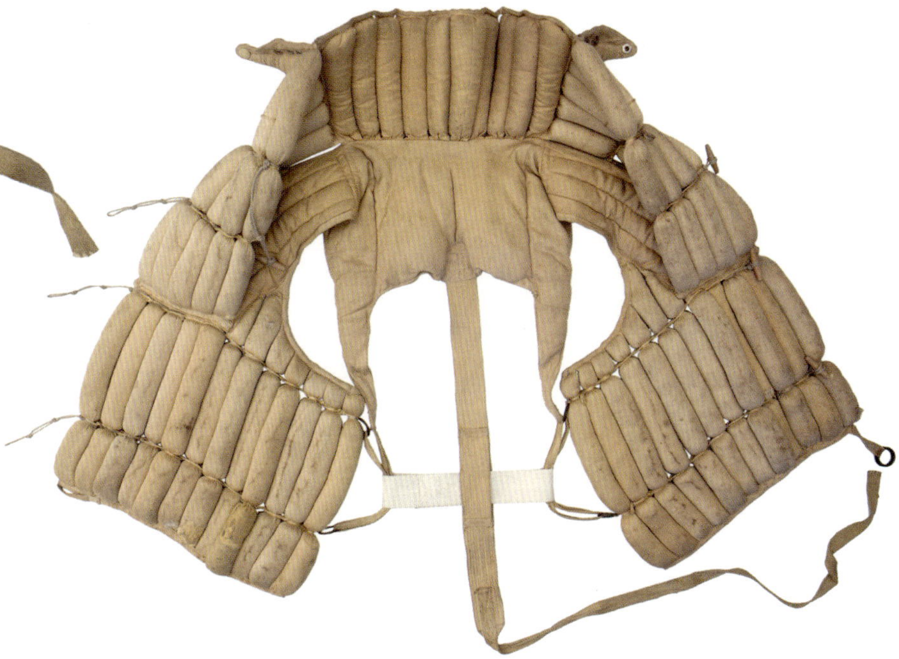

5. The vest was closed with three short wooden pegs on the left front side that hooked into cord loops on the right front side.

Inflatable life preservers

Luftschwimmwesten

Model SWp 734/10-30 inflatable life preserver

The Model 10-30 life vest was a waistcoat model made of a rubberized canvas fabric developed by Dräger in 1936/37. The inflatable buoyancy chamber was an envelope that ran from the breasts to the back, and was connected with a canvas section that went over the shoulders. The left and right side breasts were joined at the front with the help of three canvas straps placed on the left side and ring buckles located at the right side. The first one was located slightly below the neck, the second slightly above the waist line and the third on the bottom edge of the vest. A strap was sewn to the center edge of the back, passed between the legs and buckled on the front edge. A compressed carbon dioxide cartridge was fixed to a cast alloy mechanism located on the bottom edge of the left front. A twist valve allowed the pilot to inflate the vest rapidly. The vest also allowed the pilot to inflate the vest using a mouth inflation hose attached to the front of the vest, near the left breast. The hose was fixed in a vertical position and the end had a one-way valve for the pilot to inflate if necessary. The design had some drawbacks, as it provided the same buoyancy on the front and back. If the wearer fell unconscious while floating, the head tended to move forward instead of falling to the back, which caused the pilot to drown. Subsequent models corrected this problem.

6

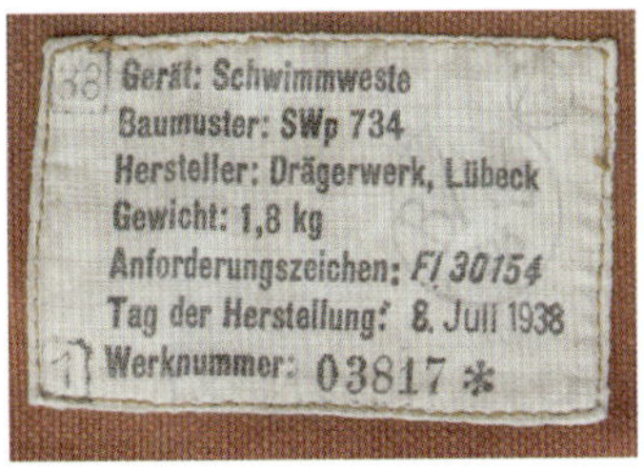

7

6. The life vest of the photos is an early production model made in brown canvas. The color changed in later production models to pale yellow in order to allow a better identification by air-sea rescue teams. The woven specification label shows a manufacturing date of 1938 with the early type nomenclature of SWp 74.

7. The mouth inflation hose was fixed to the left breast of the life vest to allow the wearer to manually inflate it if necessary. It was made of black rubber and had a one-way valve at the top.

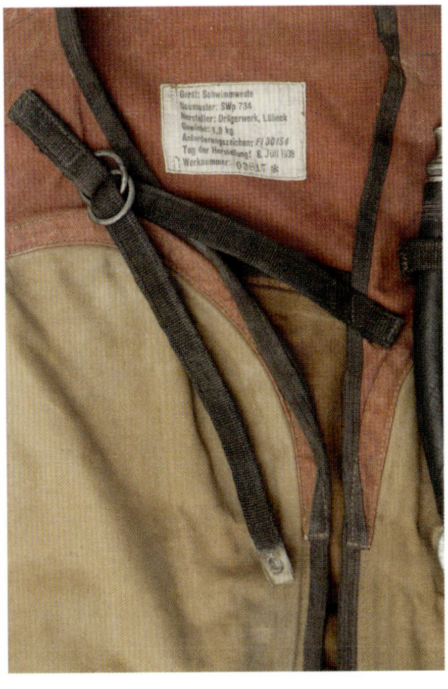

8

9

8. Detailed view of the gas inflation mechanism. A small compressed carbon dioxide cartridge was fixed to one side and operated with a twist open valve.

9. The closure was achieved by three straps and the corresponding ring buckles. The vest was intended to be used underneath the flying suit to allow the wearer to free himself from the suit in case it was necessary. The parachute harness was worn over the vest.

Model 10-30 B-2 inflatable life preserver

The B-1 and B-2 versions of the 10-20 *Schwimmveste* were developed in 1940 and 1941 respectively and offered a clear design improvement over the previous model. The basic construction was similar to the 10-30 vest, but without buoyancy on the back, except for an inflatable ring around the neck of the wearer that supported the back of the head, reminding of the allied *"Mae West"* vests. The system assured that the head was kept clear from the water and prevented the wearer from drowning. Closure was achieved by two straps and ring buckles that secured the front panels and a belt that ran horizontally around the waist with a front friction buckle. As in the previous model, the vest had a strap passed between the legs and buckled on the front edge to prevent the vest from slipping upwards. The metal mounts of the valves were replaced by plastic.

10. The jacket closed with two frontal straps with loop buckles. Late war examples had the fittings made of steel instead of cast alloy, due to the decline in the quality of raw materials.

11. The nomenclature label was made of cloth in early production models, and later replaced by an ink control stamp inside the vest in order to speed the manufacturing process and save costs. The name of the maker has been replaced by the three letter code *"BWZ"*, that stands for Auer-Gesellschaft AG, *Werk* y of Oranienburg.

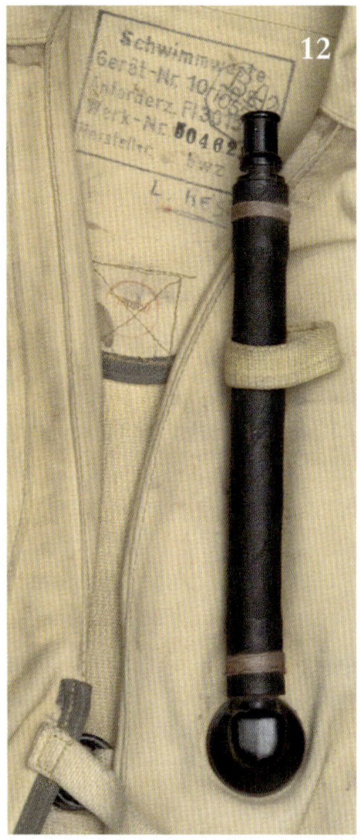

12. The mount and one-way valve of the mouth inflation hose were made of plastic, instead of the metal alloy used in previous models.

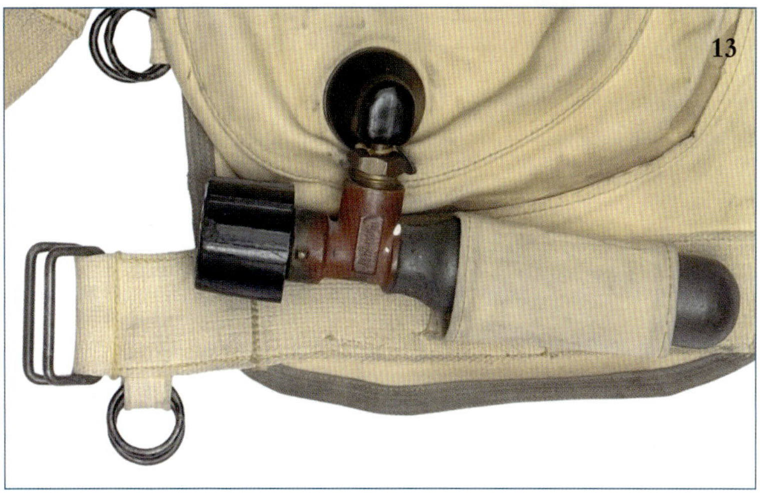

13. Detail of the markings of the mechanism to inflate the vest using a compressed carbon dioxide cartridge. A twist valve allowed the pilot to inflate the vest rapidly. Notice the plastic mounts that replaced the metal fittings of the previous models.

15. Parachutes

The parachute is not a modern invention. Even though the exact origin is unknown, the principle is so simple that excited the people's imagination throughout the ages. It was not until the invention of the balloon by the Montgolfier brothers in France during the early XVIII Century, that the parachute found a practical application. A Frenchman, Andre-Jacques Garnerin, made the first confirmed parachute descent from a balloon on October 22, 1797.

The two crewmen of the Bf 110 mount their aircraft. The pilot wears a seat-pack parachute, while the rear gunner/radioman wears a standard back-pack parachute, necessary in the cramped conditions of the rear cockpit. (Schlag aüf Schlag)

With the invention of the airplane by the Wright brothers in 1903, it was just a matter of time until aircraft of various types were making flights at air shows and fairs in the United States and Europe. Very few of these early airplane pilots carried parachutes. Despite the many dangers a pilot could encounter during flight, such as engine and structural failures, most of the pioneer aviators preferred to take their chances with a disabled aircraft and make an emergency landing wherever possible. Many airmen considered the parachute, developed previously for balloonists, to be an unreliable and cumbersome addition to his gear. Other pilots disdained the use of a parachute because they felt that it would reflect upon their faith in their plane and their abilities. This attitude remained unchanged until after the beginning of air combat in World War I.

German flyers used parachutes in the final phases of the war. The airmen were being supplied with the Heinecke parachute, manufactured by Schroeder & Co of Berlin. This parachute, designed by Otto Heinecke, a junior NCO, was tested in May 1917. The Heinecke model was a transitional device between the bulky balloon parachute, and the modern body parachute for aviators introduced after the war. It was also the first parachute to be used in quantity by airplane crewmen.

European scientists made numerous improvements in the years that preceded World War II. Modern aeronautical research and development facilities established in England and Germany began exploring basic aerodynamic and other performance criteria. The use of the vertical wind tunnel for testing parachutes originated in England where Professor A. V. Stephens built the first such structure in 1931. German experimenters appreciated the need for scientific investigations into the factors determining parachute performance, and German research was quite advanced at the beginning of the war. Notable work was accomplished by both Dr. Helmut G. Heinrich and Theodore Knacke, who continued their research in the United States after the war.

Flying personnel of the *Luftwaffe* had three basic types of personnel parachutes at their disposal: The first was the chest type. The parachute pack was a separate piece and could be attached to the harness quickly in case of emergency. It was intended for use when the back-type parachute was impractical to wear, such as confined spaces in bomber aircraft. The harness was worn by crew members during flight, and the pack was stowed in a location which allowed immediate access in case the crewmen needed to bail-out. The back-type parachute could be used by all flyers, especially pilots. This type of parachute restricted the mobility and therefore the pilot had limited view of the rear of his aircraft. The seat-type offered the pilot more mobility than the back-type, and therefore allowed greater visibility in all directions. Despite the minor improvements made in the seat-type parachutes from their introduction in the early 1920s, they still caused difficulty when moving in the cramped space of an aircraft.

A bomber crewman helps his comrade to adjust his back parachute. They are both wearing the summer one-piece flight suits. (Schlag aüf Schlag)

Seat parachutes

Sitzfallschirme

Model 30 IS 24 (FL. 30231) seat parachute

The seat type parachute model 30 IS 24 was used by fighter pilots as well as crews of other types of aircraft with the bucket recess in the seat. It was based on British models, especially the quick release mechanism of the harness, which was a copy of the Irwin mechanism. The designation 30 I stood for seat parachutes, The following letter could be *"S"* for silk or *"M"* for Mako synthetic weave, which was the type of fabric used to manufacture the canopy. The number 24 stood for the number of panels in the canopy. The parachute consisted of the following main parts: The parachute canopy, the parachute packing bag, the back flap and the harness. The harness was made of strong webbing and had several adjustment slides made of metal. The belt strap had a large quick release buckle to which four plates on the ends of the straps were inserted into the buckle.

1. These crewmen are ready to board their Heinkel 111 in a Polish field. The man on the left is wearing the harness for a chest pack parachute. The parachute was usually removed inside the aircraft and the connecting straps placed over the shoulders with the hooks secured to a metal plate on the vertical breast straps. The other crew member is wearing a seat parachute with a ring and hook style fastening system. (Militaria Arganzuela)

2. The pilot of the Ju 87 Stuka dive bomber of the photo is wearing a seat type parachute while being filmed. The photo was taken during the shooting of the propaganda film *"Besatzung Dora"* by the UFA *(Universum Film AG)*, the most important German film studio. During the war, it produced both entertainment and propaganda films.

1

2

3

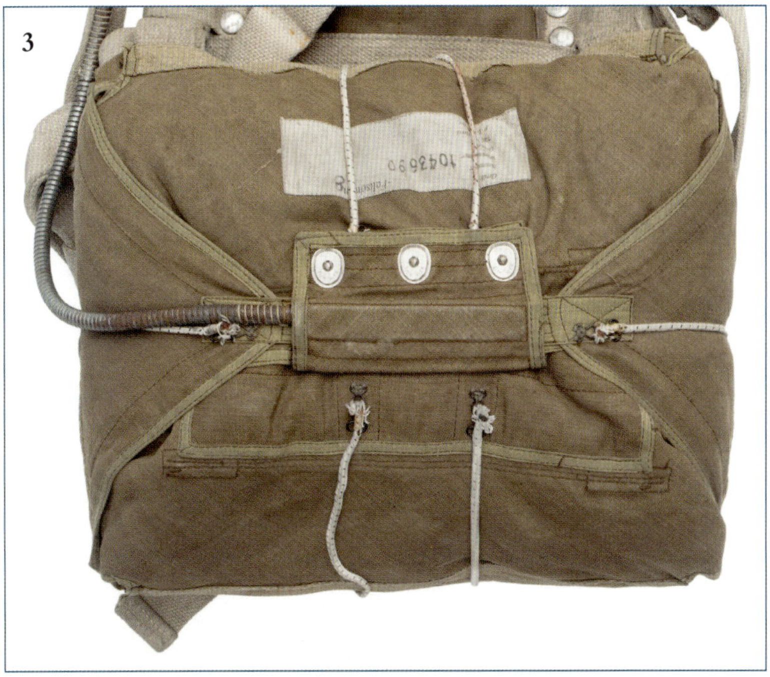

3. The parachute was sealed inside the pack by three lift-the-dot metal fasteners and had six elastic bands attached to the four sides to further secure the four closing panels of the pack. The woven specification and control label was sewn to the bottom side of parachute pack.

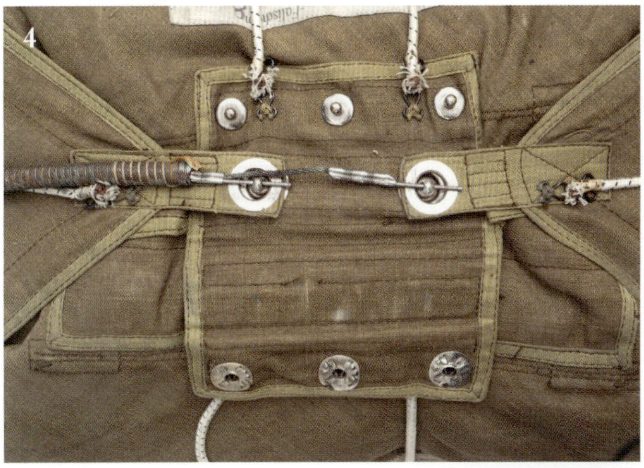

4

4. The release system of the packing bag consisted of a shield with a canvas flap. The four side flaps of the bag were placed over the packed parachute and connected by two metal eyelets to a spring system. The flaps of the parachute packing bag were also connected to spring ropes hooked to eyelets. When the rip cord was released, the flaps were freed and the spring ropes forced the flaps to fold back, activating the small chute that pulled the main parachute from the bag.

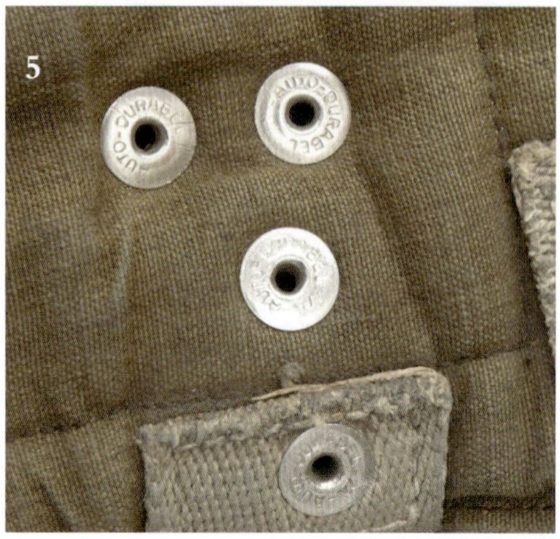

5. The harness was made of strong webbing. The canvas back panel was attached to the harness using canvas webbing loops held in place by quick-release buttons. The back panel was designed to alleviate the discomfort of the straps on the back when wearing the parachute, to hold the harness structure in place and give some warmth to the back of the wearer.

6. Detailed view of the cloth specification label sewn on one of the straps of the parachute harness.

7. The parachute release system consisted in a rip cord that was attached to the belt strap. The trapezoid grip was located on the left side of the harness belt strap and was connected to a shielded strong metal wire that reached the parachute bag to release the parachute.

8. The Fl. 30231 parachute required the pilot or aircrew member to sit on top of the parachute pack when flying. For this reason, the back of the pack had a rectangular soft cushion that was buttoned to the bottom shield of the pack for comfort. This model of parachute was used by fighter pilots and crew of other aircraft that featured a bucket recess in the aircraft seat.

8

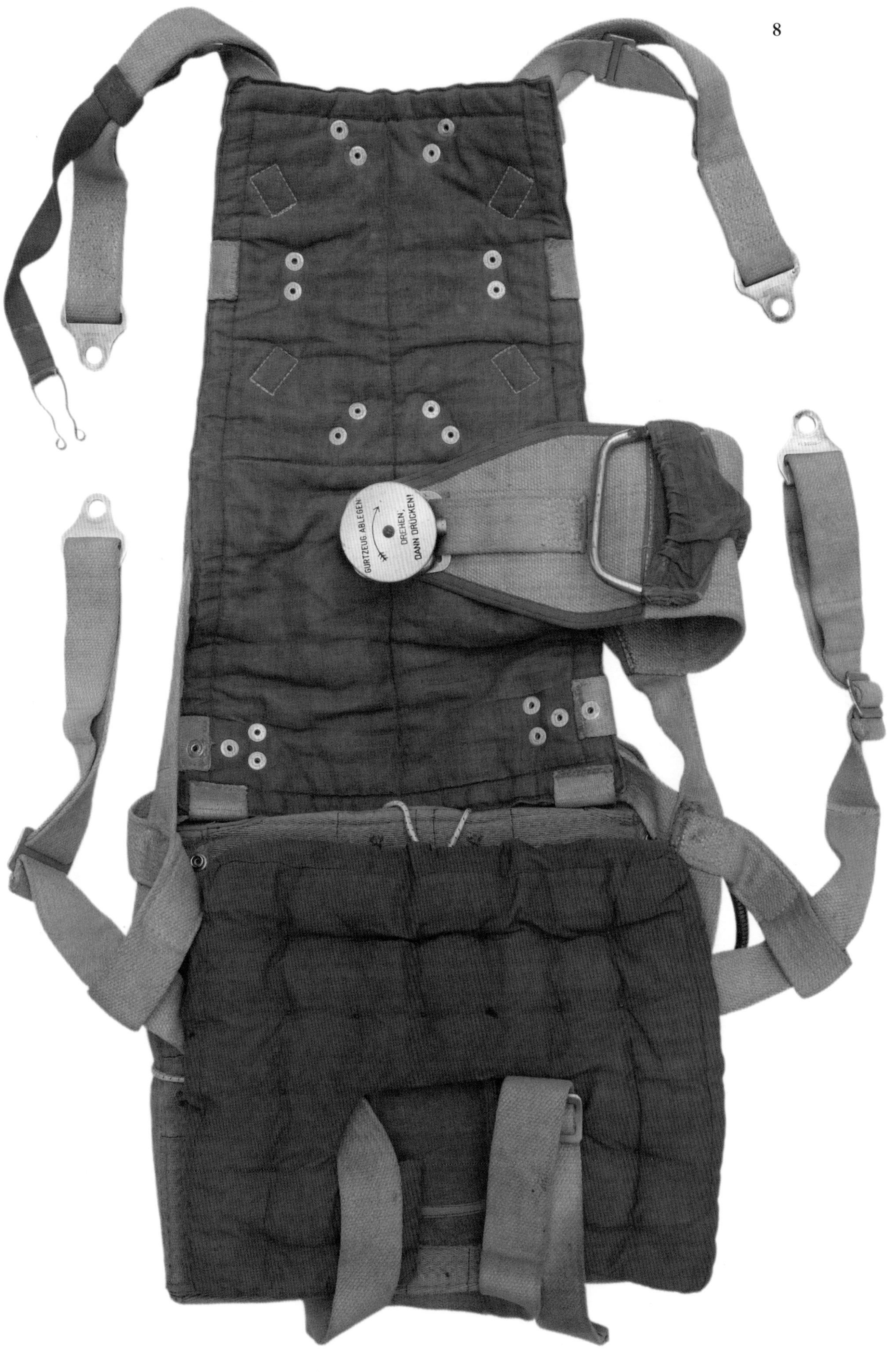

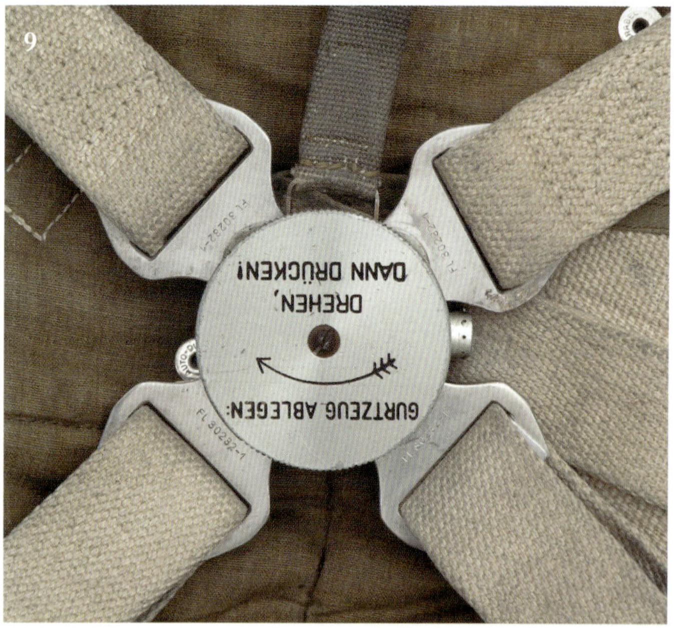

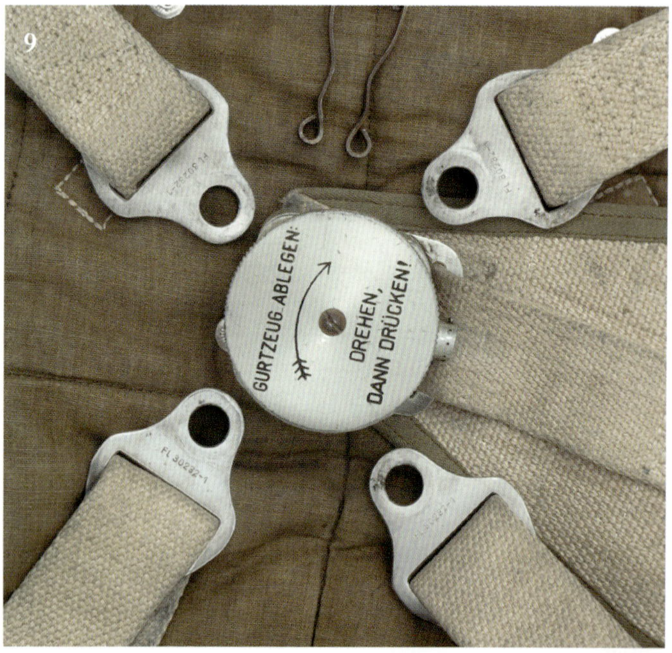

9. The quick-release mechanism was developed by two Englishmen and the patent assigned to the Irvin Air Chute Company. It consisted in a small metal box containing four spring-activated pins. When the harness was fixed in place, perforated metal tips on the ends of the two chest and two thigh straps were held in place by the pins. When the wearer wanted to release the harness, he had to rotate the front metal disc of the box 90 degrees and depress it with a sharp blow.

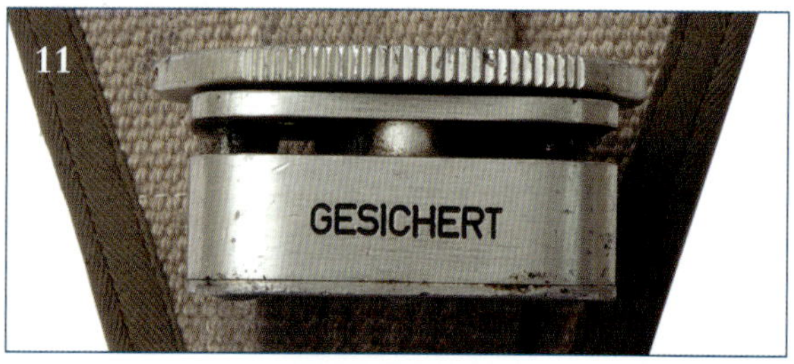

10. The photos show the safety key for the quick-release box, also known as fork. It was the only German contribution to an otherwise purely British design. When the key was inserted under the frontal disc of the box, it prevented its accidental depression and premature release of the parachute harness. When the harness was to be released, the key was withdrawn and the box could then be rotated and depressed. Ironically, the Irwin Company sold several of these quick-release mechanisms to Germany in 1937, who found them to be of superior design and was subsequently copied by German manufacturers during the war.

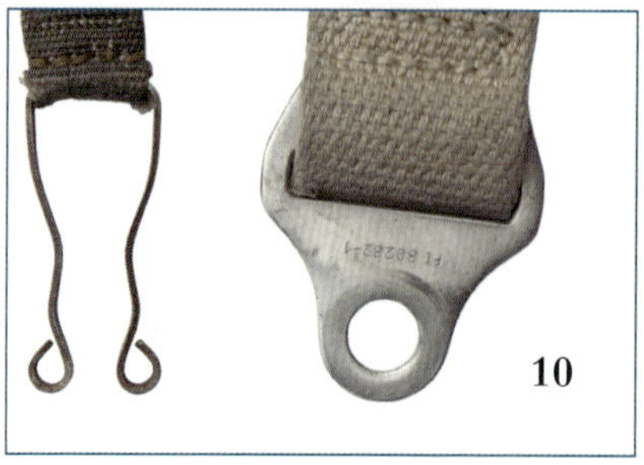

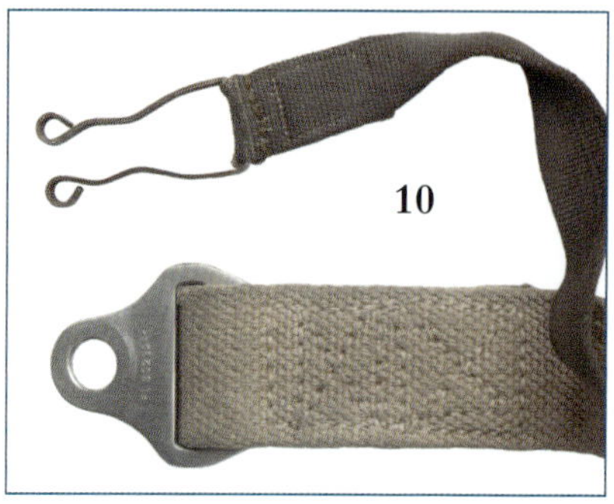

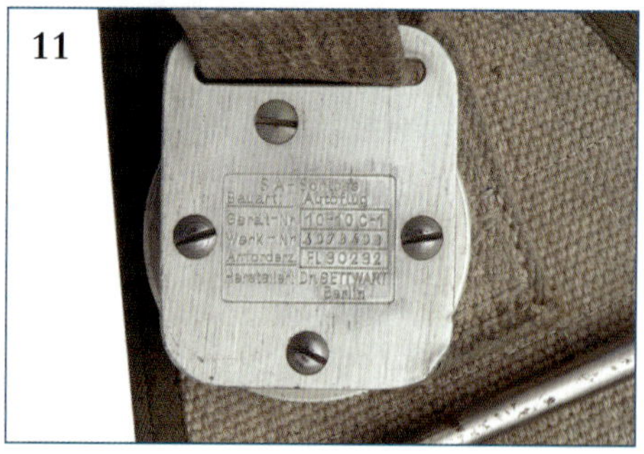

11. The face-plate had engraved instructions on how to release the harness. The inscription read: *"To release harness: Turn and push"*. On the side of the box , the wearer could see the position of the mechanism at a glance, with the red mark of the plate and the inscriptions *gesichert*, or *"safe"* and *ensichert*, or *"unlocked"*. The photo also shows the engraved spec and technical data markings found on the rear of the box.

GURTZEUG ABLEGEN-
DREHEN,
DANN DRÜCKEN!

12. The *Fallschirmtransporttasche* or parachute transport bag model TT1 was issued with all parachutes and allowed the airmen to carry and transport this delicate piece of equipment in a convenient way when it was not being worn or stored. The bag was made of heavy canvas fabric and had two handles. The large opening flap had *"lift-the-dot"* fasteners surrounding the edges as a closure system.

12

12

13

13. Detailed view of the cloth spec label, which included blank lines to write down the name of the owner of the parachute.

14

14. The snap fasteners had the words *Zieh Hier* or *"Pull Here"* stamped into the female socket.

14

Back parachutes

Rückenfallschirme

Model RH 12B (FL.30245) back parachute

The RH 12B back type parachute, also known as Rüfa 12B, consisted of a 24 panel canopy, a back packing bag and the harness. The harness was made of strong webbing and incorporated an oversized a belt strap with a quick-release system on one of the ends and a strap and a metal tip with two perforated eyelets on the other end that was inserted in the buckle. The two shoulders traps and two leg straps ended in metal tips with a single eyelet and fastened to the quick-release metal box. The parachute consisted of a khaki-colored parachute pack fitted to an aluminum tray, which was adjusted to the back of the airman together with the harness.

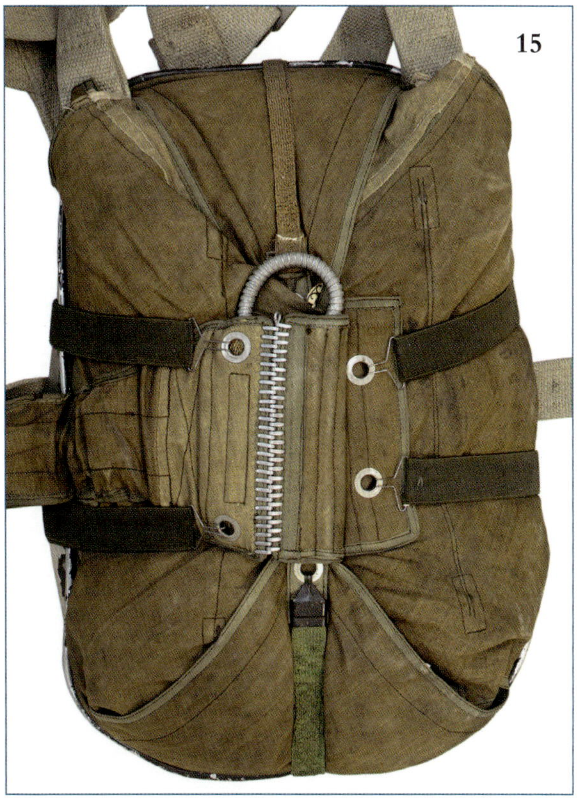

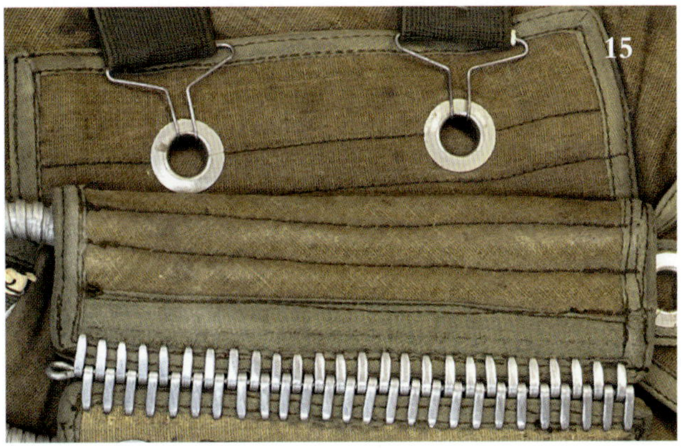

15. The pack was located to the rear of the tray and consisted of a four sided envelope-styled pack which contained the parachute. The pack was secured by means of a strong 150mm long metal zipper, which also acted as a shroud to the concealed connecting rip cord. This type of parachute was worn in aircraft which had a recess made into the back of the airman's seat.

16

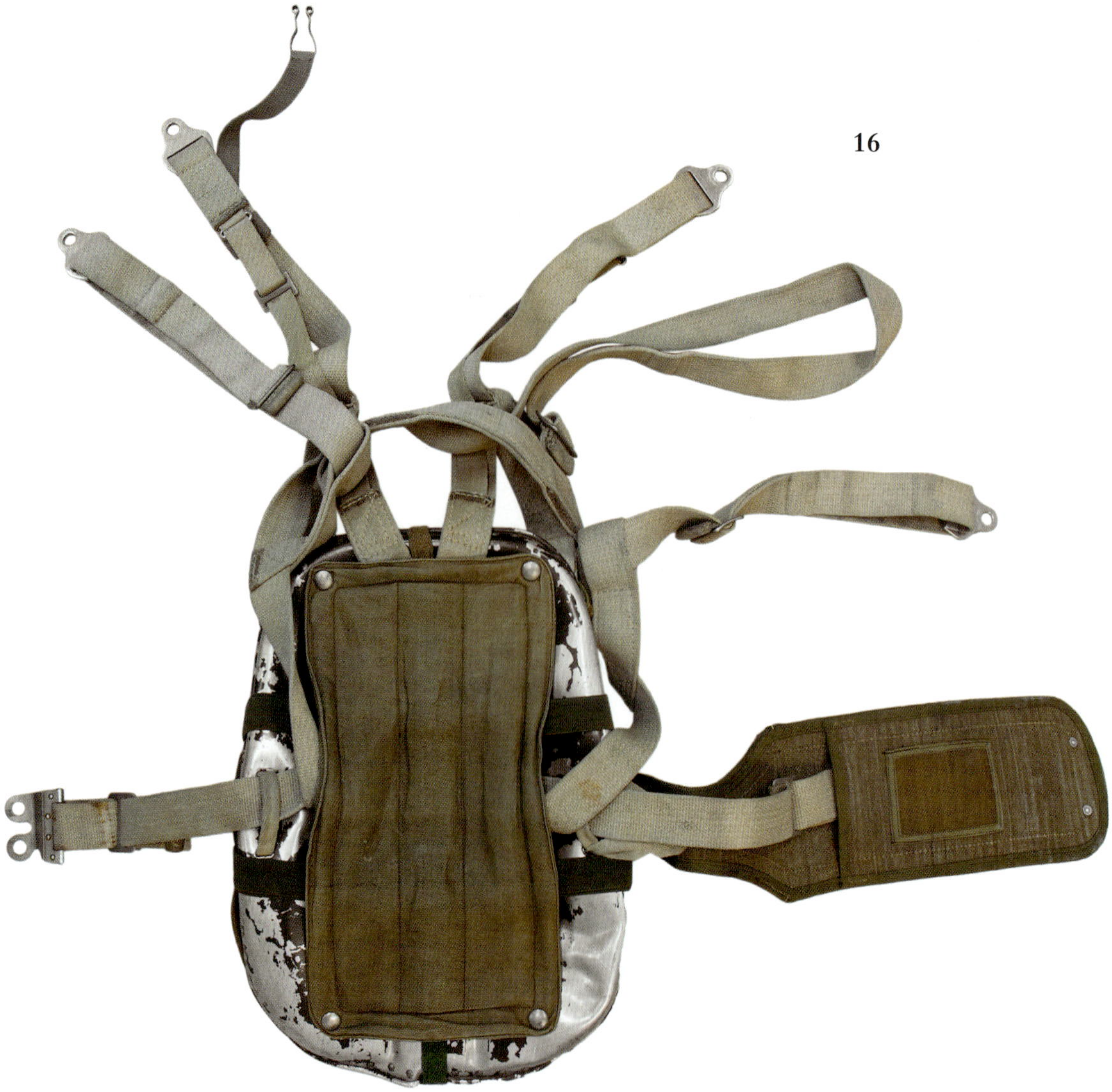

16. The tray was painted in dark green and was shaped to fit the airman's back. The parachute featured an innovative system, with the harness straps attached to the tray and the parachute bag, all of which was kept hidden beneath a padded fabric panel located between the tray and the back of the pilot. This padded panel was used as a cushion to protect the back of the wearer from the hard metal tray as well as for comfort. It was fixed to the tray by four metal press-studs, located on each corner.

17

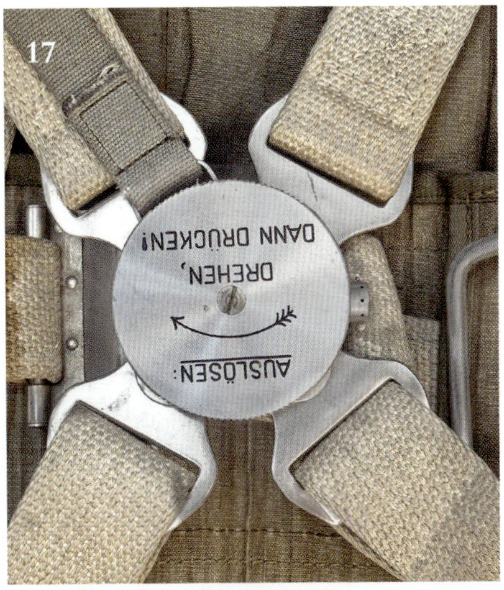

17

17

17. The quick-release system consisted in a metal box with four spring-activated pins. When the wearer wanted to release the harness, he had to rotate the front metal disc of the box 90 degrees and depress it with a strong blow. The use of a single-point quick-release box gave the wearer a considerable advantage, as it allowed him to free himself from his parachute harness without delay. This proved critical when the wearer was dragged on the ground, or if he landed on water.

17

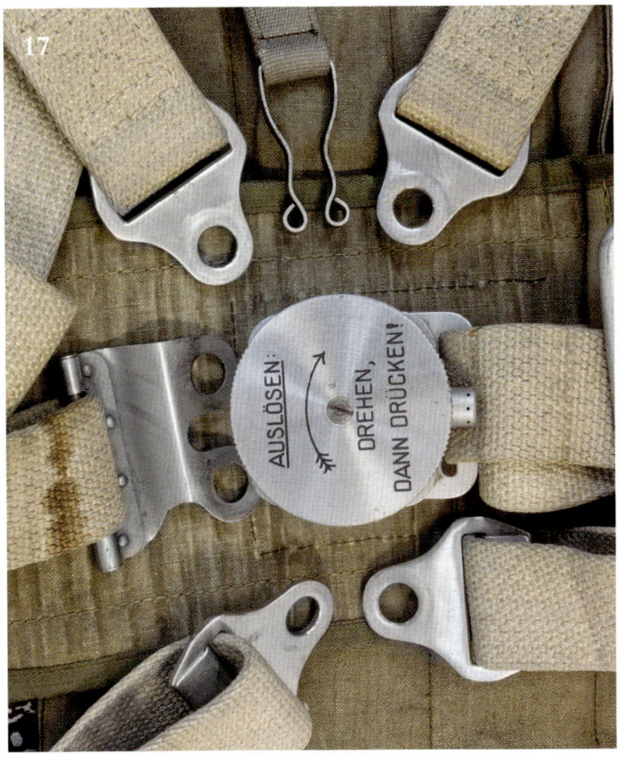

18

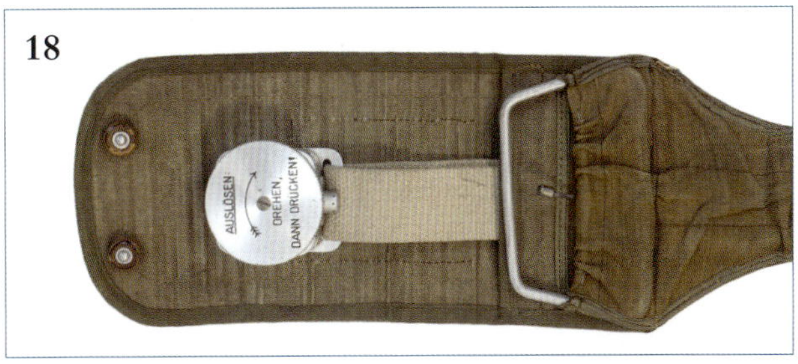

18

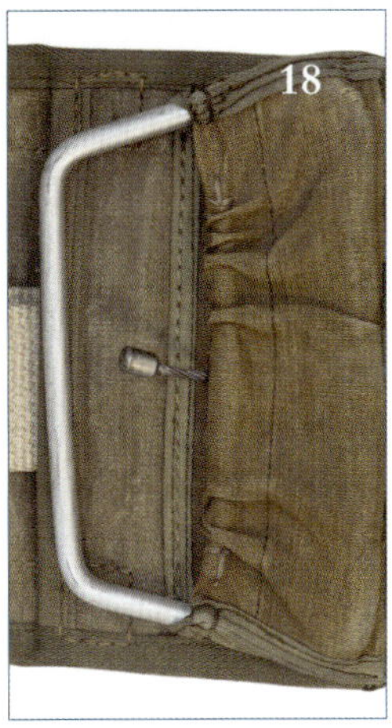

18. The rip cord extended to the left into the widening strap that held the quick-release metal box and ended over the wearer's stomach. This wide strap housed the trapezoid metal ring that pulled the rip cord. When the ring was pulled, the security threads were broken and the four flaps of the pack were turned back by the elastic cords, activating the pilot chute which pulled the main chute from the bag.

16. Operational and personal flight equipment

The navigator/bombardier of this Heinkel He 111 aircraft is giving information to the pilot. Notice that the navigator is wearing a back parachute, while the pilot wears no parachute at all. (Der Adler)

The *Luftwaffe* utilized assorted mechanical and electrical radio directional aids, primitive radars, precision target detection equipment and flight personnel were given basic training in manual navigation and map reading. Personnel who had elected or had been chosen to become flight observers undertook further blind-flight and navigational training.

Along with the mechanical and electrical radio directional navigation aids mounted on the aircrafts, the *Luftwaffe* also utilized two different models of manual flight navigation computers which were basically circular slide rulers to assist in navigation calculations, popularly known by the pilots as the Knemeyers. They were well designed pieces, with a metal frame that encircled five plastic disks and two cursors. This construction gave it a robust quality that would forgive even the most abusive treatment. The *Luftwaffe* issued a complete navigation kit to observers consisting of specially designed metal cases which opened and could be used in the confined space of the cockpits in the form of a laptop desk.

Many pilots and navigators were issued with oversized wrist chronometers with long straps which allowed them to be worn on top of the gloves or flight suits. They were produced by many well known German instrument companies.

The flyer that had to abandon a disabled aircraft, whether by bailout, a forced landing or ditching, was immediately in a very serious situation. Survival conditions were on occasions arduous, and space and weight considerations have always severely limited the type and amount of emergency equipment that can be carried. In case the flyer had to abandon his aircraft in flight, he needed essential equipment and supplies attached to his person. If he was to bring his plane down on land or

This crew member gears up for a mission. The photo demonstrates the large size of the navigation watch on his wrist. (Der Adler)

water, he had to be quick to retrieve his emergency gear. In addition to coping with difficult terrain, rough seas, and weather conditions, and his needs for food, water, and shelter, a downed aviator often found himself in a hostile area where he had to evade capture and escape to friendly or neutral territory. The *Luftwaffe* made a considerable effort to equip the crew members with personal and survival equipment for these situations. Flare pistols were an integral part of the toolkit of *Luftwaffe* crews. *Luftwaffe* crews developed an incredibly complicated signal code to communicate permutations during flights using a wide array of flares. Flight trousers had especially designed side pockets to house the flare pistol, and developed straps which were tied to the legs to increase the provisions of flares. Other elements of flight and survival equipment at the disposal of crew members were wrist compasses, used by pilots and aircrew members forced to abandon their aircraft or in crash landing situations, as well as Utility knives. They were not meant to be used as offensive weapons, but were versatile tools for crafts, medical emergencies and many other field uses.

These men are receiving training on the use of the flight computers, an important equipment designed to make navigation calculations.

Wrist watches

Armbanduhren

Tutima Glashütte wrist watch

The wrist watch was one of the most important elements of equipment for a fighter pilot or navigator. Aviators needed consistently accurate, robust and readily legible timepieces on their aircraft to determine their location and flight times. Crew members and fighter pilots were issued with oversized wrist watches that featured extra long straps which could be worn on the wrist or over the flight suits or gloves. These high precision timepieces were made by several German instrument companies, being one of the best known Tutima Uhrenfabrik AG Glashütte. The dial featured a black finish and Arabic numbers and included two registers, the left for constant seconds, and the right for 30 minutes intervals. The outer dial markings were gradated at 1/5 of a second and had skeleton pear hands.

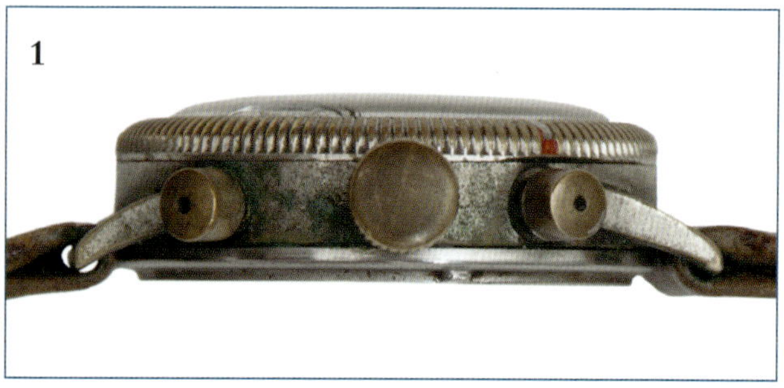

1

1. View of the case and the side crown and chronometer buttons. The upper pusher was used to start and stop the chronometer, while the lower pusher was used to reset the counter to zero. The central crown was used to wind the spring and to set the time. Notice the knurled bezel.

B-Uhr wrist watch for astronomical navigation

There were two *B-Uhr* types. The first type or Bauart A shown in the photos was issued in 1939, while the Bauart B was introduced in 1941. The *B-Uhr* had a large case with a diameter of 55 mm and was equipped with a large crown in order to allow manipulation with the flight gloves. The hacking feature, which stopped the seconds hand when the crown was pulled, was essential for a precise time setting. The oversized strap was made of brown leather. The markings on the back include the letters R.L.M., abbreviation for *Reichsluftfahrtministerium*, the name of the model and the serial number of the individual piece. Even though these timepieces cannot be considered precision watches, they were useful to pilots and crew members in the last years of the war, when the *Luftwaffe* operational radius became increasingly limited.

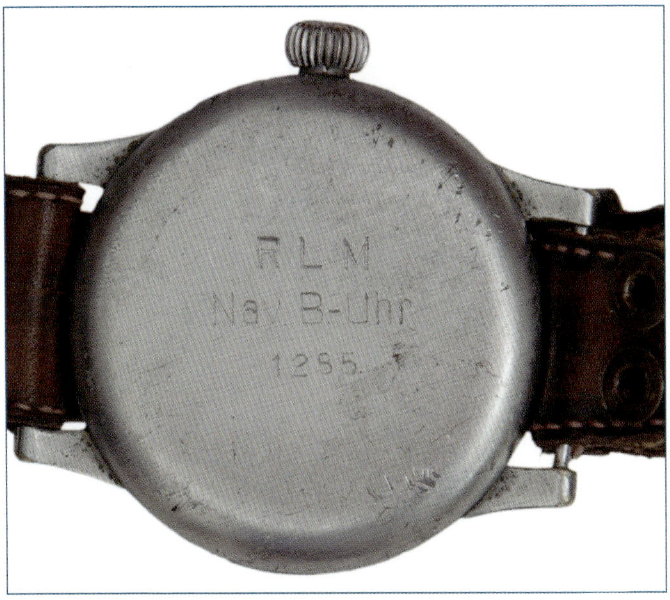

Wrist compasses

Armband-Kompasse

Model AK 39 wrist compass (first model)

The wrist compass was an essential tool for a downed aviator in a hostile area, as it was used to help him escape to friendly territory to evade capture. The designation AK stands for *Armband-Kompass* (wrist compass) while the number 39 is probably the year of issue, 1939. The compass had an oversized 61mm diameter black bakelite case with a depth of 20 mm, a weight of 80 gr and had a contoured back plate with the engraved nomenclature and other relevant data. The dial plate had a luminous gradated dial and it had a black bearing plastic bezel. The dial itself floated on a needle inside the case, which was filled with alcohol. The strap was made of black leather.

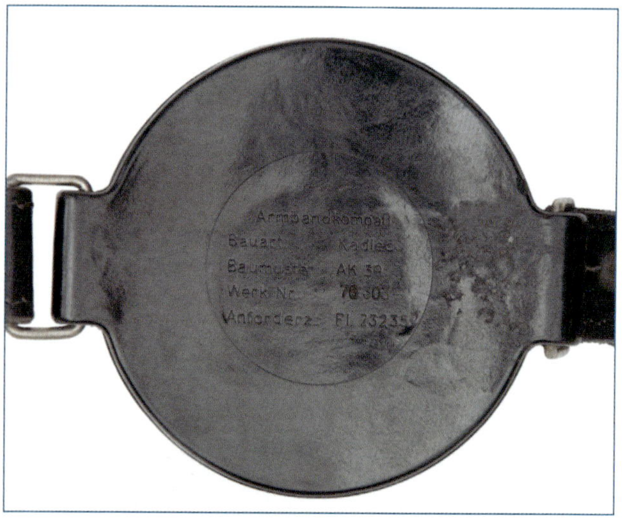

Model AK 39
wrist compass (first model variation)

At least two variants of the first model of AK 39 compass existed. The first one, shown in the previous page, had a black bearing plastic bezel, while the second variant, shown in this page, had a translucent one. This model had a black bakelite case and a contoured back plate. The case had the nomenclature and other data engraved on the back. The pilots could strap the wrist compass above their flight uniform or gloves with the help of a leather extension strap, or fix it to their belt or to any other part of their equipment, such as life preserver.

Model AK 39 wrist compass (second model)

The compass (Fl 23235-1) showed on the photos is the second of the two AK 39 main models. It allowed the setting of a course by means of two white rotating semi-circular discs located at the back. The specifications of aircraft instrument and flight accessory item nomenclature was established by the the *Reichsluftfahrtministerium*, (National Ministry of Aviation), assigning an *Anforderungszeichen* (order reference number) to each specific item, preceded by the letters FL, which stand for *Fliegermaterial*. The AK 39 was equipped with an additional, extended, strap when worn over the sleeve of the flight suits, but it was not unusual for the pilots to wear it tied to the life vest, looped around the belt or other various assorted pieces of equipment.

2

3

2. The translucent top plate had a plastic bezel that rotated for aligning directional headings. The interior of the compass was filled with alcohol. It featured a free floating clear bakelite plate with a luminous arrow pointing the north heading and 360 degree directional markings in increments of 30 degrees with luminous dots. Notice the red sighting aids, introduced in 1943.

3. View of the back of the compass, with the two white adjustable marching course half-disks. The interior white section of the bottom plate is marked with printed AK 39 designation, as well as the *Luftwaffe* requisition number, *"Fl 23235-1"*.

Model AK 39 wrist compass (second model variation)

This compass is an unmarked specimen, but shows all the features of the second model of the AK 39 *Armband-Kompass*. The plastic bezel is translucent and the sighting aides are colored in black, instead of the more usual red color. The inner dial plate is also translucent, with directional markings in a luminous color. The strap is made of black leather with a single claw buckle.

Flight navigation computers

Dreieckrechner

DR 2 flight navigation computer

The DR 2 a dead reckoning flight computer popularly known by the pilots as *KnemeyerIn*, was a triangle computer designed to make navigation calculations. Many DR 2 flight computers were designed by *C. Plath* of Hamburg. DR 2 Flight computers had 15cm of diameter, were screwed together and had a metal outer rim. They featured a compass side and a calculating side. The compass side had a rose with cardinal and inter-cardinal directional points. The aircraft symbol identified the heading of the aircraft. The outer rim had instructions for use, which were absent in later production specimens. The outer cursor had parallel sides. The calculating side had an outer ring with a logarithmic scale from 1 to 90 degrees and back to 179 degrees. The middle ring had two logarithmic speed scales, and finally the inner ring had time scales.

DR 3 flight navigation computer

The DR 3 was an improvement of the previous DR 2 model, the basic construction was the same, except for the cursors, which were wider in the pivoting points, and the joining of the discs, which used rivets instead of screws. It had a 15 cm diameter, dual sided, multi-piece, molded black and white bakelite construction, flight navigation computer with aluminum rivets. The compass side featured black bakelite outer circle with white, 360 degree numerical compass markings with cardinal and inter-cardinal directional points. The inner circle was made of white bakelite, with printed black and red 360 degree numerical compass markings, as well as the outline of an aircraft with directional arrow. Finally the top contained a cursor with a wide pivoting point. The calculating side of the computer featured white bakelite three movable inner and outer circles, all of them with printed black, red and white, numerical degrees, temperature and kilometre markings.

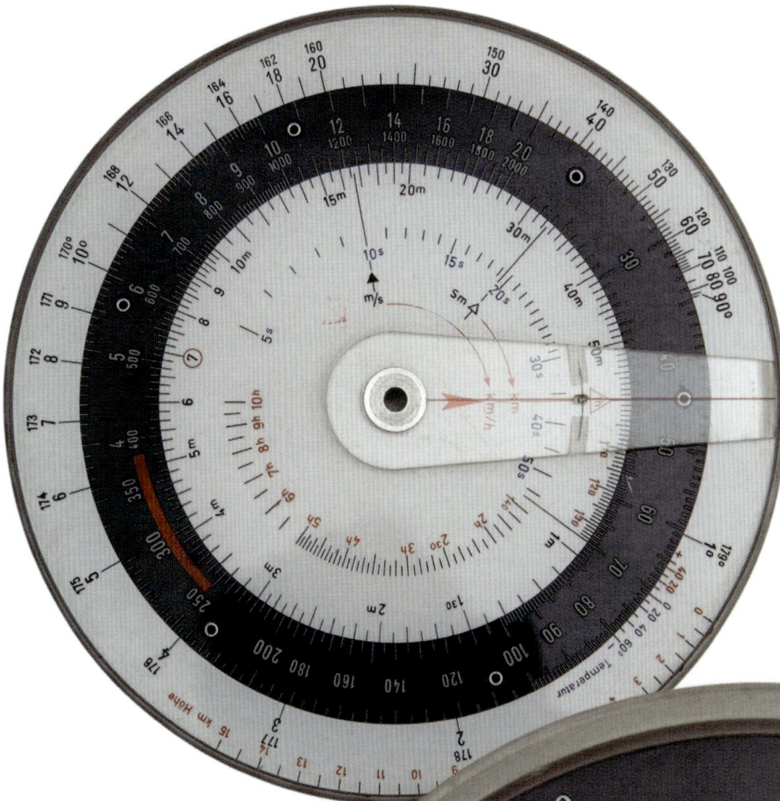

Flare pistols

Leuchtpistolen

Walther Heeres-Modell flare pistol

The *Heeres-Modell* signal pistol was developed by the *Carl Walther* company of Zella Mehlis and adopted in 1928 to replace the earlier Hebel M1894 model. The first specimens were made of steel. In1934 the material changed to aluminum alloy and finally of zinc alloy in 1943. The main purpose of the flare guns was signalling. *Luftwaffe* crews developed an incredibly complicated signal code to communicate permutations during flights using a wide array of flares. The flare pistol was also used by downed pilots to mark their location to rescue planes or by air crews to signal the presence of wounded crew members when approaching the base and radio contact was lost. Pre-war guns had commercial Walther markings and wooden grips.

4

5

4. The pre-World War II pistols were produced by Walther, and were initially made of steel with wood grip panels and later of an anodized aluminum alloy called duralumin. In 1943, the composition of the flare pistols was changed to zinc, with bakelite grips.

5. Detail of the inspection and firing proof stamps found on the right side of the chamber. German 1891 Proof Act stamps were used use between 1892 and 1939 and found on all small arms made between those two dates.

6

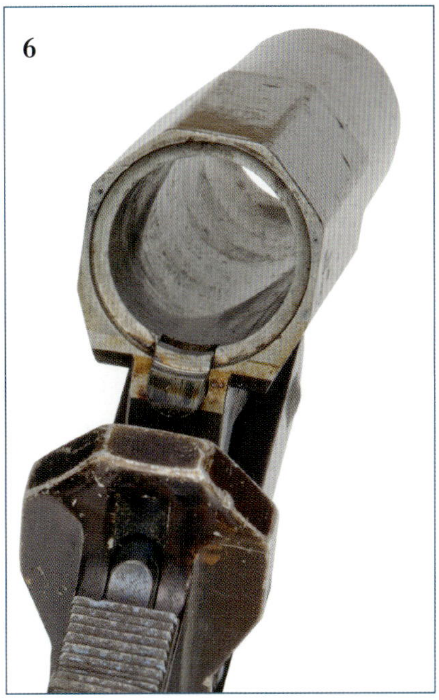

6. The pistol featured an 8cm long barrel, without including the breach. The soft-bored barrel had a diameter of 30mm with an octagonal shaped receiver end. The bottom edge of the receiver had a steel trigger with an integral trigger guard. The top reverse edge of the receiver had a pull-back trigger hammer with a pin head activator.

6

7. The forward edge of the trigger guard had an additional, steel, push, finger lever which activated an internal barrel locking mechanism and also enabled the barrel hinge to be folded forward to load the pistol.

7

8

8. The pistol of the photos was made in 1937. Pre-war guns have the commercial Walther stamp markings. The N4002 number stands for *Nachrichtenmittel* 4002, which is considered by some experts as a specific supply number of the *Luftwaffe*.

Flares

Signalpatronen

The flare pistols fired a variety of more than forty different types of signal rounds, including light, parachute, star cluster, whistling shell and smoke signals. Each of the flares had a color code and in some cases the bottom rim had a notch to indicate the type of flare, an aid when they were to be used at night. A specially designed pouch was made to contain 18 assorted flares, with six assorted flares in three rows. It was made either of black leather or green strong webbing fabric.

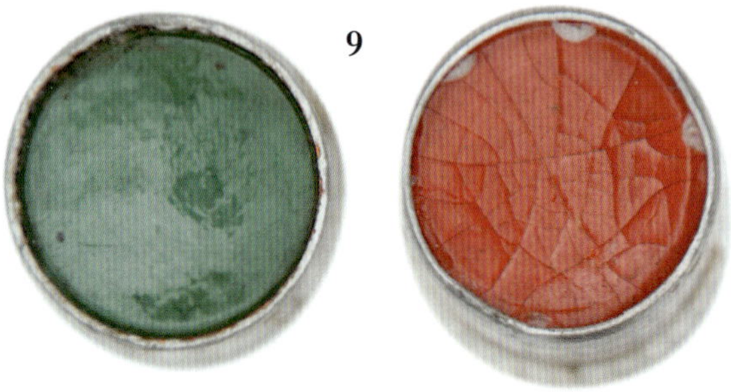

9

9. Detailed top view of red and green flares. The top and side of the flares had color codes indicating the main color of the flare for a fast identification by the user.

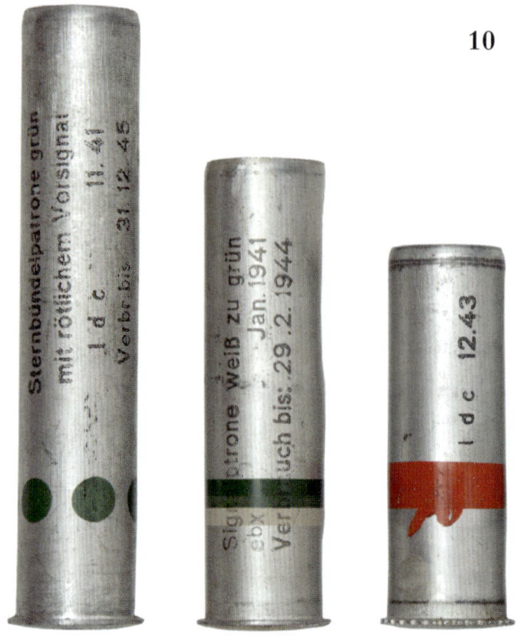

10

10. View of three different flares. The side markings and text indicated the type of flare and the colors it would display once fired. The information included the maker code and the date of manufacture. In some cases, the base of the flares was milled for easy identification in darkness.

10

11. The six green circles on the case plus the description of the top flare cartridge indicates that it fires a red flare that transforms into six green stars after reaching a distance of 90 meters. The flare on the bottom fires a white flare that transforms to green. Each flare color and pattern was meant to give a specific message. All flight personnel received training on how to interpret their meaning accurately.

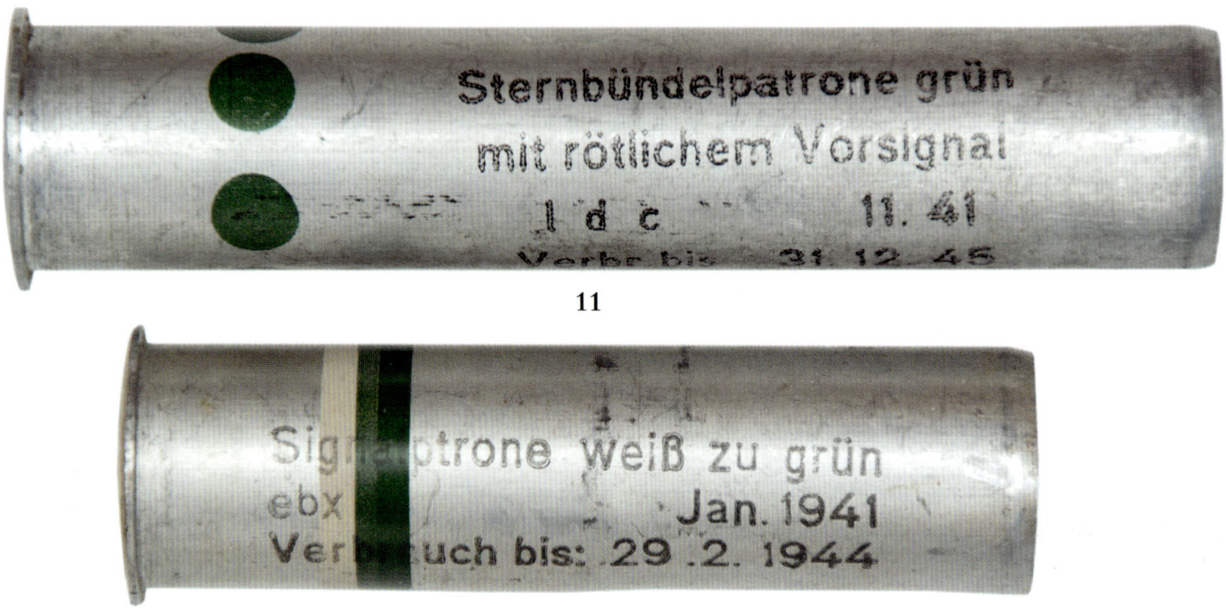

11

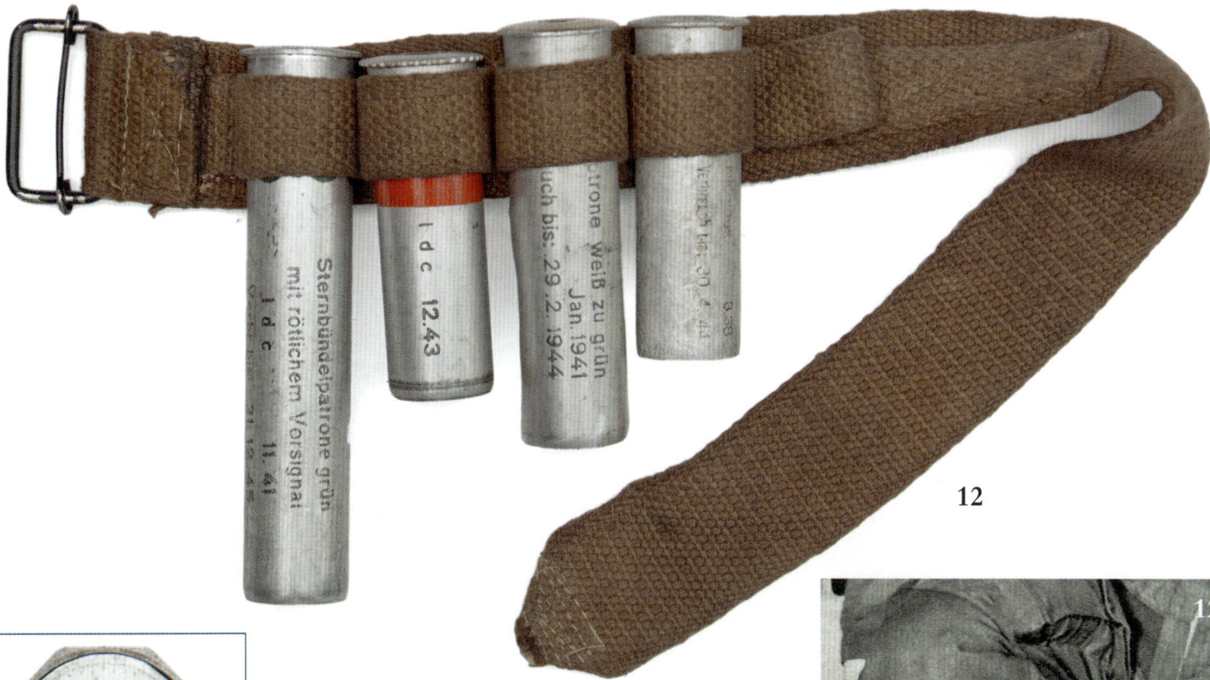

12

12. German flight crew members carried their flares in the pockets of their trousers, but often the space was not enough for the wide array of flares at their disposal. Initially, flare straps were locally field-made, but later the *Luftwaffe* issued a standardized strap for all flight crewmen. It was made of blue-grey cotton twill and had a capacity of ten flares, although early models had compartments for between six and twelve flares. The strap was tied around the leg, the flying boot or the waist , fastened with a friction buckle.

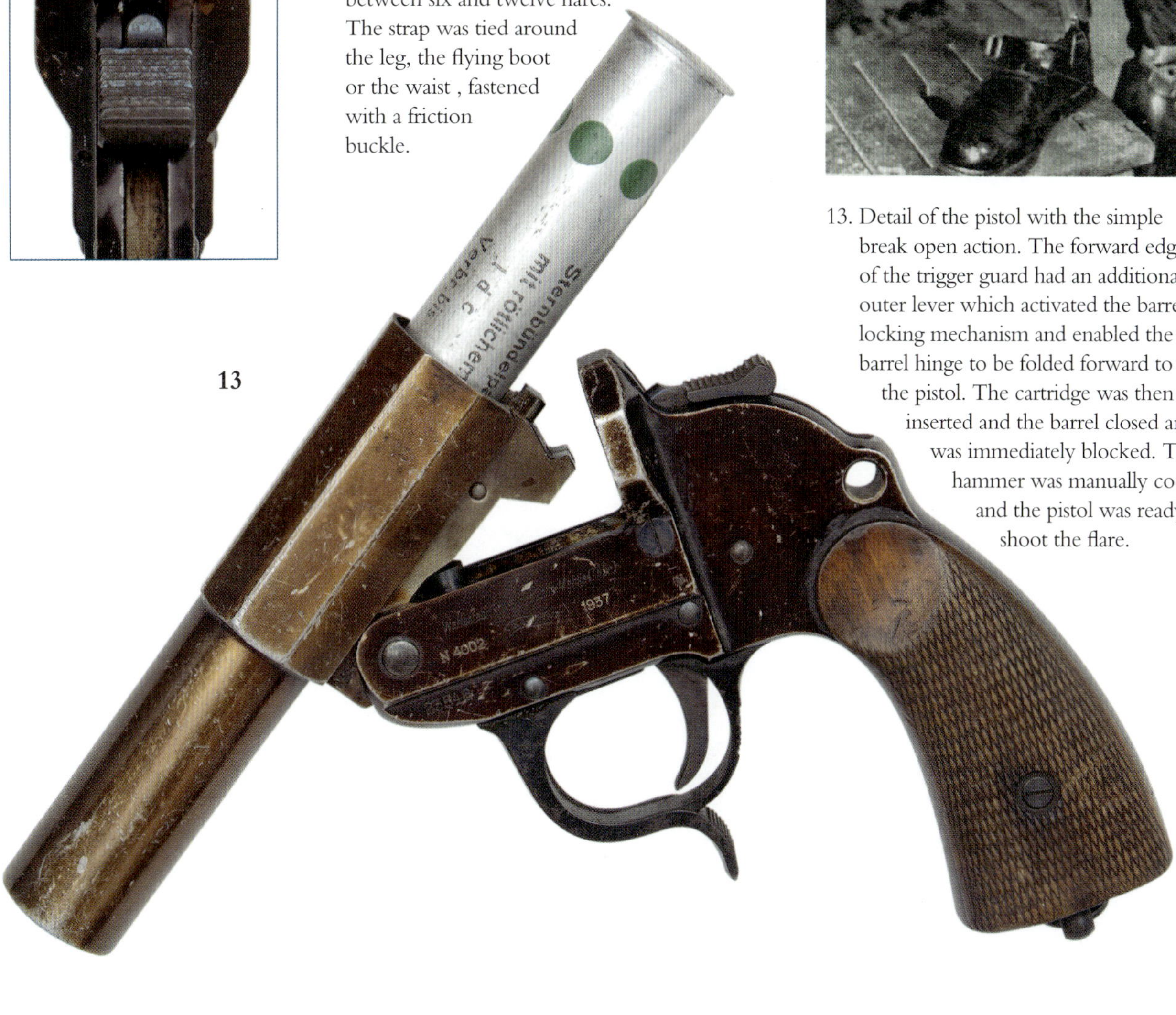

13

13. Detail of the pistol with the simple break open action. The forward edge of the trigger guard had an additional outer lever which activated the barrel locking mechanism and enabled the barrel hinge to be folded forward to load the pistol. The cartridge was then inserted and the barrel closed and was immediately blocked. The hammer was manually cocked and the pistol was ready to shoot the flare.

Utility knife

Fliegerkappmesser

The utility knife was introduced in 1937 for parachutists and aircraft crew members. The knife was also known as *"gravity"* knife because of the special design, which enabled the blade to be extended or retracted with only one hand, using the force of gravity. Two types of utility knives were made during the war. The first one was assembled with no possibility to take it apart, making the maintenance of the knives very impractical. As a result, in the summer of 1941 a take-down version of the knife was adopted, which allowed the knife to be easily disassembled for cleaning and repair.

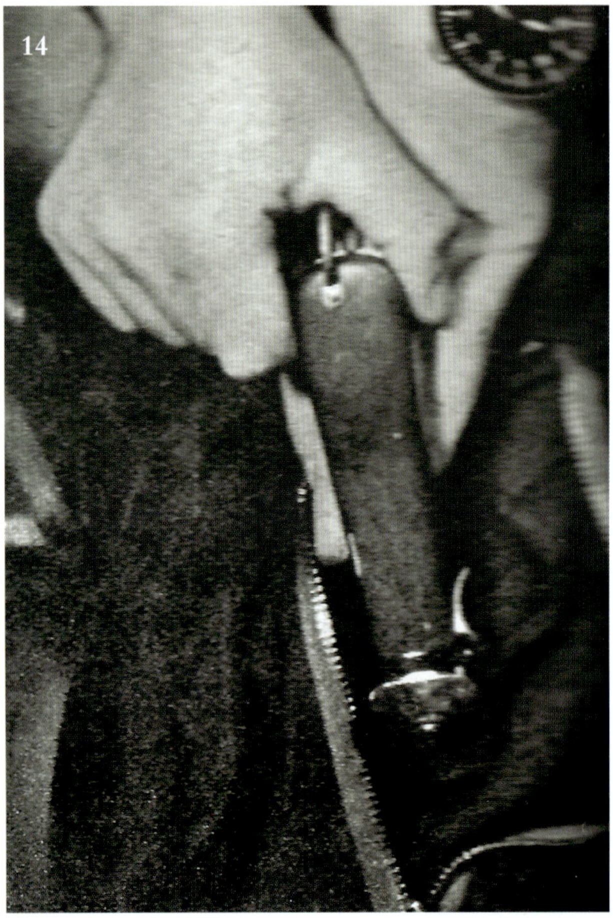

14

14

14. The blade was housed inside the grip plates of the handle and secured by an activator lever located on the side. When the knife was pointed downwards and the lever pressed, the gravity caused the blade to slide from the housing and extend. To house the blade back, the user had to hold the knife blade-up and depress the lever a second time, making it slide back in the handle. Crew members usually stored the knife in the pocket of the *"Channel"* trousers.

14

15. The knife featured nickel-plated stainless steel mounts. The grips were covered by wood plates, usually made of walnut, oak or beech, fixed to the metal plates by pins. The end of the knife had a wire loop.

16. A lanyard with metal carbine hooks on both ends was attached to the metal loop of the utility knife and fixed to a loop located in the inside of the *"Channel"* trouser pocket or tied to the belt. This way, the user always had the knife within reach.

15

16

17. A fold-out marlin spike was fixed to the narrow side of the handle, on the opposite side of the lever. Its function was to untangle rope knots, and could also be used as a prying tool. The fixed metal throat shows this specimen belongs to the first type, which could not be disassembled by the user.

17

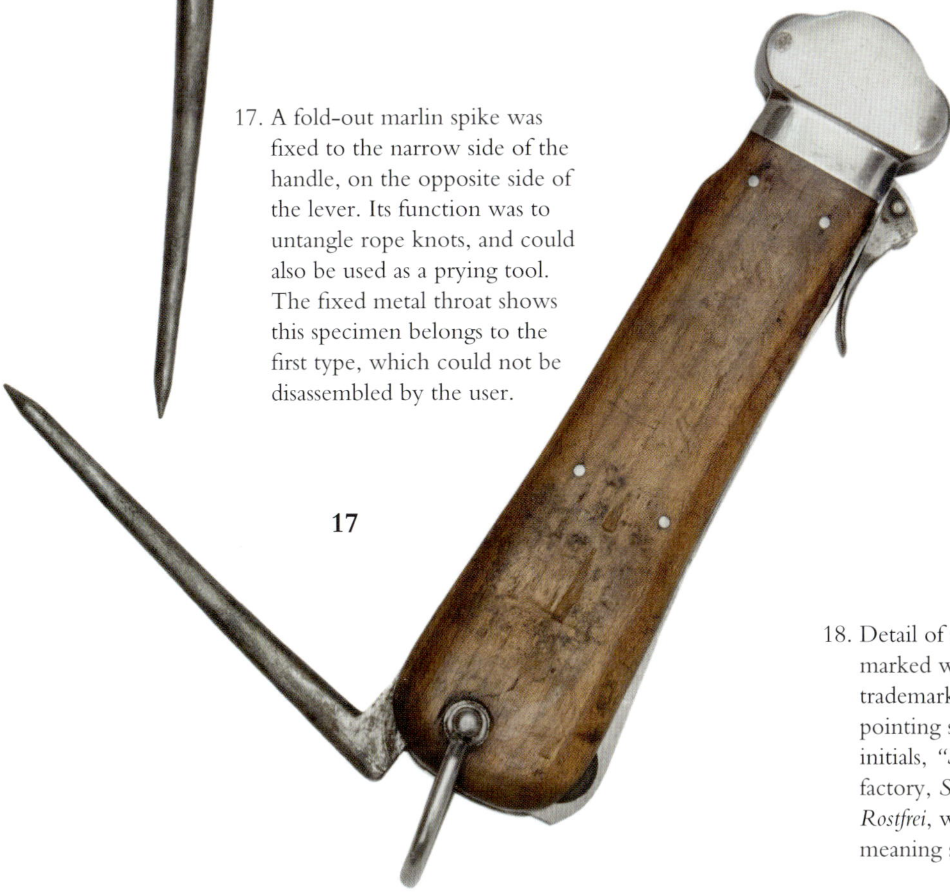

18

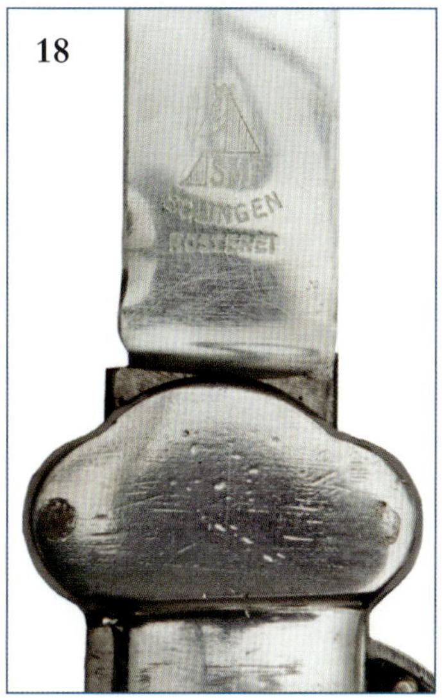

18. Detail of the blade marking.The blade is marked with the *Stocker & Co* manufacturer trademark. The king holds an upward pointing sword and is seated over the firm's initials, *"SMF"*. Below, the location of the factory, *Solingen* and below this the word *Rostfrei*, which literally translates to *"rust free"*, meaning stainless steel.

17. Pistols

The practice of carrying sidearms by the pilots and crew members doesn't seem to have been widespread. Although *Luftwaffe* aircrews were issued with sidearms, apparently the decision to wear them during combat missions depended largely on each individual. However, it is safe to assume that it was more common to carry weapons on the Eastern Front due to the hostile nature of the theater of operations, as the photographic evidence clearly shows. Equally it is assumed the practice also took place on the western front after the Allied invasion of mainland Europe in 1944. The P.08, used in the initial phases of the war, was eventually replaced by smaller types that were easier to carry in fighter aircrafts. In the final phases of the war, when the pilots were fighting over the Reich territory, they would hardly be needed.

When the Nazis gained power in 1933, the official service pistol of the German armed forces was still the outdated P.08 pistol. Even though the gun was a masterpiece of engineering, studies by the *Heereswaffenamt* showed that the design and manufacturing process was too expensive and complicated. Trials for a simpler pistol were undertaken by Walther as early as the years of the Weimar republic, and after solving some design problems, the Walther pistol was adopted on April 1940 as the P.38. The *Luftwaffe* signed several contracts to supply their troops with P.08 pistols; the most notable with Heinrich Krieghoff of Suhl in 1936 to acquire 10,000 guns. Even thought these weapons had an excellent quality, they represented an insignificant quantity of the all pistols acquired by the Air Force, compared to the more than 130,000 Lugers supplied to the *Oberkommando der Luftwaffe* by Mauser-Werke during the war.

Members of a Luftwaffe *unit have the weapons inspected by their NCO. Notice the sidearm on his belt.*

With the expansion of the war, the Wehrmacht still needed to arm a growing number of servicemen of all branches, as well as police forces and paramilitary organizations with handguns. As a result, these forces were supplied with German blowback pistols. Mauser had produced a single action conventional blowback pistol based on the Modell 1914. Even though it offered a good overall quality, it was procured in relatively small numbers, some 8,000 for the *Wehrmacht*. Other Mauser pistol supplied to the armed forces was the HSc, with a more sleek appearance. Even though most of the war production ended up in the hands of the police and the paramilitary, some made their way to the *Luftwaffe* to arm their pilots and aircrews.

But, in spite of the high amount of weapons produced by German factories, production always fell short of the needs of the country's rapidly-growing army, and thus several contracts were signed with neutral and German allied countries. Hungary had a small but competent small arms industry which manufactured all types of infantry weapons, from rifles to machineguns. The blowback adaptation of the *Frommer* pistols had been adopted by the Hungarian army as the 37M, and soon the German army secured a contract for 50,000 pistols in 1941 for a chambered in 7.65mm on behalf of the *Luftwaffe*. At the same time, the German army captured huge amounts of weapon from their enemies and also placed the weapons factories of the conquered countries under the control of the *Deutsche Waffen-und Munitionsfabriken Aktien-Gesellschaft* (German Weapons and Munitions public limited company), known as DWM. This was the case of the Belgian *Fabrique Nationale d'Armes de Guerre*, FN; the plant located in Hertal made hundreds of thousands of small arms for the Wehrmacht. Their inventory included the model 1922 pistol, a single action blowback designed by John Browning that chambered the 7,65mm cartridge. Soon after the FN factory fell in German hands, production of the weapon, designated as Pistolen 626 (b), resumed with most of the initial deliveries going to The *Luftwaffe*, which received some 100,000 by the end of 1942.

The pilot of the photo is describing combat maneuvers to his comrades using his hands. The pilot listening to his explanation is wearing a Femaru P.37 (u) holster on his belt. This Hungarian pistol was one of the models used by German pilots in the Eastern front.

German pistols

Deutsche Pistolen

2

Model P.08 pistol

The Parabellum Pistole 08 was a recoil-operated semi-automatic pistol originally designed by Georg Luger in 1898. The Luger model 1904, in 9mm caliber, was adopted by the German army *(Reichswehr)* in 1908. The pistol was accurate, but difficult and expensive to mass-produce. However, it was used extensively during the First World War. With the defeat of Germany, production for the most part ceased as the Versailles Treaty placed restrictions on the German armament industry. The advent of conscription in Germany on 1935 accelerated the production of all small arms and soon *Mauserwerke* began supplying the army of P.08 pistols at a monthly production rate of 10,000 guns. Other manufacturers joined in production, and in 1934 the *Luftwaffe* negotiated a contract for additional military pistols with the firm Heinrich Krieghoff, a company with an excellent reputation in the sport firearms business. Around 14,000 Krieghoff P.08 pistols were eventually produced until 1945.

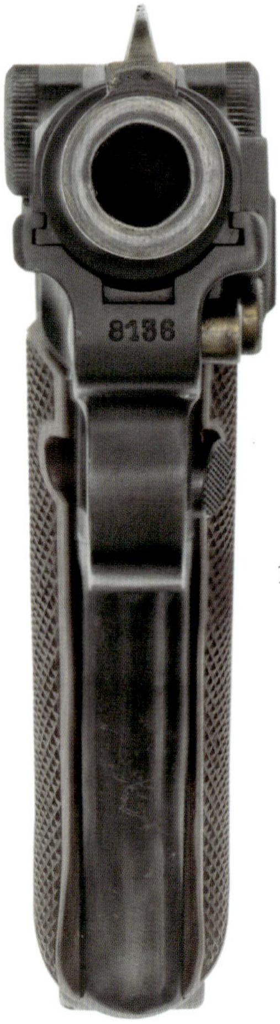

1

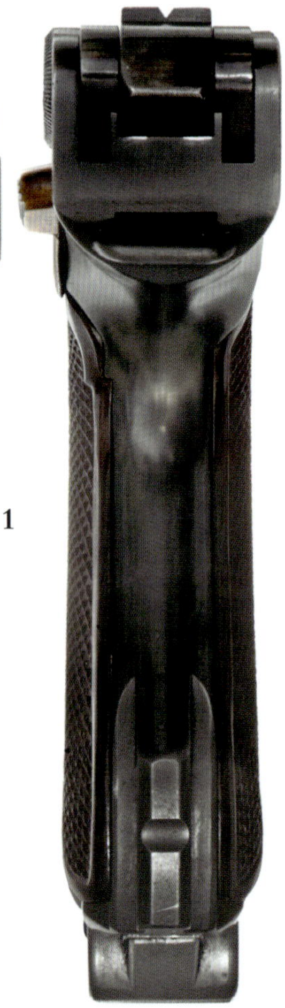

2

2. The magazine could be plated or blued and had a capacity of eight 9mm rounds. Pistols were issued with magazines with matching serial numbers. The serial number was engraved on the magazine bottom. The magazine of the photos is the extruded version, introduced around the 8,000 serial number.

3

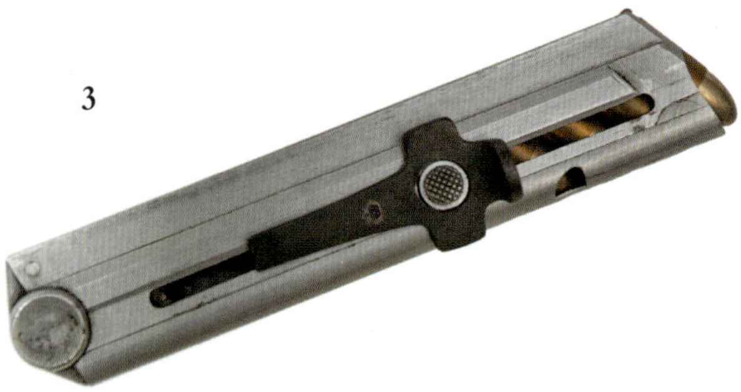

1. Front and back view of the P. 08 pistol. The serial number was engraved on the front of the frame and the side of the receiver. Notice the locking bolt on the left side of the frame. The magazine bottom clearly protrudes from the grip.

3. The P.08 tool was originally issued alongside each pistol, in a pocket inside the cover flap of the hard-shell holster. The tool worked as a magazine loader and take down utensil. Placing the hole of the tool over the load assist button of the magazine provided increased pull and made the loading much easier. It was also used to aid in the disassembly of several parts of the pistol. Magazines were marked with the serial number. The specimen of the photos includes an Eagle 2 Krieghoff proof marking.

4. There were at least seven different logos that were engraved on top of the toggle of the Krieghoff pistols over the years. The marking on the specimen of the photos consist of the sword and anchor with the letters *"H K"* on each side, and below, the legend *"KRIEGHOFF SUHL"* in two lines. The letter *"I"* is centered over the letter *"S"* and the *"U"* has a flat bottom.

5. The right side of the receiver is stamped with two Krieghoff *"L"* Eagle 2 inspection proofs flanking a single military acceptance stamp. Additional Krieghoff Eagle 2 proofs appear on the front of the right side rail and on the bottom of the barrel.

6. Detailed photo of the production year of the pistol, 1937, engraved on top of the chamber.

7. Early magazine bottoms had the Eagle 2 Krieghoff proof marking engraved upside down. In later production pistols it was turned over to read in the same direction as the serial number. The reason for this unique practice is not known.

8. The P.08 pistol used 9mm Parabellum ammunition. The boxes are pre-war commercial ammunition made by the firm *Gustav Genschow & Co A.G.* of Durlach. The brand SINOXID was the trademark of non-corrosive priming used in some German ammunition.

8

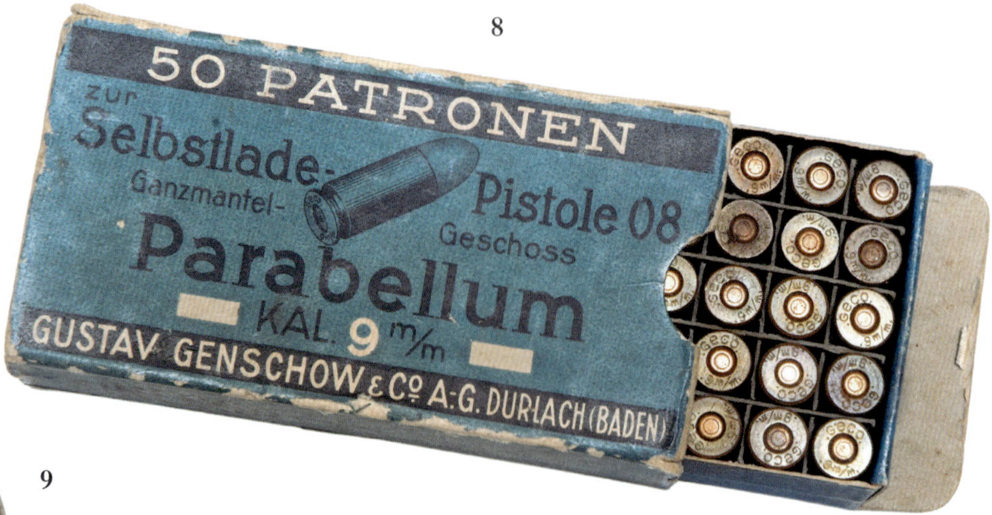

9

9. The 9mm Parabellum caliber cartridge consisted of a jacketed leadcore in a straight-sided brass case. The headstamp information in this cartridge includes the designation of *"GECO"* which stands for *Gustav Genschow & Co*, as well as the caliber.

8

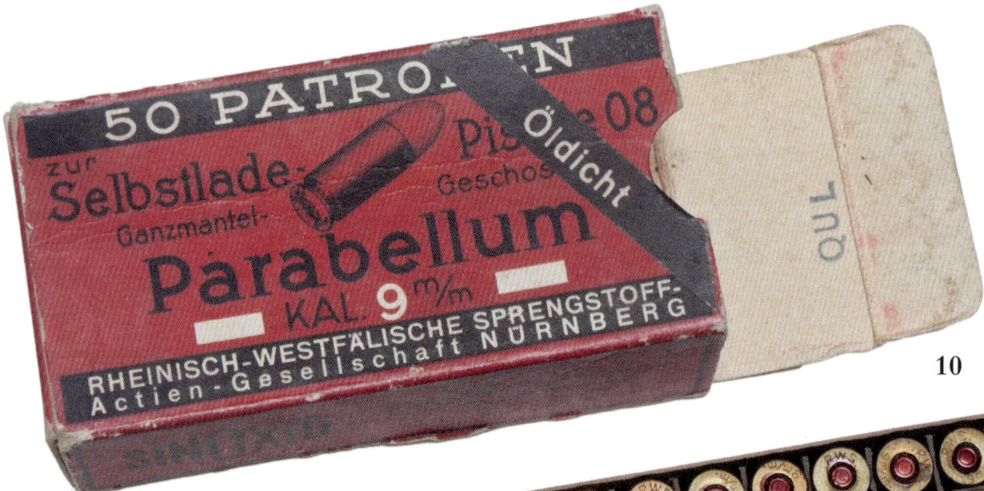

10

10. This pre-war commercial box of 9mm Parabellum ammunition has the trademark of *Rheinisch-Westfälische Sprengstoff-Fabriken A.G.* of Nürnberg and the cartridges marked with the RWS headstamp. The similarities of this box with those made by *Genschow & Co* shown in this page are not casual. RWS and GECO signed an agreement in 1927 under which the manufacture of pistol cartridges and shot shells of both companies would be manufactured in the Durlach plant of *Genschow & Co.*

11

12

11. Detailed view of the side plate and the locking bolt on the left of the frame. The serial number was engraved on the front of the frame and the side of the receiver.

12. Detail of the manual safety area of the P.08 pistol located on the left side of the frame. The surface under the lever was marked to indicate the position of the safety. When the word *"GESICHERT"* (Safe) was exposed and not covered by the lever, it was an indication that the safety was engaged.

12

13

13. The P.08 pistol was issued with a standard hard-shell holster. It had a fold back scalloped top flap with a horizontal stitched hinge to the reverse. The top had a stitched closure strap on the front, which attached diagonally to a leather roller buckle located on the center front of the holster body. An extra magazine pocket was stitched vertically along the forward edge. The holster had an internal quick release pull strap on the front body. The reverse had two slightly angled stitched belt loops. The holster of the photos is marked with the name of the manufacturer, *Gebrüder Klinge* of Dresden, is dated in 1937 and has the eagle over *"WaA142"* Waffenamt stamp.

14

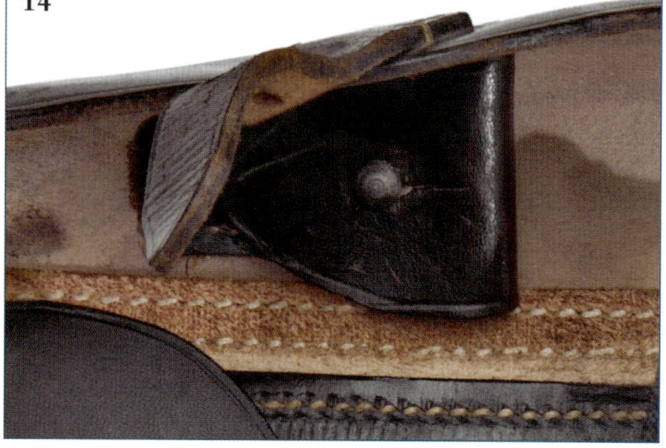

14. The interior of the top flap had a small leather pocket with a steel stud closure flap that housed the loading tool. It was used to ease the loading of the magazine and as a take down utensil.

The photo shows a Luftwaffe *music band playing their instruments, probably to entertain troops in the field. The* Unteroffizier *on the foreground is wearing a P.08 in a hard-shell holster fixed to his service belt.*

Model Mauser 1934 pistol

The Mauser Pocket Pistol first appeared in 1910, when German designers from the famous maker developed a new, simple blowback semiautomatic pistol, chambered for the 9x19mm Luger ammunition. In 1914 the pistol was redesigned and issued in 7.65mm caliber for the first time. The major changes of this new version were the redesign of the magazine and the introduction of an ejector which also held the slide in the opened position when the magazine was empty. In 1934, Mauser introduced a final version of this pistol, known as Model 1934; the major modification was the curved shape of the grip panels. At the beginning of World War II, the Model 1934 was outdated and was only adopted as a substitute standard. The *Wehrmacht* ordered only a small amount of 8,000 pieces that were used mainly by the *Kriegsmarine*, the *Luftwaffe* and other police forces.

16

15

16

16. The eight-round magazine had a machined steel follower that locked the slide open when the magazine was empty. The pistol used a 7.65mm (.32 ACP) cartridge with a bullet weight of 74 grains.

17. Detailed view of the machined steel magazine release. The logo of the manufacturer was engraved on the base plate of the magazine, which recessed into the base of the grip. The magazines were blued.

17

15. Front and back view of the Modell 34 pistol. The photo of the back shows the cocking indicator. The firing pin protruded from the orifice of the rear of the gun when the action was cocked, while it was not visible when the weapon was not cocked, providing a clear visual indication of the state of the gun.

18. View of the muzzle and front sight. The barrel retention pin head is visible below the muzzle. The complete serial number was stamped on the left front extension of the slide, while the last three digits were stamped on other parts of the pistol.

19. The pistol was marked on the left side of the frame with the *"WaA655" Waffenamt* inspector stamp, used for the company *Mauserwerke A.G. Oberndorf* from 1938 to 1941, together with the Army test proof stamp, an eagle over a swastika in a circle.

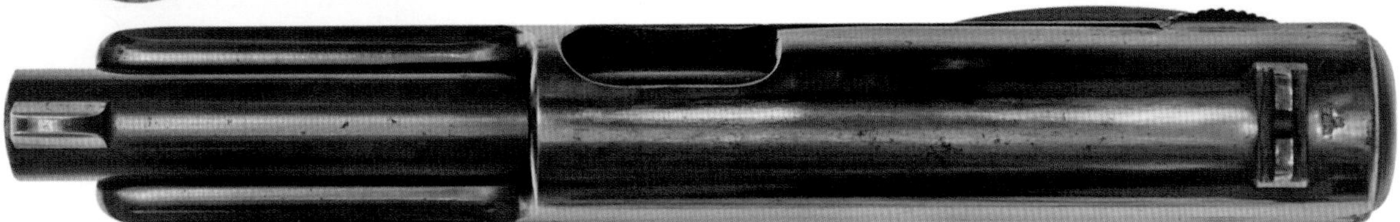

20

20. The right side of the slide had the inscription *"Cal. 7.65 D.R.P.u.A.P"*. The pistol had brown walnut grips with a checkered pattern.

21

21. One of the most notable differences between the 1934 pistol and the previous 1914 variant was the shape of the grip, which was redesigned with a slight curve to make it more ergonomic. Procurement was minimal; some 8,000 units were manufactured for the *Wehrmacht*.

22

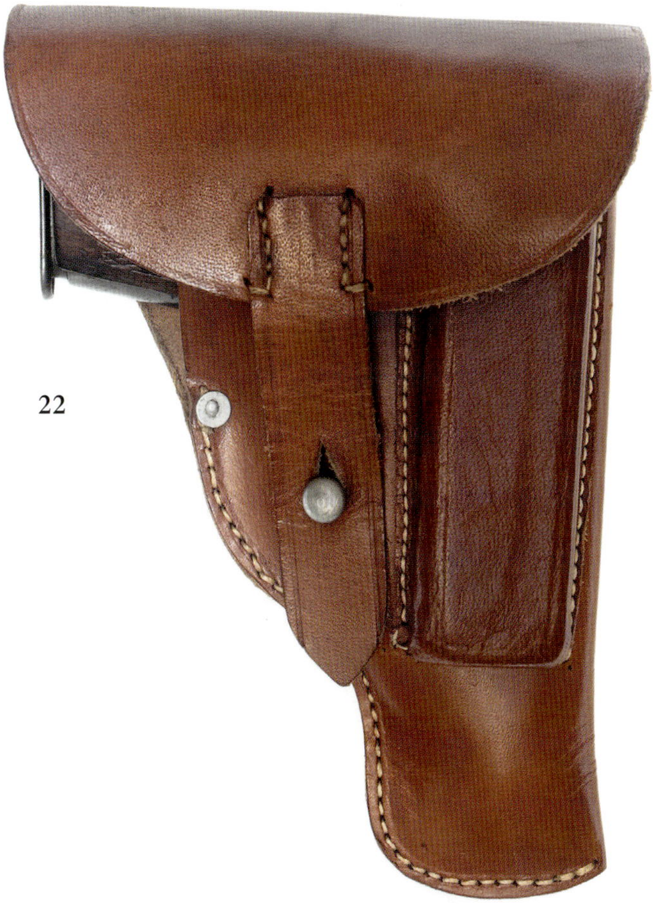

22

22. The holster was made of smooth brown leather. It featured a fold over top flap with a stitched vertical closure strap with a single eyelet. The closure strap attached to a steel stud on the holster body. It had a spare magazine pocket stitched to the right front. The back of the holster had a slightly angled vertical belt loop. The specimen of the photos bears the name *"SCHAMBACH & Co BERLIN"*, a *Waffenamt* eagle marking and is dated in 1942.

22

Model Mauser HSc pistol

The Mauser HSc was a blowback operated, compact pistol. The name HSc was an acronym of *Hahn-Selbstspanner Pistole Ausführung C*, or *"self-cocking hammer pistol, model C"*. Design and development of the Model HSc pistol took place in the late thirties at the Mauser-Werke plant in Oberndorf am Neckar, Germany. It was meant to replace the outdated single-action Model 1914/1934 pistols. The HSc went into full production on December 1940 and ended in the final days of the war. At that time, about 252,000 pistols had been manufactured. The *Luftwaffe* purchased a batch of pistols through the *Heereswaffenamt* instead of the more usual direct purchase by their own procurement department.

23

23. The magazine had a capacity of eight 7.65 caliber rounds. The magazine release catch was located at the bottom of the butt.

24

24. The safety switch was mounted on the slide. When turned down (lowered), it did not introduce a block in front of the hammer, but moved the rear part of the firing pin out of the impact area of the hammer. Also, the safety did not lower the hammer, which had to be done by pressing the trigger. If the safety was applied with the hammer down, the hammer could not be manually cocked.

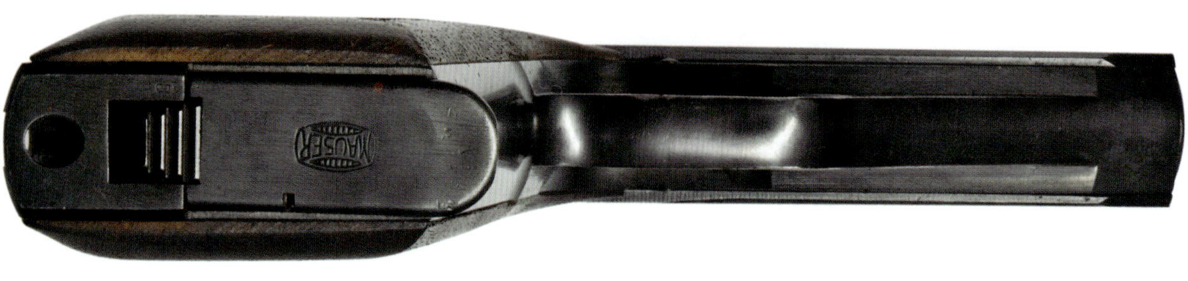

25

25. The design of the HSc pistol was very unobtrusive, so that it would not easily catch on clothing. The grips were made of walnut and were checkered.

26

26. The complete six-digit serial number was stamped on the lower front grip. The last three digits were also marked on the bottom of the barrel breech and the same three digits were electro-penciled by hand under the muzzle of the slide. The serial number and markings of the specimen of the photos denotes it was the Army variation with a production of some 4,000 pistols.

27

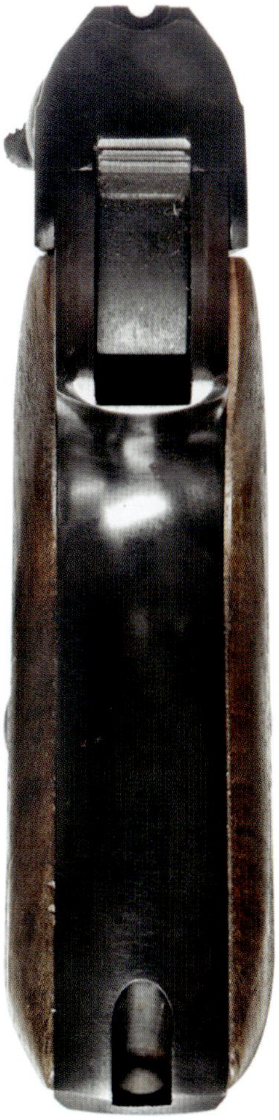

27. The hammer was concealed except for the small lip that protruded from under the slide. It could be manually cocked for a single-action first shot if desired. Due to its form and close fitting, it effectively sealed the internal mechanism against dust.

28

28. Detail of the legend on the left slide that reads *"Mauser-Werke A.G. Oberndorf a. N. Mod. HSc Kal 7,65 mm"*. The HSc pistol had a quality blue high-polish finish that gradually became rougher as the war progressed. Late war specimens had a phosphate finish.

Foreign and captured pistols

Ausländische und Beute-Pistolen

Model M 37 (u) - Fémáru pistol

The Fémáru model 37 pistol was a simple blowback operated weapon. It was developed in 1937 at the Hungarian *Fémárú Fegyver-és Gépgyár Reszvenytarsasag* arms factory to replace the Frommer-designed 29M pistol, becoming the standard Hungarian army issue pistol. With a simpler design than its predecessor, it was subsequently less expensive to manufacture. Hungary signed the Tripartite Pact with Germany in November 1940 and the Hungarian Army officially entered the war in April 1941 as an axis power with the invasion of Yugoslavia. With this alliance, the Hungarian armaments industry began to provide the Germans with all types of weapons and equipment which were for the most part distributed to second line personnel. In this context, Germany signed a contract with Hungary in 1941 for several thousand 37M pistols. German authorities requested the change of the caliber to 7.65 mm and the inclusion of a manual thumb safety catch. The pistols were designated as P.37 (u) and destined largely for the *Luftwaffe*.

29

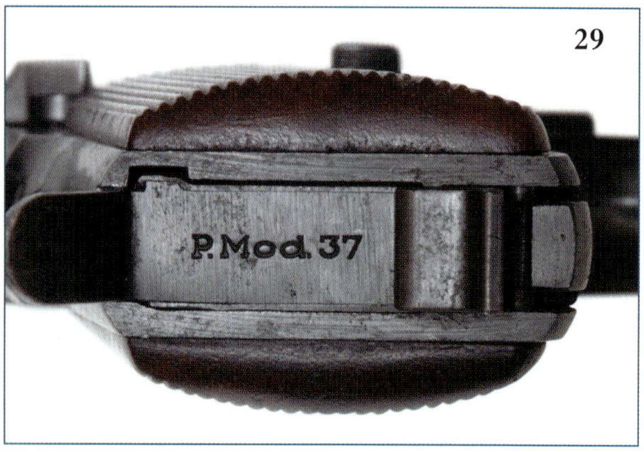

29. The detachable box magazine had a capacity of seven 7,65mm rounds. The bottom of the magazine was marked *P. Mod. 37* and featured a characteristic forward-facing finger rest. The magazine release catch was located at the base of the grip, behind the magazine well.

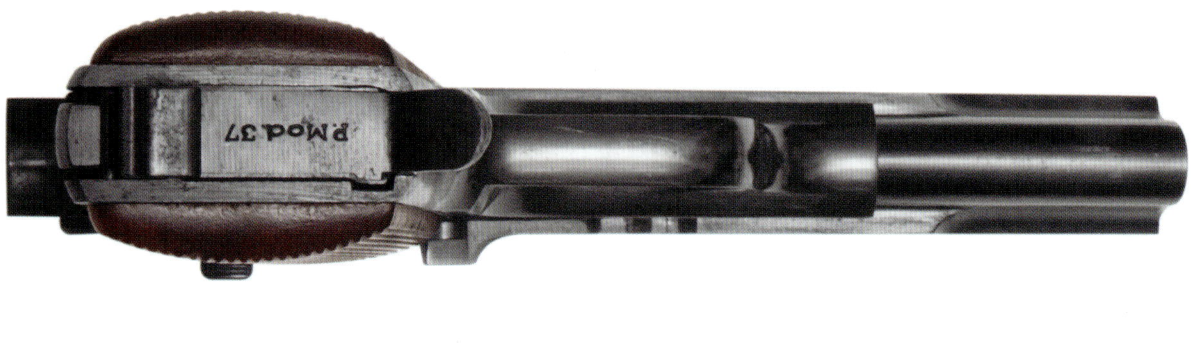

30

30. The marking on the left side of the slider was changed from the original legend *"FÉMÁRU FEGYVER ÉS GÉPGYÁR RT 37M"* to the German designation of *"P. Mod. 37 kal 7,65"*.

31

31. Detail of the muzzle and front sight, showing the tip of the recoil spring guide. The return spring was located below the barrel.

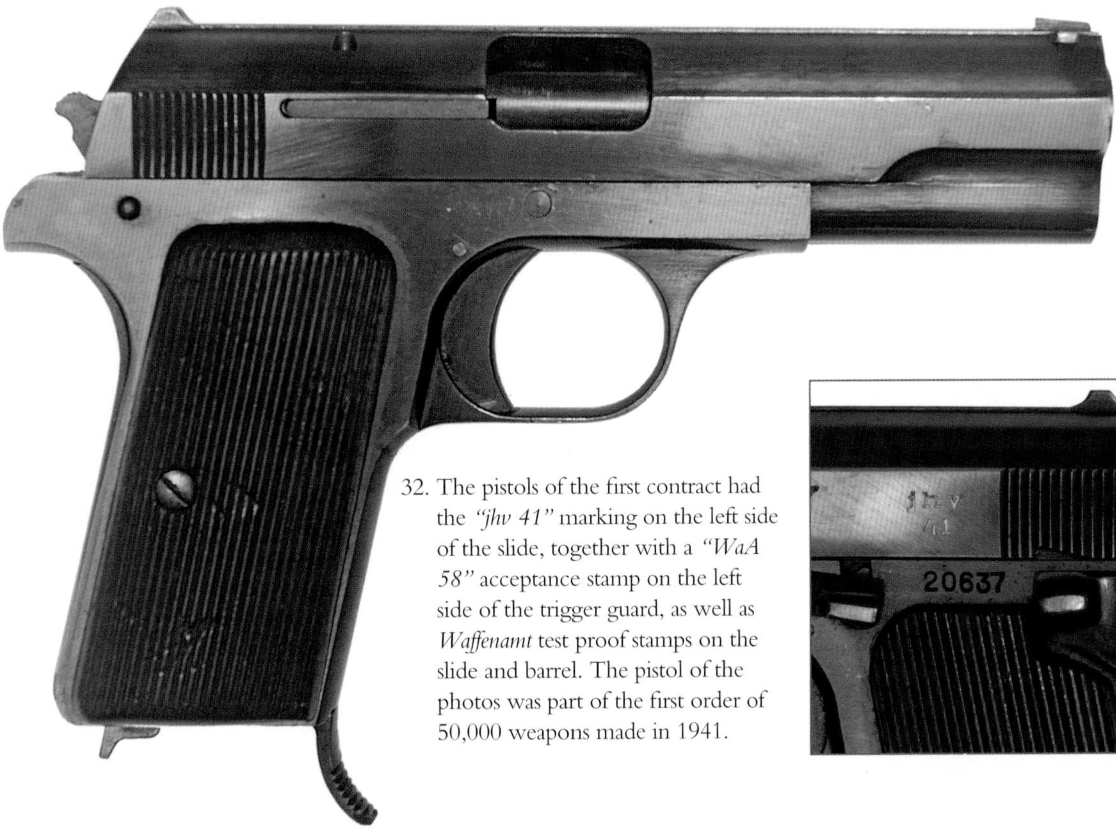

32

32. The pistols of the first contract had the *"jhv 41"* marking on the left side of the slide, together with a *"WaA 58"* acceptance stamp on the left side of the trigger guard, as well as *Waffenamt* test proof stamps on the slide and barrel. The pistol of the photos was part of the first order of 50,000 weapons made in 1941.

33

33. View of the right side of the pistol with the fully retracted slide, showing the barrel and recoil spring guide. The pistol had a high gloss finish. The grips were made walnut and featured a vertical grooving.

34. Several types of holsters could be used with the P.37 (u) pistol. The specimen of the photo is a German holster, manufactured entirely of leather.

34

35

35. The P.37 (u) pistol used the 7.65x17mm Browning cartridge. The box of the photos was manufactured in the pre-war period by the *German Rheinisch-Westfälische Sprengstoff-Fabriken A.G.* of *Nürnberg*, commonly known as RWS. The brand *SINOXID* was the trademark of a non-corrosive priming used in some German ammunition.

36. The holster was made of brown leather with cotton-linen stitching throughout body, flap and seams. It featured a pocket for a spare magazine. Visible in the inside of the flap is the ink marking indicating the pistol a designation and the caliber.

37

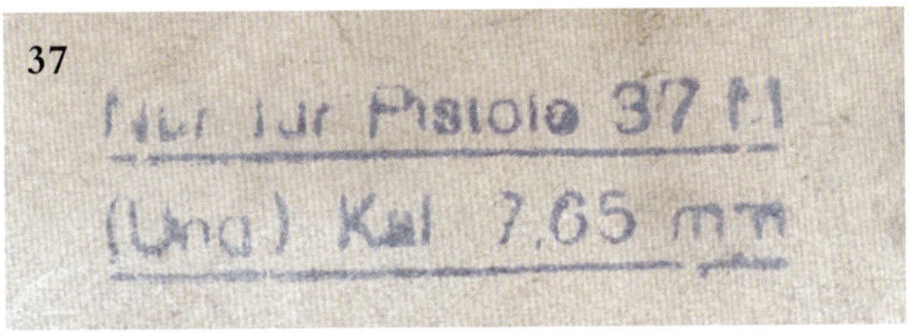

37. Detailed view of the markings found on the loop, a *Luftamp* eagle over a number 2, which corresponds to the acceptance marking of *Heinrich Krieghoff Waffenfabrik* of Suhl. The code *"jsd"* indicates it was manufactured in 1942 by *Gustav Reinhardt Lederwarenfabrik* of Berlin.

37

36

36

38

38. The Germans produced a canvas and leather version of the P.37 (u) pistol with a simpler design. The specimen of the photos has the *"cdc"* code of *Kern Klager & Co. Lederwaren* of Berlin and a manufacture date of 1941. The inside of the flap was ink-stamped with the designation *"Nur für Pistole 37M (Ung) Kal. 7.65mm."*

Several pilots pose for the camera on a cold winter day in the Eastern front. The sidearm of the man on the right is a P.37 (u) pistol with a canvas pistol holster. (Azaola)

Model M 626 (b) - Browning FN 1922 pistol

The Model 1910 pistol was developed by John M. Browning for the *Fabrique Nationale* (FN) of Belgium. In 1922, the Yugoslavian Army placed a contract for the supply of pistols. At the customer requirements, Browning modified the model 1910 pistol by lengthening the barrel and making a magazine with a capacity of two more rounds. After the invasion of Belgium in May 1940, the German army confiscated large quantities of Belgian pistols. With the capture of the FN factory in June, the occupants resumed production of a wide assortment of weapons and ammunition which was generally issued to second line troops. This was the case of the M1922 pistol, which was produced in larger numbers than any other firearm during the Nazi occupation, being the *Luftwaffe* the primary user.

39. This crewman waits for his next mission reading a magazine. The holster for his Pistole 626(b) is clearly visible on his waist. (Azaola)

40. Detail of the magazine well with the heel type magazine catch. There were three safety mechanisms on the P.626 (b) pistol: The grip safety, the magazine safety, which blocked the firing of the pistol when the magazine was removed and finally the manual safety, located on the left side of the frame and operated by the user.

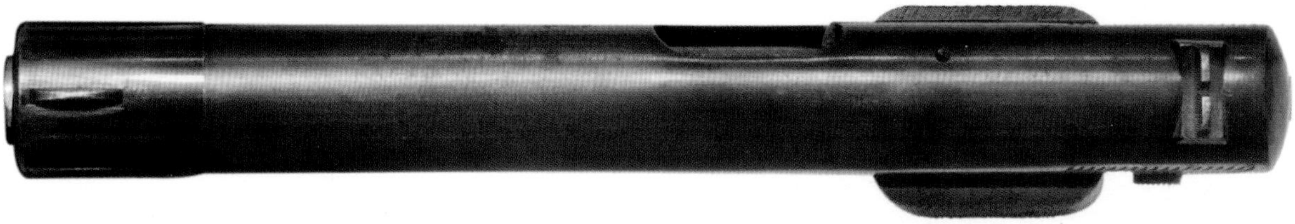

41. View of the muzzle. The P.626 (b) was a blowback operated semi-automatic pistol. The recoil spring was located around the barrel, while the trigger was a single action type.

42. The photograph shows the left side slide inscription. Also visible in the slide and frame are three *"WaA140" Waffenamt* inspector stamps and two test proof stamps consisting in an eagle with swastika in a circle. These markings were used from 1941 to the liberation of Belgium in 1944, with some 325,000 pistols produced.

43. Detailed view of the manual safety. The manual safety lever could be pushed upward, engaging with a notch in the slide which would lock it open for general cleaning. The pistol had checkered walnut grips.

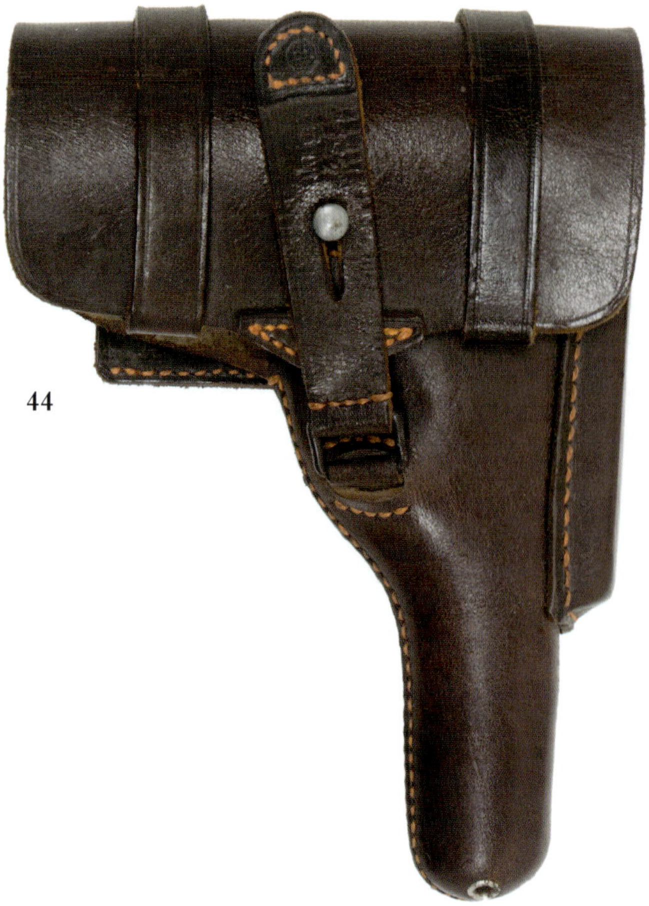

44

44. The Theurmann Patent drop-type holster featured a top flap with two vertical straps extending to the reverse of the holster. The back had a wide horizontal belt loop. Closure was achieved by an aluminum stud in the center of the top flap had and a closure strap with an eyelet fixed to the body of the holster by a small stitched rectangular metal buckle. The holster featured an extra magazine pocket stitched to the forward edge and had two small metal grommets on the bottom for a leg lanyard.

45

45. The interior of the top fold flap was ink-marked with the inscription *"Nur für lange Browning Pistole Kal. 7.65"*, which translates to *"Only for the long Browning Pistol Caliber 7.65"*.

45

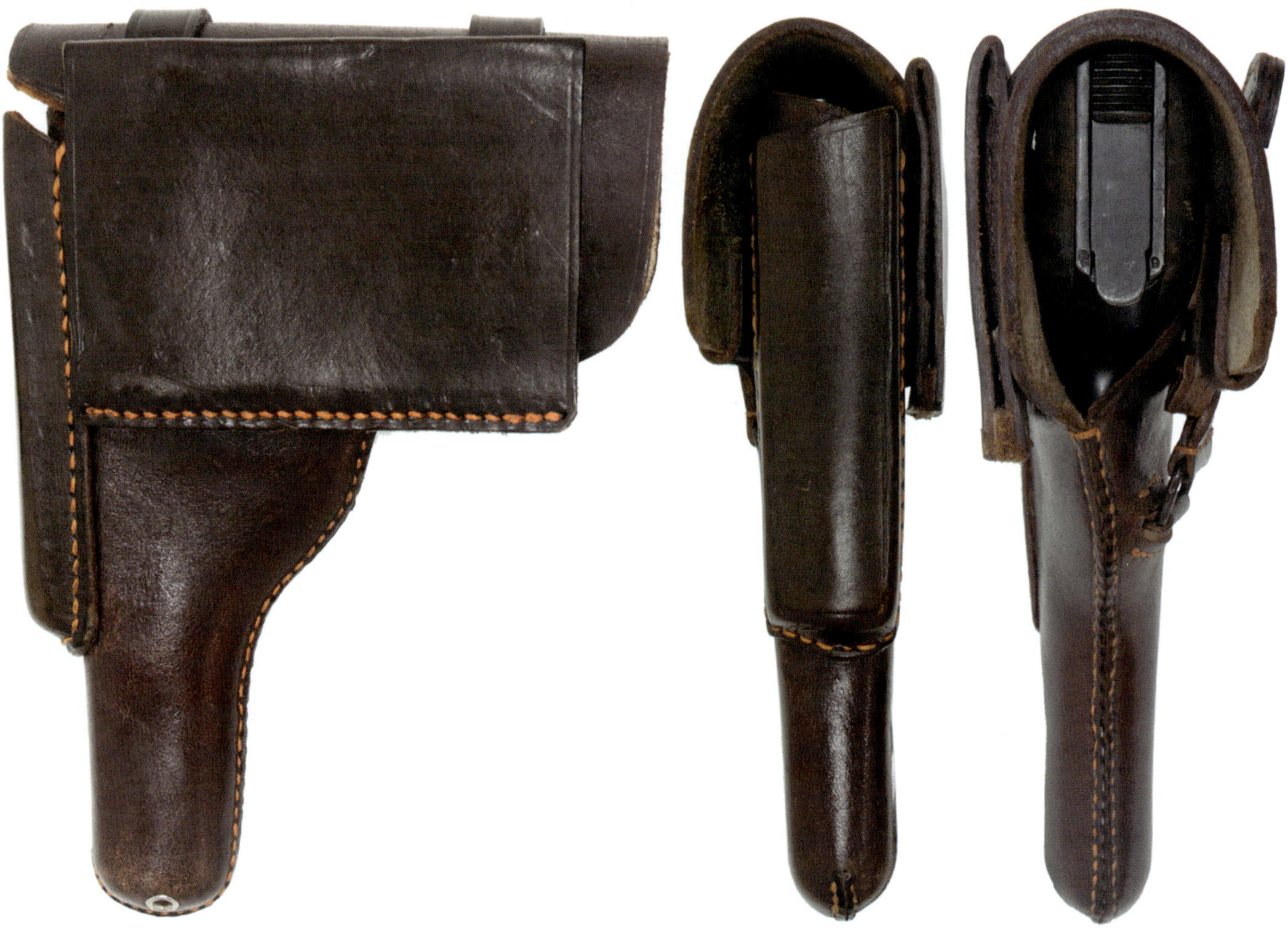

46

46. The photo shows the slide of the pistol in a fully retracted position. Notice the manual safety lever engaged in a second notch which keeps it secured in an opened position to allow a better cleaning.

Luftwaffe *fighter pilots relaxing between missions somewhere on the French coast in the summer of 1941. (Signal)*

IV. EPILOGUE
THE MEN BEHIND THE MACHINES

Their element is to attack, to track, to hunt, and to destroy the enemy. Only in this way can the eager and skillful fighter pilot display his ability. Tie him to a narrow and confined task, rob him of his initiative, and you take away from him the best and most valuable qualities he possesses: aggressive spirit, joy of action, and the passion of the hunter.

General Adolf Galland, *Luftwaffe* pilot

The words of Adolf Galland perfectly summarize the nature of the men who used the uniforms and artifacts described in this book. What was their motivation? What kept them flying one day after the other against all odds when everything around them was crumbling down? Their feats were astonishing at the time, and they become more impressive when compared to the airmen and the state of affairs of air forces around the world today, and the future trend of the air forces beginning to show in the horizon.

Combat pilots of today fly in extremely sophisticated aircraft, riddled with electronic systems, which have turned them from highly skilled and motivated hunters looking for their prey to technicians, in an environment where operating onboard computers has become more important than manning the aircraft itself. They only have a glimpse of the presence of their foes through a blimp in the multi-function display of their cockpits and they shoot them down with *"intelligent"* missiles that travel further than the eye can see, without even having to physically see the face of the enemy pilot or the aircraft they are engaging. Nowadays, at the dawn of the twenty first century, we witness the rise of a new generation of pilots, or perhaps they should be called operators, controlling unmanned aerial vehicles (the infamous drones) sitting comfortably in a base located thousands of miles away from the combat zone and controlling them remotely via computer screens and joysticks that resemble more a videogame than a real life war. The raids become an aseptic business; the operators don't need to physically know the country where they are releasing their lethal payload. In this alienated context, it is a question of time before the universal traditions of comradeship between airmen will be lost and only found in the pages of history books.

During the Second World War, pilots fought in cramped cockpits of aircraft with a deafening sound of roaring engines that needed their complete attention and skill to avoid crashing against the ground. They were often quartered in uncomfortable barracks, had little time to rest and still were able to fly their machines, engage in furious dogfights and claim an astounding amount of air victories. Some even lived to fight the next day. Men like Adolf Galland, Erich Hartmann or Hans-Ulrich Rudel. Perhaps we can begin to understand their accomplishments when we observe that they all had in common their early enthusiasm and interest in flight. This enthusiasm was enough to keep them flying against all odds. A new glider club opened near his home

This photo was autographed by Hans-Ulrich Rudel, one of the most famous Stuka dive-bomber pilot during World War II. He was the most highly decorated German serviceman of the war, Hans-Ulrich Rudel flew 2,530 combat missions claiming a total of 2,000 targets destroyed including 800 vehicles, 519 tanks and 150 artillery pieces.

and when Galland saw the gliders perform in the sky, he immediately became a member. He was so determined to learn how to fly that the nineteen miles it took him to arrive in a horse-drawn wagon never bothered him. Hartmann´s mother, a glider instructor, inoculated the love for flight to her young son, who became an instructor himself at the age of 14. Some of the most skilled pilots had close calls during their training and early service while others had such poor flight records that almost cost them their careers. Galland damaged several planes during training and suffered heavy wounds in a crash during a training flight in 1935. Rudel

This photo was signed by Adolf Galland to the co-author of this book Santiago Guillén during one of his visits to his summer vacation house in Spain. Galland never forgot his service in Spain during the civil war of 1936-1939 and visited the country as frequently as he could.

did so poorly during his training that he was initially considered unsuited to fly combat missions. These drawbacks, which would make others quit, only hardened their resolve to keep trying and succeed.

The newly formed *Luftwaffe* was the only arm of the German armed forces to be formed from scratch and therefore was forced to look back to the aces of the previous war as its source of inspiration. The First World War had created new breed of fighter, all the governments were quick to benefit from the successes of their airmen for propaganda purposes. Governments had started to award the distinction of 'ace' to those fighters who had shot down a number of enemy aircraft. The German government instituted the status of Ace to those pilots with eight air victories, becoming eligible for the highest award of the Air forces: the prestigious *Pour le Merite*. The traditions of World War I were kept alive in the new *Luftwaffe* by the presence of veterans like Ernst Udet in high-profile positions. *Major* Harry von Bulow-Bothkamp, who had commanded the *Jagdstaffel Boelcke* during the First World War, was given the command of *Jagdgeschwader 2 Richthofen*, one of the most famous units of the air forces.

The *Luftwaffe* needed a revised and expanded version of their famous aces, and the propaganda machine began to create a mythology of knightly air warriors. Göring encouraged score-chasing by pilots and the Ministry of information of Goebbels used them as propaganda material. The rivalry between the leading aces to be the pilot with most kills became a priority. Several German civil and military newspapers published ample articles about them and their feats of arms, creating a form of personality cult around them. This led to the perception of the *Luftwaffe* more as a hunting club that a military organization. The war was an opportunity for the selected few to engage in a dangerous but thrilling sport. At the beginning of the war trophies were collected. Pilots such as Molders and Galland actually went hunting in their spare time. When Galland went to Berlin to collectthe Oak Leaves to his Knight's Cross for forty victories, he joined Göring and Molders for a deer hunt at the *Reichsjägerhof* in East Prussia.

It is striking how many German pilots interviewed after the war agree that air fighting was chivalrous. Galland's chivalry is clear in his wartime encounter on the ground with Wing Commander Douglas Bader, the legless RAF ace. Shot down with several squadron mates in a melee over the Pas de Calais, Bader fell into German hands. Galland was one of the German pilots scoring kills in that action, but the wildness of the engagement made it impossible to determine Bader's conqueror. Unfortunately, in parachuting from his plane Bader had damaged his artificial legs, and asked for a spare set to be sent from England. Galland forwarded his request with a recommendation for approval, and safe conduct was offered for the aircraft bringing the legs. Sadly, the British concept of chivalry had worn thin after the bombing of London, so the RAF dropped Bader's legs along with some bombs targeting on the airfields of JG 26.

One of the most incredible feats of German aces was the enormously high number of victories. *Luftwaffe* pilots were using the same rules as others, and even perhaps stricter rules. Throughout history, when a fighter pilot achieved an air victory, the after-action report or the word of the pilot was enough to credit him with the kill. However, the system instituted by

Emil Lang obtained his 100th air victory on January 3, 1943. Awarded with the Knight's Cross of the Luftwaffe *with Oak Leaves, he flew 403 combat missions, claiming a total of 173 enemy aircraft. He was killed in action in September 3, 1944 when his plane crashed near the belgian village of Overhespen after being attacked by RAF and USAAF fighters. He is buried in an unknown grave on the German cemetery of Lommel, Belgium.*

the *Luftwaffe* required not only the word from the pilot, but also the confirmation from at least another pilot. The difference laid in the superior training and commitment and also in the conditions of the battleground in which they accomplished their air victories. Most of the aerial combat that took place in the Eastern front happened at very short distances of the battle front, as most of the missions of the German aircraft were in support of ground troops. These short distances meant that the forward bases were also close to the target area, permitting the pilots to fly multiple missions in a day and allowing multiple opportunities to score air and ground victories. Another factor was the fact that the German guideline for frontline airmen did not include any rotation or retirement from the front after a number of missions. Their policy in most cases was *"fly till you die"*. This policy hindered the possibility of a good pilot to share his knowledge with new recruits, but at the same time allowed for a high number of missions and the obvious higher amount of aerial victories. Some German pilots flew more than 1,000 missions and were shot more than 15 times themselves. The fact that the German pilots were constantly exposed to aerial combats, coupled with the enormous amount of enemy planes they had to face, especially in the first years of war, added to the high victory rate of the German air force in the Eastern Front.

Pilots such as Hannes Trautloft, Adolf Galland and many others lived through lengthy exposure to combat, the reversal of fortune when the tide turned against Germany and political dramas that would have broken even the strongest of men. In the final years of the war they fought not only the enemy but also their own corrupt leadership, which was willing to sacrifice Germany's best and bravest to their personal agendas. Aces like Steinhoff or Lützow risked death to defend their nation and, if that was not enough, voiced their opposition to the incompetent actions and decisions of the Third Reich high command, risking both their lives and their careers. The pilots were being accused for the inability to stop the bombings on German cities and for and losing the war. Galland, who always voiced his opinions and criticized the way the air war was being run, became the scapegoat. At the end of 1944, Göring dismissed Galland as *General der Jagdflieger* and appointed *Oberst* Gordon Gollob in his place. A group of the most decorated and courageous *Luftwaffe* pilots confronted Göring. Their main concern was the *Reichsmarschall's* lack of understanding and unwillingness to support his pilots against accusations of cowardice and treason. Lützow, who had been elected to act as the group's spokesman, was threatened with a court-martial. He was finally sent to Italy as a *staffel* commander and Galland was ordered to leave Berlin and instructed to await orders. His future was at stake. The intervention of Albert Speer, minister of armament and war production, made Göring reconsider his position and put the controversy and mutiny to rest.

A young pilot once wrote a letter home from the front lines explaining that he was having the time of his life. He candidly said that peacetime was going to be very boring. Time proved that his predictions were for the most part correct. Many of the most famous aces lived plentiful and adventurous lives after the war, perhaps in an attempt to replicate the thrills and dangers of the most important and central part of their vital experience. Many of them, such

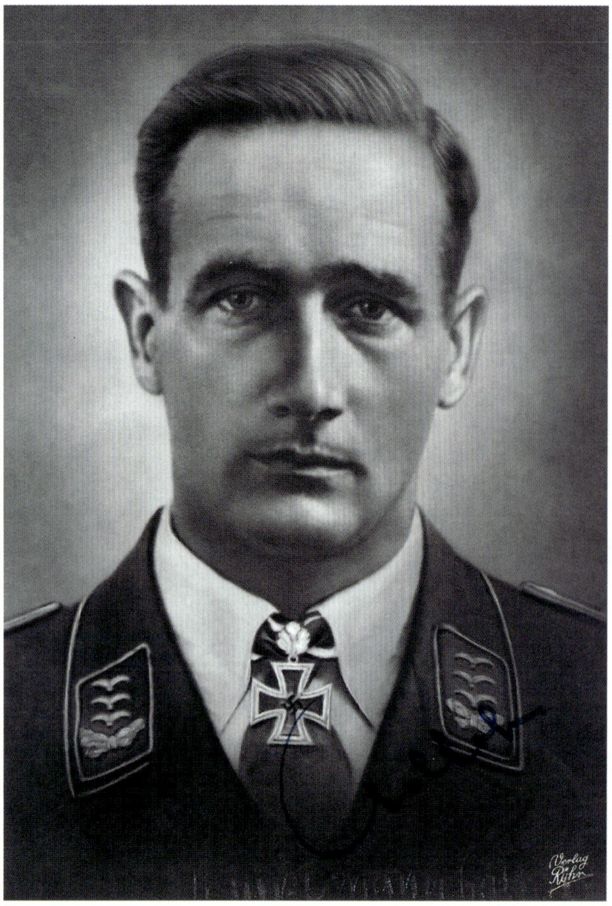

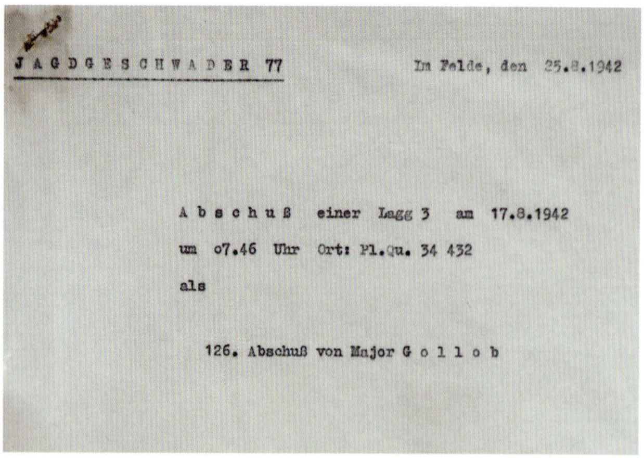

JAGDGESCHWADER 77 Im Felde, den 25.8.1942

Abschuß einer Lagg 3 am 17.8.1942
um o7.46 Uhr Ort: Pl.Qu. 34 432
als

126. Abschuß von Major Gollob

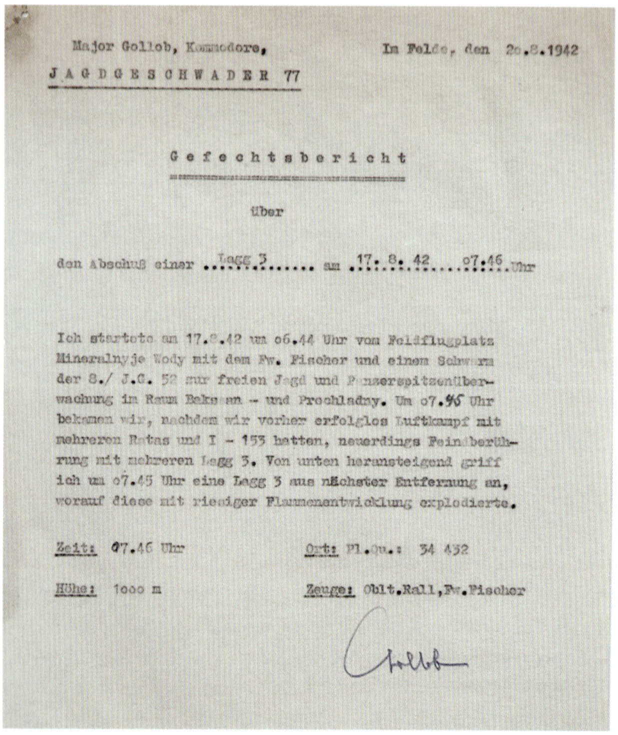

Major Gollob, Kommodore, Im Felde, den 20.8.1942
JAGDGESCHWADER 77

Gefechtsbericht

über

den Abschuß einer Lagg 3 am 17. 8. 42 o7.46 Uhr

Ich startete am 17.8.42 um o6.44 Uhr vom Feldflugplatz Mineralnyje Wody mit dem Fw. Fischer und einem Schwarm der 8./ J.G. 52 zur freien Jagd und Panzerspitzenüberwachung im Raum Beksan – und Prochladny. Um o7.45 Uhr bekamen wir, nachdem wir vorher erfolglos Luftkampf mit mehreren Ratas und I – 153 hatten, neuerdings Feindberührung mit mehreren Lagg 3. Von unten heransteigend griff ich um o7.45 Uhr eine Lagg 3 aus nächster Entfernung an, worauf diese mit riesiger Flammenentwicklung explodierte.

Zeit: 07.46 Uhr Ort: Pl.Qu.: 34 432

Höhe: 1000 m Zeuge: Oblt.Rall, Fw.Fischer

Signed photo of Gordon Gollob and one of his after-action reports as Geschwaderkommodore *of* Jagdgeschwader 77. *This Austrian born fighter ace is credited for being the first pilot to achieve 150 air victories in the* Luftwaffe.

as Erich Hartmann, Gerhard Barkhorn or Hannes Trautloft, returned to the new West German *BundesLuftwaffe* as soon as it was created in 1956. Very few of the great pilots survived the war, yet the fact that Germany's three leading aces did is testimony to their skill, determination and luck.

We would like to finish this epilogue with a story of a promising German pilot who could have had an impressive career during the war. But fate crossed his way in a combat mission on the first months of the war. The story of this pilot is accompanied by a document grouping, shown in the following pages. His name was Hans-Sigmund Storp, a *Junkers* Ju 88 pilot who was arguably the first German airman shot down over Great Britain in the Second World War.

Sigmund Storp was born in the small town of Lautertal (Goslar) on the 21st of August, 1914. After completing high school, 17 year old Sigmund began to study at the Warnemünde civil aviation school to obtain a pilot license. In reality, the school trained seaplane pilot candidates for the Navy, but had to cover-up its true intentions to circumvent the Versailles treaty. Storp ended up enrolling in the Navy and consequently joined the light cruiser *Köln* as a cadet in late 1932 for a cruise around the globe. The tour lasted a full year, stopping in ports across the Mediterranean Sea and the Atlantic, Pacific, and Indian oceans. In 1934, Sigmund was appointed as *Fänrich zur see* (Officer Candidate of the Navy) and sent to the Flensburg-Mainz Naval Academy to complete the officer course.

He finally obtained his pilot wings in 1935 and was immediately abducted to the *Luftwaffe*, as it occurred with most of the Navy pilots. Göring was in the process of taking away control of all aviation assets not only from civilian outfits, but also from the Army and the Navy. Every asset related to flight, including the pilots, had to be handed over to Göring. In his own words, *"Everything that flies belongs to me!"* On the first of October of 1935, the former *Kriegsmarine* officer candidate was promoted to *leutnant* of the *Luftwaffe* with an order signed by the *Reichsminister der Luftahrt und Oberbefehlshaber der Luftwaffe* himself, Hermann Göring, and destined to a maritime reconnaissance unit.

In 1936, after a civil war broke out in Spain, Storp´s crew was one of the first to march as volunteers to fight in the Iberian Peninsula as part of the Condor Legion. He was a member of the AS /88 unit (*Aufklärungsstaffel* AS / 88) air reconnaissance unit, equipped with He 59 and He 60 seaplanes. The first two aircraft and their crews arrived to the port of Cadiz aboard the vessel *Wighert* in October of 1937. Their primary duty was to protect German cargo vessels in Spanish waters along the strait of Gibraltar area, from the port towns of Cadiz to Almeria. Soon, the unit was sent to the Malaga sector, where they were had an active role in the conquest of the city of Malaga. It was during this campaign when Siegmund Storp had his first close call. On February

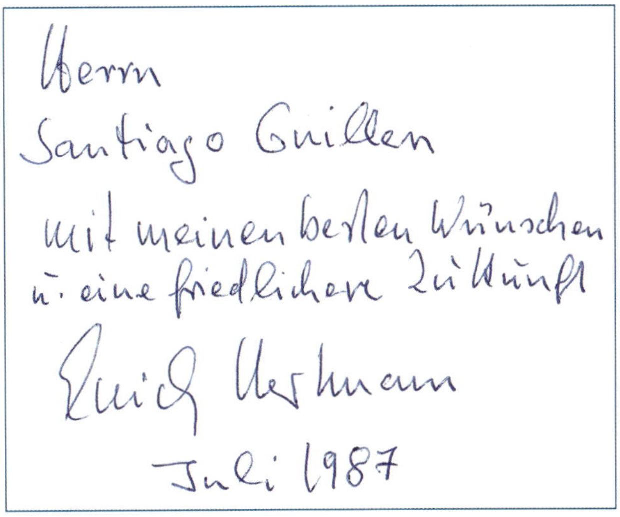

Autographed photo and dedication to Santiago Guillén by Erich Hartmann. Flying a Bf 109 fighter he claimed 352 kills in 1,404 combat missions, making him the highest-scoring fighter ace in the history of aerial warfare.

5, 1937 Storp was flying his He 60E along with the He 59B-2 aircraft of *Leutnant* Dieter Leich in an anti-submarine reconnaissance mission in protection of the Nationalist cruiser *Canarias*. Storp's seaplane, bearing the numeral 512, was decorated with a large black circle with painted skull and crossbones and named *"Fiera del Mar"* (Beast of the sea). The mission was going as planned, when suddenly a Soviet manufactured *Polikarpov* I 15 fighter from the Republican air-force manned by the American mercenary pilot Charlie Koch attacked both planes. The He 59B-2 was hit and plunged into the sea, but not before striking the left port wing of Storp's plane, which had to make a forced landing close to the *Canarias*. He was rescued by the ship's crew with slight wounds and the aircraft was towed onboard.

The next months saw the arrival of more seaplanes and crews, but also of good news for Siegmund. On April 1, 1937 he was promoted to *Oberleutnant*. The promotion certificate was again ink-signed by Hermann Göring. After completing his six month tour, Storp was sent back to Germany, where he was appointed as a flight instructor in the *Luftwaffe* flight school of Travemünde, transmitting the experience gained during the Spanish war to his young students. In 1939, after the Spanish civil war ended, the new ruler of the country, General Franco, decided to express his gratitude towards the German legionaries in the form of military awards. Storp was one of the few legionaries awarded with the individual *"Medalla Militar"* (Military Medal) as opposed to the more usual collective medal. He was also awarded the *"Medalla de Campaña"* (Campaign Medal) for his outstanding service. The Italian government, which also sent volunteer troops to fight in Spain, awarded him with the *"Ordine della corona D'Italia"*. Lastly, his country also awarded the young officer with the Spanish Cross in Gold with Swords in recognition for his service in Spain. The war soon broke out in Europe with the invasion of Poland and Siegmund Storp added another decoration to his list. On September 28, 1939 he was awarded with the Iron Cross 2nd Class. Storp had been transferred to the *Luftflotte 2*, commanded by *General der Flieger* Hellmuth Felmy. Due to his brilliant record, he was selected to be part of the *Erprobungskommando 88* experimental unit (later re-designated as I./ KG 30), created in the Rechlin airfield to test the new Ju 88 bomber in combat conditions.

Göring was informed of the teething problems encountered with the Ju 88 and the need to solve them before attempting to fly in combat missions. Soon, news of the sinking of the *HMS Courageous* by the U-29 submarine and later the daring attack on Scapa Flow in which the battleship *HMS Royal Oak* was torpedoed and sunk by the U-47 submarine commanded by Gunther Prien arrived. The popularity gained by the *Kriegsmarine* in these high profile missions prompted the commander of the *Luftwaffe* to demand a mission that would deliver a blow to the Royal Navy and earn popularity and military laurels for him and his organization. On October 15, 1939 the opportunity arrived. Reconnaissance aircraft reported that a battleship, possibly the *HMS Hood*, was about to enter the Firth of Forth, a strategic estuary located in the May Island, Scotland that included the naval base at Rosyth and the Forth Rail bridge. It was 11:55 in the morning of Monday October 16, 1939. Twelve *Junkers* Ju 88A-1s of the first *Staffel* of *Kampfgeschwader* 30 (1./ KG30) took off from their base on the German coastal area of Westerland to attack the vessels. Leading the raid was *Hauptmann* Helmut Pohle, with *Leutnant* Sigmund Storp as his second-in-command (His Ju 88A-1 was identified with the numerals 4D + DH). Just the day before, Storp had re-

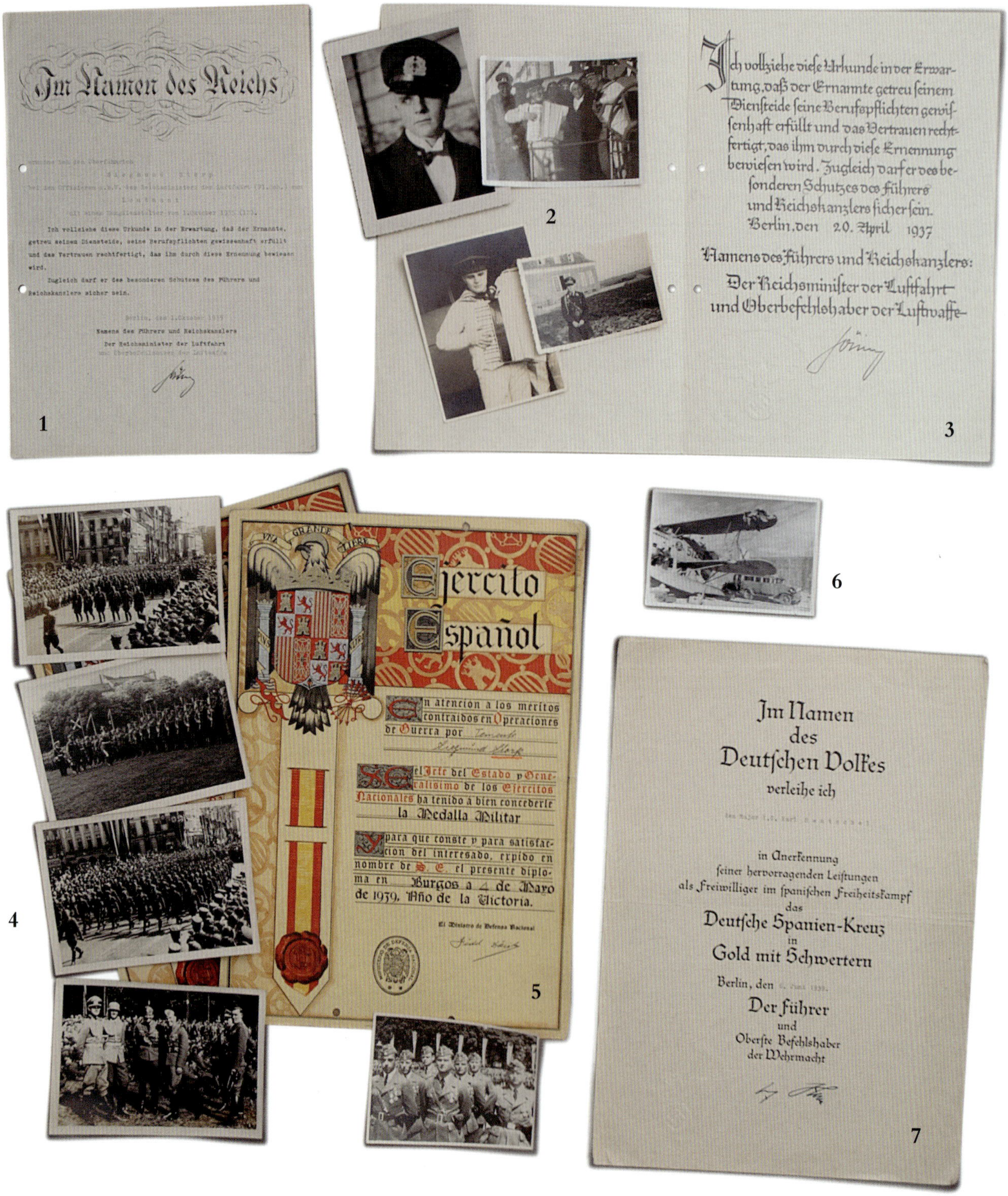

1. *Promotion certificate to* Leutnant *of the* Luftwaffe *signed by the* Reichsminister der Luftfahrt und Oberbefehlshaber der Luftwaffe, *Hermann Göring.*
2. *Photographs of Storp as a* Fähnrich zur See *of the* Kriegsmarine.
3. *Promotion certificate to* Oberleutnant, *ink-signed by Hermann Göring.*
4. *Photos of the Parade held in Berlin to welcome the Condor Legion veterans and the award decoration ceremony held at Doeberitz.*
5. *Award certificates of the individual* "Medalla Militar" *(Military Medal) and the* "Medalla de Campaña" *(Campaign Medal), awarded to Storp.*
6. *Photo of Storp's* "Fiera del Mar" *seaplane with the damaged port wing caused by his fellow airman after suffering an attack by a Republican fighter.*
7. *Spanish Cross in Gold with Swords award certificate, issued in 1939 in recognition of Storp's service in Spain.*

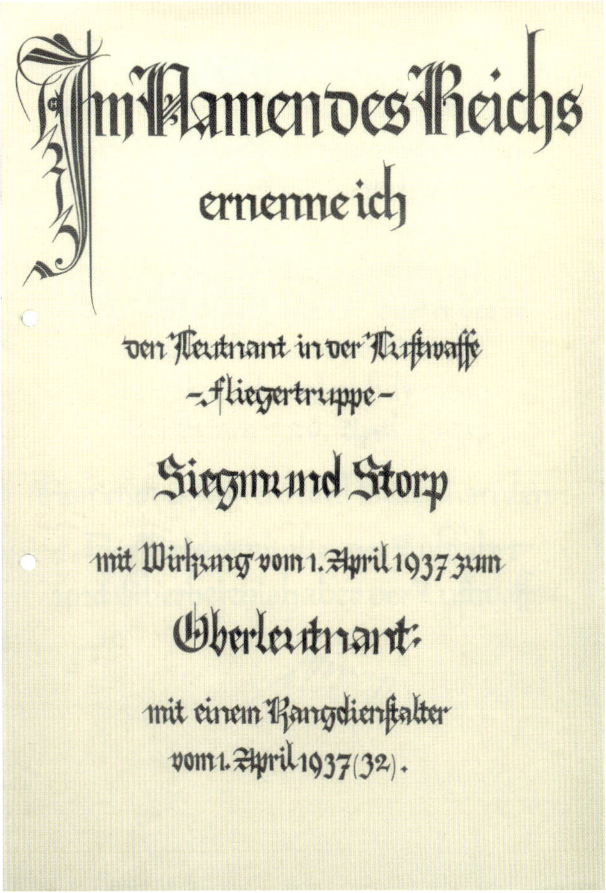

Im Namen des Reichs
ernenne ich
den Leutnant in der Luftwaffe
-Fliegertruppe-
Siegmund Storp
mit Wirkung vom 1. April 1937 zum
Oberleutnant.
mit einem Rangdienstalter
vom 1. April 1937 (32).

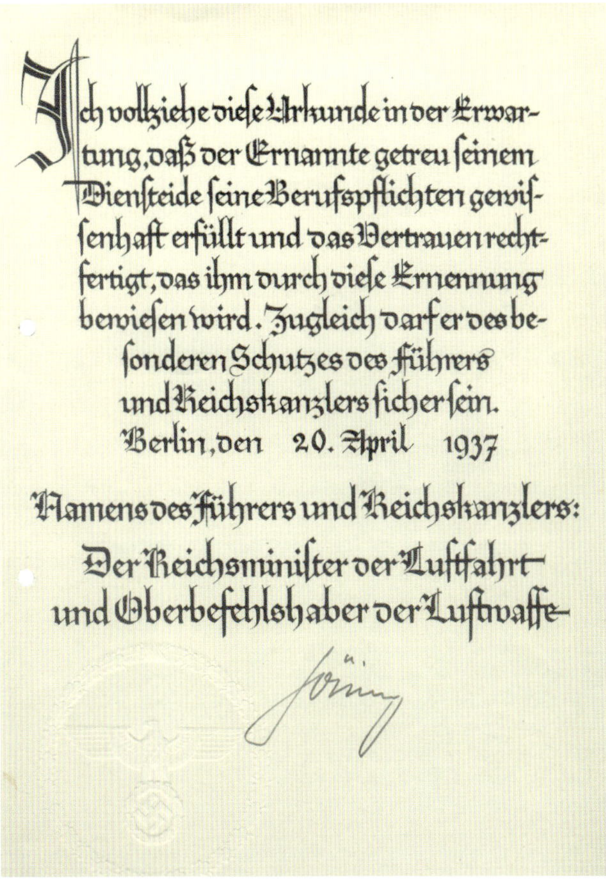

Ich vollziehe diese Urkunde in der Erwartung, daß der Ernannte getreu seinem Diensteide seine Berufspflichten gewissenhaft erfüllt und das Vertrauen rechtfertigt, das ihm durch diese Ernennung bewiesen wird. Zugleich darf er des besonderen Schutzes des Führers und Reichskanzlers sicher sein.

Berlin, den 20. April 1937

Namens des Führers und Reichskanzlers:
Der Reichsminister der Luftfahrt
und Oberbefehlshaber der Luftwaffe

Göring

Detailed photo of the promotion certificate to Hauptmann *of the* Luftwaffe *ink-signed by Hermann Göring. Sigmund Storp was a prisoner of war when he was promoted and received his collar and shoulder board in the Canadian POW camp of Bowmanville, Canada via the Red Cross in January 1940.*

This photo shows Sigmund Storp during his internment in a Canadian Bowmanville POW camp. He received his Hauptman *collar rank and shoulder boards via the Red Cross and wore them in his uniform for the duration of the war.*

ceived news that he had been awarded with the Iron Cross 1st Class. The medal certificate was personally signed once more by *Generalfeldmarschall* Hermann Göring.

At 12:15 the attackers, arriving in several sections, had reached the outskirts of the Firth of Fourth and headed inland. The German Intelligence had informed them that the area would be free of fighters. The information was completely faulty. Supermarine Spitfires of 603 squadron *'City of Edinburgh'* were rapidly scrambled from Turnhouse Aerodrome, as well as aircraft of the 602 squadron *'City of Glasgow'* based at Drem in East Lothian. The pilots had the order to intercept any aircraft approaching to the area. The three JU 88 commanded by Pohle arrived first, watching several targets in the waters of the Firth, some of them just below the bridge. They were the cruisers *HMS Southampton, HMS Edinburgh* and the destroyer *HMS Mohawk*. Pohle picked out the *HMS Southampton* and took a steep dive to attack the vessel, placing a 500 kilogram bomb on the deck. But the bomb failed to explode, and in turn sliced through the decks and flew out the flank. A few moments later, Lieutenant Hans Storp led the second section to attack the ship from the west. The Spitfires were heading their way.

1. Daily Express newspaper press release of the first three Germans shot down in Britain, with a photo taken at the Military Hospital at Edinburgh castle.
2. Official Luftwaffe *Map showing the Firth of Fourth area in Scotland where the raid that resulted in the capture of Storp took place.*
3. Page from a local magazine with pictures of the facilities of the Windermere Prisoner-of-war camp.
4. A group of German military personnel pose for a photo at the Canadian Bowmanville Prisoner-of-war camp. Storp is the fourth from the left.
5. The photo shows Sigmund Storp playing piano at the Scottish camp surrounded by other German prisoners.
6. Detailed view of the Firth of Fourth Estuary where the failed raid took place.
7. Award certificate of the Iron Cross 2nd Class.
8. Award certificate of the Iron Cross 1st Class signed by Hermann Göring.
9. Promotion certificate to Hauptmann *of the* Luftwaffe *signed by Hermann Göring.*
Storp received the promotion during his confinement in the Canadian Bowmanville Prisoner-of-war camp.

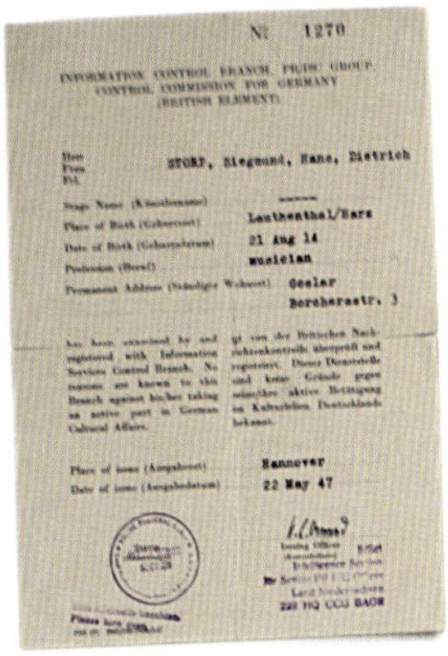

1

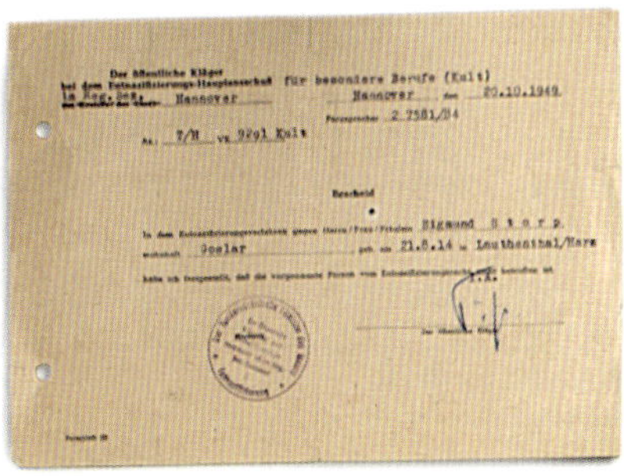

2

3

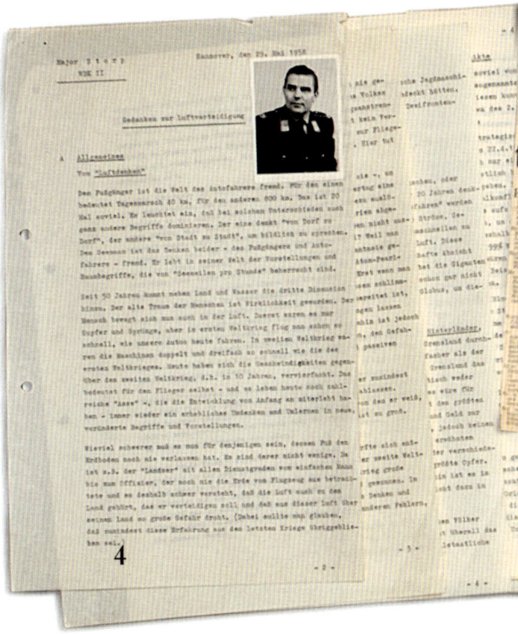

4

Daily Express 21.8.1961

FLASHBACK TO 1939: GERMAN RAIDERS CAPTURED

Ex-PoW turns to the Luftwaffe again

5

Nordwestdeutsch

Kampfflieger schreibt Symphonie

6

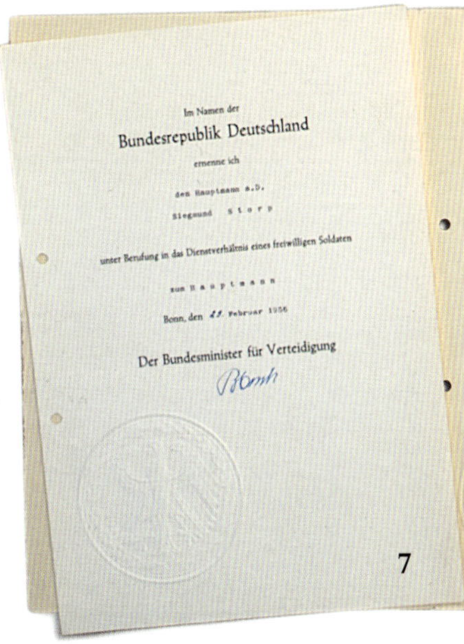

Im Namen der

Bundesrepublik Deutschland

ernenne ich

den Hauptmann a.D.

Siegmund Storp

unter Berufung in das Dienstverhältnis eines freiwilligen Soldaten

zum Hauptmann

Bonn, den 21. Februar 1956

Der Bundesminister für Verteidigung

7

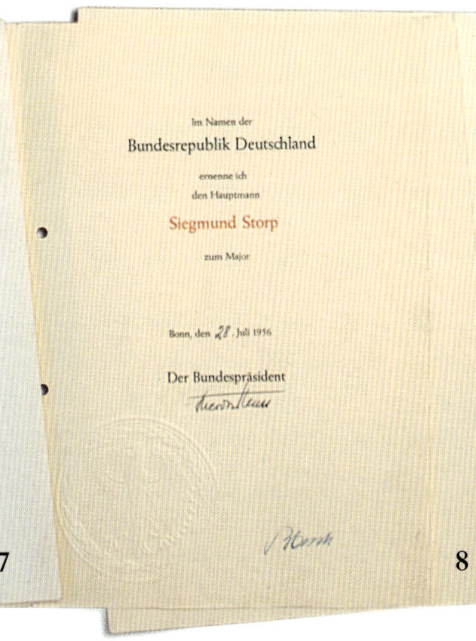

Im Namen der

Bundesrepublik Deutschland

ernenne ich

den Hauptmann

Siegmund Storp

zum Major

Bonn, den 28. Juli 1956

Der Bundespräsident

8

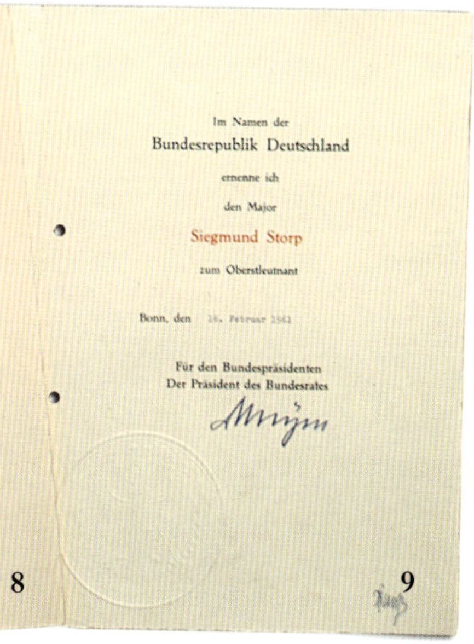

Im Namen der

Bundesrepublik Deutschland

ernenne ich

den Major

Siegmund Storp

zum Oberstleutnant

Bonn, den 16. Februar 1961

Für den Bundespräsidenten

Der Präsident des Bundesrates

9

1. Document of the Information Control Branch of PR/ISC Group, Control Commission for Germany issued in 1947, clearing Sigmund Storp of any wrongdoing during the war.
2. German denazification document referred to Sigmund Storp issued in 1949.
3. Official Certificate of Discharge document issued by the allied authorities in 1946.
4. Files of Storp from his service period in the Bundesluftwaffe.
5. Newspaper article informing of Storp's enrollment in the new German Air Force.
6. Newspaper article of Storp's musical activities in the Bundesluftwaffe, *with photos of the choir and orchestra he organized.*
7. Government Certificate issued in February 1956 reinstating Storp's wartime rank of Hauptmann.
8. Promotion certificate to Major *issued in July 1956.*
9. Promotion certificate to Oberstleutnant *issued in February 1961.*

Flight Lieutenant Patrick Gifford, of 603, attacked Storp´s aircraft, hitting his port engine and killing his gunner. The plane plunged into the ocean. Gifford had just shot down the first enemy aircraft over Britain in WWII. Another pilot, Flight Lieutenant George Pinkerton of 602, shot down a second bomber, taking down Helmut Pohle´s plane and killing his crew. The attack caused slight damage to two cruisers, *HMS Edinburgh* and *HMS Mohawk*, and to the destroyer *HMS Southampton* even though all three ships sustained direct hits. In turn, three JU88 were shot down. Storp was rescued from the sea with two of his crewmen, Köhnke and Hielsher, by a fishing boat. His savior, a courageous fisherman called John Dickinson, was given a gold ring– a family heirloom- by Storp as a form of gratitude for saving his life. The three became the first German airmen made prisoners by the British in the war. Pohle was also rescued, bleeding from facial wounds suffered in the crash. The wounded German pilots were taken to the Miltary Hospital at Edinburgh castle. During their stay at the hospital, Pinkerton and Gifford visited Storp and Pohle, who appreciated the gesture and thanked them for the visit, stressing the universal bonds that held all pilots together.

Storp´s participation in the war had ended. He was initially transferred to the Windermere Prisoner-of-war camp. The facilities included a piano, and Sigmund, a long time accordion player and music enthusiast, decided to study music. Soon, he formed a small orchestra with other prisoners with musical skills, organizing classical music concerts in the camp. Storp was definitively transferred to the Bowmanville Prisoner-of-war camp in Canada. On the 1st of January 1940 he received his promotion to *Hauptmann*. He wore the new rank in his inform, brought to him via the Red Cross, for the remainder of his internment in the Canadian camp.

After the end of the war, Sigmund Storp had to wait until 1947 to be released. He returned to Germany and studied in the Detmont Conservatory of Music. He finished his piano studies in 1950 and began to work as a music professor at the Goslar institute. At the same time, he was a professional pianist, playing with many classical music orchestras. In 1956, when the new German air force, the *BundesLuftwaffe*,was created, Storp followed the steps of many of his fellow veteran comrades and enrolled with the rank of *Haupttman* (Captain). He was promoted to Major in 1956 and ended his military career in 1970 as *Oberstleutnant* (Lieutenant-Colonel). He ended up his days teaching piano lessons in his countryside home at Engesen, in the lower Saxony.

This photo was taken after the "Fiera del Mar" seaplane was towed from the battleship Canarias *to the port for repairs.*
Visible on left port wing is the damage caused by the He 59B-2 of Leutnant *Dieter Leich, who collided with Storp´s seaplane during his descent after being hit by an enemy fighter.*

This happy pilot is about to take a good bite out of his fruit as a reward after arriving to his airbase from a successful mission. (Signal)

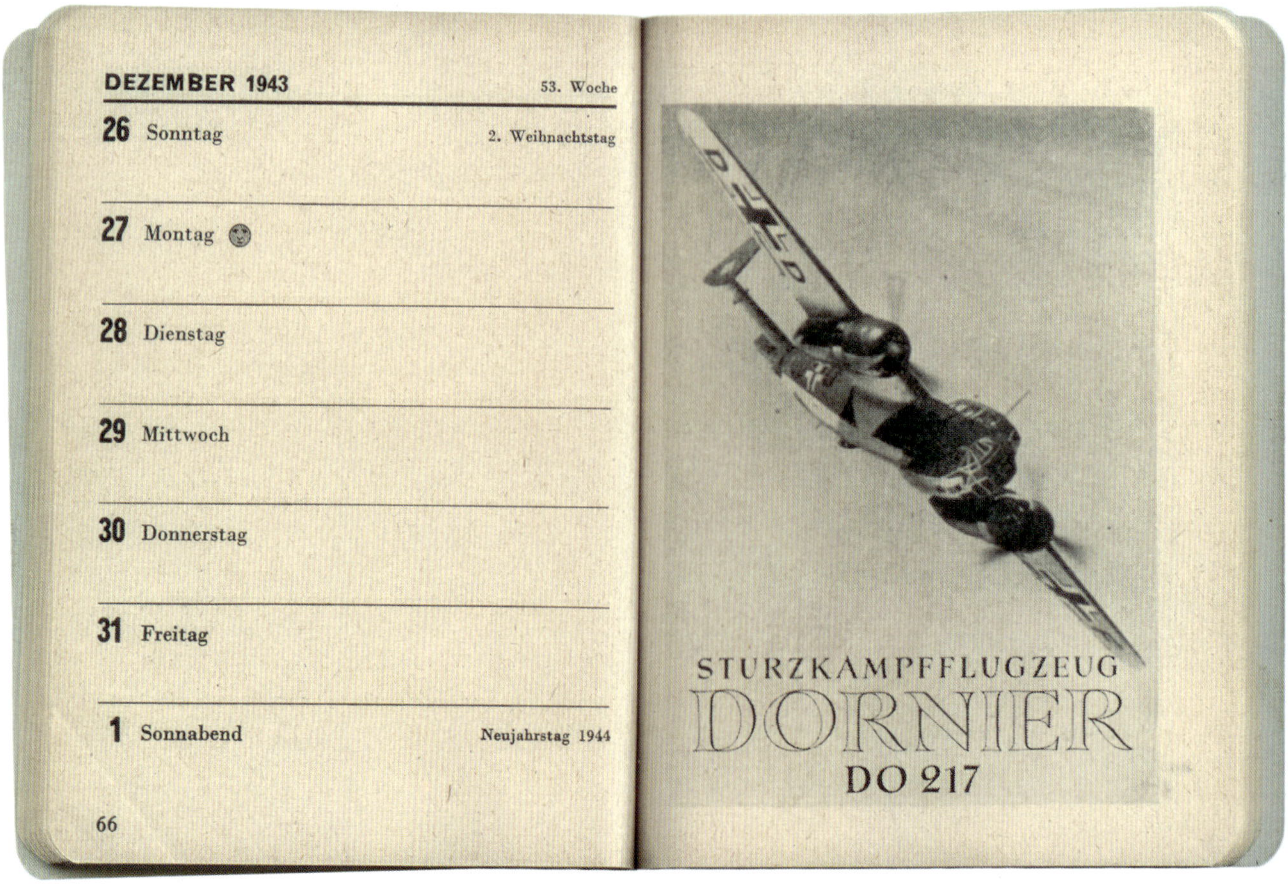

1943 official pocket year book of the National Socialist Flyers Corps or Dienst-Taschenbuch des-Fliegerkorps *published by order of the NSFK leadership.*

BIBLIOGRAPHY

AILSBY, Christopher J.
A collector's guide to the Luftwaffe
Surrey, England
Ian Allan Publishing, 2006

ANGOLIA, John R. and SCHLINCH, Adolf
Uniforms and Traditions of the Luftwaffe (3 Volumes)
San Jose, USA
Roger James Bender, 1996

Buckton, Henry
Birth of The Few
Ramsbury, UK
Airlife Publishing, L.T.D., 1998

BUNGAY, Stephen
The most dangerous enemy. A history of the battle of Britain
London, UK
Aurum Press, 2001

DAVIS, Brian L.
Uniforms and Insignia of the Luftwaffe Volume I: 1933-1940
London, UK
Arms and Armour Press, 1991

DAVIS, Brian L.
Uniforms and Insignia of the Luftwaffe Volume II: 1940-1945
London, UK
Arms and Armour Press, 1995

GIBSON, Randall
The Krieghoff Parabellum
USA
Gibson, 1980

LAUREAU, Patrick
Legion Condor. The Luftwaffe in Spain 1936- 1939
Crowborough, UK
Hikoki Publications Ltd, 2000

MARKHAM, George
Guns of the Reich
London, UK
Arms & Armour Press, 1991

MURRAY, Williamson
The Luftwaffe 1933-45: Strategy for Defeat
London, UK
Brassey's Inc., 1996

PRODGER, Mick J.
Luftwaffe vs. RAF: Flying Clothing of the Air War, 1939-45
Atglen, USA
Schiffer Publishing, Ltd. , 1997

PRODGER, Mick J.
Luftwaffe vs. RAF: Flying equipment of the Air War, 1939-45
Atglen, USA
Schiffer Publishing, Ltd. , 1998

PRODGER, Mick J.
Vintage Flying Helmets: Aviation Headgear Before The Jet Age
Atglen, USA
Schiffer Publishing, Ltd. , 1995

RECIO CARDONA, Ricardo
Blitzkrieg, Guerra Relámpago (1939-41)
Madrid, Spain
Acción Press, 2006

STEDMAN, Robert F.
Kampfflieger: Bomber Crewman of the Luftwaffe 1939-45
Botley, UK
Osprey Publishing, 2005

STEDMAN, Robert F.
Luftwaffe Air & Ground Crew 1939-45
Botley, UK
Osprey Publishing, 2002

SWEETING, C.G.
Combat Flying Clothing: Army Flying Clothing during World War II
Washington D.C., USA
Smithsonian Institution Press, 1984

SWEETING, C.G.
Combat Flying Equipment: U.S. Army Aviator's Personal Equipment, 1917-1945
Washington D.C., USA
Smithsonian Institution Press, 1989

WAR Department
Handbook for Combat Air Intelligence Officers
Harrisburg, Pennsylvania, USA
AAF Air Intelligence School, 1944